The Business and Marketing Environment

The Business and Marketing Environment

Adrian Palmer

and

Ian Worthington

McGRAW-HILL BOOK COMPANY

London · New York · St Louis · San Francisco · Auckland
Bogotá · Caracas · Hamburg · Lisbon · Madrid · Mexico · Milan
Montreal · New Delhi · Panama · Paris · San Juan · São Paulo
Singapore · Sydney · Tokyo · Toronto

Published by
McGRAW-HILL Book Company Europe
Shoppenhangers Road, Maidenhead, Berkshire, SL6 2QL, England
Telephone (0628) 23432
Fax (0628) 770224

British Library Cataloguing in Publication Data

Palmer, Adrian
Business and Marketing Environment
I. Title   II. Worthington, Ian
658.8
ISBN 0-07-707442-4

Library of Congress Cataloging-in-Publication Data

Palmer, Adrian James.
The business and marketing environment/Adrian James Palmer, Ian Worthington.
     p.   cm.
Includes bibliographical references and index.
ISBN 0-07-707442-4
1. Marketing. 2. Export marketing. 3. Organizational effectiveness. 4. Marketing research.
I. Worthington, Ian. II. Title.
HF5415.P234   1992
658.8-dc20   92-9025 CIP

 234 HWV 9432

Typeset by Computape (Pickering) Limited, North Yorkshire
and printed and bound in Great Britain by BPCC Hazells Ltd.

CONTENTS

AUTHORS

Adrian Palmer is Senior Lecturer in Marketing at De Montfort University Leicester Business School.

Ian Worthington is Senior Lecturer in Business Environment at De Montfort University Leicester Business School.

CONTRIBUTORS

Ian Clark is Senior Lecturer in Industrial Relations at De Montfort University Leicester Business School.

Bob Hartley is Principal Lecturer in Marketing at De Montfort University Leicester Business School.

Mary Mulholland is Senior Lecturer in Law at De Montfort University Leicester Law School.

PREFACE

This book is intended for the student who wants to learn about how marketing fits into an organization and the much wider environment in which the organization itself operates. After an overview of the basic principles of marketing, the book explores the diversity of social, economic, political and technological factors, the reading of which makes marketing management a combination of an art form and a science. The aim of the book is to make the reader aware of the nature of these increasingly turbulent factors which marketing management cannot afford to ignore. Suggestions are made of frameworks for use in assessing the marketing environment to help decision-making on such matters as new product development, pricing policy, etc.

The book fills a gap between two broad categories of books. On the one hand, there are numerous excellent books which look inwardly at the principles and practices of marketing but make only a very brief analysis of the nature of the environment to which these principles and practices are designed to respond. On the other hand, there are many texts on the organization in its environment, most of which suffer from a lack of focus on specific problem-solving needs within an organization. This book focuses on the needs of marketers by analysing the organization's environment as it affects them.

The readership envisaged for this includes first-year degree students and HND students following a foundation course in marketing or business studies. Students following a non-business subject such as engineering or science who undertake ancillary studies in marketing and business studies will also find this book of great value.

Adrian Palmer and Ian Worthington

MARKETING: AN OVERVIEW

1.1 WHAT IS MARKETING?

Marketing has become an all-embracing business discipline in Western economies, adopted by large sections of both the private and public sectors. The Chartered Institute of Marketing defines marketing as

The management process which identifies, anticipates and supplies customer requirements efficiently and profitably.

The first part of this definition entails the company looking outward and studying the nature of existing and potential markets, while the second part requires it to look inward to ensure that it manages its resources effectively in order to meet those needs that have been identified in the market. Strategic marketing management is the process of ensuring a good fit between the opportunities of the market-place and and the abilities and resources of the organization.

Despite its increasing importance as a business discipline, marketing is not universal; nor has it always been with us. Before looking in more detail at what is meant by marketing orientation, we need to consider some of the business disciplines that have preceded the dominance of marketing orientation.

Today, the needs of the consumer assume primary importance. Earlier, however, the need for cost reduction was emphasized during periods of what can be called production orientation, and the need for aggressive selling of a company's output assumed overwhelming importance during periods of what was sales orientation (see Figure 1.1).

1.2 PRODUCTION ORIENTATION

Marketing as a business discipline has much less significance where goods are scarce and considerable unsatisfied demand exists. If a company is operating in a stable environment in which it can sell all that it can produce, why bother spending time and money trying to understand precisely what benefit a customer seeks from a product and trying to anticipate future requirements? Furthermore, if the company has significant monopoly power, it may have little interest in being more efficient in meeting customer requirements. The state monopolies of Eastern Europe are frequently accused of producing what they imagined consumers might want and what was convenient for their organizations to produce. Thus, in car production, Eastern and Western design standards increasingly diverged; the East German Trabant car satisfied very few of the car-buying public's needs, yet in some countries the waiting list was up to 20 years long. Protected by monopoly power, the company had little incentive to improve its product or

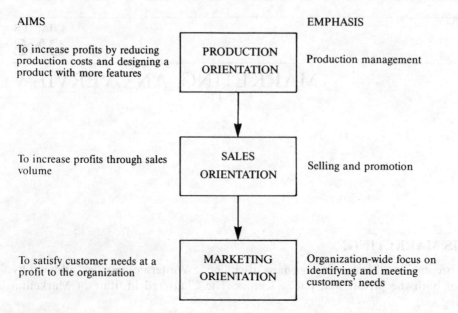

AIMS   EMPHASIS

To increase profits by reducing   Production management
production costs and designing a
product with more features

To increase profits through sales   Selling and promotion
volume

To satisfy customer needs at a   Organization-wide focus on
profit to the organization   identifying and meeting
                                                                    customers' needs

Figure 1.1   The development of the dominant business environment

to produce it more efficiently. This was in sharp contrast to the West German market, where increasing competitive pressure resulted in an excess supply of cars relative to demand. Western manufacturers have had to modify their product to reflect the changing needs of consumers, whether this be for improved performance, additional features or increased reliability. To attract the customer, a lower sales price and higher product quality could be achieved only by efficient production: those companies that succeeded in supplying consumer requirements efficiently made a profit which ensured their survival, and those that didn't would eventually cease production as independent entities. With the reunification of the two Germanies and the creation of a single German market, the production orientation of the Trabant came to an abrupt end as consumers exercised their newly found spending power and freedom of choice by buying the products of its Western competitors.

In Britain, production orientation was common until the 1920s, when a shortage of goods and a lack of competition resulted in a sellers' market. The world depression of the 1920s and 1930s had the effect of tilting the balance of supply and demand more in favour of the buyer, resulting in sellers having to address the needs of increasingly selective customers more seriously. Production orientation in Britain has been associated with some of the nationalized industries, which have faced very little effective competition. The telephone service was frequently accused of paying insufficient attention to changing consumer needs—for example the provision of a rapid repair service or a choice of telephone handset designs. Before 1980, the Post Office had a monopoly in the provision of telephone handsets, with the result that they were dull and didn't do all the things that consumers sought. With the removal of this monopoly, consumers were able to buy or rent handsets that reflected their life-styles and individual performance requirements.

Production orientation sometimes returns to an otherwise competitive market during periods of shortage. The shortage could be caused by factors such as strikes, bad weather or simply a sudden increase in demand relative to supply. For example, during a prolonged strike by bakers in Britain in 1973, the bakers remaining in production were able to sell all that they could produce. These bakers moved away from providing specialized products for different segments of the markets, ensuring wide availability and a consistently high quality: instead, there was a tendency to produce large batches of uniform bread in order to minimize production costs. Channels of distribution were limited to those that were easy for the baker rather than advantageous to the consumer. The extent of price discrimination was much reduced. In short, a form of production orientation had temporarily returned to dominate the business environment.

1.3   SALES ORIENTATION

Faced with an increasingly competitive market, the natural reaction of some business organizations was to shout louder in order to entice customers to buy its stockpile of goods. No thought had yet gone into examining precisely what benefits a customer was seeking to obtain from the purchase of a product—product policy was still driven by the desire to produce those products which the company felt it was good at making. However, in order to shift its stockpiles, the focal point of the business now moved away from the production manager to the sales manager. The company sought to increase effective demand through the use of various sales techniques. Advertising, sales promotion and personal selling were increasingly used to emphasize product differentiation and branding. Above all, sales techniques were used to create a greater awareness of the brand among the perceived group of customers.

Sales orientation was a move away from a strict product orientation, but it still did not focus on satisfying customer needs. Little effort was made to research these needs and devise new offerings which were customer-led rather than production-led.

Sales orientation has been in evidence in a number of areas of the economy. Supermarkets have often grown by heavy advertising of their competitive price advantage, supported by aggressive sales promotion techniques within their stores. It was only in the 1970s and 1980s that supermarkets as a whole seriously addressed the needs that customers sought to satisfy in a supermarket, such as the range of goods offered, the availability of car parking, speed of checkouts, and quality of after-sales service. Similarly, the package holiday industry during much of the 1970s and 1980s was based on a sales mentality—heavy advertising and discounting were used to sell holidays which the companies thought consumers wanted and which were much easier for them to provide. More recently, travel companies have recognized that selling on the basis of a low price alone is not adequate. They are now responding to identified consumer needs by offering guaranteed standards of hotel, compensation schemes for delayed departure and a better service by representatives at holiday resorts. Much of this is much more difficult for the company to provide and will cost the customer more, but it represents a shift away from sales orientation towards marketing orientation.

If a company were to identify consumer needs and provide a product offering that satisfied these needs, then consumers would want to buy the product, rather than the company having to rely on intensive sales techniques. In the words of Peter Drucker (1973),

The aim of marketing is to make selling superfluous. The aim of marketing is to know and understand the customer so well that the product or service fits him and sells itself. Ideally, marketing should result in a customer who is ready to buy. All that should be needed is to make the product or service available . . .

1.4   MARKETING ORIENTATION

Marketing orientation came to be the dominant business discipline as increasingly competitive markets turned to the buyers' favour. It was no longer good enough for a company simply to produce what it was good at, or to sell its products more aggressively than its competitors.

Some of the elements of marketing orientation can be traced far back to the ancient Greeks, the Phoenicians and the Venetian traders. In modern times, marketing orientation emerged in the relatively affluent countries among products where competition between suppliers had become great. It became an important discipline in the USA in the 1950s and has since become dominant around the world. In a marketing-orientated business environment, a firm will survive in the long term and make a profit only if it ascertains the needs of clearly defined groups in society and produces goods and services which satisfy identified customer requirements. The emphasis is on the customer wanting to buy rather than on the producer needing to sell.

Marketing orientation is used to describe both the basic philosophy of the business and the techniques which the business uses.

1.5 MARKETING AS A BUSINESS PHILOSOPHY

Marketing as a philosophy puts the customer at the centre of all the organization's considerations. Basic values such as the requirement to identify the changing needs of existing customers and the necessity to search constantly for new market opportunities are instilled in all members of a truly marketing-orientated organization, covering all aspects of the organization's activities. Thus, in a fast-food retailer the training of serving staff would emphasize those items—such as the standard of dress—which research had found to be particularly valued by existing and potential customers. The personnel manager would have a selection policy that sought to recruit staff who fulfilled the needs of customers rather than simply minimizing the wage bill; the accountant would investigate the effects on customers before deciding to save money by cutting stockholding levels, thereby possibly reducing customer choice. It is not sufficient for a company merely to appoint a marketing manager or set up a marketing department: viewed as a philosophy, marketing is an attitude of mind which permeates the whole business organization.

1.6 MARKETING AS A BUSINESS PRACTICE

Marketing is associated with a range of specific techniques. For example, market research is a technique for finding out about customer needs, but it loses a lot of its value if it is conducted by a company that has not fully embraced the philosophy of marketing. Similarly, marketing management provides a series of specific techniques covering advertising, pricing, the design of channels of distribution and new product development, some of which are considered later in this chapter.

1.7 PRIVATE AND PUBLIC SECTOR MARKETING

Marketing orientation first achieved importance in industries that produced largely undifferentiated products: with growing competition in their markets, survival meant researching the needs of specific segments of their markets and developing products to meet that segment's needs. The soap powder and cigarette markets were early adopters of marketing orientation for this reason. Over time, more and more markets have become competitive, and increasingly this has applied also to much of the public sector. Many non-statutory public services have faced competition for some time. A number of Britain's nationalized industries, such as British Rail, have come to face ever-growing competition from the private sector. This, combined with the requirement for greater accountability, has encouraged the adoption of marketing orientation by most nationalized industries.

Many public sector services such as museums and leisure services are increasingly being given clearly defined business objectives, which makes it much more difficult for them to continue doing what they like doing rather than what the public they serve wants. Marketing orientation has been most rapidly adopted by those public sector services that provide marketable goods and services, such as swimming pools and municipal bus services. It is much more difficult—though still possible—to adopt marketing orientation where the public sector is a monopoly provider of a statutory service. In the provision of hospitals, the government is moving towards allocating resources to hospitals that are popular with patients—those that provide an efficient service which meets the needs of patients will grow, while those that don't will gradually lose resources. Only time will tell if government policies will shift the health service away from its historical acceptance of production orientation.

In other public services, it may be even more difficult to introduce a marketing discipline. The

VICTORIA & ALBERT MUSEUM DISPLAYS NEW MARKETING ORIENTATION

Museums in Britain have traditionally been seen as guardians of our culture, and the curator as one who preserves the history of our culture for future generations. Managing a museum has been viewed as a long-term mission with educational objectives, and the idea of basing exhibitions on their short-term popularity with visitors tended to be met with resistance from curators.

The days of dull exhibits being displayed in dusty glass cases is rapidly disappearing, however, as this sector of the public services takes on board a much greater marketing orientation, brought about by changes in the museums' environment. Visitors' expectations of a museum have changed with the emergence of a wide range of private sector theme museums offering elaborate displays; the relatively high prices charged by museums such as the Jorvik Viking Centre in York indicated that a significant segment of the population was prepared to pay for a museum offering a higher standard of presentation. At the same time, the political environment was changing, with government trying to move as many public services as possible towards a business-like orientation.

Against this background, the Victoria & Albert Museum in London appointed its first marketing manager in 1988. Marketing principles and practices were used to achieve the museum's aim to double the number of visitors from 500,000 in 1990 to 1 million in 1995 and then to 5 million by the year 2000. A marketing plan was developed after undertaking considerable market research. A strategic plan was adopted to target specific groups by creating highly visible, highly segmented events which would attract new audiences as well as build repeat audiences.

One result of this strategy was the creation of the Tsui Gallery of Chinese Art in June 1991. Market research carried out by NOP into visitor expectations revealed that visitors were interested in thematic displays rather than the traditional chronological shows. Carrying marketing practices further, the exhibition earned sponsorship of £1.25 million from Hong Kong businessman TT Sui and was supported by a £30,000 poster campaign and the distribution of leaflets in Chinese restaurants throughout London. By adopting these marketing techniques, the V & A felt confident of attracting a segment of the population that might not otherwise have visited the museum, as well as generating additional revenue which will contribute towards the long-term cost of maintaining existing collections and acquiring new ones of national importance. It appears that the V & A is successfully achieving its objectives by adopting a marketing orientation.

core of the work carried out by the police force, the fire brigades and the armed services cannot easily be subjected to the test of market forces. It is difficult for the consumer to exercise any choice over who polices their town, and equally difficult in practice for local authorities to subcontract provision via a competitive tender.

1.8 THE MARKETING ENVIRONMENT

Marketing orientation, then, requires organizations to monitor their environment and to adjust their offering so that consumer needs are fulfilled at a profit to the organization. But what makes up the marketing environment? Kotler (1988), for example, defines a business organization's marketing environment as

the actors and forces external to the marketing management function of the firm that impinge on the marketing management's ability to develop and maintain successful transactions with its customers.

Here, marketing has to look both inwardly and at the outside world. Within the company, its structure and politics will affect the manner in which it responds to changing consumer needs. A firm that assigns marketing responsibilities to a narrow group of people may in fact create internal tensions which may make it less effective at responding to changing consumer needs than one where marketing responsibilities in their widest sense are disseminated throughout. The whole issue of the internal environment of marketing is examined in detail in Chapter 4.

The external environment comprises all of those uncontrollable events outside the business which impinge on its activities. Some of these events have a direct effect on the firm's activities: these can be described as the immediate external environment. Others, beyond the immediate environment but nevertheless affecting the firm, can be described as the indirect external environment (see Figure 1.2).

The immediate external environment would include suppliers and distributors; some of these the firm would deal directly with, while others, with whom there is currently no direct contact, could nevertheless influence the firm's policies. Similarly, the company's competitors would have

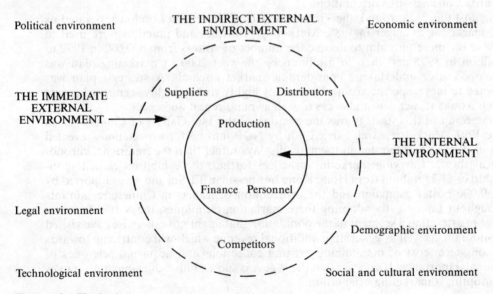

Figure 1.2 The business organization's marketing environment

a direct effect on its market position and would form part of the immediate external environment.

To give an example, a manufacturer of television sets would need first of all to identify who its competitors were: both direct competitors, in the form of those producing similar designs of television, and competitors with products that satisfy broadly similar needs—the need for entertainment—such as compact disc/video players. The company would need to monitor the competitors in terms of their quality, design, price, etc.; it may have decided in advance on a strategy of being either an innovator or a follower. To make the most of new opportunities, it would monitor new product developments by its suppliers—new designs of integrated circuits which it could incorporate into its models, for example. It would also probably be continually monitoring other potential suppliers to ensure that it was able to buy the quality of components that it required from the lowest-cost source. A manufacturer of this type would not typically sell the equipment directly to the final consumer: instead, it would distribute them through dealers who could offer local availability of stock, sell it aggressively and provide an after-sales service. In the television industry, the changing size and sophistication of the intermediaries would be an external and uncontrollable event to which the industry would have to respond, for example by offering different packaging to meet the needs of the growing catalogue store sector.

Beyond this immediate external environment is a whole set of factors which will indirectly affect the company's relationship to its markets—the indirect external environment. The firm may have no direct relationships with politicians as it does with suppliers; yet the actions of politicians in passing new legislation may have profound effects on the markets the firm seeks to serve. The indirect environmental factors cover a wide range of nebulous phenomena; they represent general forces and pressures rather than institutions which the business relates to directly. One of these forces is the demographic environment. Changes in the size and age structure of the population are critical to many business organizations; for instance, a retailer of fashion clothing would need to be able to predict the size of different age segments so that resources could be shifted towards growing segments and away from declining segments. The company might study the demographic environment by analysing changes in birth rates and the migration of people between different parts of the country and, within any area, between urban and rural areas. With an analysis of these trends, the company will be in a better position to predict likely turnover for a new shop in a specific location in five years' time than if it had assumed that past performance would simply be repeated.

A whole range of indirect environmental forces can be identified. Many of them overlap, and the extent to which they are given labels is to some extent arbitrary. Many analysts have divided these factors into four categories and used the acronym PEST to describe them—the Political, Economic, Social and Technological environments. This book additionally considers the legal environment as an area of concern in its own right, although it is of course linked with the other elements; the political environment creates much of our legislation, while it in turn influences a firm's economic, social and technological environments. The demographic environment is similarly considered to be an important area worthy of analysis in its own right.

1.9   THE TOOLS OF MARKETING MANAGEMENT

The subsequent chapters of this book are concerned with analysing the indirect marketing environment. In this chapter, a brief analysis is made first of the means by which the environment is monitored through marketing research, and second of the tools that marketing-orientated firms use to adapt their offerings to satisfy the needs of their target customers. For a more comprehensive overview of these tools, the reader is recommended to consult one of the many books available, especially Lancaster and Massingham's *Essentials of Marketing* (1988) and Kotler and Armstrong's *Principles of Marketing* (1989).

1.10 MARKETING RESEARCH

In order to be able to respond to a constantly changing environment, a business organization must collect information on which it can base decisions. Marketing research has seen major growth in recent years for at least three reasons:

1. Markets have become larger, with national replacing local markets and—increasingly—European-wide markets replacing national ones as the basis on which products are launched. Larger markets mean greater risk, which can be reduced by having greater access to information.
2. In some cases, technology and the development of economies of scale has increased the threshold at which a new product can be launched into a market; for example, a new medium-sized family car requires very efficient large-scale production methods if it is to be competitive, which in turn means a high minimum volume and high risk.
3. The environment in which a company operates is changing at an increasingly rapid rate.

Marketing research does not produce answers—it can only produce information that may help decision-makers and allow them to make decisions that are based on something more than a hunch. Marketing research can lose much of its value if it is not set clear objectives and managed and communicated effectively. For this reason, marketing information systems are created to manage the flow of information to meet the needs of decision-makers—both for planning future activities and for controlling current operations. Marketing information systems are discussed more fully in Chapter 13.

Market research should be distinguished from *marketing research*: the former is essentially confined to the task of quantifying the size and nature of markets, while the latter is much wider and includes research into all aspects of a company's marketing activity—the effectiveness of its advertising and sales promotion activity, for example. In determining its marketing research needs, an enterprise should identify which elements of the marketing environment are critical to its success. A firm's aims and objectives—or mission statement—will give an indication of the general areas that should be the subject of regular information collection. These will then be refined into more specific information needs—for example the level of disposable income, or attitudes towards diet. The programme will involve two basic types of research: secondary (or desk) research, and primary (or field) research. A company would normally start with secondary research.

1.10.1 Secondary research

This is research that has been collected by somebody else, at some other time, for some other purpose. Although the information is to some extent out of date by the time the company receives it and is probably not quite what was wanted in the first place, secondary research is popular on account of its relatively low cost. Government sources provide a wide variety of secondary data, although their quality and availability have been declining in recent years. Some typical sources of secondary data are shown in Table 1.1.

Table 1.1 Secondary marketing research: some examples of sources

Sources	Material provided
Monthly Digest of Statistics and *Annual Abstract of Statistics*	General background statistics on topics such as population trends, employment, production, expenditure and overseas trade. These are a useful starting point before consulting more specialized statistical sources.
Business Monitors	Monthly, quarterly or annual reports produced by the government on sales figures for over 4000 individual products and services.
Regional Trends	An annual government publication showing regional variations in current and projected population, housing, employment, production, investment, health and education, etc.
General Household Survey	An annual publication based on a survey of about 15,000 households, containing information on housing, employment, education and household expenditure.
Mintel	Privately produced research reports on selected markets indicating size of market, structure and trends.
Trade associations	Most industries have some form of trade association and many provide regular information on market conditions for their industry—for example, the Association of British Travel Agents undertakes research into holiday-buying intentions and sells the results to its members.

1.10.2 Primary research

If secondary data do not yield sufficient information, the company must then turn to relatively expensive primary data collection. The four main types of primary data collection are survey research, observation, experimentation, and qualitative techniques.

Survey research A survey can be undertaken to achieve a number of aims. It could be carried out to judge reaction to a proposed new product or awareness of a brand name, or to learn about the public's attitude towards an important point which may affect a new product launch. A survey involves carefully defining research objectives and designing a questionnaire which can be administered by mail, telephone or personal communication. Sometimes a company seeking to reduce its costs will undertake its research in conjunction with a number of other information-seekers through an Omnibus survey.

Observation Observational research involves no interaction with the subject of the research—instead, the researcher views and listens to situations and records human behaviour. It is frequently used to monitor the activity of competitors, for example where a shopkeeper makes a note of the prices being charged at nearby shops. Other uses include measuring pedestrian and vehicle flows by proposed retail outlets and observing the behaviour of consumers when using a product.

Experimentation Experimentation techniques can be applied at a number of levels. In a consumer panel, blindfold tests are used to identify individual consumer preferences. At a higher level, experimentation can be used in a scientific manner to compare different marketing strategies between areas that are identical in terms of all other environmental variables.

Qualitative techniques   Where a company seeks to probe people's attitudes and feelings, an unstructured interview—either on a one-to-one basis or in a group—may be the most appropriate method of research. Cultural values are constantly shifting, and a qualitative technique may be useful for example in probing the attitudes of ethnic minorities towards buying package holidays.

1.11   MARKETING INTELLIGENCE

In addition to collecting relatively 'hard' data about the market in which it operates, a business organization will need to acquire some relatively 'soft' information regarding ideas and trends in its environment. Proposed changes in legislation, new product offerings by competitors and the emergence of new competitors are all issues that cannot be picked up easily through a formalized marketing research system, yet each may be critical to the fortunes of the company. Intelligence of this nature can be gained in a number of ways. A survey of the media, especially the trade press, may pick up pertinent developments; some companies subscribe to cuttings services which take extracts from published media. A second major source of intelligence is the company's own workforce, especially sales personnel who are in day-to-day contact with the market-place and can obtain information on current trends. A company must ensure not only that such intelligence is collected and collated regularly, but also that it is rapidly disseminated to those who can act on it. Intelligence-gathering procedures are discussed more fully in Chapter 13.

1.11.1   Internal reporting system

An organization routinely collects information which could be of value as an input to a marketing information system. By use of postcode analysis, an analysis of the addresses of enquiries and customers can help to build up a profile of the existing customer base. A company selling to industrial markets could analyse sales orders to identify trends between different sectors, between different parts of the country or between small and large companies, for example.

1.12   SEGMENTATION

A central aim of marketing orientation is to meet the needs of customers. Different customers have different needs which they seek to satisfy. To be fully marketing-orientated, a company would have to adapt its offering to meet the needs of each individual. In fact, very few firms can justify aiming to meet the needs of each specific individual: instead, they aim to meet the needs of small sub-groups within the population. These sub-groups are referred to as 'segments'. A segment, then, represents a group of customers with similar needs to which the company responds with a product offering designed to meet the specific needs of the targeted group. A three-dimensional segmentation of the population in terms of sex, income level and environmental awareness is illustrated in Figure 1.3.

The development of segmentation and target marketing reflects the movement away from production orientation towards marketing orientation. When goods were scarce and the emphasis was on producing them as cheaply as possible, companies produced one homogeneous product which sought to satisfy the needs of the whole population. In the early days of mass production of cars, the emphasis was on keeping costs down through economies of scale—production capacity was initially limited, and people were only too happy to buy a uniform black car, something which until then would have been no more than a dream for most of them.

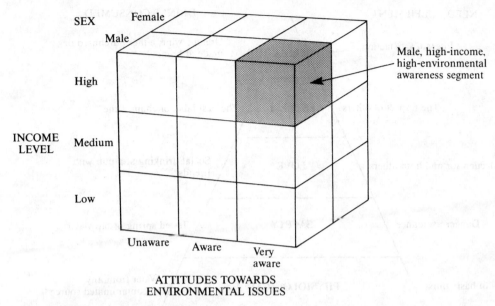

Figure 1.3 Hypothetical segmentation of population by income, sex and attitudes towards environment issues

Over time, increasing affluence has increased customers' expectations. The customer was no longer satisfied with the homogeneous black car, but instead was able to demand one that satisfied an increasingly wide range of needs—not just for transport, but for speed, excitement and as a status symbol, among many others. Furthermore, society was becoming much more fragmented—the 'average' consumer was becoming much more of a myth—as incomes, attitudes and life-styles diverged. This fragmentation can be related to changes in the basic levels of need that are being satisfied at different stages of a society's development. A society that is surviving at the most basic level of existence will be in a position to demand no more than basic commodities which satisfy its members' need for food and shelter. When these needs can be satisfied, individuals seek to satisfy social and esteem needs—to enjoy friendships with others and to earn their respect. Once *these* needs are met, individuals may seek to satisfy a need for internal contentment.

Maslow (1943) identified the dominant level of needs that motivate an individual's purchasing decisions. The Hierarchy of Needs model (Figure 1.4) illustrates the changing basis for aggregate demand as a society progresses with particular hypothetical reference to the drinks market. This figure indicates how we might understand the emergence of specialized, higher-value drinks as a reflection of the changing needs of members of a society.

The Hierarchy of Needs model is no more than a conceptual model. It is difficult to measure the nature of the needs motivating an individual, and even more so when the motivations of societies as a whole are being analysed. Nevertheless, the marketer must recognize that consumers in Western developed countries are likely to be seeking to satisfy a much wider range of needs than those in a developing country.

Alongside the greater fragmentation of society, technology is increasingly allowing special products to be produced for ever smaller segments. Initially, Henry Ford did not have the technology to offer anything more than one basic model of car in one colour—black. To have produced variations on the basic model would have meant stopping the production line and

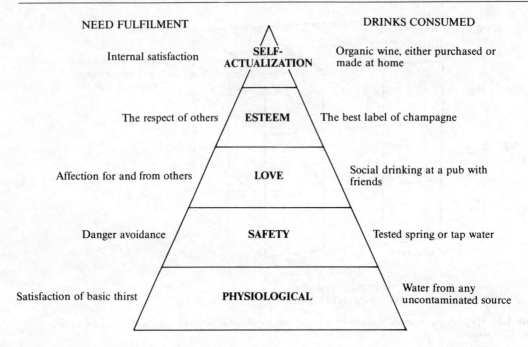

Figure 1.4 A hierarchy of needs model: application to the drinks market

expensive retooling. Today, computer-controlled production methods allow Ford to produce many variants of the same basic model. So the 'Popular' version of the Ford Escort is aimed at the budget-conscious company buyer or the household seeking a cheap run-around. The XR3 model is aimed at the needs of a younger, more affluent segment which seeks excitement and status out of a car. The Ghia is a more refined car aimed at the needs of the affluent, elderly male segment. Some short-run models are aimed at quite specific segments—the Cosmopolitan was aimed at the needs of career-minded women, for example. In addition to these basic model types, Ford is able to offer a range of engine sizes and colours to meet the needs of very small segments.

1.13 TARGET MARKETING IN PRACTICE

The ever more diverse needs of consumers mean that firms must become increasingly scientific in seeking out and addressing small groups. The process of target marketing has three stages:

1. *Market segmentation*—dividing the population into distinct groups of consumers
2. *Target selection*—choosing which of the many possible segments to address
3. *Positioning*—adopting a position relative to its competitors in offering products to a particular segment

1.13.1 Market segmentation

The purpose of dividing the population into segments is to identify groups with similar needs and who will behave in a similar manner when presented with a product offering. The aim is to create segments where the difference within each segment is less than the difference between segments. There is no universal basis for segmenting markets; the basis adopted will vary from one product to another, and the most appropriate basis will be the one that is best at predicting consumer behaviour. Nor is there any universal basis for determining the optimum number of segments—in some markets such as fresh vegetables, relatively few segments can be identified compared with the large number possible for perfumes. It is pointless for a company to identify a large number of segments that are too small in their own right to be economically viable.

Some of the more commonly used bases for identifying segments in consumer markets are shown in Table 1.2.

Table 1.2 Bases for segmenting consumer markets

Bases for segmentation	Comments
Age	Widely used—e.g. holidays—Club 18–30 and Saga
Sex	Many obvious examples such as clothing; often also used more subtly as a basis for segmentation—e.g. cars, alcoholic drinks
Household structure	The size and structure of a household—e.g. economy-size packages aimed at the young couple with a family; convenience meals for single-adult households
Social economic groups	A widely used basis which takes account of a person's occupation, arguably an important influence on spending power and consumption pattern. The commonly used classification is: (A) Higher managerial, administrative and professional (B) Intermediate managerial, administrative and professional (C1) Supervisory, clerical, junior administrative or professional (C2) Skilled manual workers (D) Semi-skilled and unskilled manual workers (E) State pensioners, casual workers
Geodemographics	Where a person lives can be correlated with his or her spending pattern; e.g. postcodes are used to define ACORN codes. Each code represents a particular life-style
Education	Very important for newspapers—e.g. *Sun v. Guardian*
Benefit segmentation	Different segments can buy the same product but seek different benefits—e.g. fashion as against timekeeping as a primary benefit from watch-buying
Rate of usage	Frequent users of a product such as rail-users will require a different marketing programme compared to a non-user—reliability and price discounts against the need for timetable and fare information
Loyalty status	Groups that remain loyal to one specific brand as against those who are prepared to switch brands

1.13.2   Target selection

Defining segments of the market is only a preliminary to deciding which specific segments to aim to satisfy. Large companies with adequate resources may choose to address a large number of segments; for example, Ford provides a number of variants of each car to satisfy a large number of different segments. Smaller companies may choose to target only one or two segments at a time—Aston Martin and Morgan are examples of companies who offer a much more limited product range to a small number of segments.

The choice of a target segment will involve the company looking inwardly at its strengths and weaknesses and outwardly at the opportunities and threats in its environment. For each segment, the company will need to determine whether it is growing or declining. This in turn may involve having to read the demographic environment (to predict what will happen to the size of that particular age group), the economic environment (will this group be getting richer or poorer than the average?) or possibly the political environment (will the government intervene in this market with legislation?)

This book addresses the question of how a company can analyse an increasingly turbulent business environment in order to select the groups of customers it should aim to serve, and how it should adapt the products it offers to meet their changing needs.

1.13.3   Positioning

A company can address the needs of a particular segment in a number of ways that are acceptable to that segment. The company could simply copy the other competitors in the market by imitating their marketing programmes. Alternatively, it could seek to differentiate itself from the competition slightly. A company producing breakfast cereal may try to give its product a slightly different flavour and build up a 'fun' image which may position it away from other cereals focusing on value for money. British supermarkets are typically evaluated by potential customers by two sets of criteria: the perceived price levels charged, and the quality of service offered in terms of range of goods, quality of merchandise, opening hours, store environment, etc.). The relative positions of some of the main UK competitors are plotted schematically in Figure 1.5.

Product positioning in its fullest sense involves a number of tools which a business organization uses to address its market and to differentiate its products from its competitors. These tools are known as the 'marketing mix'.

1.14   THE MARKETING MIX

Environmental factors are those that are beyond the control of the marketer, who must monitor and respond to change in them. Response is brought about by using the elements of the marketing mix. Kotler (1988) gives the following definition:

The Marketing Mix is the set of controllable variables that the firm can use to influence the buyer's response.

The marketing mix is commonly accredited with four principal elements—the '4 Ps' of Product, Price, Promotion and Place. Each of these itself contains a number of elements, so marketers talk about the 'product mix' and the 'promotion mix'. Some marketers have defined the elements of the marketing mix in slightly different ways; the end result is usually similar, even if the method of classifying the elements differs.

A marketer is a person who, partly through scientific research and partly through inspiration, creatively mixes these elements to produce offerings that satisfy consumers' needs at a profit to the business. The essence of managing the marketing mix lies in providing each segment of the market with the mix of product, price, promotion and place characteristics that most suits its needs (see Figure 1.6).

1.14.1   Product

To a marketer, a product includes both tangible goods and intangible services. A product can be viewed at a number of levels. At the most basic level, it may comprise a plain generic item—such as a radio. Customers would expect to buy more than this basic offering, however: they would

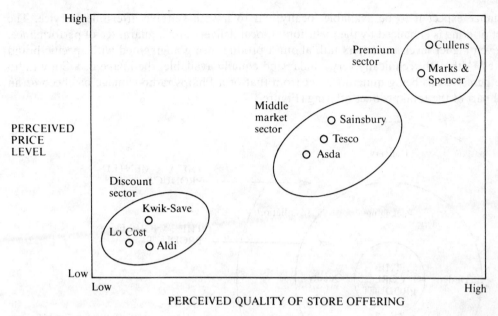

Figure 1.5 A hypothetical product positioning map for UK supermarkets

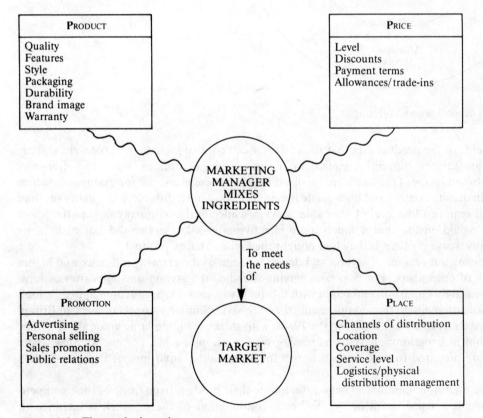

Figure 1.6 The marketing mix

for instance expect it to be available locally and to have a suitable after-sales service. The product offering is enhanced by the inclusion of local delivery and a guarantee of performance. At an even higher level, marketers talk about a product being augmented with specific brand attributes. Although technically very similar and equally available, the image of a Sony radio may be perceived as being quite different from that of a Philips radio—image has become an integral part of the total product offering (Figure 1.7).

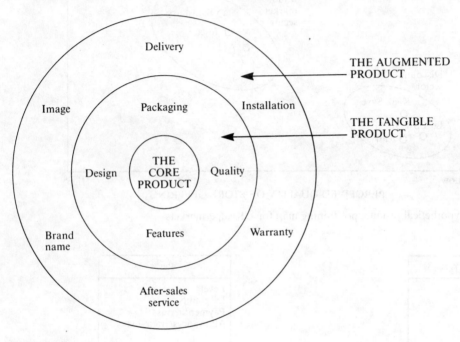

Figure 1.7 The total product offering

The elements of the product mix that the marketer can control include quality levels, styling, special design features, durability, packaging, range of sizes or options, warranty, after-sales service and brand image. Trade-offs are involved between these elements; for example, one firm may invest in quality control and high-grade materials to provide a durable, top-quality product which would require a low level of after-sales service, while another company might offer lower quality but would ensure that a much more effective after-sales service did not make their customers any worse off than if they had bought the higher-quality product.

The increasing importance of styling and design is a sign of the growing affluence and higher expectations of consumers. For a person buying a radio, the styling and appearances have become increasingly important compared with the quality of sound reproduction, as people look more and more for a design that complements their life-style. Similarly, the retail scene in Britain underwent considerable change during the 1980s, with stores spending large amounts of money on refurbishment programmes. With increasing wealth, shopping has become an area where consumers are prepared to pay more in return for a pleasanter environment in which to buy goods.

Brands are used by companies to help differentiate their product from those of their competitors. A brand is a name, term or symbol, or a combination of these, which is intended to differentiate the goods of one seller from those of all other sellers. Consumers are willing to pay more for an established product with unique attributes and consistent quality standards than for an unbranded product. With increased wealth, consumers have looked increasingly to products that carry a brand image. Sometimes the image is more important than the tangible product itself, and does a lot to convey a message about the life-style of the purchaser—perfumes and training shoes are often selected for their life-style associations rather than for the tangible qualities of the product.

The fragmentation of society referred to earlier means that companies must offer a wider range of product options. A brewery can no longer produce just a couple of brands of bitter and lager—it also has to meet the needs of groups who want high-strength lagers, non-alcoholic lagers, low-calorie drinks, traditional cask-conditioned 'real ale' and lagers with exciting life-style associations.

The product mix may need to be altered to reflect more widely changing social and cultural values. Cosmetics have traditionally been considered a purely feminine product. However, just as with fashion clothing some years earlier, it is now being seen as acceptable for males to buy cosmetics for themselves. Although many of these cosmetics are essentially the same as those that have traditionally been purchased by women, manufacturers have repackaged and reformulated the product to appeal to the new male market.

Sometimes changes in the legal environment require the product mix to be altered. New homes are not typically sold on their thermal efficiency, but a gradual tightening of the building regulations over time has forced house builders to improve insulation levels.

With regard to the product mix of firms in general, the 1970s and 1980s saw a growing emphasis on short-life, high-fashion designs. Clothing, home furnishings and electrical equipment are just three sectors where products were selected to fulfil fluctuating life-style requirements. It can be argued that short-term fashionability represents needs felt by the relatively young segments in society—that older segments tend to value durability rather than fashionability. The changing age structure of most Western European countries, with increasing proportions of elderly people, may therefore bring about a general shift in emphasis from fashionability to durability as the cultural norm.

1.14.2 Pricing

Of all the elements of the marketing mix, only price brings revenue into a company—the others result in expenditure. If the selling price of a product is set too high, a company may not achieve its sales volume targets; if it is set too low, volume targets may be achieved, but no profit earned. Setting prices is a difficult part of the marketing mix. A starting point is to consider the market price for a product; the economists' approach to free-market price determination is described more fully in Chapter 5.

While market forces impose a constraint on the ability of marketers to fully exploit the price element of the marketing mix in highly competitive markets, the marketer in an imperfectly competitive market uses pricing policy to achieve three basic objectives.

1. Get a product accepted by a market
2. Maintain market share against competition
3. Earn profits

As the relative emphasis placed on each of these objectives is likely to change during the life of a product, the price charged is itself likely to change. Relatively undifferentiated new product launches may require a relatively low price at first to tempt people to try the new product. Once customers have developed a loyalty towards that brand, the company will try and increase the selling price in real terms, capitalizing on the brand loyalty which it has built up. Confectionery (such as Whispa and Hob Nob biscuits) and magazines (such as *Bella*) frequently follow this price pattern. Marketers refer to this as a saturation—or penetration—pricing strategy. An alternative is to start with a relatively high price to capitalize on the product's uniqueness and novelty value; as more competitors move into the market, the price is gradually reduced to protect market share and allow access to further segments of the market. This type of pricing strategy (known as prestige pricing or skimming) is often used for new high-technology products—fax machines, home computers and video cassette recorders have all followed this pricing pattern.

The pricing of a firm's product will depend on the stage in the life-cycle for the market as a whole. If the market is new and growing, there will be relatively less pressure on prices than when the market becomes mature or saturated, where the level of competition will impose a strong downward pressure on price levels. Figure 1.8 depicts a typical product life-cycle and the pressure that is placed on pricing decisions by the extent of competition in the company's business environment.

Bases for price determination There are three basic approaches to determining a price for a product:

1. What it costs to produce
2. What the competition is charging
3. What customers are prepared to pay

Production costs set a minimum limit on the price a company will charge. What the customer is actually willing to pay sets the maximum that the company can achieve. Within these two limits is the area of price discretion open to the company.

Costs The idea of basing prices on production costs can be more difficult than would first appear. Some products involve a high level of fixed costs relative to variable costs and pose problems when it comes to cost allocation. Airport operation is a good example. The fixed costs of maintaining the runway, navigation facilities and terminal buildings form a high proportion of total costs, which need to be allocated between different types of output—landing facilities for private aircraft, scheduled/charter aircraft and freight aircraft, for example. It can also be argued that it is more expensive to provide landing facilities at the peak period, as equipment is being provided for only a short productive period and its cost cannot be spread over other output.

Within an organization that has high fixed costs, there is likely to be argument among departmental managers over how these costs should be allocated. BAA (formerly British Airports Authority) is a good example of an organization where the allocation basis has frequently changed.

A further problem of using costs as a basis for pricing is that it can be difficult to predict how much it will actually cost to produce a product. In some markets it is necessary to print price lists that will apply for some months in advance; yet all cost information is of a historic nature. Tour operators publish price lists which they would expect to last for up to a year; yet the price of important inputs such as fuel can vary greatly during that time. Therefore they often include in their price the right to charge a supplement if the cost of key items—in this case oil and foreign exchange—increases beyond a specified amount. A company can also overcome the problem of basing prices on unpredictable cost levels by organizing itself for more frequent price changes. Oil companies, for example, have developed the ability to adjust the forecourt price of petrol at very short notice in response to movements in the cost of oil.

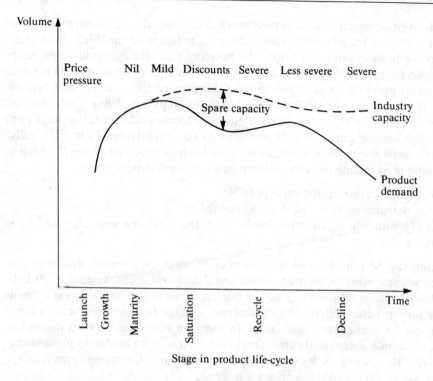

Figure 1.8 The product life-cycle and its effects on pricing

A strict cost-based pricing system does not allow a company to charge different amounts to different groups according to their willingness to pay. Nevertheless, it is the basis of many pricing systems; for example, builders charge for time and materials at a standard rate plus a fixed percentage for a profit margin.

Competition The nature of the business environment in which a firm operates will influence the extent to which prices will be set by reference to those of competitors.

At one extreme, in a perfectly competitive market, the firm will have to take its prices from the market. A company selling basic commodities such as fruit and vegetables from a market stall will find it very difficult to charge anything other than the going rate—anything less than this rate and there will be no profit margin left to make it worth their while selling; anything more and they will be unlikely to sell any. In an undifferentiated commodity market, it is very difficult to persuade a customer to pay more than the going rate; the price must be taken from what the competitors are charging, or the firm must seek to differentiate its product in some way. The methods by which market equilibrium prices are determined are examined in more detail in Chapter 5.

In some markets where there are relatively few companies, it is common for one firm to become the acknowledged price-leader, while others act as price-followers. The followers wait for the leader to make a price adjustment and then generally follow to a varying degree in terms of amount and timing. In the UK new car market, Ford has been acknowledged as the traditional price-leader—other car manufacturers wait to see what action Ford takes before adjusting their prices.

Price discrimination   A profit-maximizing company seeks to discover the maximum price that a particular consumer is prepared to pay for a product. So long as this is sustainable in the longer term, this represents the profit-maximizing price. The haggling that takes place in many Arab and Far Eastern markets is part of the process whereby the seller tries to determine the highest price that each potential purchaser is prepared to pay. Haggling of this kind is not a typical characteristic of a Western approach to business. Instead, companies define a number of segments of the population which represent different groups who respond in different ways to a particular price. A high-income group may be prepared to pay slightly more for a basically similar product than a segment composed of students or the unemployed. The degree to which a company can discriminate its pricing between different segments will depend on:

- the extent to which product differentiation is possible
- the extent to which potential customers can be segmented
- the ease or difficulty with which customers buying in a low-price segment can resell to a higher-price segment

Price discrimination can be implemented in a number of ways. A common method is to discriminate between groups based on their economic and demographic characteristics. British Rail's practice of charging different prices for young people, families and pensioners is a good example where very little product differentiation is needed (except for some restrictions concerning which trains can be used at the lower fares). In common with other services that offer similar discounts (for example, cinemas, theatres and hairdressers), it is possible to prevent the product being sold from the low- to the high-price segment—students, for example, must carry an identification card while using a reduced-price train service.

The ability to resell is greater in the case of tangible goods. In order to overcome this problem, companies differentiate their product slightly in order to appeal to the needs of different groups, and the differentiated products are given differential prices. Customers buying fountain pens as gifts are likely to be prepared to pay more than those shopping around for a pen for their own use; the products aimed at the two groups can be differentiated by including a gift box for the former—adding a small amount to the cost of production, but a relatively large amount to the price.

Companies frequently discriminate between users at different times and in different places. At times of peak demand, a firm may be able to sell all it can produce, so it will seek to charge a premium price; at off-peak times, where there is a high price elasticity of demand, prices may be reduced to stimulate demand. This is particularly characteristic of service industries, which have relatively high fixed costs—the electricity supply companies are an example of organizations that reduce charges during off-peak periods when demand becomes relatively price-sensitive. The 'Happy Hour' custom, in which some pubs charge lower prices in the early evening, is another attempt at stimulating demand where spare capacity exists. In some cases, of course, periods when demand is greatest could also correspond to periods when costs are greatest—as mentioned above, the electricity supply companies would argue that their costs are also greater in the peak periods.

BRITISH RAIL ARRIVES AT MARKET-BASED PRICES

British Rail has often been accused of confusing its customers by offering so many different fares. For a return journey from Leicester to London, for example, no fewer than 23 different fares are charged. A number of market segments have been identified and a distinctive marketing mix has been developed for each. Thus, the business traveller typically has a need for the flexibility of travelling at any time of the day; because an employer is often picking up the bill, this segment is less price-sensitive. Some segments of the business market demand higher standards of quality and are prepared to pay a higher price for first class travel or for an executive package which includes additional services such as meals and car parking. Leisure segments are on the whole more price-sensitive and more prepared to accept a lower standard of service offered; for example, the student segment is charged a lower fare in return for accepting restrictions on the times when they travel.

A keen eye is kept on the competition in determining prices. The student is more likely than the business person to accept the coach as an alternative—the Leicester to London student rail fare of £10 is pitched against the student coach fare of £7.75, the higher train fare being justified on the basis of a superior service offering. For the business traveller, the comparison is with the cost of running a car, parking in London and, more importantly, an employed person's time. Against these costs, the full fare of £41 (return) appears to be relatively good value. For the family market, the competition is considered to be the family car, so a family discount railcard allows the family as a unit to travel for the price of little more than two adults.

The underlying cost of a train journey is difficult to determine as a basis for pricing. The provision of the track and terminals represents high fixed costs which can be allocated to individual trains by a number of methods. British Rail currently recognizes that trains operating in the morning and afternoon peak periods cost more to operate, as the fixed costs of track, terminal and vehicles used solely for the peak period cannot be spread over other off-peak trains. The underlying costs of running commuter trains has been publicly cited by British Rail as the reason for increasing season ticket charges by more than the rate of inflation, although the fact that commuters often have no realistic alternative means of transport may have also been an important consideration.

The political environment has had an important effect on British Rail's pricing policies. Before the 1960s, railways were seen as essentially a public service and fares were charged on a seemingly equitable basis which was related to production costs. Fares were charged strictly on a cost-per-mile basis, with a distinction between first and second class, and a system of cheap day returns which existed largely through tradition. Since the 1960s, British Rail has moved away from social objectives with the introduction of business objectives. With this has come a recognition that pricing must be used to maximize revenue rather than to provide social equality. The strict relationship between distance and price no longer exists following the advent of market-led fares. In its applications of pricing policy, British Rail has been held out as an example of good railway business practice. Many overseas governments still hold that railways are a vital part of the public infrastructure, and that prices should reflect wider public needs and should not be determined by market forces.

Price discrimination by place can occur where people in one area have a greater willingness to pay for a product than those in other areas. Regional differences in spending power have led some national store chains to have different price lists for different regions. Sometimes further price discrimination is made between stores on the basis of their location within a town, those with a good central location being able to command higher price levels than those in a secondary position. Hotels have traditionally charged more in areas where demand is strongest, such as central London. Scheduled airlines operating between two points may consider the two termini to represent completely different markets. The London-based market for travel to New York is quite different from the market based in New York for travel to London, and the two markets are therefore often priced at different levels.

1.14.3   Distribution strategy

The question of how to get a product from the manufacturer to the final consumer can be broken down into two separate issues:

1. Which intermediaries to use in the process of transferring the product from the manufacturer to final consumer: this is referred to as the design of 'channels of distribution'.
2. How physically to transport and handle the product as it moves from manufacturer to final consumer: this is referred to as 'logistics' or 'physical distribution management'.

Channels of distribution   Channels of distribution comprise all those people and organizations involved in the process of transferring the title to a product from the manufacturer to the consumer. Sometimes products will be transferred directly from manufacturer to final consumer—a factory selling specialized kitchen units directly to the public would fit into this category. Alternatively, the manufacturer could sell its output through retailers, or, if these are considered too numerous for the manufacturer to handle, it could deal with a wholesaler who in turn would sell to the retailer. Sometimes more than one wholesaler is involved in the process.

Intermediaries perform the following functions:

- Making products locally available to consumers
- Breaking down the large volumes produced by the manufacturer to the small volumes required by the final customer
- Providing sales support at a local level
- Providing an insight into what could be for the manufacturer a new and strange market— important for exporters
- Financing stock
- Processing of goods—e.g. cutting timber to size
- Offering an after-sales service locally

These functions are of varying levels of importance in different markets. In some cases the manufacturer will be able to manage quite adequately without intermediaries. The design of a channel of distribution will be influenced by:

1. *The type of product*   For fast-moving consumer goods, customers will be less willing to travel far to obtain a particular brand—an extensive network of outlets will be necessary. On the other hand, customers may be prepared to travel further to seek out higher-value consumer durables.
2. *The nature of the product*   Bulky and perishable products will be less capable of being handled by large numbers of intermediaries.
3. *The abilities of intermediaries*   If the product is very specialized, it may be difficult to obtain intermediaries who can handle the product effectively—ski tour operators have often sold their holidays direct to the public, claiming that travel agents have insufficient knowledge and training to sell them effectively.
4. *The expectations of consumers*   For some products, consumers expect to buy from an intermediary which offers a choice of products from a number of producers, as in the case of books and holidays. This could make direct selling of one company's products direct to the public more difficult. Consumers may furthermore have expectations about what constitutes an acceptable channel through which to buy a product; attempts to sell cars and houses through supermarkets have failed partly for this reason.

In many markets, different channel structures can exist side by side. Commemorative porcelain products are frequently sold direct to the public by means of advertisements in magazines. Manufacturers of the same type of product can also be found selling them through retailers and indirectly through retailers via wholesalers. In this case, the company selling direct may find a niche product to sell, or may present the offer so as to appeal to a particular segment which is more responsive to the idea of ordering by mail.

Channel design is constantly adapting to changes in the business environment. A major change during the past two decades has occurred in the size of intermediaries. In many market sectors, multiple retail outlets have become dominant, often at the expense of the smaller unit. Grocery retailing and DIY retailing are two areas where this has been particularly significant. Table 1.3 gives some indication of the trend towards concentration in distribution more generally.

Table 1.3 Retail turnover by type of outlet, 1980–1987

	1980		1984		1987	
	(1)	*(2)*	*(1)*	*(2)*	*(1)*	*(2)*
Single outlet	225,907	19,231	218,700	24,863	213,378	29,522
Small multiple	76,216	8,548	70,235	10,431	69,384	12,180
Large multiple	66,130	31,978	60,793	47,500	62,706	62,925

(1) Number of outlets
(2) Turnover (£m)
Source: 'Retailing in the UK', *Key Note Market Review*, (1990, Table 1.7).

Economies of scale in purchasing and promotion have been important causes of the increase in concentration. Where retailers have become more concentrated and individually more powerful, there has been a tendency for them to deal directly with manufacturers, rather than through wholesalers. The turnover of a large grocery supermarket can be more than that of a large wholesaler, leaving the latter to cater for the small- and medium-sized retailer.

The way in which goods pass through the channel of distribution has changed. Before the advent of strong branding, a manufacturer would aggressively sell a product to a wholesaler, who would buy and stock the product on what it considered to be the merits of the product. The wholesaler would in turn aggressively sell the product to the retailer, who would buy on the basis of his experience and what he thought he could profitably sell to his customers. This is known as a 'push' strategy of distribution. With the advent of branding, the manufacturer was able to cut out the uncertainty associated with the intermediaries by appealing to the final consumer directly through the medium of advertising. The final consumer would then go to a retailer and demand a specific brand rather than accept the generic brand which the retailer tried to push. The retailer, having had a specific brand demanded, will in turn order that brand from the wholesaler, who in turn will order from the manufacturer. This is known as a 'pull' strategy. In this situation, the intermediaries become merely dispensers of pre-sold goods. The two strategies are compared in Figure 1.9.

More recently, the growing strength of retailers has put them at the focal point of the channel of distribution. By building up their own strong brands, large retailers are increasingly able to exert pressure on manufacturers in terms of product specification, price and the level of

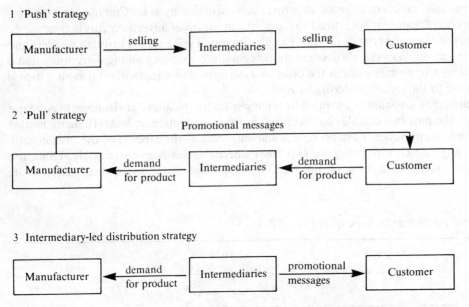

Figure 1.9 'Push' and 'pull' strategies of distribution

promotional support. It is estimated that in Britain the four largest grocery retailers may account for over half of the sales of a typical manufacturer of fast-moving consumer goods. The dependency is not reciprocated, with very few retailers relying on one single supplier for more than 1 per cent of their supplies.

While large retailers have been consolidating their position, the 1980s have seen the development of small specialist niche retailers. These have concentrated on such specialist items as ties, fine cheeses, sportswear and bags. A number of factors have contributed towards the development of these niche outlets. Greater affluence has meant that consumers are able to express a desire for individualism which may be incompatible with a purchase from a large mainstream retailer. Although large retailers have often tried to enter niche markets, they have often not had the flexibility of movement open to the smaller company.

It would be wrong to analyse channels of distribution primarily in terms of confrontation between companies involved at different levels. Movement towards integrating the different levels has occurred in a number of ways. In its most simple form, integration can occur through agreement over operational matters—standardization of pallet sizes and packaging methods to suit the needs of manufacturer, wholesaler and retailer is one example. More recently, the bar coding of products allows all intermediaries to process goods by a common standard much more efficiently. Sometimes the agreement takes the form of a voluntary buying chain set up to act as a wholesaler on behalf of a group of retailers; Londis and Nisa are examples.

Channel integration could occur through common ownership of different stages in the channel of distribution—a manufacturer, for instance, buying its own retail outlets. Although this has occurred on a number of occasions during the past decade, for example the Corah textile group establishing a chain of shops under the Harcourt name to sell its products—the more common trend has been for companies to concentrate on what they are best at doing. The Burton Group, for example, decided that it was better at selling clothes rather than making them; similarly, Asda—originally founded as a dairy to which retailing was later added—decided that its capital could be better employed in exploiting economies of scale in retailing rather than in operating dairies.

A very significant source of channel integration has come about through the development of franchising. It is estimated by the British Franchise Association that the number of franchise outlets has increased from under 2,000 in 1978 to around 16,000 in 1988. This has reflected a growth in franchising in the USA, where sales through franchised outlets now account for 32 per cent of all retail sales. Franchising involves a company with a proven business format—known as a franchisor—selling the right for somebody else—the franchisee—to use the brand name that has been established. The franchisee agrees to pay a capital sum in advance for this right and additionally usually agrees to pay a proportion of turnover and/or profits to the franchisor; it will also agree to buy most of its supplies from the franchisor. Franchising grew rapidly during the 1980s, especially among service-based industries such as fast food, car hire and dry cleaning and among the emerging niche markets such as ties and lingerie. The growing interest in the importance of small business units helped franchising during the 1980s, for the typical franchisee is a small entrepreneur who takes significant responsibility for ensuring the profitable operation of his or her franchise.

Retail formats go through life-cycles, just like any normal product. Forms of retailing are born and eventually die in response to changes in the business environment. Thus, full-service retailing went into decline with increasing real wage levels, to be replaced by the self-service store. With increasing car ownership and rising aspirations of consumers for greater choice, the supermarket is approaching the end of its life-cycle, being superseded by the larger out-of-town hypermarket. The concept of the department store appears to be at a point of maturity, overshadowed by the emergence of small niche outlets. Catalogue shops are a relatively recent innovation in Britain, resulting from the increasing cost of city-centre floor space and rapidly gaining social acceptability as a method of shopping. Developments in technology may allow further innovation in the home shopping sector, allowing it to exploit the growing number of money-rich, time-poor households. There are signs that, in areas such as financial services, insurance companies are able to use information technology to target specific groups with sales offerings and achieve a sale with good after-sales service, without the need to deal through the traditional intermediary of the insurance broker.

Physical distribution management   Aside from considerations of which intermediaries are to be involved in transferring goods from the manufacturer to the final consumer, there is the question of how they are to be physically handled. The design of a physical distribution system begins by considering the needs of the customers which it seeks to meet. These needs can be specified in terms of parameters such as reliability of delivery, time taken to deliver from the placing of an order and the condition in which goods are delivered. Physical distribution management involves balancing the need to maximize these benefits to consumers against the need to minimize costs.

The basic elements of a physical distribution system are shown in Figure 1.10 and comprise six basic elements which are used in designing an optimum system:

1. *Suppliers* A marketing-orientated system will have to balance the need to be close to customers against the economies of scale that may be achieved from having one central point of supply. Technology is increasingly allowing multiple supply points to produce goods close to the market. In the case of bread baking, the supermarket has itself become the point of production, meeting the requirements of customers for freshly baked bread.

   Where markets are turbulent, the distribution system may incorporate those suppliers that

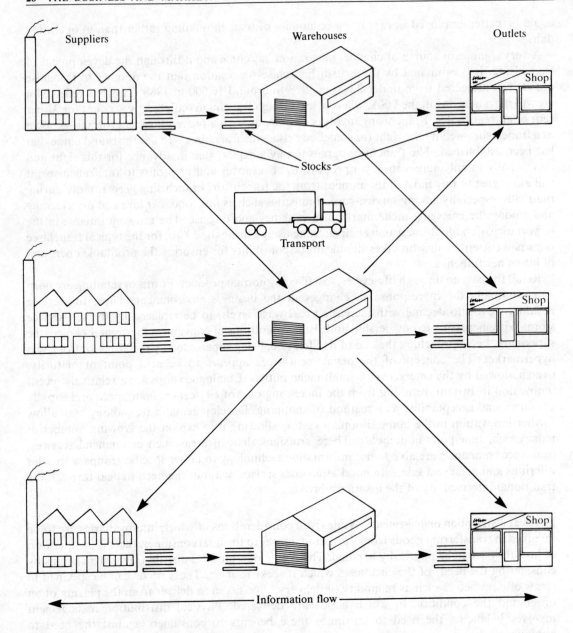

Figure 1.10 The elements of a physical distribution system

are closest to the customer rather than necessarily the cheapest sources of production. High-fashion clothing sold in Britain is more likely to be sourced from within Europe, allowing rapid delivery to a changing market, whereas basic items such as plain standard shirts or trousers may be sourced from lower-cost but more remote areas such as the Far East or Eastern Europe.

2. *Outlets* These can range from the individual household to the largest hypermarket.

3. *Stocks*   These need to be held:

   (a)   to balance seasonal patterns of production and consumption;
   (b)   to provide rapid availability of goods to customers;
   (c)   to provide contingencies against disruptions of production.

   A physical distribution system has to balance the need to hold large stocks in order to be able to fulfil customer orders against the cost of excessive stockholding. The tendency towards specialized products aimed at small segments of the market has meant that much higher stocks have to be held if the company is going to be able to rapidly satisfy an order for each variant. At times of high interest rates and capital shortage, there is pressure to keep stockholding to a minimum. In rapidly changing markets, such as fashion clothing, there is a tendency to keep stock levels at a minimum level to guard against large stocks of goods suddenly becoming obsolete because of a change in tastes.

4. *Warehouses*   These are incorporated into a system to provide a break-of-bulk point, and to hold stocks. A company must decide on the number and nature of the warehouses that are incorporated into its system, in particular the balance between the need for local warehouses as against the need for efficiency savings which favour large warehouses. Automation of warehouses with the development of computerized picking systems is increasingly favouring larger warehouses. A typical national supermarket would now include just half a dozen strategically located warehouses in its distribution system to serve a national chain of outlets.

5. *Transport*   This moves the stocks from manufacturer to retail outlet and sometimes—as in the case of mail order or home delivery of milk—to the home of the final consumer. Transport is becoming an increasingly important element of the distribution system, with goods tending to travel for longer average distances within the system. Road haulage has become the dominant form of goods transport within Britain, accounting in 1988 for 60 per cent of all tonnage carried (or 82 per cent of all tonne-miles) (Department of Transport, 1990). The strength of road transport has been helped by the increasing size and efficiency of lorries and the progressive development of the motorway network. Very few distribution systems include rail as an important element of their physical distribution system: the railways are mainly confined to relatively low-value, high-volume products such as aggregates and coal. The opening of the Channel Tunnel may increase the opportunities for rail transport by eliminating the need for goods to or from Europe to be transhipped at the port. The choice of a mode of transport involves balancing the costs of a mode against the benefits of that mode in terms of speed and reliability of delivery.

6. *Information flow*   The requirement to respond to customer requirements rapidly, while at the same time keeping down stockholding levels, demands a very effective flow of information. The development of 'just in time' (JIT) systems has been possible only with the improvement of data flow. The development of bar codes has achieved notable results in this respect. A supermarket now knows minute by minute the state of stocks for all of its products and can order replacement stocks—by a computerized data link—for delivery from a regional distribution centre the following day. Similarly, the regional distribution centres can rapidly reorder stocks from their suppliers. The development of JIT systems has not only allowed a more reliable level of availability of goods to the final consumer, but has also allowed retailers to reduce warehouse space provided within shops. Because it is no longer necessary to hold large stocks locally, warehouse space can be turned over to more valuable sales floor space.

The role of specialized physical distribution management firms   Physical distribution is a specialized activity which can often be carried out more efficiently by a company that is independent of the manufacturer or intermediaries. The last two decades have seen many manufacturers identifying their core business activities and concentrating their management and financial resources on these. Physical distribution management has often been seen as a relatively peripheral activity, with the result that many companies have hived the activity off to a specialist organization such as TNT or subsidiaries of the National Freight Corporation. Cash has often been raised for investment in the core business by selling vehicle fleets and warehouses to the distribution company.

Because specialist distribution companies usually work on behalf of a large number of companies, they can achieve significant economies of scale compared with the free-standing operation of a single manufacturer. Warehouses can be built to a more efficient scale, and peaks and troughs in demand can be reconciled more easily within a larger and more broadly based organization. The company also benefits by being able to use staff with a level of specialist knowledge that may not be achievable within a manufacturing company.

1.14.4   Promotion strategy

A company must choose a strategy to promote the benefits of buying its product to its target market. The choice of a promotion strategy raises the following issues, each of which will be examined in turn:

- What is the purpose of the communication?
- What message is to be said?
- How is it to be said?
- Where is it to be said?
- When is it to be said?
- How much money is to be allocated to the promotion effort?
- Who is to manage the promotional effort?
- How is the promotional effort to be evaluated?

The tools of promotion can be divided into four main elements:

1. *Advertising*   This can be defined as any paid form of non-personal promotion of a product by an identifiable sponsor. It includes the principal broadcast media of radio, television, press, posters and the cinema. Many people would include the growing medium of direct mail in this category.
2. *Sales promotion*   These are short-term incentives used to boost sales of a product. Typical incentives are selective temporary price discounts, gift and coupon offers and samples. This element of the promotion mix has been growing rapidly, and expenditure on sales promotion in the UK now exceeds that spent on advertising.
3. *Public relations*   This is defined by the Institute of Public Relations as 'the deliberate, planned and sustained effort to establish and maintain mutual understanding between an organisation and its public'. The public can in turn be divided into a number of special interest areas—for example the financial public, the media public or the government public.
4. *Personal selling*   This is a presentation on a one-to-one basis with a view to a sale. Personal selling is particularly important in industrial marketing where products may be relatively complex and the decision-making unit more diverse than for a consumer sale.

What message is to be said?   The starting point for developing a message is to ask what its purpose is. The aim could be to create awareness of a brand name without expectation of a short-term payback. On the other hand, the aim could be to encourage target customers to make a purchase in the very short term. Advertising is good at building up brands over the long term, whereas sales promotion activity is good at achieving short-term sales. The latter could in fact be in conflict with long-term brand building where discounts and special offers may be perceived as devaluing the product.

Secondly, the company must try and differentiate its products from that of its competitors by identifying a unique selling proposition (USP). Within the soap powder market, a number of basically similar products have chosen particular attributes to stress in their advertising—the

---

GREEN ADVERTS MAKE CONSUMERS SEE RED

The dominant theme of messages in adverts tends to reflect the attitudes of a society at any one time. Environmentalism became an important issue in Britain during the late 1980s, and for many companies this required a change in emphasis from earlier campaigns which had focused on the desirability of power and wealth creation in its own right.

Faced with the changing tide of public opinion towards the environment, many advertisers sought to associate their products with 'green' benefits. The transformation of advertising messages was particularly noted in the car sector.

Adverts for new cars during the early 1980s had capitalized on individuals' need for power and status by stressing the speed and acceleration of a model. An advert by Peugeot depicting a car travelling at speed through a burning field with the catchline 'Takes your breath away' epitomized the dominant mood of the mid-1980s. With a change in attitudes towards the end of the 1980s, however, cars were increasingly being promoted on the basis of their claimed environmental credentials. Speed and performance became less dominant themes, and in their place the emphasis was put on the ability to run on unleaded petrol. The slogan 'Takes your breath away' acquired a double meaning—environmental campaigners pointed out that the pollution produced by a Peugeot would easily do this. Vauxhall led a number of manufacturers in targeting family purchasers of cars by stressing the benefits to children of a lead-free environment. The importance of promoting an environmentally friendly car was further recognized with the development of catalytic converters and the incorporation of messages about the benefits of catalytic converters into many manufacturers' advertising, especially the Volkswagen Audi group.

In trying to develop green credentials, many car manfuacturers pushed their message beyond the credibility of their audiences. Having set in motion a green promotional platform, car manufacturers were judged by an increasingly critical audience. Vauxhall—although claiming it was offering 'green' cars, still received adverse publicity for selling cars which—although running on unleaded petrol—had unnecessarily high-performance engines, adding to the greenhouse effect.

In an attempt to reduce the level of misleading claims appealing to the public's green consciousness, the Advertising Standards Authority issued revised guidelines. Friends of the Earth achieved good publicity for itself—but bad publicity for its targets—by promoting its 'Green Con Awards'. An early recipient in the motor sector was the Halfords chain of car shops and service centres. Its publicity had attempted to give it green credentials by stressing the benefits to the environment of having a car's engine adjusted by Halfords to run on unleaded fuel. The publicity backfired when Friends of the Earth pointed out that, by promoting more motoring in itself, Halfords was significantly contributing to environmental pollution.

unique ability to destroy odours, to prevent colours fading and to work at low temperatures have all been used as USPs.

Messages have to respond to the continually changing values of the target market. Changing attitudes towards healthy living have resulted in the advertising message for many products, such as soft drinks and cheese, placing less emphasis on taste and more on the product's health benefits.

The message is just one element—but an essential element—of the positioning of a brand. The product specification, packaging and pricing must all be reflected in the message that is used to position the product.

How is it to be said?   The sales message must be conveyed in such a way as to appeal to the target market to which it is aimed. Within any country, the message must reflect the values of different segments of the population. An advertisement for the *Sun* newspaper will use very different techniques of communication from those used for *The Times*. An advert for bank current accounts aimed primarily at a young market will use different imagery from an advert for the same account aimed at a more elderly segment. Between different cultures, techniques of communication are likely to differ. Thus, the British tend to respond to promotion that incorporates humour, the American culture is more responsive to a brash, hard-sell type of message, and the French treat sex as an expected element of the sales message for a wide range of products. Imagery that works successfully in one culture may fail abysmally in another. Cuddly dogs have positively added to the image of a wide range of products from paint to toilet rolls in the UK, but in Japan they would associate the product with an inferior and disliked animal.

The nature of the message will influence which element of the promotion mix is used. Announcement of an innovative new product launch may be best achieved by means of public relations activity, while a complex message about the attributes of an industrial capital good may be best achieved by means of personal selling.

Within each element of the promotion mix, a number of different methods can usually be used to convey a message. In the case of advertising, the medium of television is preferable where movement and colour are likely to form an important selling proposition—image-building for a car, for example; a printed medium may be more appropriate where it is necessary to provide more comprehensive information which can be referred back to.

Where is it to be said?   A company seeks to minimize the cost of getting its message through to a specified target market by ensuring a close match between its target market and the audience of the available media. Audiences and target markets can be defined according to any of the segmentation criteria referred to earlier. Within the national press, each newspaper has its own distinctive audience; even the *Sun* and *Daily Mirror*, although superficially appearing to be quite similar, have somewhat different audiences, with the *Sun* having a relatively young and male-dominated readership compared with the *Daily Mirror*.

The ability of marketers to aim their messages at clearly defined targets has been improving since the early 1980s. Technological refinements and better working practices have allowed national newspapers to operate economically with much smaller circulations than hitherto, each addressing an audience with unique characteristics. Technology has also allowed the national press to develop regional supplements to their titles, allowing a greater degree of geographic segmentation for advertisers.

The most precise form of targeting a message is provided by direct mail, which has grown rapidly with the increasing power of computers to manage large databases. The Direct Mail Information Service estimates that expenditure on direct mail rose to £979m in 1990.

In some instances, the choice of advertising medium may be influenced by legislation or voluntary codes of conduct. Thus, the Independent Television Commission Code of Advertising Practice does not allow cigarette advertising on television. This has forced the bulk of advertising expenditure for cigarettes into press and poster advertising, although sponsorship of sports events allows tobacco companies to get their name before television audiences.

When is it to be said?   Consideration needs to be given to the timing of a campaign. Promotional expenditure usually increases when the target market most feels a need for the product—for example, lawn mowers in the springtime and perfumes in the run-up to Christmas. For products that face a relatively uniform annual demand pattern, a company can choose between a strategy of spending uniformly throughout the year, or concentrating promotion into short bursts.

Within a particular campaign, the precise timing of promotional activity must reflect the target market's life-style. The weekend has been the traditional time for buying household durables; thus, Friday has been a popular time to advertise in the national press. It may be considered desirable to get a message across to the target market before they go out for the day—an attraction of the national newspapers which is now challenged by breakfast television.

How much money is to be allocated to the promotion effort?   There are three approaches to determining the amount to be spent on the promotion element of the marketing mix of a product: affordability, competitive parity, and product needs.

The first of these approaches reflects an attitude that is found in many organizations—especially smaller firms—in which promotion is regarded as something approaching a luxury. When times are good the promotion budget is increased, but when a downturn occurs that budget is one of the first to be cut. The rationale for this could be that, as most forms of promotion are inherently speculative, it may be difficult to raise capital for speculative activity during a period of downturn. On the other hand, the need for promotion may be much greater at a time when it is becoming more difficult to achieve a sale and when there is a much higher level of activity from competitors, all of whom may be sending out additional messages.

Some industries occasionally see significant sudden increases in promotional spending, often to communicate a change in one of the other marketing mix elements, such as a new price level or a new variant of a product. Sometimes increased spending could result from one company trying aggressively to build a market share, to which competitors feel they must respond with increased promotional spending if they are to maintain their own market shares.

The actual promotional needs of a product are a good basis for determining the budget to be allocated to it. The marketing mix strategy could in fact place very little emphasis on promotion; for example, a manufacturer of own-brand soap powder such as Albright and Wilson will not need to spend as much on promotion as Proctor and Gamble. During the lifetime of a product the promotional needs are likely to fluctuate, with much greater demands during the launch and possible future relaunch periods. In addition, promotional needs can fluctuate very rapidly in response to changes in the business environment. Egg producers facing consumer worries over the safety of eggs have been forced to increase their promotion budgets to communicate a message of reassurance.

Who is to manage the promotional effort?   The mounting of a promotional campaign demands a number of specialist skills, such as media planning, copywriting and the production of material. Many of these skills are not to be found in most companies, so the task of promotion is often subcontracted to an agency with a clear set of promotional objectives. Other advantages of using an agency include the separation of a creative advertising culture from the mainstream company culture with which it would probably be difficult to reconcile. An outside agency is also able to take a much more objective and fresh approach to the promotional needs of a product and can more easily cope with peaks in workload. Against these advantages, the cost of using an agency and disagreement over the interpretation of promotional objectives have led some large companies to keep campaign management in-house.

How is the promotional effort to be evaluated?   The effectiveness of promotional effort can be assessed only by reference to the original promotional objectives—e.g. to increase awareness, or to produce a short-term increase in sales effects. The process of evaluation can be divided into two aspects: measuring the effectiveness of communicating a message to the target market, and measuring the effect on sales. The former can be done relatively easily by means of tracking surveys, but the latter is much more difficult, requiring the company to try and isolate all other factors that might have resulted in a change in sales.

REVIEW QUESTIONS

1. Select one company with which you are familiar. To what extent is that company marketing-orientated? What would it need to do to become more marketing-orientated?
2. Of what relevance is marketing to the public sector?
3. What forms of marketing research might a manufacturer of bicycles use in designing new products?
4. What advantages does franchising offer a company wishing to expand in the fast printing sector?
5. Outline the stages that are likely to be involved in developing a new snack food.
6. What is the difference between selling and marketing?

REFERENCES

Chisnall, P. M. (1985a), *Marketing: A Behavioural Analysis*, 2nd edn, McGraw-Hill, Maidenhead, Berks.
Chisnall, P. M. (1985b), *Strategic Industrial Marketing*, Prentice-Hall, Englewood Cliffs, NJ.
Crimp, M. (1985), *The Market Research Process*, Prentice-Hall, London.
Department of Transport (1990), *Transport Statistics*, London: HMSO.
Drucker, P. F. (1973), *Management: Tasks, Responsibilities, Practices*, Harper and Row, NY.
Greenley, G. E. (1986), *The Strategic and Operational Planning of Marketing*, McGraw-Hill, Maidenhead, Berks.
Howard, J. A., and Sheth, J. N. (1969), *The Theory of Buyer Behaviour*, John Wiley, NY.
Kotler, P. (1988), *Marketing Management: Analysis, Planning and Control*, 6th edn, Prentice-Hall International. Englewood Cliffs, NJ.
Kotler, P., and Armstrong, G. (1989), *Principles of Marketing*, 4th edn, Prentice-Hall, London.
Lancaster, G., and Massingham, L. (1988), *Essentials of Marketing*, McGraw-Hill, Maidenhead, Berks.
Maslow, A. H. (1943), 'A theory of human motivation', *Psychological Review*, July.
Stern, L. W., and El-Ansary, A. I. (1982), *Marketing Channels*, 2nd edn, Prentice-Hall, Englewood Cliffs, NJ.

CLASSIFICATION OF BUSINESS ORGANIZATIONS

2.1 INTRODUCTION

To many people, 'marketing' is most commonly associated with large private sector organizations that have the resources to engage in costly promotional exercises. In fact, the marketing concept is embraced by a wide range of organizational types, from the owner of a small corner shop deciding which new lines to sell to a multinational construction company tendering for a large contract. Marketing is embraced by the private sector, and increasingly by the public sector.

Marketers need to understand the diversity of organizational types. Why?

1. Different types of business organizations will be able to address their potential customers in different ways. Lack of resources could inhibit the development of some new products; or the objectives of the firm—either formal or informal—may influence its offerings to the public.
2. As sellers of materials to companies involved in further manufacture, marketers should understand how the buying behaviour of different kinds of organizations varies. A small business is likely to buy equipment in a different way from a large public sector organization.
3. Marketers should be interested in the structure of business units at the macroeconomic level. It has been argued by many economists that a thriving small business sector is essential for an expanding economy and that the effect of domination by large organizations may be to reduce competition and innovation. Marketers should therefore be interested in the rate of new business creation and trends in the composition of business units.

There are many approaches to classifying organizations which would satisfy the marketer's interests identified above. Organizations could be classified according to the size of the unit, however measured, or the type of industry they are engaged in. However, a good starting point is to look at their legal status, a classification that is often closely related to the size of a company, the resources available and the objectives of the company.

2.2 THE LEGAL STATUS OF ORGANIZATIONS

The legal status is important because it influences the methods by which the business raises its capital, determines who owns it and decides on the method of control—three vital elements of the company's trading operations.

The first major division is between private sector organizations, which are owned by private individuals in one form or another, and public sector organizations, which are instruments of government.

2.3   PRIVATE SECTOR ORGANIZATIONS

2.3.1   The sole trader

The most basic level of organization is that of the sole trader. In fact, the concept of a separate legal personality does not apply to this type of organization, for the business and the individual are considered to be legally indistinguishable. The individual carries on the business in his or her own name, with the result that he or she assumes all the rights and duties of the business. Thus, if the business is sued for breach of contract, this amounts to suing the individual, and if the business does not have the resources to meet any claim, the claim must be met out of the private resources of the individual.

Becoming a sole trader requires the minimum of formality, and for this reason it can be difficult to tell how many of them there are at any one time. The most commonly used indication is VAT registrations, although this does not give a complete picture as businesses with a turnover of less than £35,000 (1991/92) do not need to register. Little formality is required to maintain a business as a sole trader; for example, there is no obligation to file annual accounts, other than for the assessment of the individual's personal tax liability.

It has been estimated that about 80 per cent of all businesses in the UK are sole traders, although they account for only a small proportion of gross domestic product. In some sectors of the economy they are the dominant business form, as with corner shops, window cleaners and hairdressers. Sole traders can grow by taking on additional employees—there is no legal limit on the number of employees they may have, and there are many examples of sole traders employing over 100 people. At the other extreme, it is sometimes difficult to determine just when a sole trader business unit comes into existence, with many sole traders operating on a part-time basis, some 'moonlighting' outside the gaze of the Inland Revenue.

Marketers should recognize a number of important characteristics of sole traders. First, they tend to have limited capital resources. Risk capital is generally provided only by the sole proprietor, and additional loan capital is often only made available against security of the individual's assets. In the new product development field, this type of business has very often made new discoveries, only to be unable to see the product through to production and launch on account of a lack of funds. If a new product does make it into a competitive market, this type of business may face competition in price, promotional effort or product offering from larger and better resourced firms. The larger firm is likely to have greater resources to mount a campaign to see off a newer competitor.

Being relatively small, the sole trader may suffer by not being able to exploit the economies of scale available to larger firms. On the other hand, many sole traders aim for those sectors where economies of scale are either unimportant or non-existent, for example painting and decorating, hairdressing and outside catering. In many personal services, smallness and the personal touch plus the fact that many small businesses do not need to charge their customers VAT can be strong selling points.

The small sole trading unit could also find that it is too small to justify having its own expertise in many areas. Many do not have specialists to look after the accounting or advertising functions, for example. Furthermore, the goals and policies of the business can become totally dominated by the sole trader. Although goals can be pursued determinedly and single-mindedly, the sole trader presents a narrower view than may be offered by a larger board of directors. The goals of a sole trader may appear very irrational to an outsider, inasmuch as many such individuals may be happy to continue uneconomic ventures on emotional grounds alone. Very small caterers, for example, might be financially better off drawing unemployment benefit;

but being a sole trader may satisfy wider goals of status or the pursuit of a leisure interest.

Many sole traders fail after only a short time, often because of the lack of management skills of an individual who may well be an expert in his or her own field of specialization. Others continue until they reach a point where lack of expertise and financial resources imposes a constraint on growth. At this point, they may consider going into partnership with another individual, or setting up a company with limited liability.

Sole trader or employee? It can sometimes be difficult to decide whether a person is a self-employed sole trader or an employee of another business enterprise. There can be many advantages in classifying an individual as self-employed. Tax advantages could result from being able to claim as legitimate business expenses items that are denied to the employee. The method of assessing income tax liability in arrears also usually favours the self-employed. For the employer, designation as self-employed could save on National Insurance payments; it also relieves the employer of many duties that are imposed in respect of employees but not sub-contractors, such as entitlement to sick pay, notice periods and maternity leave.

The problem of distinction is particularly great in the building industry, and for various part-time workers such as market research surveyors. The courts would decide the matter on the basis of the degree of control the employer has over the employee. If the employer is able to specify the manner in which a task is to be carried out, then an employment relationship exists; if, however, the required end result is specified but the manner in which it is achieved is left up to the individual, then a contract for services will exist—in other words, self-employment.

2.3.2 Partnerships

Two or more persons in partnership can combine their resources and expertise to form what could be a more efficient business unit. The Partnership Act 1890 defines a partnership as 'the relation which subsists between persons carrying on a business with a view to profit'. Partnerships can range from two builders joining together to a very large accountancy or solicitors' practice with hundreds of partners. In practice, the maximum number of people that can form a partnership is limited by legislation to 20 (although certain professional partnerships may exceed this number).

Partnerships are generally formed by contract between the parties, although where this is not done the Partnership Act 1890 governs relationships between the partners. Among the main items in a partnership agreement will be terms specifying:

1. The amount of capital subscribed by each partner
2. The basis on which profits will be determined and allocated between partners
3. The management responsibilities of each partner—some may join as 'sleeping partners' and take no active part in the management of the business
4. The basis for allocating salaries to each partner and for drawing personal advances against entitlement to profits
5. Procedures for dissolving the partnership and distributing the assets of the business between members

Despite this internal agreement between partners, a partnership in England and Wales does not have its own legal personality. As a consequence, the partners incur unlimited personal liability for the debts of the business. Furthermore, each partner is jointly liable for the debts incurred by all partners in the course of business. An added complication of a partnership is that the withdrawal of any one partner, either voluntarily or upon death or bankruptcy, causes the automatic termination of the partnership. A new partnership will come into being, as it would if an additional partner were admitted to the partnership.

Because of the lack of protection afforded to partners, this form of organization tends to be relatively uncommon, except for some groups of professional people, where business risks are low and for whom professional codes of practice may prevent the formation of limited companies. Partnership is a particularly common form of business organization with accountants, solicitors, dentists and small building contractors.

2.3.3   Private limited companies

It was recognized in the nineteenth century that industrial development would be impeded if investors in business always ran the risk of losing their personal assets to cover the debts of their business. At the same time, the size of business units had become larger, causing the idea of a partnership to become strained. The need for a trading company to have a separate legal personality from that of its owners was recognized from the Middle Ages, when companies were incorported by Royal Charter. From the seventeenth century, organizations could additionally be incorporated by Act of Parliament. Both methods of incorporating a company were expensive and cumbersome, and a simpler method was required to cope with the rapid expansion of business enterprises which was fuelling the Industrial Revolution. The response to this need was the Joint Stock Companies Act 1844, which enabled a company to be incorporated as a separate legal identity by the registration of a memorandum of association and the payment of certain fees. The present law governing the registration of companies is contained in the Companies Act 1985. Today, the vast majority of trading within the UK is undertaken by limited companies.

When a limited company is created, it is required to produce a memorandum and articles of association. The memorandum regulates the relationships of the company with the outside world, while the articles of association regulate the internal administration of the company.

The memorandum of association   This statement about the company's relations with the outside world includes a number of important provisions.

The first item to be considered is the name of the company. If it is a private limited company, the name must end with the word 'Limited' (or *Cyf*, its Welsh equivalent for companies registered in Wales). A number of restrictions exist on the company's choice of name; for example, the name must not cause confusion with an existing company or suggest a connection with royalty. The trading name will very often be quite different from the registered name, in which case the company is required to display the name and address of its owner at its business premises, on its business stationery, and to customers and suppliers on request.

The second important element of the memorandum is a statement as to whether the liability of its members is limited, and if so what the limit of liability will be in the event of the company being wound up with unpaid debts. The majority of companies are limited by shares: members' liability to contribute to the assets of the company is limited to the amount—if any—that is unpaid on their shares. An alternative is for companies to be limited by guarantee: in these companies, the liability of each member to make up for any shortfall in assets in the event of the company being wound up is limited to the value of his or her guarantee. This type of company is comparatively rare, and is found mainly among non-profit-making organizations, such as professional and trade associations. An even less common type of company is that where the liability of members is unlimited. Because the members of such companies have unlimited liability for the company's debts, they are liable to lose their personal assets—a problem that gave rise to the limited liability company in the first place. There has however been an increase in the number of unlimited companies since 1967, because the Companies Act of that year exempts them from filing their accounts with the Registrar of Companies, and hence from publicizing their financial affairs.

The third important element of the memorandum is the objects clause. This is particularly important because it specifies the scope within which the company can exercise its separate legal personality. There are two principal consequences of having an objects clause. First, the clause protects investors who can learn from it the purposes for which their money is to be used; and second, it protects individuals dealing with the company, who can discover the extent of the company's powers. Any act which the company performs beyond its powers is deemed to be *ultra vires* and therefore void. Thus, even where the directors of a company were in agreement with a contract that was beyond its powers, the contract itself would be void unless the members of the company had formally changed its memorandum of association to include the activity with which the contract is concerned.

The principal of *ultra vires* was amended by the Companies Act 1985, s. 35, so that any person who enters into a contract with a company that is outside its objects but is sanctioned by the directors of the company will be able to enforce it against the company, providing he or she did not know that the contract was beyond the company's powers. In practice, it is common for the memorandum to contain an objects clause that is drafted in a deliberately broad manner, allowing considerable freedom for the directors to move away from their traditional business area. Nevertheless, marketers within limited companies would be wise to check their memorandum of association to ensure that diversification is allowed by their objects clause.

The Articles of Association   While the memorandum regulates the relationships of the company with the outside world, the articles of association regulate the internal administration of the company—the relations between the company and its members and between the members themselves. The articles cover such matters as the issue and transfer of shares, the rights of shareholders, the meetings of members, the appointment of directors and the procedures for producing and auditing accounts.

Companies seeking to expand by acquisition may need to check the articles of the company they are seeking to acquire. The articles may for instance restrict ownership of shares by any one person to a fixed percentage of the total, as has been the case in many newly privatized companies. Different shares may attract different voting rights, so that, despite acquiring a majority of shares, the acquiring company is not able to obtain effective control of the company. The Trust House Forte company, for example, has owned a majority of the shares in the Savoy Hotel group for some time. However, most of the shares it holds carry no voting rights, while it does not hold a majority of the voting shares: it has therefore been unable to exercise control over the Savoy group.

Directors   A company acts through its directors, i.e. persons chosen by shareholders to conduct and manage the company's affairs. The number of directors and their powers are detailed in the articles of association, and so long as they do not exceed these powers, shareholders cannot interfere in their conduct of the company's business. The articles will normally give one director additional powers to act as managing director, enabling him or her to make decisions without reference to the full board of directors.

The secretary   Every company must have a secretary, on whom the Companies Acts have placed a number of duties and responsibilities, such as filing reports and accounts with the

Registrar of Companies. The secretary, who is the chief administrative officer of the company, is usually chosen by the directors.

Shareholders   The shareholders own the company, and in theory exercise control over it. A number of factors limit the actual control that shareholders exercise over their companies. It was mentioned earlier that the articles of a company may discriminate between groups of share-holders by giving differential voting rights. Even where shareholders have full voting rights, the vast majority of them typically are either unable or insufficiently interested to attend company meetings, and are happy to leave company management to the directors, so long as the dividend paid to them is satisfactory.

Company reports and accounts   A company provides information about itself when it is set up through its memorandum and articles of association. To provide further protection for investors and people with whom the company may deal, companies legislation imposes a duty on companies to provide subsequent information.

An important document which must be produced annually is the annual report. Every company having a share capital must make a return in the prescribed form to the Registrar of Companies stating what has happened to its capital during the previous year, for example by describing the number of shares allotted and the cash received for them. The return must be accompanied by a copy of the audited balance sheet in the prescribed form, supported by a profit and loss account which gives a true and fair representation of the year's transactions. Like the memorandum and articles of association, these documents must be available for public inspec-tion, with the exception of unlimited companies, which do not have to file annual accounts. Also, most small companies with a turnover of less than £1.4 million or a balance sheet total of less than £0.7 million or fewer than 50 employees need only file an abridged balance sheet and do not need to submit a profit and loss account. Most medium-sized firms with a turnover of less than £1.4 million or a balance sheet of less than £2.8 million or fewer than 250 employees may omit details of their turnover and gross profit margin.

In addition to providing the annual report and accounts, the directors of a company are under a duty to keep proper books of account and details of assets and liabilities.

Advantages and disadvantages   Comparisons between sole traders and partnerships on the one hand and private limited companies on the other can be made at a number of levels. First, formation of a limited company is relatively formal and time-consuming, whereas for a sole trader there is the minimum of formality in establishing a business. The added formality continues with the requirement to produce an annual return and set of accounts. On the other hand, limited company status affords much greater protection to the entrepreneur in the event of the business getting into financial difficulty. Raising additional funds is usually easier for a limited company, although personal guarantees may still be required to cover loans to the company.

A SMALL BUSINESS BY DESIGN

Like many small businesses, James Allen set up his interior design business in London on a very small scale, starting off by undertaking work in his spare time. He was very much a small sole trader. Before long, he decided to turn his interest into a full-time business and set up a private limited company with the minimum per-missible equity capital—£100. Although the business was now legally separate from himself, he still had to offer his private house as security against a bank loan which he needed in order to finance his working capital.

The business grew by winning a number of large contracts. However, a design contract for a building contractor worth £70,000 turned into a major problem for Allen when the contractor went into liquidation owing the business £50,000. This in turn meant that Allen was unable to pay his creditors or to repay his bank loan. As a result, the business had to close when creditors forced the appointment of a receiver to wind up the limited company. At this point Allen lost the control of his business that being a director and the majority shareholder had previously given him. The receivers took control and eventually liquidated the available assets in order to reimburse creditors. However, the value of the assets was not enough to reimburse them in full, and Allen himself lost all of the capital that he had put into the business. Although the bank was able to recover its loan from Allen personally (on account of the security it had over his house), limited company status protected him from claims made by other unpaid creditors

---

2.3.4 Public limited companies

The Companies Act 1985 recognized that existing companies legislation did not sufficiently distinguish between the small limited company and the large multinational firm. So the concept of the public limited company—abbreviated to PLC—came about. The basic principles of separate legal personality are similar for both private and public limited companies, but the Companies Act 1985 confers a number of additional duties and benefits on public limited companies.

The difference is partly one of scale: a PLC must have a minimum share capital of £50,000 compared with the £100 of the private limited company. It must have at least two directors instead of the minimum of one for the private company.

Before a public limited company can start trading or borrow money, it must obtain a 'business certificate' from the Registrar of Companies, confirming that it has met all legal requirements in relation to its share capital.

Against these additional obstacles of the public limited company is the major advantage that it can offer its shares and debentures to the public, something that is illegal for a private company, where shares are more commonly taken up by friends, business associates and family. As a private limited company grows, it may have exhausted all existing sources of equity capital, and 'going public' is one way of attracting capital from a wider audience. During the latter part of the 1980s, many groups of managers bought out their businesses, initially setting up a private limited company with a private placement of shares. In order to attract new capital, and often to allow existing shareholders to sell their holdings more easily, these businesses have often been re-registered as public companies.

For the marketer, PLC status has a number of strengths and weaknesses. Many companies highlight PLC status in promotional material in order to give potential customers a greater degree of confidence in the company. Another major strength is the greater potential ability to fund major new product developments (discussed in more detail in Chapter 3). Against this, the PLC is much more open to public examination, especially in the financial community. Management may have plans that will achieve a long-term payback, bringing it into conflict with possibly short-term objectives of City institutions. Management could end up being influenced unduly by short-term financial market considerations rather than long-term market factors. Indeed, a number of companies have recognized this problem of PLC status and reverted to private status by buying back shares from the public (for example, the Virgin Group in the late 1980s).

Today, although public limited companies are in a numerical minority, they account for a substantial proportion of the equity of the limited company sector and cover a wide range of industries that typically operate at a large scale—for example banking, car manufacture and property development.

2.3.5 Franchising

In franchising, an organization known as a franchisor sells the right to market a product under its name to another organization, known as a franchisee. The term 'franchising' refers to a special relationship between the two companies. In terms of their legal status, the companies themselves could be any one of the types previously described. The franchisor is more likely to be a public or private limited company, while the franchisee is more likely to be a sole trader, partnership or private limited company. The franchisor and franchisee have legally separate identities, but the nature of the franchise agreement can make them very interdependent.

Franchising is a rapidly growing type of business relationship, and the British Franchise Association estimates that it now accounts for over 20 per cent of retail sales in the UK. Franchising offers a ready-made business opportunity for the entrepreneur who has capital but does not want the risk associated with setting up a completely new business. A good franchise operation will have a proven business format and will already be well established in its market. The franchisee will be required to pay an initial capital sum for the right to use the name of the franchisor; this may sometimes seem high, but it represents a relatively less risky investment than starting a completely new business. It has been estimated by the British Franchise Association that, whereas 90 per cent of all new businesses fail within three years of starting up, 90 per cent of all franchisees survive beyond this period.

In addition to the initial capital sum, a franchise agreement will usually include provisions for the franchisee to purchase stock from the franchisor and to pass on a percentage of turnover or profit. The franchisor will undertake to provide general marketing backup (see Figure 2.1).

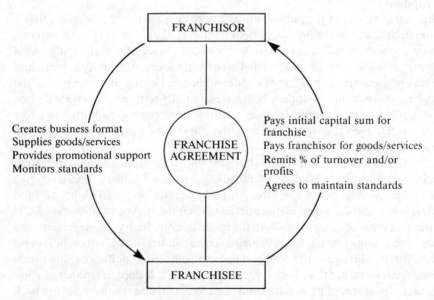

Figure 2.1 The elements of franchising

Franchising has been popular with companies seeking a rapid expansion of their distribution outlets without tying up large amounts of their own capital—niche retailers such as Tie Rack and Benetton grew rapidly in the UK in the 1980s on this basis. It is also attractive for a company where point-of-sale service is very important, the argument being that an individual will be much more highly motivated to provide a good level of customer service if his or her personal profits are directly dependent on it, rather than if they simply reported through a management hierarchy to head office, from which effective control would be difficult to exercise. The value of personal service has been recognized in catering franchises such as Burger King and Kentucky Fried Chicken, dry cleaning (Sketchley) and fast printing (Kwik Print and Prontaprint).

2.4 PUBLIC SECTOR ORGANIZATIONS

Government has traditionally been involved in providing services that cannot be sensibly provided by market forces—for example defence, education and basic health services. Government involvement has however developed beyond providing these basic facilities to providing goods and services that could arguably be supplied just as effectively by private sector organizations. Goods and services offered by the government by way of trade are generally provided by some form of public corporation—as distinct from a government department, which generally retains responsibility for the provision of essential public services.

Public sector organizations take a number of forms, embracing government departments and agencies, local government, nationalized industries and all other undertakings in which central or local government has a controlling interest. This chapter will focus on those public sector organizations that supply goods and services to consumers; those government organizations that are primarily policy-making in nature will be considered in more detail in Chapter 8, which deals with the political environment. In between those branches of government responsible for providing goods and services and those responsible for policy are an increasing number that are involved in both. For example, many public services such as health authorities are increasingly selling services at a profit, although this is not their primary function and represents a small part of their total turnover.

Table 2.1 General government expenditure as a percentage of GDP, 1946–1987

	% of GDP
1946	23.9
1950	19.8
1955	20.3
1960	19.7
1965	20.9
1970	22.3
1975	26.4
1980	23.6
1985	22.9
1987	22.3

Source: *Economic Trends (1991)*, no. 21, reproduced with the permission of the Controller of HMSO.

The importance of public sector organizations varies from one country to another, and within the UK their importance has varied through time in terms of their share of gross domestic product. Table 2.1 shows that, after a surge in growth in the late 1940s, public sector expenditure gradually declined in relative importance during the 1950s before starting to grow again in the 1960s and 1970s, peaking in the late 1970s. In 1987 the total expenditure of all public sector organizations represented 21 per cent of GDP, employing over 1.3 million people and being responsible for 18 per cent of all investment in the economy. Since that date, the importance of public sector organizations within the UK economy has continued to decline.

Public corporations take a number of forms and are created by Acts of Parliament, or occasionally by Royal Charter. The exact status, function, power and authority of each corporation can be determined only by reference to the statute that created it. Sometimes public corporations are in fact limited companies in which government owns all of the shares.

2.4.1   Nationalized industries

One large but declining sector comprises the nationalized industries. These are organizations producing goods and services for consumers which are owned by central government. Together, they employed 800,000 people in 1985 and accounted for 5 per cent of GDP, compared with 9 per cent in 1979.

Government first became involved in industry for largely pragmatic reasons. Thus, in 1913 a key shareholding in the Anglo-Iranian Oil Company—the precursor of British Petroleum—was acquired to ensure oil supplies to the Royal Navy. During the interwar years, the Central Electricity Board, the British Broadcasting Corporation and the London Passenger Transport Board were created to fill gaps which the private sector had not been capable of filling. Whereas the reasons for the creation of these early nationalized industries were largely pragmatic, the early post-Second World War period saw the creation of a large number of nationalized industries for increasingly ideological reasons. The model for these industries was an organization to be run professionally along business lines, subject to a board which was appointed by a minister, accountable to Parliament through him and funded by Treasury-guaranteed capital at a fixed rate of interest. Nationalized industries were expected to break even, taking one year with the next. During the Labour government of the early postwar years, the state acquired control of the coal, electricity, gas, iron and steel industries and most inland transport. Some industries returned to the private sector during the Conservative governments of the 1950s, while others were added by subsequent Labour governments.

The term 'nationalized industry' has been traditionally applied to industries where the government has exercised day-to-day control over activities, as it did with electricity and coal mining following nationalization in 1948. Direct control of such industries no longer occurs, having been replaced by formally constituted corporations. Thus, the National Coal Board (now British Coal) was created with its own constitution, controlled by a semi-autonomous board of management appointed by the government and theoretically accountable to Parliament through its annual report to the House of Commons Select Committee on Nationalized Industries. Other nationalized industries have been created using the provisions of the Companies Acts; for example, the former National Bus Company was a private limited company in which the government owned all of the shares.

In a few cases, public corporations have some private sector involvement; the Austin Rover group, for example, operated as a private limited company with the government owning 96 per cent of the shares and private individuals the remaining 4 per cent.

The 1980s have seen a great demise in the role of nationalized industry. Just as ideology brought about the creation of nationalized industries in the postwar period, the Thatcher years were dominated by the ideology that industry was of necessity more efficient if it was responsible to private owners rather than the government. Consequently, many nationalized industries have been sold off to the private sector. Quite typically, the industry would have first been reconstituted into Companies Act format prior to privatization, with a shareholding structure. The method of selling the shares to the private sector has varied between different organizations. Some, such as British Gas and British Telecom, have been sold by offering shares direct to the public. Others, such as the National Freight Corporation and a number of former National Bus Company subsidiaries, have been sold to their management and employees. A few, such as Austin Rover and the Royal Ordnance factories, have been sold to another organization—both of these to British Aerospace, which was itself the result of an earlier privatization. In a number of cases, a nationalized industry has been reorganized with the aim of selling off some of its more peripheral, but marketable, assets. This has happened with British Rail, where separate companies were formed for the hotels, shipping and hovercraft businesses prior to selling them off to private sector organizations.

The sale of nationalized industries (see Table 2.2) has been a major feature of the 1980s, accounting for the declining importance of the public corporation in the UK. Those remaining have proved difficult to sell for a variety of practical and ideological reasons. Thus, the nuclear generating sector of the electricity industry was omitted from electricity privatization because the private sector was not prepared to underwrite the long-term risks associated with decommissioning nuclear power stations. Privatization of the coal and rail industries has been delayed largely because of the underlying unprofitability of the industries, faced with competition from other means of transport in the case of British Rail, and from relatively cheap imported coal in the case of British Coal. Both industries have been substantially reorganized to operate in a businesslike manner, with goals and a management structure more resembling a PLC than a traditional nationalized industry. In the case of the Post Office, ideological objections have been raised at the prospect of the Royal Mail letter delivery service being owned by a private sector company. This has not however prevented the Post Office from being reorganized along business lines, with private limited companies being formed for the main business units, one of which—Girobank—has been sold off to the Alliance and Leicester Building Society, while another—the parcel delivery service—has been restructured to act more like one of the private parcel companies with which it is having to compete in an increasingly competitive market.

The role of marketing within public corporations has been influenced by the nature of the market in which they operate. Following the late 1940s nationalizations, marketing was seen in many of the nationalized industries as being very secondary to production. The relative unimportance of marketing was often associated with some degree of monopoly power granted to the industry. In these circumstances, public corporations could afford to ignore marketing. However, as production of the basic industries caught up with demand and the economy became more deregulated during the 1980s, consumers increasingly had a choice between suppliers offered to them. For example, the deregulation of the coach industry in 1981 and the growth in private car ownership have placed increasing competitive pressure on British Rail, and hence an increasing importance for the company to become marketing-orientated; BR has increasingly been set profit objectives rather than unspecified social objectives.

What could be seen as either a strength or a weakness for the public corporation marketer has been finance for investment and new product development. Investment comes mainly from government—either directly, or through guarantees on loans from the private sector. Profits earned have not necessarily been ploughed back into the business. Since the 1930s, the public

Table 2.2 Key privatization sales

Date	Organization
1979	ICL
1980	Ferranti
1981	British Aerospace
	Cable and Wireless
1982	Amersham International
	Britoil
	National Freight Corporation
1983/4	Associated British Ports
1984	British Telecom
	Jaguar
	Sealink
1985	Vesper Thorneycroft
1986	BA Helicopters
	British Gas
	National Bus Company
	Swan Hunter
	Royal Ordnance
1987	British Airports Authority
	British Airways
	Rolls-Royce
	Leyland Bus Company
1988	British Steel
	Rover Group
1989	Regional Water Companies
1990	English and Welsh electricity supply companies
1991	Powergen
	National Power
	Scottish electricity companies

Note: This is not a complete list of privatizations. In some cases, the sale of shares was phased over a number of periods.

sector has been seen as one instrument for regulating the economy, cutting back or increasing investment to suit the needs of the national economy rather than the needs of the particular market the corporation is addressing. As well as limiting the amount of investment funds available, government involvement has also been accused of causing delay because of the time it has taken to scrutinize and approve a proposal; by the time approval had been granted, the investment could have been too late to meet changed market conditions.

Public corporations are perceived as an instrument of government, and although theoretically they may have an independent constitution, government is frequently accused of exercising covert pressure in order to achieve political favour. Fuel prices, rail fares and telephone charges have all at some time been subject to these allegations, which make life for the marketer more difficult because of the confused objectives.

2.4.2   Regulated public limited companies

It was noted above that many nationalized industries have been reconstituted to PLC status and sold to the private sector. However, they often retain features of government control which differentiates them from other PLCs. In some of the privatized companies, the government retains a 'golden share'. This effectively gives the government power of veto in vital areas for a specified number of years; for example, in the case of Rolls Royce, it allows the government to limit foreign ownership or the holding of large blocks of shares by any one individual. It has been used to prevent take-over bids for a company which would allow the company to fall into the control of an organization that the government considers undesirable. The existence of a 'golden share' can significantly affect the value of a newly privatized business. The government retained a golden share in the newly privatized Jaguar company, which it used to block proposed take-over bids. However, it relinquished the share in 1990, leaving the way open for Ford to push up the value of Jaguar and eventually take it over.

A second difference occurs where public utilities have been the subject of privatization. These have sometimes effectively transformed a public monopoly into a private monopoly. In addition to privatization, a dominant theme of the 1980s has been the liberalization of markets and the curbing of monopoly power. Consequently, the privatized public utility companies have been watched over by newly created regulatory bodies which have varying degrees of power to set price levels and establish the standards of service to be provided by the company. Gas, electricity, telecommunications and water supply each have their own regulatory body. In the case of Ofgas, which regulates British Gas, the latter is allowed to increase gas supply charges to customers to fully reflect changes in energy prices, whereas the price for non-gas services (e.g. maintenance) can be increased only by the rate of inflation less 2 per cent. The newly privatized companies have tried to lessen their dependence on government-regulated activities by diversifying to unregulated markets. For example, water companies have invested in hydraulic engineering companies and in street-cleaning businesses.

2.4.3   Local authority enterprises

In addition to providing basic services such as roads, education, housing and social services, local authorities play a number of roles in providing marketable goods and services in competitive markets. For a long time, local authorities have operated bus services and leisure facilities, among others. Initially such services were set up for a variety of reasons—to provide a valuable public service, to help stimulate economic development or to earn a profit to subsidize the local rates. Where a project was too large for one authority and benefited neighbouring authorities, a joint board might be formed between the authorities. This sometimes happened with local-authority-controlled airports, for example the East Midlands Airport.

Increasingly, local authorities are being forced to turn their trading activities into business-like units, separately accountable from the rest of the local authority's responsibilities. In the case of local authority airport operations, the government has passed legislation in the form of the Airports Act 1986, requiring local authorities to create limited companies into which their assets will be placed. Like any limited company, they will be required to appoint a board of directors and to produce an annual profit and loss statement. It was also the government's intention that, by creating a company structure, it would be easier to introduce private capital, or indeed to sell off the business in its entirety to the private sector. This has already occurred in the case of a number of local authority bus companies.

Even where separate business units have not been created, local authority services are being exposed to increasing levels of competition. Operations in such areas as highway maintenance, refuse collection and street cleaning must now—following the Local Government Act 1988—be put out to competitive tender. Consequently, the existing local authority workforce finds itself competing against outside private sector organizations. The legislation requires that in these circumstances a direct labour organization should be accountable separately from the rest of the authority's activities. The management of these direct labour organizations must study the market carefully to judge the likely price at which its competitors will bid.

In other areas of local authority services, clients are being offered greater choice. With the advent of local management of schools, the governing bodies of schools are adopting—if somewhat grudgingly—a marketing orientation to ensure that the service they are offering is considered better than neighbouring schools to which pupils would have the choice of attending. Only by attracting clients can they ensure funding for their school.

2.5 QUANGOs

A 'quasi-autonomous national government organization' (or QUANGO) is one step removed from a public corporation. A QUANGO typically has a constitution created by Parliament defining its objectives, powers and procedures for nominating members of its governing body. The QUANGO generally fulfils a socially necessary role, while having considerable independence from government on day-to-day matters. After declining in number in the early 1980s, the latter part of the 1980s saw a growth in their numbers, often by taking activities out of the hands of the civil service or local authorities and creating an accountable business unit. Thus, civil service activities such as the Driver and Vehicle Licensing Centre have been reconstituted as executive agencies, and polytechnic higher education corporations have taken over the role previously provided by local authorities. The policy-forming functions of QUANGOs is considered in more detail in Chapter 8, which covers the political environment.

2.6 CO-OPERATIVE SOCIETIES

Consumer co-operative societies date back to the mid-nineteenth century, when their aims were to provide cheap, unadulterated food for their members and to share profits among members rather than hand them over to outside shareholders. The number of co-operative societies grew during the latter half of the nineteenth century but has declined during recent years as a result of mergers, so that in 1987 there were only about 200 co-operative retail societies.

Each co-operative society is registered under the Industrial and Provident Societies Acts and not the Companies Acts and has its own legal personality, very much as a private limited company. The main contrast between the two comes in the form of control of the society. An individual can become a member of a co-operative by buying one share and is then entitled to one vote; further shares can be purchased, but the member still has only one vote, unlike the private limited company, where voting power is generally based on the number of shares held.

A variation on the consumer co-operative is the producer co-operative, sometimes formed by groups of farmers to market their produce more effectively than they could achieve individually.

2.7 OTHER TYPES OF ORGANIZATION

A few other forms of organization exist. Building societies are governed by the Building Societies Acts, which have evolved over time to reflect the changing role of building societies. They were for some time seen as being almost monopoly providers of money for house purchase, with strict regulations on the powers of the society in terms of its sources of funds and the uses for which loans could be advanced. With the liberalizing of the home mortgage market, building societies now have wider powers of lending and borrowing. As a result, societies have had to embrace the marketing concept in a way that was previously seen as unnecessary. The Building Societies Act 1986 further allowed building societies the possibility of converting to public limited company status, eliminating the remaining controls imposed by the Building Society Acts.

Charities that are registered with the Registrar of Charities are given numerous benefits by the government, such as tax concessions. They have taken on board many of the practices of marketing, such as their increasingly sophisticated communications strategies and trading activities. The aims of charities are normally much more complex than a profit-motivated organization. This often influences the ways in which money is raised and production organized. For example, Barnardo's runs coffee shops where providing training for the disadvantaged staff is seen to be as important as providing a fast service for customers or maximizing the profits of the outlet.

REVIEW QUESTIONS

1. For what reasons might a manufacturer of fitted kitchens seek PLC status? What are the advantages and disadvantages of this course of action?
2. How might a local authority try to introduce a marketing orientation to its residential homes for elderly people?
3. Critically assess the benefits to the public of turning a branch of the civil service with which you are familiar into an executive agency.
4. Why has franchising become such an important business relationship in the UK?

FURTHER READING

Davies, S. (1988), *Economics of Industrial Organisation*, Longman, London.
Donnelly, G. (1987), *The Firm in Society*, 2nd edn, Pitman, London.
Harden, G. (1987), *Business Organisation and Management*, Phillip Allen, Oxford.
Newell, M. (1984), *The Economics of Business*, Pan, London.
Thomas, R. E. (1987), *The Government of Business*, 3rd edn, Phillip Allen, Oxford.

CHAPTER
THREE
ORGANIZATIONAL GROWTH

3.1 INTRODUCTION

Organizations have an almost inherent tendency to grow. The reasons for this are varied—managers may feel the need to boost their own career prospects, or the owners of a business organization may see growth as a means of increasing the value of their business. Growth can take many different forms, and the rate and type of growth will have an influence on the marketing function of a business. This chapter will first seek to understand the diverse nature of objectives and the effect they may have on patterns of growth. It will then consider the methods by which organizations grow, the implications for marketing of growth, and the limits to growth that a company may face.

3.2 THE OBJECTIVES OF ORGANIZATIONS

All business organizations exist to pursue objectives of one kind or another. It is important for the marketer to understand the nature of organizational goals, as these will affect, among other things, the way the organization makes purchases, sets prices or pursues a market-share strategy. Whether a firm is selling to, or competing with, another firm, a study of its objectives will help to understand how it is likely to act.

Very broadly, organizational goals can be classified into three categories:

1. Those that aim to make a profit for their *owners*
2. Those that aim to maximize benefits to *society*
3. Those that aim to maximize benefits to their *members*

The specific objectives of business organizations are now considered in more detail.

3.2.1 Profit maximization

It is often assumed that business organizations will always try to maximize their profits, through a combination of maximizing revenue and minimizing costs. It is often thought that the pursuit of profit maximization is the unifying characteristic of all private sector businesses; indeed, economic theory is very much based on the notion of the profit-maximizing firm.

However, the simple model of profit maximization is open to question, even if it is recognized for the moment that it may be of only marginal relevance to organizations that exist largely for the members' or community's benefit. First, the profit-maximizing objective must be qualified by a time dimension; a firm pursuing a short-term profit-maximizing objective may act very differently from one that is seeking to maximize long-term profit. This may be reflected in a differing emphasis on R & D, new product development and market development strategies. Whether or not a company is able to pursue long-term profit-maximizing objectives will be influenced by the nature of the environment in which it operates. The financial environment of the UK and the emphasis on short-term results has caused UK organizations to pursue much more short-term profit goals than firms in, say, Japan, where the nature of organizational funding allows a longer time for projects to achieve profits. Similarly, a company operating in a relatively regulated environment—such as patented medicines—will be in a stronger position to plan for long-term profit maximization than one that is operating in a relatively unpredictable and uncertain deregulated market.

A second major criticism of the dominance of profit maximization as a business objective is that maximization is not observed to occur in practice. In most business organizations there is a separation of ownership from management, whereby the managers of the company have little or no stake in the ownership of the company. Thus, the managers may be able to pursue policies more in line with their own self-interest so long as they make sufficient profit to keep their shareholders happy. Instead of pursuing maximum profits, therefore, the managers of the company may pursue a policy of maximizing sales turnover, subject to achieving a satisfactory level of profits.

3.2.2 Market share maximization

Market share maximization may coincide with profit maximization, in cases where there is a close correlation between market share and return on investment. It has been suggested that this occurs in the UK grocery retailing sector. There are other instances, however, where there is a less straightforward relationship between market share and profitability—for example in the UK retail travel agency sector, where both the market leader and small specialist retailers have achieved reasonable returns on investment, but many medium-sized firms have faced below-average returns.

There are circumstances and reasons why a firm may pursue a policy of maximizing market share independently of a profit-maximizing objective. Domination of a particular market may give stability and security to the company, and this might be regarded as a more attractive option for management than maximizing profits. Building market share may itself be seen as a short-term strategy to achieve longer-term profits, given that there may be a relationship between the two.

The objective of market share maximization may influence a number of aspects of a firm's marketing mix. For example, it may cut prices and increase promotional expenditure, accepting short-term losses in order to drive its main rivals out of business, thereby leaving it free to exploit the market.

3.2.3 Corporate growth

As a business grows, so too does the power and responsibility of individual managers. In terms of salaries and career development, a growth strategy may appear very attractive to management, not only for managers' own self-advancement, but also as an aid to attracting and retaining a high calibre of staff. However, such enthusiasm for growth could lead the owners of the business to pursue diversification into unknown and possibly unprofitable areas.

3.2.4   Satisficing

Given that the managers of a business are probably not going to benefit directly from increased profits, the argument has been advanced that managers satisfice rather than maximize profits; i.e. they achieve certain targets for sales, profits and market share which may not coincide with profit maximization. Provided that sufficient profit is made to keep the shareholders happy, managers may pursue activities that satisfy their own individual needs, such as higher-status company cars, or they may pursue business activities that give them a relatively easy life, or add to their ego. To achieve these diverse individual objectives, part of the firm's profit which could be paid out to shareholders is diverted and used to pay for managerial satisfaction.

The extent to which satisficing represents an important business objective can be debated. It can be argued that in relatively competitive markets, competitive pressures do not allow companies to add the costs of these management diversions to their selling prices—if they did, they would eventually go out of business in favour of companies whose shareholders exercised greater control over the costs of their managers. Only in stable and relatively less competitive markets can these implied additional costs be borne by adding to prices. In fact, a growing tendency has been for the owners of a business to give senior managers of the business contracts of employment that are related to profit performance. While this may lessen the extent of the apparent conflict of objectives for management, a trade-off may still have to be made where, for example, a decision has to be made on whether to spend more money on company cars for managers: should they spend the money and get all of the benefit for themselves, or save costs in order to increase profits, of which they will receive only a share?

Satisficing behaviour can have a number of implications for the marketer. Buying behaviour in any business organization is likely to be complex, but companies that are satisficing are likely to attach relatively greater importance to the intangible decision factors such as ease of order, familiarity and the level of status attached to a particular purchase, than to the more objective factors such as price and quality.

3.2.5   Survival

For many organizations, the objective of maximizing profit is a luxury for management and shareholders alike—the overriding problem is simply to stay in business. Many businesses have had to close not because of poor long-term profit potential, but because of short-term cash flow problems. Without a source of finance to pay for current expenses, the longer-term profit maximization cannot be achieved. Cash flow problems can arise for a number of reasons, such as unexpected increases in costs, a fall in revenue resulting from unexpected competitive pressure, or a seasonal pattern of activity which is different from what was predicted. The effect is to influence marketing decisions in a number of ways; for example, pricing decisions may reflect the need to liquidate stock regardless of the mark-up or contribution to profit. An advertising campaign to build up long-term brand loyalty may be sacrificed to a cheaper sales promotion campaign which has a shorter payback period.

3.2.6   Loss-making

A company may be part of a group that needs a loss-maker to set off against other companies in the group which are making profits that are heavily taxed by the Inland Revenue. Situations can arise where one company makes a component that is used by another member of the group:

although the company may make a loss, it may be more tax-efficient for it to continue making a loss than for it to buy in the product at a cheaper price from an outside organization.

3.2.7 Social objectives

Occasionally commercial organizations have overt social objectives of one form or another, usually alongside a resource objective—for example, a requirement that the organization must at least break even. Charities such as Oxfam, while having as a clear objective the maximization of revenue, also state their aims in terms of which groups they are working to benefit. Where they engage in trading activities (such as Oxfam shops), their social objectives may result in their buying supplies from disadvantaged groups (e.g. in the Third World countries), even though these may not be the most commercially profitable sources.

Traditionally, many commercial companies have had social objectives imposed by their owners. For example, Quakers such as Cadbury and Rowntree sought to maximize the moral welfare of their workforce. In modern times, the Body Shop has an objective not to support experiments on animals, an objective that pervades many aspects of the company's marketing, including new product development and promotion. Even businesses that for the most part are pursuing profit objectives may adopt social objectives in some small areas of activity, such as running a sports or social club for its employees.

3.2.8 Maximizing benefits to consumers

An overriding objective of a marketing-orientated organization is to maximize consumer satisfaction. However, this has to be qualified by a second objective, which is normally to earn profits. In the case of consumer co-operatives, maximizing the benefits to customers has had a significance beyond the normal marketing concept of maximizing consumer satisfaction. The co-operative movement was originally conceived in order to eliminate the role of the outside shareholder, allowing profits to be passed back to the customers through a dividend which is related to their spending rather than their shareholding. Any action that maximized the returns to the business by definition maximized the benefits to the consumer.

The importance of consumer co-operatives has declined since the 1950s for a number of reasons. The co-operatives appeared very attractive to consumers at a time when firms were essentially production-orientated and when the demand for goods exceeded their supply. With the reversal of this situation, however, other retailers with greater organizational flexibility and a more overt marketing orientation have attracted custom by offering additional services to customers, often associated with lower prices.

3.2.9 Maximizing public benefits

In many government and charity organizations, it is difficult to talk about the concept of profit or revenue maximization. Instead, the organization is given the objective of maximizing specified aspects of public benefit, subject to keeping within a resource constraint. Public sector hospitals are increasingly coming to embrace the marketing concept, but it is recognized that it would be inappropriate for them to be given a strictly financial set of objectives: instead, they might be given the objective of maximizing the number of operations of a particular kind within a resource constraint. Similarly, a charity campaigning for improved road safety may set an objective of maximizing awareness of its cause among important opinion formers.

There is frequently a gap between the publicly stated objectives of a public sector organization and the interpretation and implementation of these objectives by the staff concerned. As in a private sector organization, management in the public sector could promote secondary objectives which add to the managers' own individual status and security, rather than maximizing the public benefit. A manager of a hospital may seek to maximize his use of high technology because this may be perceived as enhancing his career, even though the public benefit could be maximized more efficiently with simpler technology.

In recent years more pressure has been put on public services such as education and defence to operate according to business criteria. Marketing has begun to assume greater importance in a number of ways. Providers of public services are increasingly being set quantified objectives which reflect the needs of their clients. Improved research methods to find out more about client needs, and more effective communication of their offering to clients, have been part of this process towards greater marketing orientation. Many public services have themselves become major consumers of services as peripheral activities such as cleaning and catering have been subcontracted out. This has resulted in the growth of a market-orientated service sector. Very often, the management and staff previously providing an ancillary service within a public sector organization have bought out the operation from their employer and now have to sell the service back to the authority. Their objectives have changed from a vague notion of maximizing public benefit to one of maximizing their own profit.

3.2.10 Complexity of objectives

In practice, a business organization is likely to be pursuing more than one objective at any one time. Furthermore, objectives are likely to change through time. A marketer needs to be able to identify those that are influencing the behaviour of a company, and this can present a number of practical problems.

The first place to look for a statement of a company's objectives might be its memorandum and articles of association. This statement is required by the Companies Acts for all limited companies and includes an objectives clause. In practice, companies frequently draw up their objectives clause in a way that is so wide that the company can do almost anything.

A more up-to-date statement of objectives may be found in the annual report and accounts which all companies must produce annually. This must include a directors' report, which may give an indication of the goals the company is working towards.

3.3 GROWTH OF ORGANIZATIONS

3.3.1 Reasons for growth

Many factors can contribute to the growth of an organization.

1. The markets in which the business operates may be growing, making growth in output relatively easy to achieve. In addition, in a rapidly growing market, if an organization simply maintains a constant output, its market share will be falling. Growth may be considered not so much a luxury as a necessity if the firm is to maintain its position in the market-place. This could be particularly important for industries where economies of scale are an important consideration.
2. A critical mass may exist for the size of firms in a market, below which they are at a competitive disadvantage. For example, a retail grocery chain which is aiming for a broad market segment will need to achieve a sufficiently large size in order to obtain bulk discounts from suppliers which can in turn be passed on in lower prices to customers. Size would give

economies of scale in many areas such as advertising, distribution and administration. Many new businesses may include in their business plan an objective to achieve a specified critical mass within a given time period.

3. An overt policy of growth is often pursued by organizations in an attempt to stimulate staff morale. An expanding business is more likely to be able to offer promotion prospects, which will allow a high calibre of staff to be recruited and retained.

4. In addition to the formal goals of growth, management may in practice pursue objectives that result in growth. Higher rates of growth can bring greater status and promotion prospects to managers of an organization, even if a more appropriate long-term strategy may indicate that a slower rate of growth is preferable.

5. Some organizations may grow by acquiring competitors in order to limit the amount of competition in a market where such competition is considered to be wasteful. An important reason behind the merger between British Airways and British Caledonian Airways was the desire to reduce excess capacity over common sections of route.

3.3.2 Types of organizational growth

Two basic growth patterns for organizations can be identified—organic growth and growth by acquisition—although many businesses grow by a combination of the two processes.

Organic growth Organic growth is considered to be the more natural pattern of growth for an organization. The initial investment by the firm results in profits, an established customer base and a well-established technical, personnel and financial structure. This provides a foundation for future growth. In this sense, success breeds success, for the rate of the firm's growth is influenced by the extent to which it has succeeded in building up internally the means for future expansion. All aspects of the business can be said to evolve gradually; for example, the accounting and finance function may initially be under the day-to-day control of one person, but as the organization expands it becomes necessary to develop specialist areas within accounting, each with its own section head.

In terms of marketing, organizations may grow organically by tackling one segment at a time, using the resources, knowledge and market awareness gained to tackle further segments. Ansoff's (1957) product expansion grid provides a framework for studying the ways in which a firm can expand its output. Typically, it would first seek to achieve the highest level of penetration of an existing segment with its established product range. Then it would seek to exploit additional market segments with its established products. Having established its position in a market, it may proceed to develop new products for its existing markets. Once these opportunities are exhausted, the firm may seek to grow by diversifying into new products for new market segments.

A firm may grow organically into new segments in a number of ways. Many retail chains such as Sainsburys have grown organically by developing one region before moving on to another: Sainsburys grew organically from its southern base towards the northern regions, while Asda grew organically during the 1970s and early 1980s from its northern base towards the south. Other organizations have grown organically by aiming a basically similar product at new segments of the market—as Thomson Holidays has done in developing new holidays for the youth and elderly markets. An example of an organization which has gone beyond this stage to offer new products for its existing customers is Marks and Spencer, which, after attacking new geographical segments, has offered new products in the form of financial services to their established customer base.

Growth by acquisition   The rate of organic growth is constrained by factors such as the rate at which the market served by the organization is growing. A firm seeking to grow organically in a slowly developing sector such as food manufacture will find organic growth more difficult than one serving a rapidly growing sector such as computer software. Also, companies with relatively low capital requirements will find organic growth relatively faster.

Growth by acquisition may appear attractive to businesses where organic growth is difficult. In some cases it may be almost essential in order to achieve a critical mass which may be necessary for survival. The DIY retail sector in the UK is one where chains have needed to achieve a certain size in order to achieve economies in buying, distribution and promotion. Small chains have not been able to grow organically at a sufficient rate to achieve a critical mass, resulting in their take-over or merger to form larger chains. The market leader—B & Q—has seen mainly organic growth, while the Texas chain has acquired a number of smaller chains, such as Unit Sales.

Growth by acquisition may occur where an organization sees its existing market sector contracting and seeks to diversify into other areas. The time and risk associated with starting a new venture in an alien market sector may be considered too great; acquiring an established business could be less risky, allowing access to an established client base and technical skills.

It was noted earlier that growth in itself may be seen as good for developing staff morale in allowing career progression. The company may formally encourage growth by acquisition for this very reason, while staff may have informal objectives directed towards this end. Acquiring new subsidiaries could satisfy this objective for a company that is operating in otherwise static markets.

Growth by acquisition can take a number of forms. The simplest is the agreed take-over, whereby one firm agrees to purchase the majority of the share capital of another company. Payment can be in the form of cash or shares in the acquiring company, or by some combination of the two. A take-over can be mutually beneficial where one company has a sound customer base but lacks the financial resources to achieve a critical mass while the other has the finance but needs a larger customer base. Many take-overs occur where the founder of a business is seeking to retire and to liquidate the value of the business.

A take-over bid occurs when the acquiring company writes to shareholders in the target company, offering to purchase their shares. If sufficient shareholders agree, then the take-over proceeds. The board of the target company also writes to its shareholders giving its recommendation on whether or not to accept.

While the majority of take-overs are agreed, circumstances often arise where the take-over is contested. This particularly affects public companies whose shares can be bought and sold openly. Typically, a cash-rich firm would identify another company which it recognizes as underperforming because of poor management. Its argument for a take-over is based on the appeal of its proven management style being applied to the underperforming assets of the target company, thereby increasing the profitability of the latter's assets. Disputed take-overs can become very bitter affairs, with each side trying to prove its own performance while denigrating that of the other party. The battle is often made even more vitriolic because of contrasting cultural styles: for the target company, exposure of its management style and practices may be seen as a new and unwelcome event. This response may represent the firm's desire to remain independent.

During a contested take-over bid, the marketing strategy can be significantly affected during the short term. To prove the ability of the existing management, marketing programmes may focus on boosting short-term market share, possibly at the expense of long-term brand-building. Communication programmes can become aimed at the financial community as much as the final consumer, as in the contested take-over bid for Allied Lyons by the Australian Elders IXL, where adverts for the firm's diverse product range were amended to include the Allied Lyons name, aimed at associating the company with a much broader portfolio of brands than may have been appreciated by members of the financial community. New product launches may be brought ahead of the ideal launch date in order to impress the financial community.

For public companies, the stock exchange imposes strict rules about how a take-over bid may be conducted; these are covered by the City Code on Take-overs and Mergers and monitored by the Panel on Take-overs. Thus, an acquiring company cannot simply quietly acquire shares in a company until it has achieved a majority shareholding: it must declare its holding once it has reached a 10 per cent holding and must make a formal take-over offer once it has acquired 30 per cent. The offer document itself is tightly prescribed in terms of the information it must contain.

A merger is a variation on a take-over where two existing companies agree to set up one new company which will issue shares to the shareholders of each of the existing companies in agreed proportions and in exchange for old shareholdings. Many agreed take-overs show characteristics of a merger, and it is difficult to strictly distinguish between the two. In the UK retail DIY sector, both the Boots company and WH Smith had been expanding their separate chains of DIY stores organically (Payless and Do it All respectively). This method of growth had failed to achieve the critical mass necessary to compete effectively with the market leader, B & Q. The two owners therefore agreed to merge the two companies, with a new board of directors and shares allocated equally between the two parent organizations.

3.3.3   Horizontal and vertical integration

Amalgamations between firms can take the form of horizontal integration, vertical integration or diversification. Horizontal integration occurs when firms involved in the same stage of manufacture of a product amalgamate to achieve greater economies of scale and—subject to Monopolies Commission approval—to reduce the level of wasteful competition in a market. The merger between Sky Television and British Satellite Broadcasting falls into this category. Vertical integration occurs when a company acquires either its suppliers (backward integration) or its distributors (forward integration). Tour operators integrating backwards have ensured the provision of aircraft capacity by acquiring or setting up their own airlines, while others have integrated forwards by acquiring travel agents. Diversification occurs where firms have acquired firms operating in unrelated sectors, the purpose of the acquisition being to spread risk through a balanced portfolio of activities. Figure 3.1 depicts possible growth patterns for a brewery.

Diversification as a reason for amalgamation has become increasingly important over the past 30 years. Table 3.1 shows the changing relative importance of the three types of take-over.

3.4   SOURCES OF FINANCE FOR GROWTH

As far as the private sector is concerned, there are two basic methods of financing growth. On the one hand, companies can raise risk capital (often referred to as equity capital) from share-holders, for which a relatively high rate of return will be required. To supplement this, they can use a second and relatively less expensive form of loan finance, which must be repaid regardless of the fortunes of the company. The relationship between the two is referred to as 'gearing'. A company that has a high amount of loan finance relative to equity is said to be highly geared. An optimum balance exists between the two types of finance, although this varies between different industrial sectors.

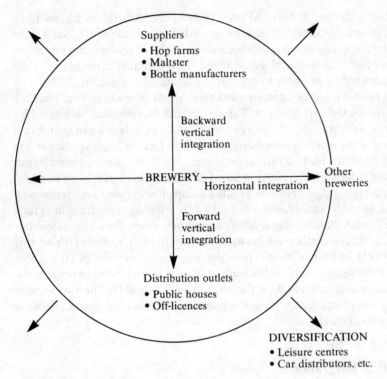

Figure 3.1 Possible growth patterns for a brewery

Table 3.1 Percentage of proposed mergers, 1965–1987, by number and by value of assets to be acquired

	Horizontal		Vertical		Diversified	
	% of amalgamations	% value	% of amalgamations	% value	% of amalgamations	% value
1965–69	82	88	5	5	13	7
1970–74	72	75	5	4	23	21
1975–79	62	67	9	7	29	26
1980–82	64	68	5	2	31	30
1987	67	80	3	1	30	19

Source: Annual Report of the Director General of Fair Trading, reproduced with permission of the Controller of HMSO.

3.4.1 Equity capital

The sole trader or partnership can raise fresh capital by forming a private limited company and selling shares in the company. The sale of shares cannot be advertised to the public, so they have to be placed privately. For smaller companies, blocks of shares are often sold to relations or business associates. New opportunities to gain access to equity share capital have been provided through a relatively new type of intermediary—the venture capital company. These intermediaries develop an understanding of the opportunities for investment in smaller private companies and provide the link—and often also the management support—through which investment from cash-rich organizations such as pension funds is provided.

To gain access to significant amounts of new equity capital from a much wider financial community, a private company may 'go public'. Becoming a public company requires the passing of a special resolution by the shareholders and amending the articles of association to take out those restrictions that apply to a private company.

To acquire a full listing on the stock exchange, a considerable amount of time and money must be spent to meet the requirements of the Stock Exchange Council. These basically aim to ensure that anybody considering buying shares in the company is adequately informed about the record, current position and future prospects of that company. A detailed prospectus, including five years of trading figures with audited accounts, must be produced.

The actual sale of shares can take place in a number of ways. The commonest method is the *offer for sale* to the general public, whereby a specified number of shares is offered at a fixed price, usually underwritten to guarantee the share income to the company. Other methods are the *sale by tender*, which involves selling the shares to the highest bidders, and *placement* with financial institutions. The cost of raising fresh equity through a share issue can be considerable, reflecting the work of the accountants, bankers, solicitors and underwriters involved. For a typical share sale valued at £2 million, between 5 and 10 per cent would be lost in issuing expenses.

An alternative to obtaining a full listing on the stock exchange is to seek a listing on the Unlisted Securities Market (USM). This is less costly to the company, and the level of financial information required is lower. Another alternative is the Third Market, introduced in 1987 to cater for the smaller and relatively young companies which had not yet acquired a track record and were typically looking for smaller sums of up to £1 million. Although forming part of the stock exchange, both of these markets represent a greater level of risk to the stock market investor. They have however become very popular with companies, as Table 3.2 shows.

An alternative method of raising fresh equity capital for an established business is to call on existing shareholders to subscribe for additional shares. This is known as a *rights issue*, and shareholders are given the right to purchase additional shares at a specified price in proportion to their existing shareholdings.

Table 3.2 Value of issues on unlisted securities market

	£m
1982	86
1983	164
1984	159
1985	181
1988	303
1990	40

Source: *Financial Statistics*, reproduced with permission of the Controller of HMSO.

3.4.2   Retained earnings

Free enterprise idealists would argue that a company's profits should be distributed entirely to its shareholders so that they can decide how they should be reinvested. In practice, companies tend to retain a proportion of profits for reinvestment within the business; they are encouraged to do this by tax advantages. The amount distributed to shareholders in the form of a dividend tends to be kept at a stable level, meeting a norm for that particular industry and the expectations of shareholders.

While retained earnings may seem an easy source of finance for a company, there is a danger that, if it does not achieve an adequate internal return on these earnings, it may become the subject of a take-over bid from another company which considers that it could manage the capital of the business more effectively.

3.4.3   Loans

For the small business, loans for expansion may be obtained from family and friends. However, when loan requirements exceed this source, commercial loans are sought and some form of security against the loan is usually required.

Debentures are loans to a company carrying interest at a fixed rate and are often repayable on a specified date. Debenture holders receive priority over shareholders for annual income payments and when the assets of the business are liquidated. Some—called *mortgage debentures*—are backed by a particular fixed asset belonging to the company as security, while others are secured by a floating charge on the company's assets in general. In the event of default on payment, the lender has the right to take over the security offered and sell it in order to repay the outstanding loan. Other debentures, known as *loan stock*, are unsecured, and their holders are in the same position as trade creditors in ranking for repayment in the event of liquidation, although they are still ahead of shareholders.

A common feature of the 1980s was the *management buy-out* whereby autonomous companies were created by the management and employees of a large group buying part of the business of their former employers. These were often very highly geared, with the management putting in relatively little of their own equity capital relative to the loan capital provided by a merchant bank. Such buy-outs often involved very complex financing, with the merchant bank seeking a route by which its minority shareholding could be floated very quickly afterwards, or by which assets of the newly formed business could be sold off to repay the loans. This method of financing growth was very attractive when the economy was expanding and interest rates were relatively low, but the high gearing spelt difficulty for many companies when the economy took a downturn and interest rates rose. Companies could not defer payment of interest on loans in the way that they could defer paying a dividend to the risk-taking shareholders.

In Britain, many buy-outs were formed among retailers during the boom periods of the 1980s when consumer spending was at an historically high standard. Faced with a downturn in consumer spending a few years later, these companies did not have the flexibility to postpone payment of interest. Instead, they had to indulge in stock reductions and price discounting to keep cash flowing in. Sometimes they succeeded, but on other occasions receivership followed, as with Lewis's department stores and the jewellers Easthope & Co. In other cases, the finances of the business had to be restructured, usually to the detriment of the shareholders, as occurred in the case of the MFI furniture group during 1990.

3.5 JOINT VENTURES

Diversification into new business areas can be risky even for a cash-rich business. The company may lack the management skills necessary in the market it seeks to enter, while the barriers to entry may be too high to be an acceptable risk. One way forward is to set up a joint venture where companies with complementary skills and financial resources join together. A new limited company is formed with shares allocated between the member-companies and agreement made on where the financial and human resources are to come from. A good example is provided by the agreement between the supermarket group Sainsburys and the clothing and furnishings shop British Home Stores to create the Savacentre chain of one-stop shops selling both product ranges under one roof. Sainsburys also used a joint venture in a different way to establish its Homebase operation. Although it had the cash to develop a chain of DIY stores on the scale that was necessary to ensure viability, it had no experience in this field. It therefore joined with the Belgian DIY company BM SA which was seeking to enter the British market, and the aims of both companies were thereby satisfied.

A joint venture is commonly used where a company seeks to enter an overseas market. It has frequently been used by European car manufacturers who have set up joint companies to manufacture and sell cars in developing countries. The car manufacturer Fiat, for example, established itself in the East European market by setting up a joint venture with the Polish government to build FSO cars.

Where new markets emerge and risks are very high, a company may succeed only if it has a very large individual backer, or if a consortium of firms pool their financial and technical resources to create a new company. Satellite television broadcasting is a very high-risk area. The only British-based company—British Satellite Broadcasting—was formed from a consortium that included electronics and publishing companies.

3.6 LIMITS TO GROWTH

Most organizations pursue growth to a greater or lesser degree. However, there are limits to how far and how fast a company can grow. Growth by acquisition, being relatively risky, can reveal limits beyond which a company cannot sustain growth. Growth by acquisition is commonly associated with high borrowings, resulting in a high level of gearing. The use of relatively cheap debt capital may be attractive while the company is profitable, but it can leave the firm dangerously exposed when conditions deteriorate. Faced with a fixed charge for interest, it may be forced to liquidate some of its assets by disposing of subsidiaries in order to raise cash to meet its interest payments. Many companies that grew rapidly during the 1980s by acquisition using borrowed capital have been forced to contract with the economic slowdown of the early 1990s. Organizations that grew organically at a slower rate, without reliance on such a high level of borrowed capital, have fared relatively better.

The ability of the management structure of a company to respond to growth sets a further limit to growth. Many companies have benefited from having as managing director a dynamic personality during a period of rapid growth, only to find that the organization needs a much broader management base once it has passed a critical size. Companies such as Next and Amstrad may have suffered because their management structures have not grown to meet the needs of a very different type of organization. If a company does not restructure itself as it grows, diseconomies of scale may set in.

Legislative constraints may limit the ability of an organization to grow in its core markets. In Britain, take-overs and mergers in which one company can control up to 25 per cent of a market, or where the assets to be acquired exceed £30 million, can be referred by the Office of Fair Trading to the Monopolies and Mergers Commission (MMC). The Commission would then have six months to investigate whether the take-over would result in a reduction in competition prejudicial to consumers or whether it would be against the public interest in a wider sense. It could recommend to the Secretary of State for Trade and Industry that a proposed merger be blocked. In the case of existing monopolistic situations, the Commission can recommend divestment of assets or other action to reduce the undesirable elements of monopoly power.

A recent example of a company forced to divest certain assets involved the Rank Organization. Rank acquired Mecca Leisure during 1990, giving it significant monopoly power in the operation of bingo halls and clubs within the London area. In order to reduce this monopoly position, Rank was forced to sell off some of its London bingo halls.

The European Community is assuming increasing power in vetting proposed mergers. Articles 85 and 86 of the Treaty of Rome in general prohibit anti-competitive practices, such as price fixing, market sharing and limitations on production; but, as in the UK, take-overs and mergers may be allowed where a monopoly situation is counteracted by an overall public benefit. The European Commission, which oversees implementation of Articles 85 and 86, can prohibit mergers where the combined turnover exceeds ECU200 million or where the company will have over 25 per cent of a national market. In Britain, the European Commission has intervened to force British Airways to sell some of the routes that it acquired from British Caledonian, even though the take-over had previously been approved by the MMC.

With the development of the single European market (see Chapter 7), monopolies and mergers are being assessed by the European Commission in terms of Europe-wide competition. The Commission can now investigate—and require advance notification of—cross-border take-overs where the combined worldwide turnover of the two companies exceeds ECU5 billion, where the smaller company has an EC turnover of ECU100 million and where less than two-thirds of the combined turnover originates in one member-state.

3.7 THE RESURGENCE OF SMALL BUSINESS

The term 'small business' is difficult to define. In an industry such as car manufacture, a firm with 100 employees would be considered very small, whereas for a firm of solicitors it would be considered very large. The term is therefore a relative one, based typically on some measure of numbers of employees or capital employed.

Despite the tendency of firms to grow, the 1980s saw renewed interest in the role of small businesses within the economy. It is suggested that many of Britain's competitor countries can attribute the success of their economies to having a strong small business sector. The dynamic economies of the Far East have particularly strong small business sectors. During the 1980s there was a significant increase in the number of small businesses, especially in the expanding services sector. Table 3.3 shows the significance of small businesses in the main sectors of the UK economy.

Advocates of small business argue that they are important to the economy. In the first place, they generally offer much greater adaptability than larger firms: with less bureaucracy and fewer channels of communications, decisions can be taken rapidly. A larger organization may be burdened with constraints that tend to slow the decision-making process, such as the need to negotiate new working practices with trade union representatives, or to obtain board approval for major decisions. As organizations grow, there is an inherent tendency for them to become more risk-averse by building in systems of control which make them slower to adapt to changes in their marketing environment.

Table 3.3 Distribution of firms by size of turnover, 1985 (%)

	Turnover size			% of total stock of businesses
	Up to £¼m	£¼–1m	£1m+	
Agriculture, Forestry & Fishing	91.1	8.0	0.9	9.5
Mining, Quarrying & Public Utilities	55.5	23.3	21.1	0.1
Manufacturing	69.1	18.8	12.3	10.6
Construction	86.5	10.3	3.2	14.3
Services	83.4	11.4	5.1	65.4
All businesses	83.0	11.7	5.2	100.0

Source: *Business Monitor* (1987). Reproduced with permission of the Controller of HMSO.

Second, it is argued that small businesses tend to be good innovators. This comes about through their greater adaptability, especially where large amounts of capital are not required. This is often true of the service sector, where typical low-cost innovations have included video film rental services and home delivery fast-food services. Small firms can also be good innovators where they operate in markets dominated by a small number of larger companies and where the only way a small business can gain entry to the market is to develop an innovatory product aimed at a small niche. The soap powder market in Britain is dominated by a small number of large producers, yet it was a relatively small company that identified a niche for environmentally friendly powders and introduced innovatory products to the market.

Third, most large firms started off as very small businesses, so it is important to the health of the economy that there is a continuing supply of growing companies to replace those larger firms that die. This partly explains some of the concessions that governments have made to the small business sector. These include a lower rate of corporation tax for firms with a taxable profit of less than £250,000 p.a., allowing them to reinvest more of their profits. Small firms with a turnover of less than £35,000 p.a. are exempt from the need to charge value added tax, and have been freed from a whole range of duties that apply to larger companies, especially those relating to employment rights. To encourage the development of new businesses, a wide range of supportive innovations have been launched by central government, including the Enterprise Allowance and various training schemes sponsored by Training and Enterprise Councils. Locally, Enterprise Agencies have been created to give support to new businesses from existing firms.

The change in the structure and organization of industry and commerce, the growing emphasis on specialized services and the application of new technology have all tended to encourage small business. Flexible manufacturing systems are increasingly able to allow a business to function at a much lower level of output than previously. An example is printing, where new production processes have allowed entrepreneurs to undertake small print runs on relatively inexpensive machinery. The success of the small printer has been further encouraged by the proliferation of small business users of printed material requiring low print runs and a rapid turn-round of work. The tendency for large companies to subcontract functions such as cleaning and catering in order to concentrate on their core business has also given new opportunities to the small business sector.

It is not only the small entrepreneurs who have been creating new small businesses: larger organizations have also recognized their value and have tried to replicate them at a distance from their own structure. In the bus operating industry, large operating units have typically had a culture which has made the organization slow to respond to its changing environment. Following liberalization of the industry in 1986, many larger companies set up small subsidiary companies which had an inherent adaptability to respond to changing markets. Many local authorities have created small businesses to take over clearly defined functions, such as tourism promotion and economic development. Similarly, many educational establishments have established research companies at arm's length from the organizational structure.

While small businesses have certainly seen a resurgence during the 1980s, it should also be recognized that they have a very high failure rate. A study by Ganguly (1985) indicates that small firms are significantly more likely to fail than larger ones, when measured by the size of their turnover. Based on a survey of UK firms undertaken in 1980, this study found that among the smallest firms—defined as those with a turnover of under £13,000—a quarter of all firms in this category failed within one year. The failure rate for firms with a turnover of between £15,000 and £49,000 was halved to 12 per cent in a year, and continued to decline as the size of the business unit grew. Only 3.6 per cent of all firms with a turnover of between £500,000 and £2 million failed during the year. More recently, the National Audit Office (1988) has examined the life expectancy of small firms set up with assistance under the Enterprise Allowance schemes. In the five-year period ending 1987/8, 330,000 people set up new businesses under the scheme, but 47,000 of these, or 14 per cent of the total, had dropped out of the scheme during their first year. It has been estimated that only 57 per cent of these new firms survive beyond three years. Similar evidence emerges from an analysis of VAT registrations, which shows that only just under one-third of businesses set up in 1980 were still registered ten years later.

3.8   TESCO STORES: A CASE STUDY

This case study is presented in greater depth to illustrate many of the points that have been raised in this and the preceding chapter. An analysis of the growth of Tesco Stores illustrates:

- The diversity of legal entities that the company has adapted at different stages of development
- The range of strategies that have been used to bring about growth
- The change in the company's marketing mix that has occurred in response to changes in its marketing environment

The basis for the existing business of Tesco was founded shortly after the First World War when Jack Cohen left the flying corps with just £30 of capital. His first taste of civilian entrepreneurship came with his decision to invest most of his £30 in the bulk purchase of tins of surplus war rations. These he proceeded to sell from a barrow in the street markets of London.

As a sole trader, Jack Cohen needed the minimum of formality to get his business started. Furthermore, large capital investment was not required at a time when the typical retail unit was very small and selling through markets was commonplace. The products he sold were basic commodities which did not need a large investment to create a distinctive and differentiated brand.

The name 'Tesco' was first used by Jack to differentiate the tea he sold from that of his competitors. The name was derived by taking the first two letters of his own surname and prefixing it with the initials of the owner of the tea importing business from which he bought his tea—T. E. Stockwell. Jack Cohen was buying a commodity in bulk from the importer, repackaging the tea and selling it under a brand name.

Further growth came by building up his sales to other market traders in addition to the sales he made to the final consumer. Cohen acted as a middleman, or wholesaler, operating from a small warehouse. Success came from his being able to spot a good bargain and to fill his warehouse with cheap goods which he would resell to London street traders. Channels of distribution at this time tended to be based on a push strategy, in which entrepreneurs needed to actively sell products to the next stage in the chain of distribution.

It became clear to Jack that he would be capable of selling considerably more stock and making more profit if he had more outlets. In 1930, therefore, he opened his first shop in an arcade in Tooting, South London. To do this and run his wholesale business would have been stretching the financial and managerial abilities of his sole trader status. He therefore decided to take on a partner—Sam Freeman—to buy and run the Tooting shop. The following year he formed another separate partnership with a nephew—Jack Vanger—to open a second shop in Chatham, followed by a third shop in London with Michael Kaye as his partner.

In 1932 Jack formed two private companies to run his two core businesses. Tesco Stores Ltd was created to run the retail business, which by 1938 had grown to a chain of 100 shops. Growth had been fuelled by attracting private equity capital and using retained profits. The second private company—J. E. Cohen Ltd—was established to run the growing wholesale business.

Backward vertical integration occurred when Jack Cohen became involved in businesses that supplied the wholesale and retail businesses. In 1942 Railway Nurseries (Cheshunt) Ltd was set up when farmland was bought to supply Tesco with fresh vegetables. A couple of years later, Goldhanger Fruit Farms Ltd in Essex was created to supply Tesco as well as other retailers with fresh and canned fruits.

Numerous private companies now existed to run the Tesco businesses, and in 1947 all were brought together in one holding company—Tesco Stores (Holdings) Ltd. The holding company held the share capital of the subsidiary companies which had been built up over the previous years. To provide additional equity capital for future growth, the holding company became a public company in December 1947 by offering 250,000 shares of 5p nominal value at 75p each to the general public. The money provided by the share issue was used to develop larger stores, in particular the new style of self-service store which was modelled on the American example and which proved increasingly successful for Tesco. The company had developed its own brands in a number of product areas such as tea and dairy products, but still relied on selling other manufacturers' products at lower prices than competing retailers.

In the postwar period, the role of the retailer was changing as manufacturers sought to develop strong brands and to promote the benefits of their brands direct to the public. The power of the retailer to influence the decision of the customer was being reduced with the development of mass media aimed at the final consumer, particularly following the introduction of commercial television in the mid-1950s. Distribution strategies were changing from 'push' to 'pull'. Tesco aimed to make branded goods available to consumers at the lowest possible price—the company's motto became 'Pile it high and sell it cheap'.

The main constraint on offering lower prices was the existence of resale price maintenance, which allowed manufacturers to control the price at which its products were sold to the public by retailers. The abolition of resale price maintenance in 1964 was to be extremely beneficial to Tesco's marketing strategy, in which price was seen as a key element of the marketing mix. Further shares were sold during the 1950s and 1960s, allowing the company to expand rapidly and to open supermarkets in most towns throughout Britain. A major rights issue in January 1991 raised £572 million from existing shareholders to fund further expansion and to reduce the level of gearing. As the company's core business of selling groceries and household goods approached saturation, the company diversified into related areas such as petrol sales and in-store coffee shops.

The bulk of Tesco's growth has been organic in nature: as management abilities and financial reserves were built up, they were used to develop more stores and to enter different stages of the distribution process. On occasions, however, growth has come about by acquisition. For example, the Hillards group was acquired in May 1987. The addition of 40 Hillards outlets allowed Tesco to expand rapidly in parts of Yorkshire where it was poorly represented at the time.

Tesco PLC is now the second largest grocery retailer in the UK after Sainsburys, owning about 400 stores (of which 100 are superstores), employing 48,000 staff and selling 20,000 lines, of which about 3,000 are own-brand products. Market traders such as Jack Cohen's original business still exist alongside Tesco, and it is possible to observe a number of changes that Tesco has had to go through to reach its present position.

In order to grow, Tesco had to offer some unique advantage over its competitors. In the early days this was based on low prices, and this price orientation was emphasized as late as 1977 when Tesco initiated a price-cutting war among the major supermarkets. More recently, Tesco has sought to differentiate itself by offering a better quality of service. Most new development of the 1980s was focused on large out-of-town superstores offering a wide choice of products with easy car parking facilities. A lot of money has been invested in developing the company's own-brand products, of which many in the late 1980s were differentiated by being promoted as healthy life-style products.

As it has grown, Tesco has been able to achieve greater economies of scale in distribution and promotion. It has also used size to exert greater power in the chain of distribution and to achieve competitive pricing. Instead of aggressively pushing goods through the chain, Tesco has sought to pull customers into its stores, specifically by stressing the unique advantages of shopping at Tesco.

REVIEW QUESTIONS

1. What problems for the marketing management of a furniture manufacturer might arise from rapid growth?
2. In what ways can the sources of finance for a business influence its marketing effort?
3. In what ways have the objectives of newly privatized industries changed compared with those that previously existed?
4. What are the problems and opportunities for marketing management arising from a policy of growth through diversification?
5. Contrast the strengths and weaknesses of small and large companies in the marketing of soft drinks.

REFERENCES

Ansoff, H. I. (1957), 'Strategies for Diversification', *Harvard Business Review*, pp. 113–24, vol. no. 35.
Davies, S. (1988), *Economics of Industrial Organisation*, Longman, London.
Fairhurst, D. W. (1986), *Business Resources*, Heinemann, London.
Ganguly, P. (1985), *Small Business Statistics and International Comparisons*, Harper & Row, New York.
National Audit Office, Department of Employment/Training Commission (1988), *Assistance to Small Firms*, HC 655, HMSO, London.
Office of Fair Trading (1990), *An Outline of UK Competition Policy*, OFT, London.
Penrose, E. T. (1980), *The Theory of the Growth of the Firm*, 2nd edn, Basil Blackwell, Oxford.
Scott, M. (ed.) (1986), *Small Firms, Growth and Development*, Gower, Aldershot.
Storey, D. J. (1988), *Entrepreneurship and the New Firm*, Routledge, London.

FOUR
THE INTERNAL ENVIRONMENT

4.1 INTRODUCTION

This chapter examines how a business organization's internal environment influences its marketing goals. It is important for marketing to analyse the organizational environment in which it functions, for two reasons.

First, because marketing is concerned with satisfying consumer needs, it is essential that the internal environment of an enterprise reflects this, and therefore shows a character and structure that enables ease of communication and response to changing customer needs and tastes. In this respect, the organization and strategic management of the employment relationship—that is, how jobs and functions are ordered—plays a significant role. This area is covered in Section 4.3.

Second, if it is accepted that a coherent internal environment facilitates the meeting of a company's marketing goals, then it is likely that a poorly organized or highly rigid and inflexible structure will inhibit the meeting of such goals.

The internal ordering of an organization's human resources is of significance because it contributes directly to the external image and customer perception of that organization. In particular, the successful pursuit of customer needs reflects the dynamic integration of such needs into all functions within a company.

Thus, the philosophy of an enterprise concerning the management and development of human resources has a crucial inhibitive or positive role with respect to that enterprise's marketing ambitions.

M & S TURNS ALL STAFF INTO PART-TIME MARKETERS

Satisfying customer needs is of paramount importance to Marks & Spencer. This need is integral to all activities performed by the company's employees, irrespective of which specialist function they work in. As an employer, Marks & Spencer sees itself as a facilitator. This involves providing services for its employees in order to facilitate them in performing their work effectively. The firm provides hairdressing, banks and chiropody services for staff members, and other activities such as training, development and supervision, all of which contribute directly to the organization by helping employees to satisfy customer needs. A simple manifestation of the combined effect of these provisions, which highlights their importance for marketing, is the fact that it is difficult for customers shopping in Marks & Spencer on a Saturday or near Christmas to distinguish between part- and full-time workers: hence the needs of the customer can be met equally effectively by both.

This chapter is divided into three parts.

First, the emergence of management theory and practice in what can be described as the 'production-orientated' firm is examined in Section 4.2. In production orientation the division of labour as devised by Adam Smith and the principles of scientific management as devised by Frederick Taylor dominated management thought. The limitations of production orientation are described and related to the emerging need for marketing, with production orientation giving way to sales and then marketing orientations (as described in Chapter 1).

Second, unitary M-form and matrix frameworks are considered as forms of internal structure in Sections 4.3 and 4.4. Here, the aims and objectives of each framework are examined and explained in relation to the successful pursuit of customer needs. In particular, the internal organization of resources is examined with respect to the imposition of internal information and 'transaction' costs on the whole organization by one particular function. Such costs may inhibit the successful pursuit of customer needs if they are not identified and minimized by management. The benefits and drawbacks of each are examined in relation to the needs of marketing.

In Section 4.5, marketing is considered within the ambit of human resource management. This seeks to illustrate how the integration of the management of human resources and marketing into all central functions can assist in the pursuit of customer needs by encouraging all employees within functional areas to think and act beyond the limitations of their function. Thus, at the operational level, aspects of the management of human resources and marketing are decentralized throughout the organization. It will be shown that such an approach can enhance the firm's marketing by giving it an internal dimension to complement its external dimension.

4.2   INTERNAL STRUCTURE: THE PRODUCTION-ORIENTATED ORGANIZATION

Since the Industrial Revolution, the majority of goods and (latterly) services have been produced in a central workplace: the factory or office. This centralization created the need for three things:

1. The division of labour in production
2. The management and supervision of that labour
3. The factory system

Each of these points is explained below.

The work of Adam Smith (1776) is central to an understanding of the division of labour. His simple 'pin' example illustrated how overall production could be greatly increased by individual units of labour specializing in the production of just one component of the pin (see Figure 4.1).

THE SEVEN STAGES OF THE PRODUCTION PROCESS

1   Drawing out the wire
↓
2   Straightening the wire
↓
3   Cutting the wire
↓
4   Rounding one end of the wire
↓
5   Grinding one end to receive the head
↓
6   Making the pin head
↓
7   Connecting the pin head to the wire

Figure 4.1   Pin production: the division of labour as described by Adam Smith

In the production of a pin there are at least seven separate processes. By organizing for each of these processes to be performed by the same man or men all the time, the overall production of pins can be greatly speeded up. If each man attempted to make the whole pin himself, he would probably be able to produce only a few dozen each day, whereas with the division of labour thousands of pins could be produced. This contributed to a great reduction in the cost of pin production.

The specialization of labour, by increasing the rate at which component parts of the pin could be produced, in turn enabled the factory owner—the entrepreneur—to further reduce the average cost of each pin produced as the fixed costs of production and the variable cost of machines could be spread over an increased level of output.

Smith laid particular stress on the production benefits of the division of labour, to the neglect of other management concerns. Production became increasingly centralized as the Industrial Revolution progressed, and it became clear that, in order for the production and cost benefits of the system to be reaped, someone had to ensure that labour performed efficiently and productively. These became issues of concern, from behavioural and institutional viewpoints, precisely because the concept of productive efficiency largely ignored human concerns except in the emphasis it placed on increased production via familiarity and repetition. Issues of quality control, work incentives and productivity were initially ignored. All three are central not only to a company's production, but also to the success of the marketing of its finished goods or services.

In order to ensure consistency of quality in production set against output targets, it became necessary for production in the centralized workplace to be managed and supervised. Hence, the *production orientation* developed. This is concerned largely with overcoming problems in production which Smith either rationalized away or failed to identify because of his concern with production.

In addition to their management and supervision functions, entrepreneurs co-ordinate different stages of production in the correct combinations so as to avoid production bottlenecks. This may create the need for detailed management and production incentives at various stages in the production process. In summary, centralized production requires the full-scale use of Smith's concept of the division of labour; but in order for the entrepreneur to reap its cost and efficiency benefits, labour has to be organized and supervised. These activities are performed by 'management'.

Notwithstanding the limitations of production orientation, Smith's division of labour concept does provide the basis for marketing and the management of the employment relationship to become separate areas in management, specializing in defined functions. As with the pin-makers, 'marketing' (in so far as it was practised) was seen as a specialist element of the management process, to be performed more efficiently by the division of management responsibilities.

4.2.1   The emergence of production management

The centralization of production and provision has created the need for specialization in production together with its organization and supervision. Thus, in addition to a horizontal division of labour—that is, between workers specializing in the production of different components of one good—a vertical division of labour developed between workers engaged in producing goods and services and those concerned with ensuring that output is efficiently produced. This latter group has become known as 'management'. Essentially, the primary task of a person acting in a management function is to ensure that labour employed under his or her supervision works effectively. Thus, management functions revolve around the effective organization and supervision of employees in a particular span of control. 'Supervision' describes the formal and informal introduction of controls over labour. These controls can be of three types: simple, technical and bureaucratic.

Simple controls
Direct personal supervision
● e.g. of factory operatives

Technical controls
Controls imposed by the monitoring and production capacity of equipment
● e.g. scanning equipment in supermarkets

Bureaucratic controls
Controls imposed where employees need to document their performance
● e.g. the completion of time sheets/sales reports

Each form of control enables employees operating in a managerial capacity or function to regulate the performance of employees under their span of control. For example, simple supervision facilitates visual monitoring of performance; technical controls enable productivity comparisons between workers; whereas bureaucratic controls assist in the monitoring of absenteeism and measures of individual productivity. Thus, in the present context, management is concerned with the supervision and regulation of work performance. What follows is an examination of the concept of management, including comments on its scientific development and the consequent neglect of marketing.

Production orientation concerns the division of work and its assignment to different groups of workers. Both of these developments are essential for large-scale production because they are crucial for saving time in production. In utilizing such time-saving devices, production is divided into constituent elements, which are then allocated to different groups of workers. Therefore, management does three things:

1. It creates an intermediary role for itself, between production and the market that buys its output.
2. By creating many individual and separate tasks, it gains control of the labour process.
3. By reducing the centrality of any one individual or group of workers, it ensures lower production costs.

Management thought developed considerably through the work of F. W. Taylor (1964), who developed the concept of 'scientific management'. Taylor suggested that any work process required two essential features: 'conception' and 'execution'. He further argued that in the centralized workplace the two features should be strictly separated.

Thus, conception in production relations—that is, the organization and division of production—should be in the hands of managers and the entrepreneur. By contrast, the execution of work is a function of productive 'shopfloor' labour. In many ways the analysis goes further, suggesting that each production or provision stage should be stripped of conceptual thought on the part of labour performing it. Therefore, overall production should consist of many individual and minute stages.

Labour is collectively more efficient if individually it specializes in one element of production. Each attempt to stimulate productive efficiency by extending the division of labour creates a new labour process, which can be controlled only by management. This is so because only management is deemed to possess the necessary conceptual skills, whereas labour is considered to be purely functional. Thus, production management is essentially a self-fulfilling prophecy. Only managers can conceptualize the use of the division of labour, and only management can conceptualize the problems its use creates for the control of the labour process. So scientific management, which dominated academic thought until the 1960s and manufacturing until much later, is concerned primarily with production, its control and efficient organization.

4.2.2 The emergence of marketing management

Many important areas such as the management of human resources and marketing developed as a consequence of the dominance of scientific management. Indeed, Henry Ford, the leading exponent of the method, was, in the initial stages of his firm's operation, bereft of both marketing and human resource management. 'Fordist' large-scale production thrived upon standardized long-run products for mass consumption. Any marketing that did exist was limited to selling and delivering the cars. With the growth in the size and complexity of business units, however, new areas of management emerged, as did a new focus towards sales and marketing orientations.

The latter-day development of important areas such as employment relations and marketing together with their management have to be examined in the context of the technological requirements of the workplace, for it is these that dictate the pace of technological change and development. These in turn were derived from the needs of the market. Personnel management and marketing management have both developed as functional adjuncts to the central organizational role inherent to production orientation.

As a consequence, these areas are not always staffed by qualified professionals. Similarly, depending on an organization's market success and standing together with its internal management structure, the profile of marketing can vary considerably. The greater the apparent predominance of production orientation, the more marginal are areas such as marketing and personnel seen to be. In the 1990s this is still true for low-margin industries such as textiles, retailing and hosiery, where many production units are small-scale market followers.

The philosophy of production orientation dominated business in the UK and USA throughout the long postwar economic boom. West Germany, Japan, France and Italy have all (re)developed their industrial bases in the postwar period. Similarly, all four have utilized the core concept of production orientation, and yet all have done so in unique ways, each adding a new dimension to it. West Germany utilized a system of industrial banks to forge direct links between industry and finance; France and Italy have both espoused systems of central state involvement, ownership and indicative planning; whereas Japan has regarded people management as being of pre-eminent importance to the success of production orientation.

As most nations developed during the postwar period, the nature of competition in Western markets began to alter. As countries developed industrially, export and individual domestic markets became arenas for increased competition. This was particularly the case in the UK and USA.

In this situation, the focus for management shifted from production alone, to the selling and then marketing of outputs.

The entry of European and Japanese producers to the UK and US auto market actively opened up the issue of marketing, marketing management and a marketing orientation to a sector where previously informative and persuasive advertising had been sufficient to attract customers. It can be argued that those auto manufacturers who actively embraced the need for marketing during the difficult conditions of the mid-1970s and early 1980s were better able to survive and maintain a reasonable market share.

Within management, marketing management and the management of human resources became central concerns of and adjuncts to scientific management. Production alone became less central during the 1980s once over-capacity became a major concern. In boom conditions demand was assumed to exist; thus, 'Fordism', the euphemism for standard long-run production, has undergone significant structural alteration as producers and suppliers have begun to recognize the need to cultivate consumer demand, satisfy increased consumer sovereignty and generally market their output. These qualities are essential if the organizational need of profits is to be met.

In the post-Fordist era, production management has been reformed and developed in two ways, both of which seek to meet the marketing needs of companies. Flexible specialization and flexibility in production create a fusion of marketing management and the management of employment relations.

4.2.3   Flexible specialization

This describes a situation where the benefits of long-run production can be attained over shorter runs. Flexible specialization is largely the result of advanced technology, the application of which enables firms to reduce set-up costs and times.

Put simply, flexible specialization takes a standardized product and differentiates it from its competitors. This can be done by producing limited editions (popular in car production), the music market (especially for 12-inch and CD singles) and clothes. (Benetton used the system extensively to develop their innovative style in the early 1980s.) The customer receives a standard product plus some unique element. For example, a car may come with distinctive body panelling, spoilers and a series name, whereas a CD single may contain alternative versions of the standard single or additional live tracks available only on that format. The years 1989 and 1990 saw some record companies releasing different versions of a CD single. Companies controlling the products of Tom Petty, REM and the Rolling Stones all undertook such an exercise. Warner Brothers released REM's 'Losing my Religion' on a CD in two versions: one of these contained three live songs in a limited edition. Successive REM singles from the *Out of Time* album underwent similar treatment. The result was a collection of 12 live tracks, that is, a limited edition live album. Similarly, the Rolling Stones' 'Highwire' single proved to be a successful vehicle to promote the live hits album *Flashpoint*: successive versions of the CD single contained additional and alternative tracks to those on the album.

Flexible specialization in production fits neatly with the concept of 'segmentation', whereby customers with similar needs are identified and targeted with a defined and differentiated product (see Section 1.12). It requires good market research and a workforce that is highly motivated, skilled and able to adapt to frequent changes in production demands.

4.2.4   Flexibility in production

The second reform of production management is flexibility in production. This is concerned with increased division in the labour force between what can be termed 'core' workers and 'peripheral' workers. The former are required to show 'functional flexibility', whereby labour is able to move between different areas of production and between different levels of skill hierarchy. This is clearly a challenge to techniques of scientific management, which emphasize routine, single-task performance. In return for functional flexibility, core workers receive more secure employment status and better chances of promotion.

'Peripheral' workers exhibit numerical flexibility: the company can plug in and unplug them as required. The characteristics of such employment include fixed-term contracts, part-time work and seasonal employment. It is a challenge of marketing management to ensure that the

NISSAN: A FLEXIBLE FIRM

The Nissan company, based in the UK at Washington, Tyne and Wear, is a leading exponent of flexibility in production. Nissan is a good example because car production is the area in which 'Fordist' principles started. At Nissan there are very few grades of worker. As a consequence, a defined skill and status hierarchy does not exist. Employees, both in management and in production, are required to be functionally flexible. The central objective of functional flexibility is to ensure that the daily production targets are met. If on any day production is behind schedule, workers move between functions to speed up production.

Flexibility agreements often require delicate employee relations policies as well as good relations with trade unions. The EETPU (Electrical, Electronic, Telecommunications and Plumbing Union) has pioneered flexibility agreements in the UK.

---

deployment of additional peripheral workers is based on an accurate forecast of customer demands. Flexible specialization can operate within the wider ambit of flexibility at the workplace; the success of both depends on effective marketing management and management of employee relations.

The central arguments of the advocates of flexibility or the flexible firm are twofold. First, inflexibility in a workforce creates excessive costs due to rigid work demarcation; hence productivity may suffer. Second, because of the first point, any good that passes through various stages of production can be held up by production difficulties arising from shortages or industrial action affecting one element of production.

In terms of core employees, both deficiencies can be overcome by functional flexibility, whereas in relation to peripheral workers, their 'plug in/out' characteristic enables production to be altered in response to market needs.

4.2.5 From production goals to marketing goals

The discussion of scientific management emphasized the self-fulfilling role of production management to the detriment of marketing management and the management of the employment relationship. As markets have become more competitive, organizations have become more concerned with the management of the employment relationship and the need for effective marketing management. Thus, the division of labour is being applied to management via the growth of separate management areas such as personnel, marketing, sales and finance. The internal organization of these management functions, their internal consistency and interrelationships are described in the following section. The strengths and weaknesses of various structures are examined with regard to marketing and the management of human resources and how organization and customer needs can be met.

4.3 THE INTERNAL ORGANIZATION OF RESOURCES AND MARKETING GOALS

The production of a good or service is the primary goal of a production-orientated firm. The scientific approach has been augmented by growing concern in two areas.

First, the attraction and retention of customers have become central concerns of business; thus, firms must examine how they can retain and improve their market share. Successful performance here requires ensuring that the company offers a product which meets the needs of the customer in the market. This is particularly important in mature product markets or service markets where there is a high degree of substitutability.

Second, and related directly to the first point, management must ensure that its employees are in tune with the company's marketing needs and ambitions. Here the development of employee relations policies espousing quality production, training and development, customer care and the need for employee flexibility are dominant themes.

Thus, in competitive markets a major challenge for management is to retain its company's market share. In relation to meeting and setting marketing goals and objectives, it is important to examine how firms can assemble their internal resources and how this ordering can complement or detract from marketing goals.

The remainder of this section contains a brief discussion of organizations, their structures and components.

4.3.1   The components and structure of a business

In the first part of this chapter it was shown that production within the centralized workplace tends to be 'non-separable'; that is, it results from an application of the division of labour. Organization is therefore required if the production of a good or the provision of a service is the result of more than one labour process.

The centralized workplace is a social entity which has been designed to accomplish particular goals. In addition to the formal organizational goals—e.g. to achieve an adequate level of profits—intra-organizational goals may exist.

Thus, different functions within organizations have their own individual, specific and defined goals. For example, the stock department may wish to hold large amounts of stock so that salespeople can quickly respond to customer needs, whereas accounts and finance may argue that such a goal is wasteful in terms of the firm's space and resources. The personnel department may bid for financial and human resources in order to develop a staff training programme on customer care, whereas other departments may see such a resource bid as wasteful in that it yields no apparent or immediate financial return.

It is therefore clear that goals of individual functions within an organization represent

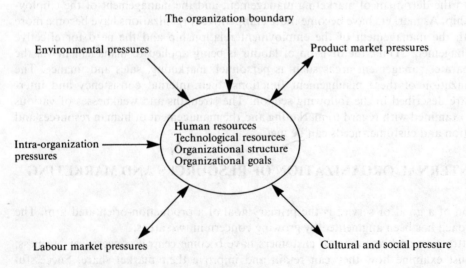

Figure 4.2   The components of a business organization

sub-goals or intra-organizational goals which operate individually within a wider organizational context. The power distribution context between different functions will greatly influence the profile of particular functions.

There are four components of a business organization (see Figure 4.2).

1. *Human resources* As companies are social entities, they are made up of *people*—their human resource. If the firm is to meet its various goals it must use its human resources to the best of their skills and aptitudes. In this regard the role of personnel management is crucial.
2. *Technological resources* The second element is that of *technology*. The level at which technology operates, together with its rate of innovation in combination with human resources, determine the economic pace at which the firm's goals can be met.
3. *Organizational structures* The *structural context* in which tasks and roles are ordered is also of great significance to the success of a company.
4. *Organizational goals* The structural context is intimately linked to the fourth element, the company's *overall purpose and function*.

The structural context of an organization is usually designed by central management and will reflect the managers' intentions and values. Thus, depending on managers' individual backgrounds, particular functions may be highlighted or neglected. Earlier in this chapter we explained how the production orientation in its initial and developed stages ignored marketing and employee relations at executive level.

While an organization's structural context and design is in the hands of central management, it must reflect corporate interests which may be larger and more widespread than those of management. For example, chemical producers may find themselves having to consider environmental questions; for the central monitor these may be of only marginal concern, but in terms of marketing, employee relations and public relations such issues are currently of central concern. Thus, within private sector monopolistic competition, a degree of managerial discretion exists, whereby the central management is preoccupied with meeting the central aims of profit maximization and organizational efficiency—but in a discretionary manner—so long as broadly based corporate goals are attained to the satisfaction of various interested parties (shareholders, non-executive directors, employees, customers and government agencies such as the Office of Fair Trading, the Monopolies and Merger Commission and the DTI).

Thus, the function or purpose of an enterprise, around which its policies and structures are designed, greatly influences its operational context. If it is inappropriate, the structural context may hinder achievement of the overall objectives of the firm.

4.4 THE GROUPING OF ACTIVITIES IN AN ENTERPRISE

The structure of a company is ultimately determined by the way in which it groups activities. There are three commonly observed structures: the functional (or U-form), the multi-divisional (or M-form) and the matrix. Each is examined below in relation to the attainment of marketing and human resource management goals.

4.4.1 Functional organization

An enterprise that orders itself around its main departments is referred to as a functional, critical function or U-form of enterprise. Here, activities are clustered together by common function. For example, all marketing activities (marketing, sales, advertising, market research) are grouped under a common function. A functional organization structure is depicted in Figure 4.3.

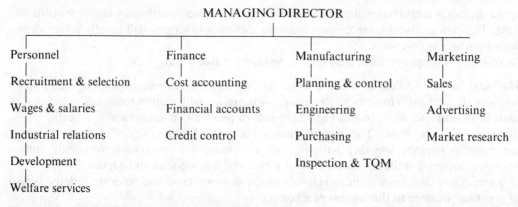

Figure 4.3   The functional structure of a business organization

   This form of structural organization represents a division of labour and management, both vertically (within a function) and horizontally (across functions). The structural form developed as management activity became more sophisticated as a response to the increase in the size and therefore the internal complexity of business units. Thus, management co-ordination by functional separation is the key feature of this type of structure. Other benefits are centralized control of functional areas, with each function having its own internal career paths and labour markets. These help to facilitate human resource goals such as staff development, identification and employee retention. Similarly, because each function is a hierarchy, it should be internally consistent and be able to meet overall organizational goals.

   One of the main drawbacks of this system is that, although each function is internally consistent, they may not all have appropriate or equal resources made available to them. Hence, marketing and personnel may exist, but the production orientation may still dominate.

   Second, sectional interests may develop into intra-function rivalries. These may impose information and transaction costs on the firm. Both of these may detract from the overall goals of the enterprise and individual functional goals. Although an organization is designed to accomplish defined goals, it is a social entity, made up of individuals performing distinct and separate activities; if the individuals performing these functional activities become isolated and functionally orientated, they may inhibit the overall performance of the organization, including the pursuit of sub-goals.

   Friction and rivalry can exist even within a particular department or function. In the case of a marketing department numerous activities co-exist; advertising, sales, new product development and promotion, market research, product research and sales promotion are the mainstay activities of a marketing department, but the perceived profile and importance of each activity may not be equal. As a consequence, within the functionally ordered organization employees may be encouraged by their own self-perception of their activity into thinking about the significance of that activity singularly, rather than about how it fits into and contributes to more global objectives. In such a situation employees outside the marketing department may have little or no knowledge or interest in the activities of marketing. This type of situation may prevent the company from attaining its full marketing ambitions. Clearly, if a functional organization of resources is to be utilized, it requires careful management and supervision by area managers, who themselves must be able to see their functional area in relation to the whole enterprise and its overall objectives.

   Thus, each function could operate in a vacuum, pursuing its own goals but not necessarily integrating them with those of other functions. For example, if marketing or personnel management are designated to be of only residual status, they may not be party to decisions of central importance and therefore could find their individual function and philosophy conflicting with that of central management. Both the multi-divisional and matrix structures are in part designed to overcome these difficulties.

4.4.2 Organization by product or service: the M-form structure

Where a business groups its internal resources around the products or services it produces, it is known as an M or multi-divisional form. In this situation each group has its own specialist functions at the operational level (see Figure 4.4.).

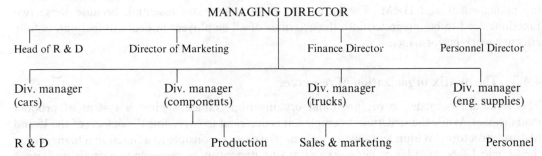

Figure 4.4 Product-centred organization structure

Within this structure, a divisional marketing manager has a dual responsibility: first to the divisional manager, and second to the director of marketing. Thus, as with employee relations and personnel, the activities of marketing may be divided into operational and strategic parts. In the routine activities of marketing, a marketing manager is responsible to the marketing manager; yet, strategically, the marketing manager is responsible to the divisional marketing director. Thus, the pursuit of company marketing policy is the operational concern of the director of marketing, whereas the daily operation is based on decisions taken at director level. This analysis is equally applicable to the management of the employment relationship, which at the strategic level is often termed 'human resource management' but at the operational level is labelled 'personnel management'.

The main benefits of the M-form are that it enables product groups to market their own output and recruit their own staff, while integrating these into a strategic business plan. This is because each function is divided into operational and strategic components, whereby senior specialists focus on corporate issues while leaving production operations with line managers. However, the M-form is not without problems.

At corporate or strategic level, executives must be able to consider issues outside their own division. This can create tension between operational and strategic constituents, the effect of which might be, for example, to prevent a marketing manager from revealing his or her true goals in order to achieve what they consider will be a better allocation of resources to their project. Thus, although the executives at strategic level should be in operational command, managers at operational levels may be able to impose an information or transaction cost on the hierarchy by opportunistic behaviour in the face of strategic decisions that are perceived to go against them. For example, managers may not fully reveal their preferences, or they may inflate resource bids. The matrix structure (see figure 4.5) is designed to overcome some of these difficulties.

To be successful, the M-form structure relies on the effective integration of functions within a division. For example, in Figure 4.4 the divisional manager responsible for components must be able to conceptualize and operationalize (make work) issues decided at executive/strategic level. This involves getting all the functional areas in the division to focus on making that division an effective contributor to the overall aims of the organization. Thus, the overall strategic aims of personnel, marketing and finance must be operationally integrated and disseminated both within those areas and to employees operating in other areas within each division. Individual employees need to be aware of how the work of other employees contributes to the overall aims of the organization and how they themselves can contribute to such aims by incorporating elements of other activities within their own functions.

Ultimately, this method of ordering resources relies on motivated employees and therefore requires extensive programmes of training and development, together with high-profile marketing management and HRM. The latter two requirements are essential, because these two functions need to be integrated into the activities of all employees in order to facilitate a fully effective work performance.

4.4.3   The matrix organization of resources

This structure is made up of functional organization framed against a system of product management. While the structure is complex, it is designed to overcome the defects of the U and M-form structures. Within any function, an employee is responsible to a functional manager for the technical aspects of his or her work and is simultaneously responsible to a product/division manager in relation to how the work is co-ordinated with other tasks in the same product area. Hence the term 'matrix'. Thus, the operation of functional areas such as marketing or personnel are integrated horizontally between different product areas in the enterprise (see Figure 4.5). So within any defined functional area practitioners will be able to disseminate best-practice marketing or personnel skills and techniques into a particular product area, while simultaneously bringing marketing and personnel issues to the attention of their product/division manager. Ease of communication can be facilitated by caucus meetings of all those involved in one particular division, that is, product managers and functional specialists operative in that area. This is sometimes known as team briefing or 'brainstorming'.

As with the M-form structure, the matrix structure relies for its success on two factors: on operationalizing the strategy, that is making it work; and on ensuring that staff members are

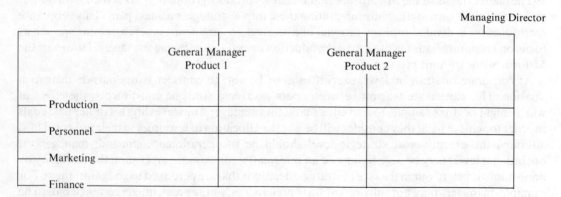

Figure 4.5   Matrix organization

motivated, integrative in thought and participative in action and thought. This latter point is crucial because it challenges the assumption of scientific management that employees, whether in management or production, can make progress only in a limited group of activities. Clearly, this is not the case if employees operating in a matrix structure are able to visualize how their work fits with that of others in a particular product division. In order that employees become communicative, integrative and participative, high-profile human resource management is essential. This is particularly significant to those employed in managerial or supervisory capacities. The goals of communication, integration and participation represent an internal self-marketing which complements the external marketing effort.

The main benefits of the matrix structure are speed of information handling and information use. Any interested party can identify the required employee quickly; thus, goals and strategies can easily be changed or modified if market conditions alter.

Perhaps the major drawback of the matrix is in its design and preparation. Employees need careful induction, selection and development in order for the full benefits to be achieved. This reinforces the need for high-profile human resource management and personnel.

4.4.4 Functional, M-form and matrix structures compared

This section has described the notion of organization and examined organization structures to show how they assist or detract in the attainment of overall corporate and functional goals and in the interrelationships of these goals. From a marketing or employee relations perspective, the M-form gives greatest operational autonomy within defined corporate strategies. On the other hand, the matrix system encourages employees and managers to consider areas beyond their own functions and creates an environment of immediate interest and concern for organizational improvement and change. This final part of the section examines organizational structures in relation to the 'costs' they can impose or allow to build up in companies.

It has already been shown that enterprises exist because of non-separabilities in production, which in turn result from the use of the division of labour as described through the production orientation of Smith and Taylor. Similarly, it has been established that non-separable production units require monitoring to ensure effective performance. This is equally the case with respect to residual management tasks in any of the structures previously described.

Rivalry and sectionalism can develop under any structure. This is particularly likely where a management residual holds defined aptitudes and skills that are not readily transferable. This may arise in either the U-form or the operational side of the M-form. By using the term 'management residual', reference is being made to a group of activities that functionally may be essential to the pursuit of the main corporate needs. For example, personnel is often characterized in this way. Personnel activity is crucial to any employing organization, but in the M-form and matrix structures its activities are integrated into main business and production areas. Thus, as an activity personnel is not free-standing except in the U-form of structure.

Functional management in areas such as personnel, finance and marketing possess resources and skills that are integral to the smooth operation of any business, but because such skills are specific to the firm they give the holders power. Hence they can make the enterprise work effectively using their specific skills within any of the structures described above, or they can use such specific skills to hold up the smooth operation of the firm. This will occur if employees do not feel integrative, communicative and participative. Such a situation represents a failure on the part of management.

Specific skills and knowledge enhance the utility and significance of a particular function. Yet, this utility and significance can be used detrimentally if a residual is not in harmony with the central monitor and the corporate goals. Thus, a group of workers on the production line, or individual managers, can act opportunistically—be self-interested—by blocking information or acting as gatekeepers to information and the pursuit of organizational goals. In such situations it is suggested that such groups are showing bounded rationality, showing sectional bias in information-processing.

The concept of bounded rationality is important for three reasons. First, the acknowledgement of its existence is a considerable improvement upon the neoclassical economic theory, which sees the firm as having a unitary character, whereby all agents are assumed to act with complete rationality as either utility- or profit-maximizers. Second, the existence of bounded rationality emphasizes the importance of management and managerial structures, because in the absence of complete rationality on the part of workers or management residuals the design of organization structures and their monitoring become the factors around which efficiency is based. Lastly, the concept recognizes—albeit, only implicitly—that different groups behave differently within what might be considered a unitary employment relationship.

In combination, the existence of specialized skills, which results in opportunism owing to the existence of bounded rationality, impose a transaction cost (the cost of 'doing') on the organization. Management is misguided to think that transaction costs can be totally eradicated; therefore central management has to ensure that their manifestations—information blockages and inefficiencies, together with functional sectionalism bias—can be effectively monitored.

It is here that the diffusion and identification of corporate goals are crucial. Employees need to identify with, and therefore to participate in, corporate objectives. Clearly, a coherent personnel policy integrated into wider strategic human resource planning is essential if functions such as marketing are to be in tune with the strategic goals of the corporation together with the operational goals of other functions. In the matrix, M-form and U-form structures the possibility of significant transaction costs exists. So under any structure central management must ensure that all employees and management residuals are working in common. In reality, this is difficult to attain; therefore, any structure must be able to accommodate and minimize transaction costs. Appropriate recruitment and selection goes a long way to satisfy this while simultaneously helping areas such as marketing to meet their operational goals. Readers seeking a fuller discussion of transaction cost economics should refer to Williamson (1981).

4.5   MARKETING MANAGEMENT AND HUMAN RESOURCE MANAGEMENT

Earlier in this chapter it was shown how the internal structure which a company adopts can either hinder or assist it in meeting customer needs. The argument developed so far suggests that there is an internal and an external dimension to marketing. Human resource management (HRM) has a significant role to play in the pursuit of both external and internal marketing needs. Here, HRM and marketing are examined in relation to how they complement one another in the quest for a performance that meets the customers' and firm's needs. Both of these needs are integral to the successful management of the employment relationship. Thus, satisfying current and (potential) future customer needs impacts upon how production is managed and organized, that is, upon how the employment relationship is considered strategically and operationally.

It has been established that marketing is so basic to the organization that it cannot be considered as a separate function, and, as Drucker (1974) has argued, marketing concerns the whole organization in terms of its final result from the customer's perspective. In order to improve the firm's final result—its product or service—marketing has to be operationally integrated throughout what were previously seen as distinct functions or internal markets.

The theme throughout this chapter has concerned the need for businesses to view their operation not just in terms of production but in terms of the delivery of a result. This changes the rationale from production to production plus the management of employees and marketing. A concentration on production alone can cause residual groups—for example, sectional groups of labour or residual management groups—to build up spheres of control or inefficiency which impair the final result. One method of addressing employees' needs and therefore the external needs of the company is through HRM.

4.5.1 The development of personnel management

Fordism encouraged organizations to see the production of long-run standard goods as the desired final result. This process contributed directly to the institution and development of task demarcation at the workplace. Demarcation can operate across tasks at a particular skill level and vertically through a skill hierarchy. One consequence of demarcation is identification with the labour process one performs—for example, craftsman, toolmaker, assembler, line worker or personnel manager. Task identification in turn creates sectionalism at the workplace, whereby different groups of workers or managers are represented by various trade unions or professional associations. Craft-based unions require a period of qualification by apprenticeship and often operate as closed or near closed shops. Essentially, craft unions exist to protect work standards and ensure that members receive wages suited to their craft status. Industrial and general unions have as their goals the general protection of members' pay and working conditions.

Within the workplace, trade unions channel any grievances that their members feel through formal contact with personnel or industrial relations managers. Thus, personnel, which historically developed as a welfare function, while primarily representing the interests of the employer, has become intimately concerned with employee grievances. This role is further complicated by the sectional nature of British trade unionism and the presence of strong shopfloor representation by lay activists—shop stewards.

It would be wrong to blame the operation of this system for the decline of Fordism and other economic problems such as de-industrialization. It should be remembered that both management and unions were happy with this arrangement. The effects of this on marketing management and the management of the employment relationship was twofold. First, marketing goals could not always be met because of production hold-ups or shortages, while marketers became apologists for their organization's poor performance. Second, the employment relationship was made up of two protagonists: the employer and the sectionally represented and fragmented employees. In some cases employees could not be blamed for low morale and poor organization: these existed precisely because of the short-sightedness of personnel management.

4.5.2 The HRM philosophy

One method of improving on this situation became popular during the early 1980s. This was a period of recession when unemployment was high, particularly in manufacturing. Industrial output was below the 1979 level and imports of manufactured goods were on the increase. It appears that some corporations that survived this recession did so because they espoused production methods and labour relations ideas distinct from mass Fordism. Flexible specialization and flexibility in production were two of the new production methods.

The labour relations ideas were broadly identified as human resource management (HRM), a philosophy that looked carefully at the internal dimension and external expression of productivity within the firm. It is designed to take the mechanical tools of personnel management and integrate them into the strategic management of the organization. Thus, an appreciation of the employment relationship and its importance to the meeting of corporate goals is gradually becoming of prime concern to central management in many organizations.

Four items follow in the discussion of HRM: its rationale and relation to personnel; HRM types; its relation to the grouping of activities in organizations; and the contribution of HRM to marketing goals and marketing management.

4.5.3   HRM and personnel management

Personnel management is concerned primarily with fitting the right person into the right job at the right time. In many companies, particularly those operating as U-forms, its activities are distinct and separate. HRM seeks to identify the employment relation together with its management as areas of central importance to corporate goals. Thus, it takes the mechanics of personnel management and integrates them within an organization's corporate objectives. These may include flexibility in production and integration of functional areas. Hence the employment relationship and, significantly, its management will become central management concerns. Clearly, the object is to improve the market performance of a company by devising structures to increase the productive performance of employees at managerial and worker levels. This is facilitated by encouraging employees to examine their role in the organization, how it can be improved and how their function contributes to the production of the final result.

Because HRM is thought to be central to a firm's economic success, the employment relation is considered strategically by senior managers. But because HRM involves all of an organization's functions—personnel, sales, marketing, accounts and production—its contents are delivered de-centrally. For example, components of personnel management such as recruitment and selection, appraisal and development are not to be considered in themselves as merely best-practice ideas within the philosophy of personnel management, but become instruments to explicitly attain corporate goals. That is, recruitment and selection techniques are examined in relation to how they contribute to getting effective marketers or accountants and to how these in turn contribute to the firm's overall performance. HRM techniques also encourage an organization to look more critically at its labour force. This may involve the implicit or explicit adoption of 'flexibility' as described above.

Essentially, HRM makes the employment relationship and its management integral to the enterprise. The previously distinct and isolated tools of personnel management become central to a firm's business or corporate plan, which may be expressed via a mission statement or a company philosophy.

4.5.4   HRM types

Guest (1989) suggested that HRM can be divided into two types: 'hard' and 'soft'. The 'hard' approach to HRM emphasizes employees as an economic resource which have to be exploited and utilized like any other factor input. Thus, 'hard' HRM is concerned primarily with the management and deployment of employees in combination with internal labour markets and a categorization of employees. Both flexibility and flexible specialization are expressions of 'hard' HRM.

'Soft' HRM is concerned more with the developmental side of the employment relationship. This side of HRM regards communication and participation as important corporate goals. Quality circles, briefing sessions, employee consultative committees, profit-sharing and employee share option schemes are all examples of this approach. In combination, these forums encourage employees to show greater identification with their employing organization and to think out of their sectional function.

By espousing the integration of functions and participation, a firm seeks to highlight the mutuality of stakeholders; therefore, the most visible expression of strategic management in the employment relation is likely to be in employee relations policies that 'talk-up' 'soft' HRM as described above. Thus, the institutionalized function of personnel management can continue to exist, but as the operational end of the strategic use of personnel management techniques.

As a consequence, it can be asserted that 'soft' HRM is really the packaging behind institutionally driven 'hard' HRM, which is concerned with the development of capabilities designed to align the identification of employees with a company's business strategy, not merely with their function within it. Clearly, 'hard' or strategic HRM is centrally conceived but disseminated through the firm by product or division managers. Yet the sophistication of HRM shows through in the recognition that a movement towards improved work performance is effectively achieved by 'soft' HRM policies operationalized through the personnel department.

4.5.5   HRM and the ordering of organization activities

The U-form, M-form and matrix structures are all rationalizations of organizational form and structure. Each is designed to meet organization needs in specific ways. Thus, each is really a strategy, and the task of management is to organize and make such strategies work—to operationalize them. The three forms can be evaluated against marketing management and HRM goals.

It has been shown that marketing management involves the conception, promotion and exchange of ideas in order to satisfy customer and organizational needs and objectives. Traditionally, within production orientation, marketing, its management and the management of the employment relationship have been undertaken by distinct internal groups. A premise of marketing management and HRM is that both are too important to be considered as distinct and separate functions; therefore, both must be integrated into general management and delivered de-centrally at line level.

In many ways, HRM has helped marketing management to attain a more central status in companies. Clearly, the U-form of structure is inappropriate to the introduction and development of HRM policies because its central theme is one of functional separation. Such a structure can work effectively, but may promote fragmentation of interest and sectionalism plus a hierarchical divide between executives, middle managers and workers. In short, the structure does not encourage individuals to think out of function.

In the M-form, resources are ordered around the goods or services produced, with each group having its own specialist functions at operational level. The dual structure or responsibility described in this section does facilitate the introduction and development of HRM policies. Figure 4.6(a) contains the original M-form structure, whereas Figure 4.6(b) shows how it has been amended to incorporate HRM.

At executive level, all functional directors are simultaneously directors of HRM. The object is to integrate aspects of R & D, marketing, finance and personnel into a coherent business and HRM strategy. This is then diffused by directors to divisional managers who, after guidance from the director of personnel, devise job designs and other elements of 'soft' HRM to integrate aspects of all the distinct functions into one another at the operational level. Thus, HRM permeates across the function boundary at the operation level.

If successful, the 'soft' HRM policies encourage employees to think and act out of function,

Figure 4.6(a)   M-form structure

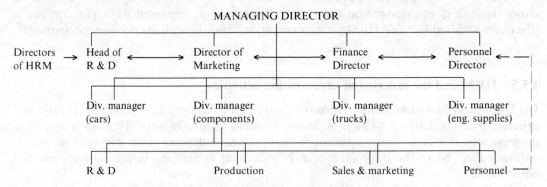

Figure 4.6(b)   M-form structure incorporating human resource management

examining how their specific function contributes to the delivery of other operational goals of the central monitor—for example, marketing and its management.

In the case of the matrix structure, functional organization is framed against product management. HRM can fit and operate within this already complex structure, as Figure 4.7 shows.

HRM philosophies can be injected into the matrix at both functional and product levels. Therefore, in any function an employee becomes responsible to a functional manager for his or her technical performance and an evaluation of it (perhaps via appraisal or brainstorming) in terms of its overall contribution to the goals of the company. Concurrently, employees are responsible to a product/division executive with reference to how their work fits into and co-ordinates with other tasks in that product area. Clearly, employees at all levels have to consider other managerial goals. In this way, a consideration such as marketing becomes increasingly decentralized into all functions, at all levels in the organization structure.

Spans of control under the M-form and matrix structure can be adopted to improve the delivery of what production management may have considered residuals such as personnel and marketing. In essence, HRM centralizes strategic thought but decentralizes strategic operations.

4.5.6   HRM, marketing goals and management

HRM methods contribute to marketing and other functional goals by raising the profile of marketing both at the central management level and within the ambit of other functions. Staff development, appraisal, customer care and total quality management (TQM) are all elements in the marketing dimension.

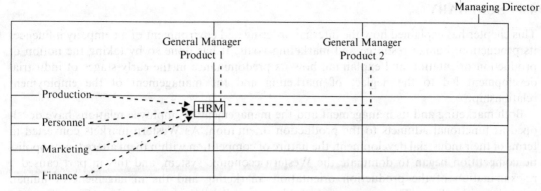

Figure 4.7 The human resource management approach to organization

Staff development and appraisal are designed to stimulate improved performance by employees which indirectly contributes to employee–enterprise identification. In many respects, employees subject to development and appraisal are marketing themselves and their function to the firm and the customer. This is of particular significance in service and tertiary sectors. Improved customer care and TQM in themselves reinforce an image of an organization to customers, suppliers and employees. Clearly, such innovations can feed into functional marketing.

STRATEGIC MANAGEMENT, HRM AND TQM AT BRITISH AIRWAYS

For an airline such as British Airways operating in the scheduled passenger market, the essential business task is to provide a service that satisfies customers' needs. Because the quality of service that scheduled carriers provide is substitutable, airlines must devise marketing strategies to retain regular business customers and also attract the less frequent traveller.

In the mid-1980s BA's strategic marketing revolved around two statements/slogans: 'We fly more people to more destinations' and 'The world's favourite airline'. These slogans informed customers that BA could meet their needs in relation to getting them anywhere, and that they were the best at doing it.

This marketing strategy was dependent upon BA employees at their booking centre, in the airport and in the plane *delivering* on the two slogans. In order for this delivery to take place, BA launched a HRM policy which highlighted customer care in the context of a total quality management (TQM) package.

Thus, all BA employees were encouraged to think in terms of customer care as well as how their contribution within the company contributed to the overall goal of providing a service that met customer needs. Clearly, the management of the employment relationship, marketing goals and strategies were linked to provide a TQM package. Such a series of integrated goals required effective internal communication and cross-fertilization of ideas, including high-profile HRM and marketing management. In the case of BA, both HRM and strategic marketing were geared towards emphasizing the quality of the in-flight service as well as the pre-service (that is, booking ease and services at the airport). The facilities that BA provides range from airport restaurant vouchers for passengers delayed because of the late arrival of incoming planes, to high-quality in-flight entertainment, including extracts of BBC news and current movies, and a high level of care and attention by flight attendants.

4.6 SUMMARY

This chapter has explained how the internal ordering and environment of a company influences its production, human resource and marketing goals. It has done so by taking the notion of production orientation and explaining how its predominance in the early stages of industrial development led to the neglect of marketing and the management of the employment relationship.

Both marketing and its management and the management of employee relations have developed as functional adjuncts to the production orientation. As Western markets converted in terms of their industrial development, the nature of competition within them altered; monopolistic competition began to dominate the Western economic system, and this in part caused a re-examination of the production orientation, marketing and the management of human resources within firms. The consequence of this re-examination was, in the face of recession and monopolistic competition, a rise in the prominence of marketing, together with an emphasis on the strategic importance of the employment relationship.

Similarly, organizations began to visualize and examine the internal ordering of their resources. Functional separation of resource areas was increasingly seen to be limited and damaging to the firm. The interrelation of apparently separate areas has become integral to the overall success of businesses. Similarly, it is critical for improving production and other essential goals such as marketing and the successful management of the employment relationship. Section 4.2 of this chapter examined organizational structures in relation to functional spans of control and apparently residual goals such as marketing and employee relations.

Production orientation alone cannot lead to the successful conclusion of a company's business. Areas such as marketing, personnel management and employee relations are integral to the delivery of a 'final result'. Marketing and a strategic approach to the management of the employment relationship in combination bridge the gap left by production orientation in relation to overall corporate goals. Section 4.5 looked at how HRM techniques contribute to production and marketing goals. Thus, the central themes of this chapter concern the need for integration of functions together with the division of and expansion of the central management role.

A consideration of the internal complexities of an organization, the integration of functions and the spans of control highlight the importance of the human dimension to the success of an enterprise. The firm cannot be characterized as a production function: its goods and services need marketing and development in response to customer preference, while human resources need developing and monitoring. The form that this development and monitoring takes can have a considerable impact on the overall success of the company. An emphasis on 'soft' HRM in combination with organizational structures which integrate marketing throughout all functional areas will considerably assist the firm to meet its production management goals. In short, such goals cannot be centrally achieved without a consideration of marketing and management of the employment relationship.

REVIEW QUESTIONS

1. On the basis of the information contained in this chapter, how would the integration of marketing with human resource goals improve the service that an airline might offer?
2. Why do you think that production management became such a dominant concept? Is it perhaps unfair to be too critical of it?
3. Which of the organizational structures described in Section 4.3 above would best meet the integration of marketing and human resource needs in:

(a) a fast food restaurant?

(b) a car manufacturer?

(c) a university or polytechnic?

4. From any work experience you have or organization with which you are familiar, do you think that the distinction between personnel management and the strategic management of the employment relationship, including marketing, is really that distinctive or new?

5. Can functional residuals such as marketing and personnel impose transaction costs on organization structures?

6. Is marketing and its management that crucial if long-run standardized production batches meet the requirements of the consumer in a secure market?

REFERENCES

Atkinson, J. (1984), 'Manpower Strategies for Flexible Organizations', *Personnel Management*, pp. 28–31.

Braverman, H. (1974), *Labour and Monopoly Capital*, Monthly Review Press, New York.

Cole, G. A. (1988), *Personnel Management*, DP Publications, London.

Drucker, P. (1974), *Effective Management Performance*, British Institute of Management, London.

Guest, D. (1989), 'Personnel Management and Human Resource Management: Can You Spot the Difference?' *Personnel Management*, pp. 40–51.

Guest, D. (1991), 'Personnel Management the End of Orthodoxy', *British Journal of Industrial Relations*, **29**(2), pp. 149–77.

Kotler, P. (1991), *Marketing Management: Analysis, Planning, Implementation and Control*, 7th edn, Prentice-Hall International, Englewood Cliffs, NJ.

Pearson, R. (1991), *The Human Resource: Managing People and Work in the 1990s*, McGraw-Hill, Maidenhead, Berks.

Sisson, K. (ed.) (1989), *Personnel Management in Britain*, Basil Blackwell, Oxford.

Smith, A. (1776), *The Wealth of Nations*, Dent Dutton, London, 1910 edn.

Taylor, F. W. (1964), *The Principles of Scientific Management*, Harper and Row, London.

Williamson, O. (1975), *Markets and Hierarchies*, The Free Press, Macmillan Publishing, London.

Williamson, O. (1981), 'The Modern Corporation: Origins, Evaluation and Attributes', *Journal of Economic Literature*, vol. 19, pp. 1537–68.

THE MICROECONOMIC ENVIRONMENT

5.1 INTRODUCTION

Economics is the study of how a society uses its resources to produce goods and services to satisfy its needs and wants. As such, it focuses on the ways in which skills, knowledge and efforts are applied to the available natural resources in order to produce those products that individuals and groups wish to consume. Defined in this way, it is clear that marketing and economics have a close affinity, and that a broad understanding of economic principles and concepts is a valuable asset to students of marketing.

In examining the economic environment in which marketing organizations function, it is useful to distinguish between those influences that operate at the level of the individual firm and those that relate to the working of the economy as a whole and thus affect firms in general. The former are normally described as 'microeconomic' factors and include the study of how markets work and how a firm's decisions are influenced by the structure of the market in which it operates. The latter are characterized as 'macroeconomic' aspects and focus on the causes and effects of aggregate decisions on production and consumption within the economy. This chapter examines some of the key influences in a marketing organization's microeconomic environment. An analysis of the macroeconomic environment is left to the next chapter.

5.2 MARKETS AND THE MARKET ECONOMY

The idea of a 'market' is a central concern for students and practitioners of both economics and marketing. While marketers tend to focus primarily on the demand side of a market and see it as 'the set of all actual and potential buyers of a product', the economist characterizes a market in terms of the interacting behaviour of two groups: those seeking to buy (or hire) products or resources, and those seeking to sell them. For the economist, the supply side of a market is no less important than the demand side, and it is the interaction of these two market forces that is seen as fundamental to the production and consumption of goods and services, and therefore to the 'allocation of resources', in what is described as a 'market economy'.

The traditional view of the operation of a market economy is illustrated in simplified form in Figure 5.1. Responding to the demands of individual consumers, firms (producers) purchase resources in the resource or factor markets and use these resources to produce goods or services which are then sold in the product markets to consumers. In the resource markets, individuals supply resources such as labour, and firms demand these resources. In the product markets these roles are reversed. Consequently, while resources flow from individuals to firms, products flow

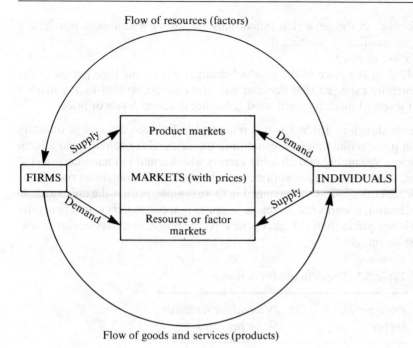

Figure 5.1   The operation of a market economy

from firms to individuals. In both cases, the linking mechanism between individuals and firms is 'price', with firms paying a price to acquire resources and individuals paying a price to acquire goods and services. Viewed in this way, price is seen as the means through which individuals express their preference for goods and services and through which firms respond to these preferences by producing the products that consumers want. Accordingly, it follows that changes in the preferences of consumers will affect the behaviour of producers and that these changes will be reflected by changes in market prices.

This perception of the role of price in reflecting consumer choice has clear implications for marketers, who see price as one of the key elements of the marketing mix and thus as one of the variables that can affect the achievement of a company's marketing and corporate goals. To this extent, the study of price formation in free markets provides a useful insight into consumer behaviour, including how potential customers see a firm's products and how much they are willing to pay for them. Thus, while price-setting in the real world may be more complex than is suggested in economists' models, an understanding of the working of the price mechanism is an essential ingredient in the analysis of how markets function.

5.3   THE BASICS: DEMAND, SUPPLY AND MARKET PRICE[1]

5.3.1   Demand

Economists define 'demand' as the quantity of a product that consumers are willing and able to buy at a specific price over a given period of time. This definition highlights some key features of the economist's view of demand:

1. Demand must be 'effective', in the sense that individuals are willing and able to purchase a product, rather than just needing or wanting it.
2. Demand is seen in relation to price.
3. A time period is involved. If the price of the product changes during the time period under consideration, it is generally expected that demand will also change, so that in any market there may be different levels of quantity demanded reflecting different levels of price.

In the hypothetical example shown in Table 5.1, this relationship between changes in quantity demanded and changes in price is illustrated by examining the demand for tomatoes in a local market over a range of prices. Assuming that all other factors which could influence consumers' decisions remain constant, it can be seen that as price falls the demand for tomatoes rises, or as price rises the demand for tomatoes falls. If, as assumed in this example, price is the only variable that could affect market demand, it seems reasonable to suppose that consumers would generally buy more of a product at lower prices than at higher prices. As the post-Christmas sales indicate, this fact has not been lost on retailers!

Table 5.1 The demand for tomatoes

Price per kilo (pence)	Demand for tomatoes (kilos per day)
100	100
80	200
60	300
40	400
20	500

While there may be markets in which this inverse relationship between quantity demanded and price may not apply (e.g. shares purchased *because* the price is rising), to most observers the economist's view of demand has intuitive appeal. Moreover, to marketers, the demand curve derived from the figures given in the table—and illustrated in Figure 5.2—is reminiscent of the buy-response curve because of its emphasis on consumer responses to changes in price. Taking the price of 60 pence, for example, it can be seen at a glance that the demand for tomatoes is 300 kilos per day and that the demand for the product falls as the price rises and vice versa. Equally, by multiplying the amount purchased (300 kilos per day) by the price at which it is sold (60 pence), it is possible to calculate what the total expenditure on the product will be at the price in question—an amount illustrated by the shaded rectangle. Since the amount spent is the same as firms receive in revenue, an understanding of the likely price–quantity relationship has obvious relevance to a business organization on both the production and the marketing sides.

5.3.2 Supply

Supply is defined as the amount of a product that producers are willing to make available to the market at a given price over a particular period of time. This definition of supply emphasizes the importance of price in determining the quantity supplied and the need to consider supply over a specific period of time. Like demand, it is argued that at different prices there will be different levels of supply, reflecting the willingness and/or ability of producers to supply a product as

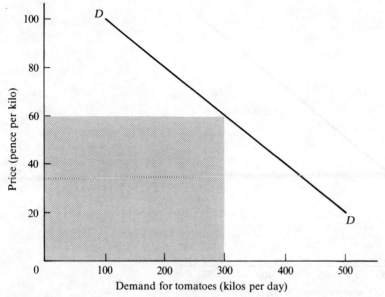

Figure 5.2 A demand curve for tomatoes

prices change. Since some producers may not be able to supply at low prices, it is reasonable to assume that as prices rise the quantity supplied will also rise, as new firms are attracted into the market-place. Moreover, this increase in the quantity supplied will be further bolstered by existing suppliers wanting to expand output to increase their profits, thus resulting in further rises in supply as prices rise.

This relationship between price and the quantity supplied is illustrated by examining the supply side of the market for tomatoes (see Table 5.2). Starting with the same assumption that price is the only variable, and that all other factors which could influence supply remain constant, it is evident that as price falls the quantity supplied falls or as price rises the quantity supplied rises. Again, while this relationship may not hold in every case—particularly when it is difficult or impossible to increase supply in the short term—in general the proposition that more will be supplied at higher prices than at lower prices appears logical. Translated into a graph shown in Figure 5.3, it can be seen clearly that the market supply curve (SS) runs in a different direction from the market demand curve, illustrating the different nature of the relationship of the two market forces with price.

Table 5.2 The supply of tomatoes

Price per kilo (pence)	Supply of tomatoes (kilos per day)
100	500
80	400
60	300
40	200
20	100

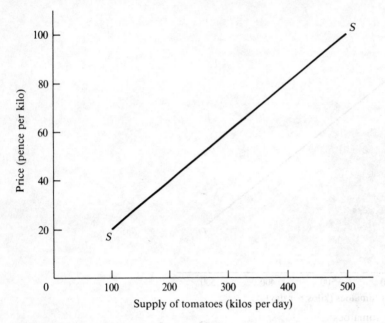

Figure 5.3 A supply curve for tomatoes

5.3.3 Market price

From the analysis in Figure 5.3, it is clear that economists view price as the common link between demand and supply. In general, consumers would prefer to purchase products at low prices, while producers would prefer to sell them at high prices. Between the two extremes, it is likely that there will be a price where the interest of the two groups will coincide. This, in essence, is the central proposition of the theory of market price. Put simply, the theory argues that in any free market there will be an 'equilibrium price' which brings into balance the quantity that consumers are willing and able to buy (i.e. demand) and the quantity that producers are willing and able to produce (i.e. supply). Moreover, the beauty of this type of market system is that when it is operating efficiently the whole process works automatically to generate such equilibrium prices, so that no centralized system for co-ordinating the multitude of individual demand and supply decisions is required as in the case of a totally planned economy.

To see how price will be determined in free markets, it is necessary to return to the example of the market for tomatoes, referred to above (see Table 5.3). At a price of 60 pence, both demand

Table 5.3 Tomatoes: demand and supply

Price per kilo (pence)	Demand	Supply
	(kilos per day)	
100	100	500
80	200	400
60	300	300
40	400	200
20	500	100

and supply are 300 kilos per day: in short, demand and supply are in equilibrium. At any price above 60 pence supply will exceed demand, whereas at any price below 60 pence demand exceeds supply. Only at 60 pence are the two equal. In this market, then, that is the price at which the interest of consumers and producers will coincide. While it is possible that for a time the price charged in the market (market price) is not the equilibrium price, it is argued that market forces will automatically push the market price towards the equilibrium position, as producers either lower their prices to get rid of excess supply or push up their prices to take advantage of excess demand. In effect, in free markets that are working efficiently, price adjustments automatically bring demand and supply into equilibrium, causing market price and equilibrium price to coincide.

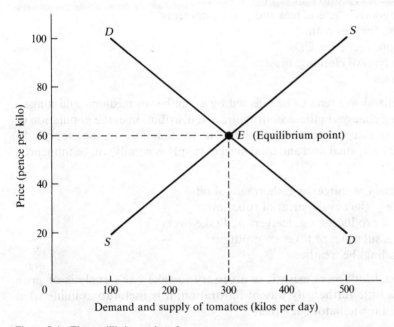

Figure 5.4   The equilibrium price of tomatoes

This interrelationship between demand and supply through price is seen quite clearly by examining the demand and supply curves for tomatoes, shown in Figure 5.4. Only at one price (60 pence) are demand and supply equal (at 300 kilos per day). This, then, is the equilibrium price, the price to which a market will always return in the short run *if* it is allowed to do so. This latter condition should not be overlooked, since it highlights the key features of the type of market under consideration, i.e. a free market which is highly competitive and is operating efficiently. In such a market, no individual producer or consumer is important enough to influence the market price: rather, it is the actions of all producers and all consumers (i.e. market forces generally) that will establish the equilibrium conditions. In the real world, as illustrated below, markets tend to be much less competitive and efficient than is suggested by this model of the free market, and consequently price will not necessarily be formed in the manner described above. Nevertheless, for students of marketing it is important to recognize that the economist's approach to market analysis is both useful and relevant, not least because it emphasizes the basic forces underlying the operation of most markets and provides a useful foundation for the analysis of more complex market situations.

5.4 CHANGES IN MARKET PRICE

5.4.1 Changes in demand and supply

Any preliminary analysis of market price starts from the assumption that price is the only variable that influences both demand and supply. In real markets, the behaviour of both consumers and producers is clearly influenced by many factors. On the demand side, for example, an individual consumer's demand might be affected by such things as:

- Changes in the level of disposable income, e.g. loss of job
- Promotional activities, e.g. advertising
- Price of substitute products, e.g. different brands of coffee
- Price of complementary goods, e.g. golf fees and golf equipment
- The weather, e.g. demand for ice cream
- The availability of new products, e.g. CDs
- Fashions and fads, e.g. styles of clothing, music
- Publicity, e.g. health scares

Moreover, total market demand will tend to be affected by a number of medium- and longer-term developments, including changes in the size, structure and distribution of the population or in the level and distribution of income and wealth in the economy. Similarly, on the supply side, the level of production of an individual firm and total market supply generally will be influenced by factors such as:

- The price and availability of resources, e.g. shortages of oil
- Changes in technology, e.g. the development of robotics
- Changes in the number of producers, e.g. mergers and take-overs
- Government policies, e.g. subsidies or taxes on producers
- Exogenous factors, including the weather

Given that these additional influences exist, it is necessary to take one's analysis of price formation in free markets a little further. By way of illustration, it is useful to examine what would happen to the demand for tomatoes, if either:

- there was a major promotional campaign which suggested that tomatoes had valuable health benefits

or

- a government report claimed that tomatoes could cause stomach ulcers

As the figures in Table 5.4 indicate, in the first case the demand for tomatoes at all the original prices has increased, as consumers respond to the persuasiveness of the marketing message. In the second case the demand at all prices has decreased, as consumers worry about the possible consequences of consuming tomatoes.

Transferring these figures to a graph (Figure 5.5), it can be seen that in both cases the entire demand curve shifts from its original position (DD), moving either to the right of the original curve (to D_1D_1) or to the left of the original curve (D_2D_2). Shifts of this nature are described by economists as *changes in demand*, with D_1D_1 being an increase in demand and D_2D_2 being a decrease. By using such terminology, economists can differentiate between (a) changes in demand which occur because of the influence of factors other than price changes and (b) changes in the quantity demanded which occur only because of price changes.

If this exercise is repeated on the supply side (Figure 5.6), similar shifts in supply will be

Table 5.4 Effect of consumers' attitudes on quantity of tomatoes demanded

Price per kilo (pence)	Original demand	New demand (after promotion)	New demand (after health scare)
100	100	200	00
80	200	300	100
60	300	400	200
40	400	500	300
20	500	600	400

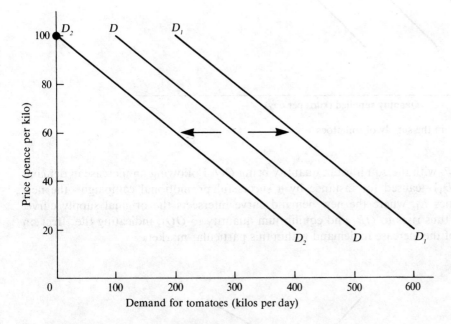

Figure 5.5 Changes in the demand for tomatoes

observed as producers respond to changes in one of the factors affecting their ability to supply products to the market. Such *changes in supply* involve either increases (S_1S_1) or decreases (S_2S_2) in supply at all prices and are represented by a movement of the entire supply curve.

Again, this notion of a change in supply is used to distinguish movements *of* the supply curve from movements *along a* supply curve, which are described as a change in the quantity supplied and which result from a change in price rather than a change in one of the other factors that affect supply as in the two cases above.

5.4.2 The effect on market price

If, in free markets, market price is determined by the interaction of demand and supply, it follows that changes in either demand or supply will cause changes in market price. Figures 5.7 and 5.8 illustrate how this occurs. In the first case, market forces initially fix the equilibrium price

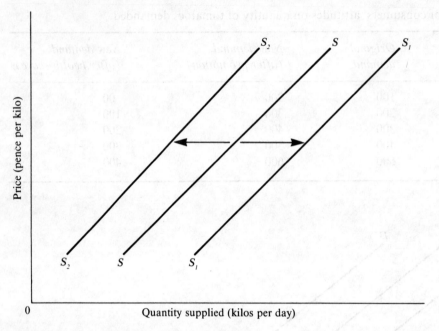

Figure 5.6   Changes in the supply of tomatoes

for tomatoes at OP, with the equilibrium quantity being OQ. Following an increase in demand for tomatoes (D_1D_1)—caused for instance by a successful promotional campaign—the new equilibrium becomes E_1, where the new demand curve intersects the original supply curve. Equilibrium price thus rises to OP_1 and equilibrium quantity to OQ_1, indicating the effect on price and output of the increase in demand within this particular market.

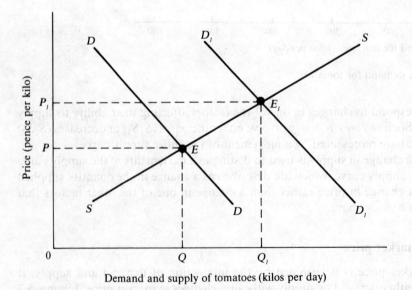

Figure 5.7   Effect on the equilibrium price of tomatoes of a change in demand

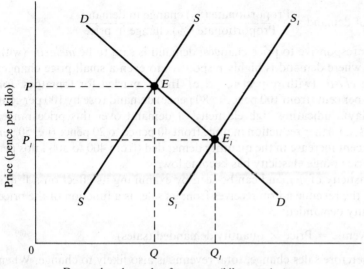

Figure 5.8   Effect on the equilibrium price of tomatoes of a change in supply

In the second example, (Figure 5.8), the change in market price is a result of a change in supply. As supply increases to S_1S_1, the new equilibrium becomes E_1, where the new supply curve intersects the original demand curve. At this new equilibrium, price moves from OP to OP_1 and equilibrium quantity from OQ to OQ_1. In short, the increase in supply in the market for tomatoes helps to reduce the market price and at the same time stimulates an increase in the quantity of tomatoes demanded (from OQ to OQ_1). To consumers operating in the market for this product, neither of these propositions from the theoretical world of the economist would appear unreasonable.

5.5   ELASTICITIES OF DEMAND AND SUPPLY[2]

5.5.1   The concept of elasticity

Whether price is increased or decreased, the decision is sure to affect consumers, suppliers, competitors and distributors, and in some cases may affect the interest of government as well. The extent to which these interested parties respond to a price change is encapsulated by the concept of elasticity. In essence, the idea of elasticity refers to the degree to which demand (or supply) changes in relation to a change in the price or some other variable such as income or the price of other goods. What is important here is to compare the proportionate (or percentage) change of demand (or supply) with the proportionate (or percentage) change in the other variable. In effect, examining elasticity represents an attempt to measure the reaction of buyers or producers to a change in one of the key factors affecting their position in the market-place. Needless to say, information of this kind could be useful to a business organization when considering possible changes in either its output or marketing strategies.

5.5.2   Price elasticity of demand

This term refers to the ratio of the proportionate (or percentage) change in demand to the proportionate (or percentage) change in price. In other words, it seeks to measure how the sales of a product respond to a change in its price. Expressed as a formula:

$$\text{Price elasticity of demand} = \frac{\text{Proportionate (\%) change in demand}}{\text{Proportionate (\%) change in price}}$$

Where demand is relatively unresponsive to price changes, demand is said to be *inelastic* (with respect to price). Conversely, where demand is highly responsive to even a small price change, demand is described as being *elastic* (with respect to price). In the market for tomatoes, for example, when price fell by 20 per cent (from 100 pence to 80 pence) demand rose by 100 per cent (from 100 to 200 kilos per day), indicating high elasticity of demand over this price range. However, at much lower prices, a further reduction in price from 40 pence to 20 pence (i.e. 50 per cent) resulted in only a 25 per cent increase in the quantity demanded (from 400 to 500 kilos per day), showing that over this price range elasticity has become low.

The significance of price elasticity of demand can be seen by examining its effect on a firm's revenue. As illustrated above, the revenue a firm receives from its sales is a function of the price at which it sells and the quantity demanded:

$$\text{Total revenue} = \text{Price} \times \text{quantity demanded (sales)}$$

Consequently, as price and therefore sales change, total revenue is also likely to change. When the demand for tomatoes was price-elastic (between 100 pence and 80 pence), the reduction in price gave rise to an increase in total revenue, since the price reduction of 20 per cent was more than offset by a 100 per cent increase in sales. However, as the price for the product fell further and demand eventually became inelastic (between 40 pence and 20 pence), even a 25 per cent increase in sales was not sufficient to compensate for the 50 per cent price reduction and, accordingly, total revenue declined. If these price changes were reversed, and prices rose instead of falling, it could be demonstrated that at high elasticities (elastic demand) total revenue falls, whereas at low elasticities (inelastic demand) total revenue rises. In effect, it is possible to characterize price elasticity of demand in terms of its effect on total revenue as price variations occur (see Table 5.5).

Table 5.5 Elasticity and total revenue

Description of price elasticity of demand	Price change	Revenue effect
High	Increase	Decrease
(Elastic demand)	Decrease	Increase
Low	Increase	Increase
(Inelastic demand)	Decrease	Decrease

5.5.3 Cross-price elasticity of demand

The price of a product is not the only factor affecting its sales. Another important variable is the price of other products, particularly where these products are substitutes (i.e. in competitive demand) or complements (i.e. in joint demand). Cross-price elasticity of demand measures this relationship, by comparing a change in the demand for one product in response to a change in the price of another product:

$$\text{Cross price elasticity of demand} = \frac{\text{Proportionate (\%) change in demand for X}}{\text{Proportionate (\%) change in price of Y}}$$

In the case of products that are substitutes, the sales of product X are likely to rise (fall) in response to a rise (fall) in the price of product Y, as some consumers switch their preferences to the product that has become relatively cheaper. This can be seen in the market for petrol, as motorists frequently shop around for the cheapest brands where price differences occur. In contrast, where products are consumed jointly (complements), the sales of product X tend to fall (rise) in response to a rise (fall) in the price of product Y, as consumers buy less (or more) of one product because of the price change of its complement.

A word of warning, however: the effect of complementarity does not necessarily operate equally in reverse. The demand for microwave meals is likely to be influenced by a change in the price of microwave ovens, but it does not follow that the demand for microwave ovens will be affected by a change in the price of microwave meals.

5.5.4 Income elasticity of demand

Income is another key influence on both individual and market demand. For example, sales of consumer durables, 'luxury' products and services tend to increase by significant amounts as consumers become more affluent; in contrast, sales of what might be described as 'inferior products', such as cheap shoes, often show a tendency to decline at such times. This idea of changes in demand in response to changes in income is encapsulated by the concept of income elasticity of demand:

$$\text{Income elasticity of demand} = \frac{\text{Proportionate (\%) change in demand}}{\text{Proportionate (\%) change in income}}$$

Where demand rises as income levels rise (giving positive income elasticities), such products are normally referred to as necessities or luxuries, with the latter having a much higher income elasticity than the former. Inferior goods, on the other hand, have negative income elasticities, given the decline in sales as income levels rise. Since an individual's willingness and ability to purchase a product will tend to vary with income, it follows that the income elasticity of demand for any product can vary from negative to positive over a range of income.

5.5.5 Price elasticity of supply

If suppliers are relatively unresponsive to an increase in the price of a product, the product is described as being inelastic in supply. If producers increase production substantially as prices rise, the product is said to be elastic in supply. Generally speaking, the time factor tends to be an important determinant of supply elasticity. In the short run in many markets it is often difficult, if not impossible, to expand production quickly as prices increase, since more investment may need to be made and more labour may have to be recruited and trained. In the long run, however, as extra factors of production become available, suppliers are better able to respond to a change in market price. In short, products tend to become more elastic in supply as time increases.

5.5.6 Some applications for marketing

The economist's idea of elasticity is concerned with measuring buyers' (or sellers') responses to changes in price or income or some other variable. Viewed in this way, the concepts described above have direct applications to the marketing of goods and services. In the case of price elasticity of demand, for example, it is clear that businesses will be concerned about how consumers respond to price changes and that this will be one of the factors that ideally ought to be taken into account when a price change is being considered (e.g. at different stages of the product life-cycle), especially in view of its potential implications for turnover and market share. Equally, consumers' responses to a change in the price of rival products (cross-price elasticity) may influence a business when fixing its own prices, particularly in highly competitive markets. Under oligopoly (see Section 5.6.3 below), for instance, companies are often tempted to fix prices around the levels charged by their main competitors and to engage in non-price competition to encourage brand loyalty and to retain market share. While a marketer may not refer to such behaviour as a reflection of a product's cross-price elasticity of demand, a combination of experience and marketing information tells the individuals setting price levels that a competitor's prices can be a key factor determining the sales of their own products in the market-place.

Income elasticity of demand is another useful idea for market planners. If, for example, a general rise in consumer income looks likely to reduce sales, a business may wish to consider future investment policies or diversification into other product areas, or the means by which it can change the image of its product so as to appeal to more affluent consumers. Conversely, if rising income levels suggest an increase in the future sales of certain products, this may help to encourage increased investment or the acquisition of new products to complement an organization's existing portfolio. Added to this, marketers often use the relationship between income levels and sales as a means of targeting a product at certain segments of a market, reflecting the view that demand is in part a function of income. In considering possible sales–income relationships, businesses can turn not only to their own internal information and market research, but also to data produced by government agencies on the current and future levels and distribution of income and wealth in the economy.

Turning finally to price elasticity of supply, it is clear that, while changes in output are more a concern of production than of marketing, marketers have a vested interest in ensuring that products are available in sufficient supply as market conditions change. If, for example, increased demand in a market forces up price, a company would be keen to exploit the situation by increasing its output to satisfy the extra demand; otherwise consumers may turn to a rival brand and market share may decline. As indicated above, the extent to which supply is able to respond to changes in market price is often a function of the time scale involved. In many agricultural markets, for instance, it is impossible to increase supply in the short term, given the nature of the product. In contrast, in other markets, such as the market for stocks and shares, it may be quite easy to increase supply immediately, as traders will respond quickly to rising prices so as to take advantage of favourable market conditions.

5.6 MARKET STRUCTURES[3]

The conditions existing in the markets for different goods and services can vary quite considerably. The market for soap powder, for example, is characterized by a small number of large suppliers and a large number of independent buyers, whereas the market for bed and breakfast accommodation has a large number of both buyers and suppliers. These differences in the market characteristics of the buyers and sellers who constitute a market are inherent in the idea of 'market structure'. In particular, it refers to:

1. The number of buyers and sellers operating in a market
2. The degree of concentration of the market in the hands of a small number of buyers and/or sellers

3. The degree of collusion or competition between buyers and/or sellers

As indicated by the analysis above, a market's structure has implications not only for the functioning of the market as a whole, but also for the behaviour of firms operating in it. To examine these aspects, it is necessary to consider some of the main types of market structure identified by economists.

5.6.1 Perfect competition

Markets are sometimes thought of as being located along an imaginary line, running from the theoretical extremes of perfect competition at one end to pure monopoly at the other end. For a market to be perfectly competitive, there must be:

- A large number of small producers, each with similar cost structures and each producing a homogeneous (i.e. identical) product
- A large number of buyers, each responsible for purchasing only a small percentage of total output
- Complete freedom for firms to enter and leave the market (i.e. no barriers to entry or exit)
- A ready supply of information for buyers and sellers about market conditions

Given the existence of these market characteristics, economists argue that no single buyer or seller is able to influence market price: rather, it is market forces as a whole that determine price, in the manner described above, and each individual supplier is forced to supply at this price for fear of losing customers (or, in some cases, available revenue). In the jargon, the firm is said to be a 'price-taker'. Moreover, because of the keen competition in the market-place, it is suggested that firms will have every incentive to be efficient and that ultimately consumers should benefit from efficient, low-cost production through lower prices. Since firms are free to enter (or leave) the market as profit levels vary, the tendency will be for any excess profits (or losses) to be eliminated in the long run and for each individual firm to make 'normal profits' (i.e. the level of profits sufficient to keep suppliers in the market, as determined by the 'opportunity cost' of their investment in production). While this may be good news for consumers, from a business point of view it is evident that perfect competition does not offer particularly good prospects for high and continued profit-making, except perhaps in markets that are slow to adjust to changes in demand.

Though in its purest form perfect competition may not exist, some markets may be described as 'near perfect', in the sense that they exhibit many of the characteristics described above (e.g. large local markets for fruit and vegetables), and it is interesting to observe that pricing behaviour in such markets often reflects the theoretical propositions of the economists. Perhaps more importantly, while not being typical of markets in the real world, the model of a perfectly competitive market provides a benchmark against which to examine the operation of markets that are less than perfect and to highlight how the existence of imperfections helps to condition market behaviour. It should not be overlooked that much of the thinking that lies behind government policies on markets in capitalist economies is influenced by a desire to remove (or at least reduce) such imperfections, in the belief that competition in markets is inherently beneficial.

5.6.2 Monopoly

At the opposite end of the scale to perfect competition lies pure monopoly. Literally speaking, a pure monopoly exists when a market is under the control of a single supplier and new firms are unable to gain access to the market because of the substantial barriers to entry, such as the monopolist's control of a resource or the high capital costs of market participation. In such a market, the large number of buyers competing with one another face a single source of supply and the absence of competition ensures that the monopolist exercises complete control over output and price. Much the same kind of situation could occur of course where a group of dominant suppliers took collective action to restrict output and by doing so influenced market price. Such an arrangement is normally referred to as a 'cartel' and is perhaps best exemplified by the Oil Producing Exporting Countries (OPEC).

In practice, such singular control over the supply side of a market rarely exists. Instead, it tends to be accepted that monopoly occurs when one firm is able to dominate a market to such an extent that other suppliers have little, if any, influence on overall output and price. (For example, in Britain the Monopolies and Mergers Commission regards monopoly as a situation where one producer or a group of producers acting together control 25 per cent of a market.) Given this dominance, the monopolist is in a position to determine the market price and as such is said to be a 'price-maker' rather than a 'price-taker'. In markets with few substitutes, where demand tends to be more inelastic, this control over the price level will be particularly pronounced and the monopolist may be tempted to go on increasing prices up to a point where profits start to be eroded. Were this to be the case, it is clear that the consumer would be at a considerable disadvantage and would probably face prices that were higher and a level of output that was lower than would have occurred in a perfectly competitive market. Perhaps not surprisingly, this ability of monopolists (and dominant firms) to act in a manner felt to be against the 'public interest' has frequently encouraged governments to take action to control or curb monopoly power, whether through legislation (e.g. anti-trust laws), policy (e.g. privatization) or administrative device.

From a marketing point of view, the existence of a monopoly would tend to imply that little, if any, marketing activity was required by the monopolist, other than to establish the most profitable level of price. However, it should be remembered that the monopolists' power does not extend to control over demand, and that promotional activities to retain or increase market demand can often be justified, particularly when some form of substitute is available (e.g. British Rail campaigns to boost InterCity travel by appealing to car drivers). Moreover, in terms of pricing policy, the monopolist may be able to make greater profits if price discrimination is possible (i.e. charging different prices in different markets). As mentioned previously, such an approach would be appropriate where:

- Discrete market segments could be identified on the basis of either time (e.g. peak and off-peak rail fares) or geographical dispersion (e.g. different beer prices in different parts of Britain) and no 'leakages' occurred between markets
- The price elasticity of demand differed in different parts of the market

While such price discrimination is by no means unique to monopoly markets, an investigation of the pricing policy of many former and present state monopolies indicates that it is a major feature of monopoly pricing and one that often reflects perceived differences in demand elasticity in different market segments.

5.6.3 Oligopoly

Between the two extremes of perfect competition and pure monopoly, there are different forms of imperfect competition. One of these is known as oligopoly. An oligopoly market is one that is dominated by a few sellers who are responsible for a large share (perhaps 100 per cent) of the total market output. What exactly constitutes a 'few' is, of course, open to question, but it seems to be accepted that the number of firms should be sufficiently small for there to be a recognition by each firm that its future prospects depend not only on its own decisions, but also on those of its rivals. This concept of mutual interdependence is seen as a key feature of an oligopoly market, and one that has an important bearing on each firm's behaviour in the market-place.

What makes oligopoly an interesting area of study is that it is a prevalent market structure in many industries in advanced industrial economies. Using what are called 'concentration ratios', which show the proportion of output or employment of the leading firms in a particular industry or product grouping, economists are able to demonstrate how just a handful of organizations can dominate in product areas as varied as detergents, cars, chemicals, oil, pharmaceuticals and beer. Yet to the consumer this situation may not be readily apparent. Faced with a wide variety of product brands, consumers may be led to suppose that a high degree of competition exists, whereas it may simply be that each of the leading producers is responsible for supplying a number of brands—a point readily demonstrated by the UK detergents market, which is dominated by two firms: Lever Brothers and Proctor & Gamble.

Supporting, if indirect, evidence of growth of oligopoly markets and the tendency towards product differentiation is provided by examining data on advertising, which show that it is in markets with a high degree of concentration and extensive branding that most advertising money is spent. MEAL's survey of the top 100 UK advertisers in 1990 contains many familiar names, with the two leading detergent manufacturers heading the list (Table 5.6).

Table 5.6 Advertising expenditure by the top 20 UK advertisers, 1990

Rank	Advertiser (holding company)	Total expenditure (£m)
1	Proctor & Gamble	54.70
2	Lever Brothers (Unilever)	53.36
3	Kellogg	47.66
4	British Telecom	39.36
5	Mars Confectionery	35.89
6	Ford	35.79
7	Kraft General Foods (Philip Morris)	35.11
8	Nestlé	34.48
9	Electricity Association (Electricity Council)	33.44
10	Vauxhall	32.50
11	Proctor & Gamble (Health & Beauty Care)	32.03
12	Birds Eye Walls (Unilever)	30.69
13	Rover (British Aerospace)	30.15
14	British Gas	30.12
15	Pedigree Petfoods (Mars)	29.85
16	Rowntree Mackintosh (Nestlé)	28.44
17	National Westminster Bank	28.13
18	Halifax Building Society	27.57
19	Gallagher Tobacco	27.13
20	Cadbury (Cadbury Schweppes)	26.06

Source: based on MEAL analysis of top 100 advertisers. Reproduced by permission of Media Register–MEAL Ltd.

Other forms of non-price competition (including free gifts, coupons, after-sales service, warranties and guarantees, sponsorship, etc.) are a common feature of oligopoly markets and are normally designed to increase or retain market share, rather than increase demand overall. Faced by stiff competition from rival organizations, an oligopolist will normally seek ways to establish brand loyalty with the use of a wide range of promotional techniques, for fear that non-reaction to the activities of a competitor will ultimately cause a fall in market share and profitability. Not surprisingly, oligopoly industries are often characterized by relatively large marketing costs.

As far as pricing is concerned, some economic models of oligopoly suggest that the inter-dependence of firms makes for price rigidity and consequently tends to force companies towards non-price forms of competition. It is argued that, while a firm's competitors would not match upward price movements in the hope of gaining extra sales, they would be prepared to match downward price movements for fear of losing market share. If this supposition is correct, it would be to the mutual benefit of all firms to leave price at the prevailing market level and to find other ways to compete for customers, even to the extent of agreeing formally to collude on price.

Empirical evidence suggests that, while price stability is often a feature of this type of market, price competition does occur on occasions. In the late 1970s and early 1980s, for example, petrol retailers in the UK engaged in a substantial 'price war' using discounts they received from the major oil refiners to cut prices at the pumps. During the same period, a price-cutting campaign by Tesco, backed up by an extensive television advertising campaign, led to a period of price competition with Asda and Sainsbury, until price stability returned to the market-place. Similarly, in the package holiday market in the mid-1980s, a fierce price war broke out between the leading rival companies, who responded to each other's price cuts to such an extent that a number of smaller tour operators who were unable to match the reduced prices were forced out of business.

While competition of this type may exist and therefore benefit the consumer, it is recognized that an oligopoly market structure may also encourage a high degree of collusion between the leading firms in areas such as pricing, market sharing and limiting new entrants. Apart from the obvious benefit to firms of reducing risk and uncertainty, such collusion could be used to maintain price levels and hence profitability, particularly if one firm (formally or informally) became a price leader and the other firms followed suit. Similarly, by agreeing joint action on reducing prices to dissuade new firms from entering the market, or by controlling distribution outlets or resorting to non-price competition to reinforce barriers to new entrants, established companies may be able to limit competition and thus maintain their control over the supply side of the market. While such activities might be justified under certain circumstances (e.g. by creating scale economies and thus cutting production costs), it is clear that such behaviour constitutes some form of restrictive or anti-competitive practice which ultimately will tend to disadvantage the consumer. Such practices, e.g. in the case of monopoly, may be subject to government influence or intervention.

5.6.4   Monopolistic competition

The idea of product differentiation is also central to the economist's original concept of monopolistic competition. Under this form of market structure, a large number of competing firms each produce a product which—in the eyes of the consumer—is differentiated from similar products supplied by its competitors. The basis of this perceived product differentiation may be quality, style, branding or some other feature, and suppliers will attempt to emphasize these differences by advertising and/or appropriate packaging. Since each firm has an effective monopoly over its own brand, the market is said to exhibit monopolistic characteristics.[4] At the same time, the large number of firms in active competition with each other, and free to enter and leave the industry, gives the market its competitive features.

Substantial criticism of the original theory of monopolistic competition—particularly the fact that in many manufacturing industries numerous differentiated products are produced by only a few firms—has given rise to revised views of product differentiation in recent years (see e.g. Lipsey 1989, Ch. 14). Consequently, the term 'monopolistic competition' now tends to refer to market structures where a small number of firms compete to sell a large number of differentiated products. In keeping with the original theory, the focus remains on product differentiation, but the emphasis is now on small-group rather than large-group competition (i.e. monopolistic competition among a few oligopolistic firms). Moreover, it is interesting to note that newer theories continue to stress the original proposition that it pays firms to differentiate their products, to advertise heavily and to engage in other forms of competitive behaviour.

5.6.5 Other market structures

As a final word, it is worth emphasizing that the discussion on market structures has concentrated essentially on the supply side of the market and has assumed for the most part that producers face a large number of independent buyers when seeking to sell their product(s). In some markets, however, the number of buyers may be very limited, or, if not, they may be responsible for purchasing a significant percentage of a company's total output (e.g. government purchases of defence equipment; the electricity industry's purchase of coal; major food retail chain purchases of food products). In cases such as these, it is clear that dominant buyers will be in a position to exercise considerable control over the price charged by producers, by threatening to turn to other suppliers if a discount is not given for bulk purchases. While in some cases such enforced price discrimination might ultimately benefit the final consumer (e.g. in the form of lower retail prices), this need not necessarily be the case, particularly if the dominant buyer operates in a monopoly market or in collusion with other oligopoly producers.

REVIEW QUESTIONS

1. What factors are likely to determine whether the demand for product is price-elastic or price-inelastic?
2. Under the theory of market price, what should happen to the equilibrium price of tomatoes if:
   (a) there is a bad harvest?
   (b) the government gives a subsidy to tomato producers?
   (c) a hot summer substantially increases consumer preferences for tomatoes?
   Draw diagrams to illustrate your arguments.
3. What is likely to happen to the pattern of demand for goods and services as income levels rise in the developing economies?
4. Using a recent survey from Mintel, examine the market supply of any major consumer product. How competitive is the market?
   (a) What forms does the competition take?
   (b) How is the product distributed?

NOTES

1   For an extended analysis, see e.g. Stanlake (1989) 5th edn.
2   See e.g. Newell (1984), Ch. 16.
3   See Hardwick *et al.* (1990), Ch. 9 and 10.

4   An example is provided by the market for T-shirts. Plain white T-shirts are frequently sold in street markets with no brand identity or advertising support. With no product differentiation, the market becomes very competitive. However, other producers (e.g. Benetton) have differentiated their product by the addition of a brand identity and image, and this gives their product a kind of uniqueness which provides a degree of monopoly power amidst substantial competition.

REFERENCES

Fuller, N. (1985), *Basic Concepts in Micro-Economics*, Checkmate/Edward Arnold, London.
Hardwick, P. *et al.* (1990), *An Introduction to Modern Economics*, 3rd edn, Longman, London.
Lipsey, R. G. (1989), *An Introduction to Positive Economics*, 7th edn, Weidenfeld & Nicolson, London.
Newell, M. (1984), *The Economics of Business*, Pan, London.
Stanlake, G. F. (1989), *Introductory Economics*, 5th edn, Harlow, Longman.

THE MACROECONOMIC ENVIRONMENT

6.1 INTRODUCTION

In a market-based economy, business organizations are one important element of the economic system. The decisions they take, along with those of consumers and governments, help to determine how the economy operates and influence the pattern of production and consumption over time. In turn, the aggregate effects of these decisions by all three groups creates the macroeconomic environment in which businesses exist, and this will have an important influence on an individual firm's operations in the market-place. The nature and influence of this economic macroenvironment, and in particular the critical roles played by government in helping to shape it, are the central focus of this chapter.

6.2 THE CIRCULAR FLOW OF INCOME IN THE ECONOMY

Markets require not only people but also purchasing power. Total purchasing power is a function of a number of factors, most notably current income, borrowing and savings, as well as the prices of goods and services. To understand consumption, therefore, it is important to appreciate how purchasing power is created and, in particular, to examine the question of income generation. To do this it is necessary to construct a basic model of income flows in a market-based economy.[1]

As a first step in the construction of such a model, it is useful to refer back to the diagram of a market economy in the previous chapter (Figure 5.1). Here it was suggested that such an economy comprised two groups: individuals and firms. Individuals (also called 'domestic households') supplied resources to firms, while firms supplied goods and services to individuals. Implicit in this was the idea that these flows of goods and services and resources are also accompanied by flows of income (e.g. wages paid to labour; revenue earned from selling products), which are determined by the prices formed in the resource and product markets. In the model below, it is these flows of income that are of central concern.

In order to simplify the analysis, it is convenient to make the following initial assumptions about income flows in a market:

1. Households earn all their income from supplying their labour to firms.
2. Firms earn all their income from supplying goods and services to households.
3. The economy is 'closed'; i.e. there is no external trade.
4. All income earned is spent; i.e. none is saved.

In such an economy it can be seen that consumption of goods and services is a function of employment and, in turn, employment is a function of consumption. Equally, since labour is employed to produce output for consumption, the output of goods and services depends on demand (i.e. consumption) by households, which, as we have seen, depends on income. In short, in a simplified market economy income, output, spending and employment are all interrelated (Figure 6.1).

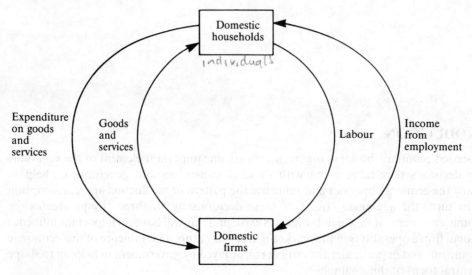

Figure 6.1   The relationship between income and spending in a simplified market economy

Despite the slightly unrealistic assumptions, it is not difficult to see that the relationships identified in the model basically explain how a market economy works. Individuals buy goods and services using income largely earned from helping to produce those goods and services; firms are able to pay this income to individuals from the income they earn from purchases by consumers. The fortunes of producers and consumers, in other words, are inextricably linked, with income flowing from firms to households and, in turn, flowing from households to firms in a circular motion. Indeed, given assumption 4 above, it is clear that consumer spending and income would be identical and that there would be no tendency for this to change if the economy operated as described.

In the real world, the process of income generation and consumption is of course far more complex and depends on a number of factors which need to be incorporated into the model. For a start, not all income earned by households is spent with domestic firms: some is saved, some is paid to the government as taxes, and some is spent on imported goods. In effect, these three activities represent 'withdrawals' of income from the circular flow and as such would cause a reduction in consumption and, therefore, ultimately in income, output and employment in the economy. Fortunately, as some income is removed from the circular flow in this way, additional income is 'injected' into the economy by domestic firms selling to foreign buyers (exports) and buying capital goods and equipment (investment) and by government spending on goods and services (government expenditure). Moreover, apart from income earned from employment, individuals also earn income from investments, property, savings and entrepreneurial activity. These various factors are shown in the revised model depicted in Figure 6.2.

Again, it needs to be stressed that even this model is still a simplified version of the real

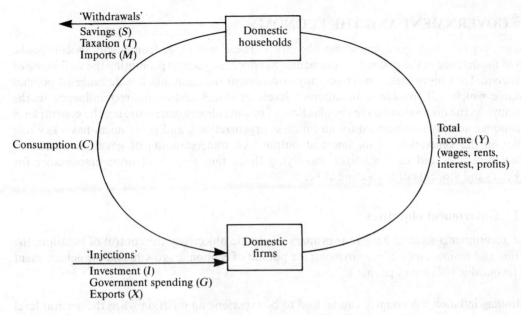

Figure 6.2   Income flows in an economy with 'injections' and 'withdrawals'

economy (e.g. firms also save; governments also invest; households also borrow on credit). But the essential point is that it emphasizes that consumption and income are related and that total demand in the economy is a function of the spending decisions not only of consumers but also of firms, government and external buyers. Moreover, decisions by any one of these groups will be influenced by a range of variables (e.g. consumers' decisions to save or spend or buy imports, government policies on taxation, etc.), so that levels of income and consumption, and therefore levels of economy activity, can vary considerably over time.

Added to this, it is important to recognize that any autonomous injection or withdrawal of income from the circular flow can cause what economists call a 'multiplier effect'.[2] If, for example, the government decides to reduce taxation, individuals will benefit from higher levels of disposable income. Assuming that some of this extra is spent with domestic firms, these businesses will receive more orders and hence more revenue, and some of this will be used to purchase additional resources (e.g. extra components, more labour). In turn, the suppliers of these resources will then receive extra income, some of which they may spend on additional foods and services or stocks. And so the income passes on to others, who will also spend a proportion of it, thus generating further income and consumption.

This multiple increase in income and consumption, brought about in this example by a reduction in taxation, can also cause an increase in investment spending by firms; this is referred to by economists as the 'accelerator effect'. As demand for consumer goods rises with the increase in disposable income, some firms will be tempted to invest in more capital equipment and stock to meet the increased consumer demands. Demand for industrial goods, therefore, will also rise as a direct consequence of the additional demand for consumer goods and will tend to be the most pronounced when businesses experiencing an increase in consumer demand have little or no excess capacity and when firms in the capital goods sector are able to meet the additional demand for plant and equipment.

6.3   GOVERNMENT AND THE ECONOMY

Like any organization, government has objectives. These may range from highly specific goals, such as the defence of the realm, to more nebulous concepts, such as promoting the well-being of its citizens. To achieve these objectives, any government normally has a wide range of policies available which will involve it in different levels of direct and/or indirect influence in the economy. As the discussion on the circular flow of income clearly demonstrates, the general level of economic activity is important for all business organizations, and government has a key role to play in the generation of income and output. An understanding of government macro-economic policies and the objectives underlying them, therefore, is of prime importance for marketers and students of marketing alike.

6.3.1   Government objectives

Most governments seem to have four primary economic objectives: the control of inflation; the creation and maintenance of employment; the pursuit of economic growth; and the achievement of a favourable balance of payments.

Controlling inflation   A country can be said to be experiencing inflation when the general level of prices is persistently rising. In Britain, for example, this situation is indicated by an upward movement in the retail price index (RPI), which is the most commonly used measure of how an average family's spending on goods and services is affected by price changes. A 10 per cent annual increase in the RPI, for example, means that over the course of a year the average family will have to pay approximately a tenth more for the 'basket' of goods and services it normally consumes. Alternatively, if its spending remained the same in money terms, by the end of the year it would have lost almost a tenth of its purchasing power. In short, inflation causes a fall in the value of money.

Inflationary tendencies can occur for a variety of reasons. On the supply side, increases in production costs (e.g. higher wage bills, rising energy and/or raw materials costs, higher overheads), if not offset by increases in productivity, may cause producers to raise their prices to maintain profit levels. If this occurs generally, then the economy may experience what is termed cost-push inflation, with production costs pushing up the general level of prices. Any attempt by the labour force to keep pace with or keep ahead of inflation—by seeking increased wages—can have a spiralling effect on prices, with wage rises forcing up prices which in turn force up wages, leading to further price rises and so on. When such an inflationary spiral occurs, price rises can become difficult to control, since neither producers nor their employees may be willing to make the first move to break the cycle.

Inflation can also be a demand-side phenomenon, with prices rising because the demand for goods and services at current prices exceeds the available supply. Such conditions of excess demand may occur for a variety of reasons, including an increase in the availability of credit, excessive spending by government and tax cuts which increase consumers' disposable incomes, thus allowing them to buy more goods and services. Should output not be sufficient to meet such an increase in demand, prices tend to be pulled upwards as the market adjusts to the new conditions. Moreover, any inability on the part of domestic producers to meet this increased demand may also result in greater import penetration, with its undesirable consequences not only for a country's indigenous firms but also for its balance of international payments.

Government concern over high levels of inflation is largely centred around its potentially adverse effects on the business community. If a country's inflation rate is persistently ahead of that of its major competitors, domestic firms will increasingly be priced out of home and overseas markets, with a resultant loss of orders, revenue and jobs, as well as a deterioration in the country's balance of payments. Added to this, the uncertainty created by a difficult trading environment makes firms reluctant to enter into long-term commitments, especially when these involve investment in fixed assets such as plant and equipment. While under the circumstances such a response may be understandable, failure to invest or reinvest can be ultimately damaging for the individual firm as well as the economy, and may inhibit attempts not only to control inflation but also to exploit any future increase in demand that results from a reduction in the general level of prices.

Maintaining employment   Unemployment is regarded as a social and economic 'evil'. Socially, widespread unemployment has been linked with such things as the increased incidence of crime, domestic strife, alcoholism and drug abuse. Economically, not making full use of a country's labour clearly represents a waste of a valuable economic resource, as well as a potential drain on the public purse. For these reasons alone, governments of all complexions are normally committed to the maintenance of a high level of employment in the economy.

Recent pronouncements suggest that few, if any, democratically elected governments now believe that full employment is attainable. Rather, the emphasis appears to have shifted towards job creation and maintenance and an acceptance that a certain level of unemployment is inevitable in technologically advanced market-based economies. A further concern has been to ensure that the correct mixture of skills is available to employers to allow them to respond to the changing demands of consumers both at home and abroad. This stress on the qualitative as well as the quantitative aspect of employment looks likely to remain a dominant theme throughout the last decade of the twentieth century.

The main causes of unemployment tend to be structural, cyclical or technological. Structural unemployment occurs when the demand for the goods produced by a particular industry declines, often because of intense foreign competition. Consequently, workers in the affected industry lose their jobs, and if their skills are very specific they may find it difficult to switch to alternative forms of employment. Much of Western Europe's textile and steel industries have suffered in this way, and the fact that these industries are often highly localized has meant that certain regions within the affected countries have experienced substantial problems of unemployment and economic decline.

Cyclical unemployment is associated with a general deficiency of demand which may signal the onset of an economic recession. As demand in the economy falls—for whatever reason(s)—increasing numbers of people lose their jobs in a wide range of businesses as firms lay off workers because of falling orders. Small firms, in particular, are very vulnerable to such a downward turn in the business cycle, and the number of liquidations and bankruptcies of small enterprises tends to grow appreciably. Even the largest firms, however, are not exempt, and many will be forced to shed labour in order to reduce their costs. The net effect is a general rise in unemployment throughout the economy, which tends to persist until an upturn in spending occurs.

As the name suggests, technological unemployment is the result of the replacement of labour with new technology. As production becomes increasingly automated, and firms seek to increase their efficiency and reduce their unit costs, some workers inevitably lose their jobs, and these are jobs that are unlikely ever to return in their present form. Recent advances in robotics and microtechnology have given renewed impetus to arguments that have been going on for centuries about the human consequences of new technologies. Moreover, as experiences in service industries such as banking and insurance indicate, the impact of technological advance is not merely confined to primary and secondary sectors but affects all areas of the economy.

The business implications of rising unemployment can vary quite considerably. On the one hand, the general deficiency of demand which gives rise to cyclical unemployment would be bad for business prospects and would affect a wide range of firms across all sectors—though not firms of liquidators and debt collectors! Equally, with structural unemployment, firms in the industry or industries experiencing a reduction in demand may be forced to slim down their activities or even close down their operations. On the other hand, investment in new technology—which may give rise to a degree of technological unemployment—would normally be regarded as a beneficial development and can help to create new products, and possibly new demand and new jobs, as well as new production methods.

Firms may also benefit from unemployment in another way. Apart from creating a pool of labour which would—if necessary—be available for recruitment, substantial levels of unemployment tend to take the pressure off wages, with workers and/or their representative organizations and associations in a weakened bargaining position in pay negotiations. Management is able to claim that wage moderation is vital if the company is to remain competitive and if further job loss is to be avoided or reduced. At least in the short term, this trade-off of jobs for moderate wage rises is likely to appeal to a majority of workers, especially in periods when inflation is under control.

HOLY LOCH CLOSURE CAUSES WIDESPREAD RIPPLES

The year 1991 was the thirtieth anniversary of the opening of the US submarine base at Holy Loch in the west of Scotland. It was also the year in which it was announced that the base was to close, bringing to an end a relationship that had evolved substantially over time. Local hostility to its establishment—bolstered by the Campaign for Nuclear Disarmament's opposition to the deployment of nuclear weapons in Britain—had, with time, given way to public acceptance of its value as an important source of income and indirect employment in the lower Clyde area. News of the speed of the closure was greeted with shock and dismay, as local politicians and public alike learned of the loss of by far the most important economic activity in the lower peninsula.

In practical terms, the base consists almost entirely of the huge repair ship the USS *Simon Lake* and the attached floating dry dock, Los Alaros. Most US Navy personnel live on the float's base, while others have married quarters ashore across the Clyde. The direct and indirect benefits of the facility to the local economy have long been recognized and provide a good example of how income expenditure and employment are interrelated.

Directly, the base employs only 150 local people, but the 2,300 US military and civilian personnel and their 2,000 dependants provide the main source of income for the town of Dunoon and the surrounding area with a population of about 17,000. According to a study by the Highlands and Islands Development Board (1990), the base generated the equivalent of 3,100 jobs, nearly 60 per cent of jobs in the Cowal Peninsula. Prime beneficiaries of the £56 million a year which it is estimated that its base contributes to the local economy are hotels, bars, shops, ferries and taxi firms.

While the potential effect of the base's closure could not be compared to a major industrial closure (e.g. a car plant or steel works), there is no doubt that the loss of income to the local economy from the high-earning US servicemen will have a significant effect on the livelihoods of some local businesses. Taxi firms, for instance, rely almost entirely on the base for their income, and it is expected that some operators will go out of business when the closure occurs.

It is, of course, too early to assess whether the revenue from the area's other industry—tourism—will compensate for the loss of income when the Americans leave. Perhaps fortunately for the west of Scotland economy as a whole, there are still Royal Navy bases at Faslane on Gare Loch and Coulport on Loch Long, which have large shore establishments. Both of these bases have large construction projects underway in preparation for the arrival of the Trident submarines which are to replace the present Poseidon vessels.

The pursuit of growth Growth is a goal shared by businesses and governments alike. Whereas firms grow in the ways described in Chapter 3, broadly speaking, economic growth occurs when there is an increase in the rate of 'real' change of a country's GDP or gross domestic product (where gross = total, domestic = within the economy and product = output of goods and services). Such output changes are generally regarded as a yardstick of a country's economic performance and as a good indicator of the living standards of its citizens. In crude terms, a rise in real output (and, therefore, income) per head of the population implies that individuals are better off. Whether this is true in reality, of course, depends not only on how the additional income is distributed, but also on one's definition of living standards.

As the circular flow of income model indicates, output is related to consumption (i.e. demand), and consequently questions of total output changes are linked to changes in aggregate demand. Since total spending in the economy is a function of spending by consumers, firms, governments and overseas buyers, changes in any one or any combination of these can help to generate growth. Given that, in most market economies, consumer spending tends to account for the lion's share of total expenditure, annual increases in the rate of growth of GDP are often largely related to actual or potential increases in private consumption. Changes in government spending or investment or in exports are, however, important contributors to growth; indeed, most governments would welcome the latter two, particularly the generation of growth that is export-led.

In principle, it would appear that a growing economy is likely to benefit domestic firms, given that they will have a share of the income generated from any additional expenditure. Nor should it be forgotten that changes in expenditure may have arisen partly as a result of the activities of producers who have been able to stimulate demand through the production and marketing of new and improved products (see Livesey, 1987, Ch. 1). However, it may also be the case that part of the increase in consumption is satisfied by extra spending on imported goods and services, which would disadvantage indigenous producers, and in some cases might even lead to their demise. In Britain, for example, which is typical of an economy whose citizens enjoy a fairly high standard of living, spending on services and household durables in recent years has tended to rise more rapidly in real terms than spending on necessities such as food, fuel and light. Much of this additional expenditure has been directed towards imports of items such as clothing, footwear and electrical goods. The result has been the continuing decline of these once prosperous industries, with the concomitant loss of jobs and output and share of world markets.

A favourable balance of payments Few, if any, countries are self-sufficient: most rely on international trade and for some such trade is vital. As the next chapter demonstrates, this trade involves movements of goods, services and capital and—as a consequence of this—movements of funds between countries. A country that exports a good or service (or imports capital funds) receives a payment which appears as a credit on its international payments account. Conversely, a country that imports a good or service (or exports capital funds) has to make a payment, and this appears as a debit (see Chapter 7). A country's balance of payments is, in effect, a net balance of credits and debits arising from its international trade over a given period of time.

Countries are said to have a balance of payments surplus if, during the accounting period, their credits exceed their debits; if the opposite is the case, they have a balance of payments deficit. Needless to say, given a choice, a government will prefer the former to the latter, but since it is impossible for all countries simultaneously to have surpluses, most governments accept that deficits are sometimes inevitable and, on occasions, may even be desirable in the short term. As a government objective, therefore, the notion of a favourable balance of payments can range from being in surplus to managing to reduce a large deficit, particularly if the latter represents the start of a general trend towards an improved trading performance.

From a business point of view, balance of payments surpluses tend to imply favourable trading conditions, with the value of exports exceeding the value of imports and the economy benefiting from the creation of jobs, additional economic growth and a general feeling of business confidence. Moreover, since any surpluses can be used to finance overseas lending and investment, these can help to generate higher levels of corporate foreign earnings in future years. Not all businesses, however, will benefit equally from a successful export performance, and the aggregate figures for a country's balance of payments can easily mask serious structural problems in particular parts of the domestic economy. Added to this, it should not be forgotten that the interests of creditor and debtor nations are intrinsically linked: countries that run large and persistent current account surpluses—because of the success of their exporters—can damage the economies of the deficit countries, and ultimately this can also disadvantage firms in the surplus countries, who may find their markets drying up and/or large-scale non-payment of debt from previous trade.

6.3.2 Economic indicators

Governments and firms share the desire to achieve their objectives; they also share the need to monitor their performances. Whereas businesses normally use balance sheets, profit and loss accounts and financial ratios as a means of assessing their achievements, governments use a range of economic indicators to help them to gauge how the economy has performed and to predict its likely course in the future. Some of the major indicators used are discussed briefly below. As will become evident, these indicators are useful not only for government but also for businesses when deciding future policies and plans, including those associated with the marketing of goods and services.

Inflation rates Inflation tends to be measured using a cost of living index which indicates relative changes in a country's overall price level over time. As mentioned previously, in Britain this involves the construction of a retail price index based on information collected about the prices of goods and services consumed by an average household and weighted according to their importance in spending terms. Since it measures the change in prices of practically all the items that people buy, it is generally seen as a good guide to the changing purchasing power of the 'money in their pockets'. Accordingly, it also tends to be used as a means of establishing annual levels of pay increase, with workers generally seeking to achieve settlements at least equal to, if not higher than, the current rate of inflation.

In recent years, increased emphasis has been placed on establishing a clearer view of inflationary trends and their causes. In Britain, for example, this has involved:

- Monitoring figures for the money supply—because of the supposed link between inflation and the amount of money in circulation
- Identifying the level of wage inflation—seen as critical in determining future price rises

- Differentiating between the 'headline' rate of inflation and the 'underlying' rate of inflation—with the latter seen as a better guide to future trends
- Comparing Britain's annual inflation rate with those of its major trading partners, especially the USA, Japan and the European Community (EC)—because of its implications for international competitiveness

Armed with such information, it is felt that governments are in a better position to take corrective action to try to reduce the level of inflation, and to persuade workers of the possible effects of inflationary wage settlements. Businesses, too, can benefit if the rate of inflation can be fully anticipated (e.g. by taking future price changes into account when deciding on contracts, or by establishing the levels of future pay rises). In practice, however, predicting the rate of inflation is not always possible, and this creates uncertainty and reduces business confidence. None the less, there is no doubt that, faced with a choice between possibly inaccurate figures and no figures at all, governments and businesses will always prefer the former, since both parties see inflation as a key economic indicator and as an important determinant of future prosperity.

Interest rates Interest rates represent the price of borrowing money from banks and other lenders. High domestic rates of interest are seen as disadvantageous in at least four main ways:

1. They deter borrowing by firms for investment purposes.
2. They increase business costs, where previous borrowing has occurred, and this may cause firms to put up their prices and risk losing customers.
3. They depress demand, by deterring consumer borrowing and by reducing the level of a person's discretionary purchasing power (through the 'mortgage effect').
4. They reduce business confidence, particularly if rates remain or look likely to remain high.

Governments tend to prefer relatively low rates of interest from both a domestic and an international comparative point of view. High comparative rates of interest, however, do attract funds into a country from overseas investors, which can help a country's balance of payments and strengthen its exchange rate. While this might help to reduce inflationary pressures (by reducing import prices), it also has the effect of making exports less competitive (by increasing export prices), which can counteract the benefit of any capital inflow into the balance of payments.

STORE CHAIN HIT BY THE RECESSION

The impact of the recession in Britain in the early 1990s was marked by rising unemployment, falling output and investment, a slump in the property market and a difficult trading environment for firms of all sizes and in all sectors of the economy. Even industrial giants such as Imperial Chemical Industries (ICI) witnessed a collapse in profits; others were less fortunate. Habitat, for example, announced the closure of almost a quarter of its outlets with the loss of about 400 jobs, while many other businesses—particularly small and medium-sized enterprises—ceased trading altogether. Even aggressive price-cutting by retailers in the January 1991 sales failed to entice consumers back into the shops: data from the Central Statistical Office indicated that the volume of goods sold by shops and stores in January was 1.4 per cent down on December.

The impact of the government's policy of high interest rates to combat inflation is well illustrated by the plight of Lewis's store group, an institution in the High Streets of northern Britain. Founded in Liverpool in 1856 by Mr David Lewis, the company later established stores in a large number of towns and cities throughout the North and Midlands, including Glasgow, Manchester, Birmingham, Leicester, Leeds, Preston and Blackpool. All the stores—with their distinctive interwar architectural style—were an integral part of their local economies and were leading advertisers in the local press.

Even a change of ownership, first by Sears in the 1960s and subsequently by a management buy-in in 1988, seemed to have had little effect on the company's fortunes. At the time of the buy-in, Lewis's had sales of around £150 million a year and was making just less than £4 million in pre-tax profits. The subsequent sale and lease-back of a number of its properties in an arrangement with Capitals and Counties, the property company, appeared to secure its financial future by allowing it to clear the costs of the buy-in.

Outward appearances seemed to suggest that the company was in a relatively safe position. In late 1990, a new store was opened in the vast shopping centre in Thurrock in Essex. At the end of January 1991, the chairman of Lewis's claimed that he was confident about the future and forecast that profits would exceed £5 million by the end of the financial year. Within days, however, the receivers had been called in by the National Westminster Bank, after the group's wages bill took the company above its overdraft limit. Unfortunately for Lewis's, high interest rates had affected the position in two major ways. Corporate debt charges from the 'bought deal'— which had been underwritten and financed by Midland Montague—were running at about £3.5 million a year. Simultaneously, the recessionary squeeze on consumer spending resulting from the government's anti-inflationary policy had caused revenue to decline substantially. In the circumstances, the National Westminster Bank felt the need to protect its own interests and that of other creditors by calling in the receivers. The expectation was that the various stores could be sold as going concerns, thus protecting the jobs of most of the employees.

Unemployment rates   As with inflation and interest rates, governments normally monitor changes in unemployment levels both domestically and internationally. Rising levels of domestic unemployment can suggest the onset of a recession, with gloomy prospects for business activity and sales. Falling unemployment may signal the beginning of an economic recovery, with favourable consequences for producers. When viewed against the unemployment levels of its major competitors, a country's own rate of unemployment may suggest that its relative position is either declining or improving, and this may reflect the underlying strength or weakness of its economy. Comparisons of this type have to be treated with care, since definitions of variables such as unemployment may differ from country to country and, indeed, may vary over time. In the 1980s, for instance, official definitions of unemployment in Britain changed around 20 times in 10 years.

Growth rates   Measurements of growth continue to underline the preoccupation that governments tend to have with their international, as well as their domestic, position. Comparative growth figures tend to be treated as a kind of virility symbol, with countries hoping to demonstrate that their annual growth rate exceeds that of their major international competitors. The assumption is that a faster growing economy is desirable and may signal comparatively higher per capita increases in gross national product (GNP)—i.e. estimated income per head of the population—thus helping to push a country further up the league table of international living standards. Yet, as with unemployment statistics, such comparisons can be misleading, not least because they do not reveal anything about the way in which income is distributed; nor do they consider the social costs associated with increased growth (e.g. congestion, pollution).

Apart from calculations of annual growth rates, governments like to monitor output changes on a very regular basis. In Britain, monthly and quarterly surveys by the Confederation of British Industry (CBI) on industry's output, investment and stock levels provide the government with a generally good indication of short-term changes in the economy, as well as a guide to possible future business trends. It is generally accepted that stable, rather than fluctuating, rates of growth are preferable, although businesses can normally cope with the latter by adjusting their stock levels. But in an economy that swings frequently from periods of slow or falling business activity to bursts of strong growth, it becomes very difficult for businesses to operate efficiently, and the uncertainty created about the future can act as a disincentive to investment.

Trade figures The balance of payments—discussed in detail in the next chapter—is seen as a symbol of a country's international competitiveness, with attention normally being focused on the 'current account', which concerns transactions in goods and services but not capital. A current account surplus or a falling deficit tends to be seen in a positive light, particularly if exports are rising at a faster rate than imports, suggesting that domestic firms may be gaining an increased share of world markets and/or competing more effectively at home.

As with other indicators, governments like to monitor performance on a monthly and quarterly, as well as annual, basis and frequently make adjustments to the statistics to take account of what are termed 'seasonal factors'. Disaggregation of the trade figures by sector and location can provide an important insight into which sectors of the economy are the most successful in trade terms and which overseas markets are the most lucrative.

Exchange rates Because international transactions occur and different countries use different currencies, it is necessary to have exchange rates which determine the value of one currency against others. As an economic indicator, a country's exchange rates—also discussed in the next chapter—tend to be regarded as a symbol of the willingness of overseas traders and investors to hold the country's currency. Falling rates of exchange against other key currencies may be interpreted as a loss of faith in the performance of the economy or the government and may put a currency under severe pressure in the foreign exchange markets. Conversely, rising exchange rates may reflect growing overseas confidence in the economy and/or government or in its future prospects. Either way, changes in exchange rates have important applications for businesses and for the economy, as indicated below, particularly because of the uncertainty they create. In this context, fixed exchange rate systems—typified by the Exchange Rate Mechanism (ERM) of the European Monetary System (EMS)—help to remove one element of the uncertainty that occurs when trading takes place across national frontiers.

6.3.3 Macroeconomic policies

In the market economies of Western Europe, the USA, Japan and elsewhere, governments generally prefer patterns of production and consumption to be determined largely by the decisions of private individuals (consumers) and firms. At the same time, given their desire to achieve certain objectives—in the belief that these are beneficial for the economy—governments often decide to intervene in the working of the market system when economic indicators appear unfavourable. As the analysis above demonstrates, decisions by governments in areas such as taxation and borrowing have important implications for the level of income and, therefore, for output, expenditure and employment in the economy. In effect, governments are able to influence the general level of economic activity, and in doing so will affect the decisions of individuals and therefore of business organizations responding to consumer needs and wants.

The ability of a government to influence the level and pattern of economic activity—both directly and indirectly—stems from the various roles it plays in the economic system. Table 6.1 identifies key areas of government involvement in business activity, with some examples.

Table 6.1 Government roles in a market economy

Key government roles in the economy	*Some examples*
1. Major user of resources	Employer; landowner; owner of capital assets
2. Major supplier of resources	Provider of technology; information; energy; land
3. Major consumer of goods and services	Purchases of public goods and services, i.e. government related goods and services
4. Major producer of goods and services	State-owned industries and services
5. Regulator and controller	Legislation e.g. consumer laws and employment laws
6. Redistributor of income and wealth	Taxation policies
7. Regulator of the economy	Macroeconomic policies

Naturally, the precise nature of government influence will vary over time and according to the prevailing political and economic conditions, with some governments seeking to play a more active and direct role in the economy, and others tending towards a more enabling and facilitating role in an attempt to improve the working of the market system. Recent experience in Britain, for instance, indicates a preference for the latter of these two approaches, and this has been exemplified by the large-scale programme of privatization and deregulation that occurred throughout the 1980s.

As far as attempts to regulate the overall level of economic activity are concerned, it is a government's macroeconomic (or demand management) policies that are of central importance, and it is vital for businesses to monitor government policies designed to influence the flow of income and expenditure, and take account of policy changes when planning their activities. Here, two distinct policy approaches are discernible:

1. Fiscal policy—which involves changes in government income and/or expenditure
2. Monetary policy—which involves changes in either the supply of money or the price of money (i.e. interest rates)

Both of these approaches have been used by Western governments in the postwar period, with varying degrees of success.

The fiscal approach to demand management uses changes in taxation and/or government expenditure to regulate total spending in the economy. Increases in government expenditure inject additional income into the circular flow and—via the multiplier effect—increase the demand for goods and services. Reductions in government spending have the opposite effect. Alternatively, demand can be stimulated by reducing taxation on income or spending (e.g. VAT), which increases the ability of consumers to purchase more products. If the government wishes to depress demand, then increases in taxation would have the desired effect.

In contrast, the monetary approach, currently in favour in Britain, uses changes in monetary conditions to influence aggregate demand. Measures that encourage and facilitate an increase in the money supply (e.g. removing or relaxing controls on credit) encourage higher spending, since borrowers (especially individuals and firms) find it easier and cheaper to obtain additional funds to finance extra expenditure. Conversely, if government is seeking to control the money supply through the control of credit, borrowing becomes harder and more expensive and this tends to reduce overall demand. Interest rate changes are designed to influence the demand for, rather than the supply of, money. An increase in interest rates depresses demand by making borrowing more expensive for both consumers and businesses; a reduction in interest rates normally has the opposite effect by encouraging higher levels of consumption and investment spending.

From the point of view of a government seeking to achieve certain desirable objectives—such as a reduction in inflation or unemployment—macroeconomic policies appear logical; but unfortunately, their implementation often brings unwanted consequences for both businesses and governments. Attempts by the British government in 1990 to reduce inflationary pressures through high interest rates helped to bring on a recession, signified by falling demand, rising unemployment, reduced levels of investment and growth and increases in the number of corporate bankruptcies and liquidations. In contrast, the decision by the former Chancellor of the Exchequer, Nigel Lawson, to cut taxes in the 1988 Budget helped to boost demand, but in doing so was said to be responsible for rising inflation and a rapidly growing deficit on the

VAT INCREASE THREATENS RETAILERS

Since its introduction in the late 1980s, the community charge (or 'poll tax') proved controversial. Consequently, following the change of prime minister in 1991, the Government, under the leadership of John Major, decided to abandon the tax and to replace it with a new form of local authority rates, and to shift some of the burden of local authority finance on to central government. To help pay for these changes, Chancellor of the Exchequer Norman Lamont announced in the March 1991 Budget that value added tax (VAT) was to rise from 15 to 17.5 per cent.

Any increase in the tax on spending clearly has implications for businesses, and while the new tax changes were welcomed by the leading business lobby groups, representatives of the retail sector claimed that the rise in VAT could force more firms 'to go to the wall'. Despite a potential and immediate boom in retail sales as shops announced 'Beat the Budget' offers, many retailers felt that the tax increase would hamper their recovery from the effects of the recession. High interest rates, coupled with the diverting effects of the Gulf War and the privatization of the electricity industry, had resulted in a squeeze on retail spending which had even affected companies like Marks and Spencer. Just at a time when the sector was confident of some kind of recovery, the additional 2½ per cent tax was announced.

While at the time of writing it is too early to predict what effect the increased tax will have on business as a whole, it is clear that retailers of goods that carry VAT can expect a difficult trading environment. Sales of non-food items such as furniture, clothing, electrical goods and fashion are expected to decline, as is the market for restaurant meals. Retailers of products that are exempt from VAT—including most food, books and newspapers—may be less affected and could conceivably increase their sales.

One thing is certain, however: in the coming weeks (and possibly months), the High Streets are likely to be full of 'sales' signs as retailers fight to attract new customers.

current account of the balance of payments, as consumers bought record amounts of imports with their extra disposable income.

A synopsis of the possible consequences of using fiscal or monetary policies to achieve particular objectives is contained in Table 6.2. The contention is not that these will *inevitably* result from the adoption of a specific policy, but that past experience suggests that they are a *likely* consequence, if only in the short term. This being the case, it is evident that an understanding of the rationale and effects of policy decisions could be of substantial benefit to business organizations when planning their activities on both the production and marketing side.

Table 6.2 Government objectives and policies

Desired objective	Chosen policy	Possible short-term consequence of chosen policy
1. To reduce or control inflation	(a) Increase taxation rates	Reduction in demand, leading to lower growth and rising unemployment; higher wage demands; possible deferred investment; reduction in rate of growth of imports
	(b) Reduce government spending	Lower growth and rising unemployment; less government investment; deteriorating public services; reduction of government borrowing
	(c) Tighter credit	Lower growth and rising unemployment; difficulties for corporate borrowers; higher interest rates
	(d) Higher interest rates	Lower growth and rising unemployment; depressed housing and related markets; deferral of investment; attraction of overseas capital and strengthening of the exchange rate which makes exporting harder
2. To reduce unemployment	(a) Reduce taxation rates	Increased demand, leading to increased jobs and output and possibly higher inflation; increased government borrowing
	(b) Increase government spending	More jobs; increased output; higher inflation; increased government borrowing; improved services; increased government debt
	(c) Easier credit	Increased demand, jobs, output, inflation and imports; inflationary housing market
	(d) Reduce interest rates	As (c); also more investment by firms
3. To improve the balance of payments	See 1(a)–(d)	
4. To stimulate economic growth	See 2(a)–(d)	

6.4 THE STRUCTURE OF THE ECONOMY

As the circular flow model has demonstrated, variations in income, expenditure, output and employment in the economy are all interrelated. It is appropriate, therefore, to conclude this analysis of the macroeconomic environment with an investigation of how changes in demand have helped to cause damages in the pattern of supply. To do this, it is necessary to examine the structure of the economy and, in particular, to consider how patterns of output and employment have changed over time.

The concept of 'structure' relates to the economy's constituent elements—often called 'sectors'—and their interrelationship. These sectors may be broadly or narrowly drawn according to requirements. At the broadest level, an economy can be divided into two sectors—the public (or government) sector and the private sector—and comparisons made of their relative size and contribution. Perhaps a more useful approach, however, is to examine changes in the fortunes of particular industries or groups of industries, since these give a much clearer view of how the economy is developing and which sectors are apparently growing or declining in response to changing market conditions. It is this latter approach that is adopted below.

A useful starting point is to divide the economy into three major sectors: primary, secondary and tertiary. The primary sector comprises all those activities directly related to the acquisition of natural resources and include those industries that produce raw materials (e.g. mining, mineral extraction, forestry, oil) and food (e.g. agriculture, fishing). The secondary sector is responsible for all other goods produced and includes the manufacturing industries, construction, water, gas and electricity. The tertiary sector comprises the service industries and covers both private sector services (e.g. banking, insurance, distribution) and public sector services (e.g. health care, education). In order to examine changes in the relative size of the three sectors, it is necessary to consider either their output (including their relative contribution to GDP) or the amount of inputs they use and, more specifically, the number of people employed in each sector.

Table 6.3 contains index numbers of UK industry output at constant factor cost for selected years in the period 1969–86. The data for 1969, 1973 and 1979 represents output at the peak of successive trade cycles and thus allow like to be compared with like; 1981 represents output during a recession and thus provides a view of how output changes during a downswing in the economy.

The figures indicate that, with the exception of coal and coke production, output in the primary sector grew over the whole of the period, with agriculture, forestry and fishing growing by about 4 per cent per annum between 1979 and 1986, despite the recession in the early 1980s. More significantly, output of mineral oil and gas grew remarkably between 1973 and 1979 and continued to grow in the early 1980s, owing to the continuing and widespread exploitation of North Sea oil as energy prices rose rapidly in the 1970s.

Output in the secondary sector during this period varies considerably. Between 1969 and 1973 all parts of the sector were growing; between 1973 and 1979, output in manufacturing, construction and mineral oil processing fell and continued to fall sharply between 1979 and 1981. Despite a recovery after 1981, output in manufacturing and construction in 1986 was still below the level achieved before the recession. Only the energy and water industries can claim an improved position by the mid-1980s, and even they experienced a fall in output betwen 1979 and 1981.

In the tertiary sector, the picture is largely one of output growth. With the exception of transport and distribution, where output fell between 1979 and 1981, and public administration, where output fell between 1981 and 1986, all sub-sectors experienced increases in output over the whole period, with banking, finance, insurance, business services, leasing and communications being particularly prominent. Given that the secondary sector is a major consumer of the output

Table 6.3 Index of output at constant factor cost* (1980 = 100)

	1969	1973	1979	1981	1986
Primary					
Agriculture, forestry and fishing	73.5	87.4	90.1	102.6	118.8
Coal and coke	148.8	114	97.6	97.3	79.3
Extraction of mineral oil and natural gas	0.3	2.2	98.7	110.3	153.0
Secondary					
Mineral oil processing	99.9	126.9	113.7	93.0	99.0
Manufacturing	103.0	114.1	109.5	94.0	104.7
Construction	117.6	122.4	105.8	89.9	102.1
Other energy and water supply	68.9	87.1	102.2	99.6	112.2
Tertiary					
Distribution, hotels, catering, repairs	92.2	107	107.9	98.4	120.4
Transport	84.8	100.8	103.6	99.0	108.7
Communication	65.5	81.8	97.2	102.2	130.8
Banking, finance, insurance, business services and leasing	66	81	95	104	154
Ownership of dwellings	80	87	99	101	107
Public administration, national defence and compulsory social security	90	99	99	101	99
Education and health services	72	82	99	101	105
Other services	76	82	95	98	120

*Market price valuations of output are distorted by taxes and subsidies. With factor costs these distortions are removed. Constant factor cost involves eliminating the effect of inflation so that the time series shows changes in 'real' output.

Source: CSO (adapted from A. Griffiths and S. Wall, 1991). Reproduced with the permission of the Controller of HMSO.

of the tertiary sector, it seems likely that levels of growth in the service industries during the period would have been higher had manufacturing and construction not suffered the decline highlighted above. Nevertheless, with annual growth rates of 2–3 per cent per annum for the sector as a whole, the service sector shows a pattern of steady growth, which stands in direct contrast to the experience of UK manufacturing industry.

These differences in growth experience between the various sectors explain why changes have occurred in the share of total output attributable to each. As Table 6.4 demonstrates, by 1986 the tertiary sector accounted for almost two-thirds of the economy's total output and its share had grown gradually over the whole period, with financial and business services expanding significantly. Some growth also occurred in the primary sector, almost entirely because of North Sea oil and gas production, but, at 5–6 per cent of total output, the sector was still the smallest. The secondary sector's share of output fell progressively after 1969 and by 1986 accounted for less than one-third of the economy's total output. As the figures indicate, much of this decline was due to the loss of output share by manufacturing industry, with its contribution to the country's GDP being a little over one-fifth by the mid-1980s (Griffiths and Wall, 1991, Ch. 1).[2]

These structural changes are further illustrated by changes in the levels of employment in the various sectors over the same period (Table 6.5). Employment in the primary sector fell from 3.6 per cent of total employment in 1969 to 2.5 per cent in 1986, largely as a result of the decline of the coal industry and fewer jobs in agriculture. Secondary-sector employment also declined,

Table 6.4 Percentage of GDP at factor cost

	1969	1973	1979	1986
Primary	4.3	4.2	6.7	5.3
Agriculture, forestry and fishing	1.8	2.9	2.2	1.7
Coal and coke	2.5	1.1	1.3	1.0
Extraction of mineral oil and natural gas	—	—	3.2	2.6
Secondary	42.0	40.9	36.7	32.2
Mineral oil processing	0.5	0.4	0.6	0.7
Manufacturing	30.7	30.0	27.3	23.0
Construction	8.4	7.3	6.2	5.8
Other energy and water supply	2.4	2.8	2.6	2.7
Tertiary	53.0	54.9	56.5	62.3
Distribution, hotels, catering, repairs	13.3	13.1	12.7	13.3
Transport	4.4	4.7	4.8	4.3
Communication	1.9	2.3	2.5	2.6
Banking, finance, insurance, business services and leasing	8.6	10.7	11.0	15.0
Ownership of dwellings	5.5	5.1	5.8	5.5
Public administration, national defence and compulsory social security	7.0	6.1	6.1	6.9
Education and health services	7.1	7.7	8.1	8.6
Other services	5.2	5.1	5.7	6.1

Source: CSO (adapted from A. Griffiths and S. Wall, 1991). Reproduced with the permission of the Controller of HMSO.

Table 6.5 Percentage share of total employment by sector

	1969	1973	1979	1981	1986
Primary sector	3.6	3.4	3.0	3.0	2.5
Secondary sector	46.8	42.4	38.5	35.4	30.4
(Manufacturing)	(38.6)	(34.7)	(31.3)	(28.4)	(24.3)
Tertiary	49.3	54.4	58.5	61.4	67.1

Source: CSO, National Income and Expenditure. Reproduced with the permission of the Controller of HMSO.

falling from 47 per cent in 1969 to only 30 per cent in 1986, with manufacturing suffering the largest number of job losses. As employment fell in both these sectors, the tertiary sector's share of employment consequently grew from 49 to 67 per cent, mirroring changing employment patterns in many other advanced industrial economies. Evidence for the late 1980s suggests that, despite a slight increase in manufacturing jobs in 1988, the decline in this sub-sector which has been evident for a generation is likely to continue into the foreseeable future.

An even more detailed account of structural changes can be obtained by examining patterns of output and employment in specific industries and their component parts. In Britain such an analysis is facilitated by the use of the Standard Industrial Classification (SIC) system introduced in 1980. Under this system, industries are divided into ten 'divisions' (e.g. division 4 is Other Manufacturing Industries), and these are then further subdivided into 'classes' (e.g. class 41 is Food, Drink and Tobacco) and into 'groups' (e.g. group 419 is Bread, Biscuits and Flour Confectionery). Analysis of the data produced by the Central Statistical Office (CSO) using this system of disaggregation thus provides a good indication of changes that are taking place in different industries and their sub-sectors over time.

Table 6.6 GDP: output-based at constant factor cost (1985 = 100)

	1979	1981	1983	1986	1988
Consumer goods industries					
Cars, etc.	121.1	95.4	98.7	97.8	116.3
Other durables	111.6	89.3	92.0	104.2	121.6
Clothing and footwear, etc.	107.6	89.0	91.6	100.2	98.9
Food, drink and tobacco	100.0	97.5	99.7	100.9	105.4
Other	100.7	90.3	92.5	103.0	119.0
Total	104.4	93.0	95.3	101.6	112.0
Investment goods industries					
Electrical	73.3	70.1	82.6	98.5	117.5
Transport	117.7	103.3	99.1	101.4	110.6
Other	115.9	96.2	93.5	97.8	107.6
Total	103.5	90.3	91.8	99.0	115.5
Intermediate goods industries					
Fuels	80.5	86.0	96.8	105.1	99.4
Materials	108.9	89.3	93.8	101.8	117.3
Total	93.9	87.7	95.4	103.5	107.8

Source: Annual Abstract of Statistics. Reproduced with the permission of HMSO.

Other official data include figures for the output of different types of industry and show the impact of cyclical fluctuations in demand. In Table 6.6, the effects of the recession in Britain in the early 1980s are manifestly evident, as is the recovery in the later part of the decade. However, as the figures clearly indicate, not all industries even in each group had similar experiences. Output in the clothing and footwear industry, for instance, declined in 1988 because of foreign competition, while other consumer goods industries witnessed an increase in output as demand in the economy grew. Moreover, the table usefully illustrates the link between changes in the demand for industrial goods and for consumer goods, with growth in the latter helping to generate increases in the demand for the former, in keeping with the accelerator principle discussed above.

In seeking an explanation for these structural developments, considerable emphasis has been given to demand and, by implication, to how increases in income which lead to increases in demand will in turn cause changes in the level and pattern of supply. It is widely recognized that as income levels rise the demand for products with high and positive income elasticities (e.g. services such as entertainment and recreation) will also rise, while the demand for other products may either fall or rise less quickly (e.g. products with low or negative income elasticities), thus causing differential rates of output growth and possibly employment. But demand on its own cannot explain all the changes identified above. Changes on the supply side, including the impact of technological developments—which permit new or improved products to be offered to the market—will also influence output, as will changes in the availability or cost or productivity of resources used to produce goods and services. Moreover, as the textile and footwear industries clearly illustrate, the effects of international competition can also be critical in determining the future prospects of an industry and its component firms. Businesses that are unable to supply products in either the right quantity or of the right quality and/or price may find consumers switching to competitive products from abroad. Over time, large-scale changes in consumer allegiance will be ultimately reflected not only in the balance of payments figures, but also in the data for output and employment of the different sectors in the domestic economy.

REVIEW QUESTIONS

1. The pursuit of growth has social costs as well as social benefits. What marketing opportunities are associated with the 'cost' of growth?
2. What are the likely consequences of a reduction in personal taxation? Will business always benefit?
3. What factors could account for the changing fortunes of the food, drink and tobacco industry in the UK?

NOTES

1 For a fuller discussion see e.g. Donaldson (1984), Ch. 3.
2 See especially the discussion of 'de-industrialization', which is linked to the declining manufacturing base.

REFERENCES

Artis, M. J. (ed.) (1989), *Prest and Coppock's the UK economy: A Manual of Applied Economics*, 12th edn, Weidenfeld and Nicolson, London.
Donaldson, P. (1984), *Economics of the Real World*, 3rd edn, Penguin Books, Harmondsworth, Middx.
Fuller, N. (1985), *Basic Concepts in Macroeconomics*, Checkmate/Arnold, London.
Griffiths, A. and Wall, S. (eds) (1991), *Applied Economics: An Introductory Course*, 4th edn, Longman, London.
Livesey, F. (1987), *Economics for Business Decisions*, London, Pitman.

SEVEN
THE INTERNATIONAL MARKETING ENVIRONMENT

7.1 INTRODUCTION

International trade has always been of importance to British businesses, but it could be argued that they must increasingly consider their business environment in international rather than purely domestic or national terms. The growing ease of movement for goods, people and information, the changing nature of the international political environment and the ever greater scale required of many business activities have all contributed towards this effect.

The international environment can affect business organizations to varying degrees and in various ways.

For domestic manufacturers, overseas markets represent an opportunity to export. The nature of the opportunity varies through time and with different destinations. The importance of export markets varies from firm to firm—some goods, such as cosmetics, are quite easily traded, whereas others, such as building materials, are more difficult. Increasingly, the producers of services are recognizing opportunities for export.

However, overseas countries represent not only an opportunity for domestic manufacturers, but also a threat. The same factors that have facilitated exports can also act to help imports, often of goods and services that were previously considered to be immune from overseas competition—such as personal banking and the water supply.

At a macroeconomic level, the amount of international prosperity can affect all business organizations, whether or not they engage in overseas trade themselves. A slowdown in the world economy can adversely affect companies supplying exporters, or the workers of companies involved in export, which in turn will affect other enterprises by lowering consumer demand. A deteriorating position of the British economy in the world can cause the government to take action—such as increasing taxes or interest rates—which affect all businesses.

Finally, all firms can be affected by the actions of international bodies. The EC is one body that is having a stronger effect on British companies; this is described more fully in Chapter 8. In addition, the government is signatory to treaties of diverse international bodies such as the International Monetary Fund and the Organization for Economic Co-operation and Development which can affect the state of the British economy.

7.2 THE BASIS FOR INTERNATIONAL TRADE

Success in international trade can help to explain the emergence and growth of many of the countries that have achieved economic pre-eminence in the world during both modern and ancient history. The Venetians, the Spaniards and later the British all saw periods of rapid domestic growth coinciding with the growth of their trade with the rest of the world.

Today, the UK, like most industrialized countries, is dependent on international trade if it is to maintain its present level of economic wealth. Some products to which we have become accustomed would be impossible to produce at home—for example bauxite, none of which is found within the country, and tropical fruits, which cannot be grown naturally in Britain. For products that fall into these categories, three possible courses of action are open:

1. Substitute products that can be produced domestically, such as steel instead of aluminium
2. Try and produce the product at home: in the case of bauxite extraction this is impossible, but with regard to tropical fruits, domestic production can be achieved, but often only at a high cost
3. Import the good from a country that is able to produce it

A similar analysis can be carried out on any other country—their imports will be another country's exports.

The nature of the products that a country such as Britain imports will depend on a number of factors. Developments in technology have seen new products such as petrochemicals assuming relatively greater significance at the expense of more traditional items such as cotton. The increasing wealth of consumers has also affected the nature of the products they buy; for example, British consumers can increasingly afford to buy exotic fruit and vegetables in place of cheaper domestically produced food.

While changing technology and tastes can explain some of the change in international trade patterns, a more fundamental explanation is found by looking at the relative ease with which a country can make a product, as compared with other countries. The idea that a country should concentrate on producing what it is good at and exporting the surplus can be traced back to Adam Smith in the late eighteenth century.

7.2.1 Comparative cost advantage: an example

For simplicity, it is assumed here that there are only two countries in the world—Britain and 'rest of world'—and that only two goods are produced—food and timber. Table 7.1 shows the hypothetical production possibilities of the two countries. It can be seen that, if Britain used all of its natural resources to produce timber, then it could produce 40 tons per year, but no food. It could, on the other hand, use all of its resources to grow 40 tons of food per year, but would produce no timber. Similarly, the rest of the world could produce 160 tons of food a year or 40 tons of timber.

The different ratios reflect the fact that Britain and the rest of the world possess different

Table 7.1 Theoretical production possibilities

	Food (tons)	or	Timber (tons)
Britain	40	or	40
Rest of world	160	or	40
World production total	200	or	80

combinations of resources. The maximum possible world output of food is 200 tons and of timber, 80 tons. However, neither country is likely to produce solely timber or solely food. For Britain to give up 1 ton of timber production will result in an increase of food production of 1 ton; however, if the rest of the world gives up 1 ton of timber production, it can increase food production by 4 tons. In this example, Britain should continue to produce timber, because the comparative cost of giving up land for food is lower for it than for the rest of the world. For Britain, the cost of 1 ton of food is 1 ton of timber; for the rest of the world, the cost of 1 ton of timber is 4 tons of food forgone. The rest of the world has an absolute advantage in the production of food (it is capable of producing more than Britain) and it also has a comparative cost advantage (because the opportunity cost of the land used is lower).

To illustrate how the production of timber and food may be divided between Britain and the rest of the world, and the pattern of trade that could take place, it will be assumed here that there are only these two countries in the world, that these are the only two goods traded, and that production equals consumption. It is assumed that timber is more valuable than food and that 1 ton of timber is worth 5 tons of food.

Table 7.2 illustrates a situation where both countries divide their resources equally between food and timber production, without engaging in trade, and contrasts this with a situation where each country specializes in the product for which it has a comparative cost advantage. It can be seen—on the terms of trade that have been assumed—that the world would be better off if Britain concentrated on producing timber and the rest of the world concentrated on producing food. Total production in this example (and, by assumption, total consumption) has increased from 300 to 360 units. This pattern would hold so long as the relative costs of production and the terms of trade remained the same. The latter could alter; where, for example, consumers valued timber products less highly than previously, timber would become a less favoured product and would be worth less in terms of food.

This has been a very simple example to illustrate how international trade can benefit all nations. In reality, substitutions take place between large numbers of countries and an almost infinite range of products. Nevertheless, the underlying principles of exporting what a country is good at producing and importing a product that can be made more cheaply elsewhere still hold true. Thus, Britain is good at producing financial services, which are sold abroad in large volume; it is not so good at producing labour-intensive textiles, which are imported in large amounts from the relatively low-wage countries of the Far East.

Table 7.2 Theoretical benefits from trade

	Original production pattern—no trade		Revised production pattern—specialization	
	Food	Timber	Food	Timber
Britain	20	20	0	40
Rest of world	80	20	160	0
World production total	100	40	160	40
Value @ 1 ton of food = 1 unit, 1 ton of timber = 5 units	100	200	160	200
Total wealth	300		360	

7.2.2 Limitations to the principle of comparative cost advantage

The previous example sought to show that the world as a whole would achieve a higher level of wealth if countries engaged in trade. In practice, the global ideas described above can become obscured by narrower national interests.

In the first place, imports can be seen as a threat to established domestic productive capacity and jobs in an industry. Short-term political pressure may restrict the ability of firms and individuals to buy in the cheapest world market, in order to protect the established industry. The Multi-Fibre Agreement which Britain signed with a number of low-cost textile manufacturing countries has had the effect of restricting the import of clothing into Britain; this has been brought about largely by the political desirability of avoiding large-scale unemployment in a number of concentrated textile areas of the country. Sometimes import controls are imposed to protect a new industry or to give an existing industry a period in which to restructure itself; the restriction on Japanese car imports into Britain was intended to give the domestic car industry an opportunity to invest in new production methods with the guarantee of a protected domestic market.

Second, strategic considerations may lead a country to restrict imports. Most Western countries have sought to preserve their own capacity to produce armaments. The British government could probably buy many of its specialized army supplies more cheaply from large, efficient overseas suppliers, especially from the USA, but it has chosen to keep relatively small production units at home. Similarly, the government has pursued a policy of self-sufficiency in food, partly for strategic reasons.

Third, governments seek to pursue a balanced portfolio of activities within their economies. Diversification away from the product in which the country has a comparative cost advantage may be sought in order to provide alternative production capacity in a new product to replace the current output when it eventually goes into decline. This may mean imposing import restrictions so that goods can be produced (more expensively) at home. Also, governments may protect industries in order to create greater employment opportunities for particular social or regional groups of the population.

Fourth, trade may not take place in some products—or may be made more difficult—because the requirements of different markets vary. National regulations on matters such as food purity and electrical safety may make it uneconomic to produce special versions of a product for an overseas market.

Transport costs act as another deterrent to international trade—producers of bulky products in areas of the world remote from alternative sources of supply will gain an added protection.

Also, national governments may artificially stimulate exports by giving export subsidies, allowing them to compete in world markets against more efficient producers. The European Community has frequently subsidized the export of agricultural products such as grain and meat to protect European farmers from competition from more efficient and less highly subsidized American and Australian farmers.

Finally, international politics may severely limit the trade that a country has with the rest of the world. Until recently, the division of Europe into western and eastern trading blocs reduced the potential for exploiting the comparative cost advantages of each.

A restriction on imports by one country can quickly bring about retaliation by its trading partners, resulting in progressively declining world trade levels. The precise methods by which trade is restricted include the following:

1. A tariff can be imposed on goods of a specified type. The British government has imposed tariffs on imports where it believed the product was being 'dumped' by the exporting country

at below its production cost. This happened during the late 1980s in the case of computer printers and colour televisions from Japan.
2. A quota on the volume of imports of a particular product can be imposed—imports of cars from Japan have been restricted on this basis.
3. Governments sometimes resort to a series of 'spurious controls' in order to try and justify their action and avoid retaliation. Faced with the political need to pacify domestic farmers, the British government has in the past sought to restrict milk imports on supposed health grounds. Sometimes governments can try to restrict imports by making the procedures for import very difficult. During the 1980s, the French government was accused of seeking to restrict the import of Japanese video recorders by insisting that they should be taken to the relatively small inland town of Poitiers for processing.

THE SUN SETS ON JAPANESE EXPORTS

Faced with the increasing import penetration, governments tend to come under pressure from indigenous producers to limit imports. Protectionist measures take a variety of forms, including tariffs, quotas and a range of administrative techniques, all of which are designed to reduce the flow of imports by increasing their price and/or reducing their availability. One such measure is the voluntary export restraint (VER), which became a popular form of protectionism in the 1980s, aimed largely at the Japanese, whose highly successive export efforts caused a considerable amount of antagonism in the USA and Western Europe.

In essence, VERs involve an agreement by the exporter to limit 'voluntarily' the amount (or value) of a product that is exported to a particular market. Such an agreement has covered the export of Japanese cars to America and parts of Western Europe for a number of years. Like all protectionist agreements, a VER is designed to help domestic producers (including saving jobs) by increasing the prices of imports that compete with their products. This is achieved by rationing the supply of imports. One benefit of this is that it allows domestic producers to increase their prices and profits, thus helping to pay for an investment programme that can help to restore their competitiveness (see *The Economist*, 6 February 1988, p. 73).

VERs, however, do not prevent exporters from taking steps to overcome the restraints they have voluntarily accepted. For much of the 1980s, for example, Japanese car makers responded to export restraints in the American market in a number of ways. First, they moved 'upmarket', by switching exports away from their smaller, more compact models towards their luxury 'gas-guzzlers', on which profits tended to be higher. Second, they invested more in productive capacity in the USA, setting up assembly plants to produce in the home market. Third, they accumulated large amounts of revenue by maintaining wide profit margins in the early years of VERs, when demand remained high and prices were increased because of the effort of the import quotas.

The second of these responses—also applied to the European market (see pp. 144)—has been the cause of a certain amount of controversy within the EC. Having established an assembly plant in Washington in the north-east of England. Nissan has moved progressively from producing vehicles from 'completely knocked down' (CKD) kits imported from Japan to assembling cars with a high proportion of local content. The essence of the company's argument is that, with such a high local content, vehicles produced in Britain are 'European' and thus are not subject to any quota agreements with member-states of the EC.

This issue was brought to a head in 1988, when Nissan began to export Bluebirds to mainland Europe from Britain. The company had previously undertaken, in negotiations with the European Commission and the UK government, to achieve a target of 80 per cent local content by 1991. The target set for 1988—when exports to the Continent were due to start—was 60 per cent local content. The French and Italian governments refused to accept that cars produced in Washington were 'European' since they had not achieved the 80 per cent level. Consequently, in their view they could not be included in the Japanaese quota arrangements. The UK government argued that Nissan had complied with their previous undertakings and produced evidence to show that the local content had reached a level of 65 per cent. The Commission agreed, and in April 1989 pronounced that the Bluebird was a 'European' vehicle, thus opening the way for the Japanese to circumvent its quota agreements.

The General Agreement on Tariffs and Trade (see Section 7.4.3) has achieved some success in freeing world trade of the barriers described above, leaving only a few specified areas in which signatories can legitimately impose import restrictions—for example, to protect infant industries and to prevent dumping of goods at below cost.

7.3 INTERNATIONAL DIRECT INVESTMENT

As an alternative to exporting goods to an overseas market, a company can instead invest in capacity to produce the goods locally. Overseas investment takes place for a number of reasons.

In the first place, a company could locate a factory where production costs are lower than at existing facilities. Ford, General Motors and Volkswagen have all invested in factories in Spain, where wage rates are significantly lower than in most other European countries. In addition to minimizing wage costs, firms could invest overseas to gain a comparative cost advantage in energy costs, or to minimize the cost of meeting pollution controls. The goods produced in such factories are frequently not consumed wholly by the local market, but enter international trade, often being exported to the investing company's domestic market.

Second, overseas investment can give access to a local market where transport costs make cheap movement of goods to that market and a rapid response to a changing market difficult. Many overseas brewers have set up breweries in Britain (or have licensed other companies to brew their beer) in order to be closer to their market.

Third, import controls may make production in an overseas market the only way of entering that market. Current import quotas imposed by the British government, and the prospect of European-wide controls by 1992, help to explain the investment of the Japanese companies Nissan, Honda and Toyota in Britain. Although many components in these factories are originally sourced from Japan, the domestically produced content tends to increase over time.

Governments frequently provide incentives for companies seeking to invest in their country. In Britain, assistance is often given to foreign investors to stimulate regional development. The Nissan and other projects have received grants and tax allowances for this purpose. In addition to the regional benefits of these investments, the British economy will further benefit by reducing the trade deficit in cars. The inflow of capital from overseas also has the effect of strengthening the value of the pound sterling.

On the other hand, opportunities for investment in overseas capacity may be constrained by a number of factors. Overseas control of a particular firm in an industry may not be allowed. This is especially true in strategic industries such as aircraft manufacture and operation; for example, investment by an overseas company in Rolls-Royce or a British scheduled airline is prohibited by the government beyond a 15 or 25 per cent holding respectively. Where investment is allowed, restrictions may be imposed on the investor's freedom to manage its business; for example, it may be required to buy all supplies locally, and there may be restrictions on the level of profits that can be repatriated to shareholders.

7.4 INTERNATIONAL INSTITUTIONS AND TRADE AGREEMENTS

Arguably the most important international institution—and one that impinges on the activities of most British companies—is the European Community. Legislation passed by the European Council of Ministers is assuming increasing importance for British marketers. Because of the importance of the European Community to Britain, the subject is discussed more fully in Chapter 8. In this section, a number of other important international institutions and agreements are described.

7.4.1 International Monetary Fund (IMF)

The IMF was established following the Bretton Woods conference in 1944 with the aims of achieving freer convertibility of currencies, improved international liquidity and a reduction in the economic nationalism that had characterized the interwar years. Each of the 141 members of the IMF is required to contribute a quota of gold and currency to a fund which can be used to provide borrowing facilities for countries facing short-term liquidity problems. The price that borrowing countries have to pay for IMF support is acceptance of the IMF's proposals for restructuring the country's economy where the problem is considered to be more than short-term. The British economy was significantly affected in 1976, when, in return for its assistance, the IMF insisted on a package of economic measures to be implemented by the British government, including a sharp reduction in government expenditure and a cut in the money supply. More recently, loans have been given to a number of Latin American countries on condition that structural reforms are implemented.

7.4.2 Organisation for Economic Co-operation and Development (OECD)

The OECD was originally set up in 1947 to administer the USA's Marshall Aid programme in Europe, but subsequently it turned increasing attention to the developing world. The OECD now has 21 members which include most of the European countries, the USA, Canada and Japan. It works by trying to co-ordinate the economic policies of members, by co-ordinating programmes of economic aid and by providing specialized services, especially information.

7.4.3 General Agreement on Tariffs and Trade (GATT)

Like the IMF and OECD, the origins of GATT lie in the early postwar period. The signatories to the agreement sought to achieve greater international economic prosperity by exploiting fully the comparative cost advantages of nations by reducing the barriers that inhibited international trade. All the signatories agreed not to raise tariffs on imported goods beyond their existing levels and to work towards the abolition of quotas which restricted the volume of imports.

  GATT has proceeded to reduce tariffs and quotas through several rounds, the most recent of which—the Uruguay round—has sought to reduce barriers to international trade in services. It has also tried to redress the distortion to world trade and the unfair competitive advantage given to subsidized exporters of agricultural products.

7.4.4 Other international agreements and institutions

A wide range of other agreements and institutions affect business organizations in Britain. Some of these will be very general in nature and will affect a wide range of enterprises; an example is the agreement to set up a European Bank for Reconstruction and Development, aimed at helping the restructuring of the emerging East European economies. Improved access to loans may help a wide range of exporters of capital equipment. Another example is where business in general—especially multinational companies—can be affected by bilateral agreements between countries on the treatment of profit taxes.

There are also very many agreements and institutions covering specific industries. An example of an institution that has a direct effect on an industry is the International Civil Aviation Authority (ICAO), to which most countries belong and which has agreed international safety standards for civil aviation. In other cases, agreements between countries can have an indirect effect on a market, as with the international agreement signed in 1990 to restrict international trade in ivory.

7.5 THE MEASUREMENT OF INTERNATIONAL TRADE

International transactions take place in goods, services and capital. As stated previously, when a country's citizens, firms and government export goods or services, income flows into that country, as it does when overseas investors decide to invest their capital in the country's assets. When any of these three groups imports goods and services or invests capital abroad, an outflow of funds occurs. A record of all these transactions in goods, services and capital between one country and those it trades with over a given period of time is referred to as a country's 'balance of payments'.

The basic structure of the UK balance of payments is shown in Figure 7.1 in simplified form.

1. *Current Account*
    (a) Visible exports
    (b) Visible imports

    Trade balance ((a) + (b))

    (c) Invisible exports
    (d) Invisible imports

    Invisible balance ((c) + (d))

    Current balance ((a) + (b) + (c) + (d))
    ---

2. *Capital Account*
    (e) Capital inflows
    (f) Capital outflows

    Net capital flow ((e) + (f))

    Balance of payments ((a) + (b) + (c) + (d) + (e) + (f))
    ---

3. *Official Financing Account*

Figure 7.1   The UK balance of payments structure

The current account records the values of goods and services traded. Goods, or visible items, include manufactured products, materials and fuels, and the differences between the value of exported goods and that of imported goods is known as the 'trade balance' or 'balance of trade'. Invisibles comprise services such as tourism, insurance, banking and shipping, together with government services (e.g. maintenance of overseas armed forces, foreign aid, etc.), specified private transfers, and interest, profit and dividends from previous capital transactions. Taken together, the trade balance and the invisible balance constitute the 'balance of payments on current account' or the 'current balance'.

The capital account comprises both outward and inward flows of capital for investment purposes, including short-term movements of capital (often known as 'hot money'), together with medium- and long-term investments of both a direct and portfolio kind (e.g. plant, premises, equipment, shares). When the net capital flow is added to the current balance, the result is the overall 'balance of payments'.

In practice, the UK balance of payments will be either in surplus (i.e. total currency inflows exceed total currency outflows) or in deficit (i.e. outflows exceed inflows). For accounting purposes, however, the account always balances, with the necessary adjustment being made in the 'Official Financing' reserves or the repayment of previous loans. Inevitably, given the volume and scope of international transactions, some errors and omissions are bound to occur in the official accounts. To compensate for these and to ensure that the account balances overall, a balancing item is normally added. In some cases this will be negative, in others positive.

Table 7.3 indicates the performance of the current account of the UK balance of payments for selected years over the period 1976–88.

Table 7.3 UK balance of payments current account

	Visible trade					Invisibles		
Year	Exports (f.o.b.)	Imports (f.o.b.)	Visible balance	Services	Transfers	Interests, profits, and dividends	Total invisible balance	Current balance
1976	25,082	29,041	− 3,959	2,244	− 786	1,560	3,018	− 941
1979	40,470	43,868	− 3,398	3,907	− 2,210	1,205	2,902	− 496
1981	50,668	47,318	3,350	3,923	− 1,547	1,210	3,586	6,936
1984	70,263	74,843	− 4,580	3,942	− 1,717	4,432	6,657	2,077
1986	72,656	81,365	− 8,700	5,631	− 2,136	5,356	8,851	151
1988	80,157	100,714	− 20,557	3,473	− 3,582	6,001	5,892	− 14,665

Source: Annual Abstract of Statistics, Monthly Digest of Statistics. Reproduced with the permission of the Controller of HMSO.

The trade statistics highlight a number of important aspects of UK external trade in recent years.

1. While the value of visible imports and exports tends to rise each year, import spending is generally rising faster than export revenues.

2. There has been a marked deterioration in the visible account since the early 1980s, as spending on imports has grown much faster than exports.
3. The invisible balance is always positive, with services and interest profits and dividends making major contributions to invisible earnings.
4. A substantial current account surplus in the early 1980s had become a very large deficit by the closing years of the decade.

In seeking an explanation for the variable performance of the visible account, it is useful to distinguish between oil and non-oil items (see e.g. Cook, 1991). An examination of the trade statistics shows that by the beginning of the 1980s the UK had a positive balance on its oil account, as the benefits of North Sea oil (i.e. reduced imports and increased exports) began to accrue. When taken together with a fairly neutral non-oil balance, during this period—as the country was entering a recession—the balance of payments on the current account was in surplus and remained so for a number of years.

Despite a substantial surplus on the oil account by the mid-1980s, the rapid growth of a non-oil deficit—largely as a result of imports of manufactured goods—led to a rising deficit on the visible account as a whole. For a while this deficit was offset by an increasing surplus on the invisible account; hence the slight overall surplus on the current account in 1986. However, the huge increase in visible imports during the economic boom of 1988, coupled with a slight decline in invisible earnings, meant that by 1988 the country had gone into deficit on the current account to the tune of £14.7 billion.

7.6 UK EXTERNAL TRADE

7.6.1 Trade patterns

Each country has its own characteristic patterns of trade, in terms of both the items it imports and exports and the countries it trades with. Over time these patterns will tend to vary in response to changes in economic, political, technological, demographic and socio-cultural conditions. At the macro level, such changes will be reflected in a country's balance of payments, which not only shows the aggregate effect of trading decisions but also helps to provide an insight into a country's relative competitiveness. To gain a clearer view of the nature of the international market-place, however, it is necessary to disaggregate the trade figures in order to monitor the changing fortunes of the different industrial sectors and to identify a country's major international competitors. To this end, this section examines UK trade from both a spatial and a commodity point of view and includes a discussion of the relevance of the findings from a marketing perspective.

An examination of the figures in Table 7.4 indicates a number of important developments in the area composition of UK trade:

- The vast majority of the UK's trade in goods is with the developed economies, having risen from about 60 per cent in 1955 to over 80 per cent by 1989.
- There has been a distinct shift towards trade with Western Europe in general, and the European Community in particular. Trade with the EC now accounts for over half of the UK's total merchandise trade.
- North America still remains an important market for traders, with the USA being the major trading partner. Significantly, while the percentage share of exports has risen slightly over the period, the share of imports from North America has tended to fall, largely because of a decline in trade with Canada.

Table 7.4 Area composition of UK visible trade (%)

	1955		1969		1980		1989	
	X	M	X	M	X	M	X	M
Western Europe	29	26	40	38	58	56	59	65
(of which: EC)	(15)	(13)	(29)	(26)	(43)	(41)	(51)	(53)
North America	12	20	17	20	11	15	15	13
(of which: USA)	(7)	(11)	(12)	(14)	(10)	(12)	(13)	(11)
Other developed countries	21	14	12	10	6	7	6	8
(of which: Japan)	(0.5)	(0.5)	(2)	(1)	(1)	(3)	(2)	(6)
Total developed economies	62	59	69	68	75	78	81	86
Oil-exporting countries	5	9	5	8	10	9	6	2
Other developing economies	31	29	23	20	12	11	10	10
Centrally planned economies	2	3	3	4	3	2	2	2

Note: Exports (*X*) are measured free on board (f.o.b.); imports (*M*) include cost of insurance and freight (c.i.f.). All figures are rounded.
Source: Annual Abstract of Statistics, Monthly Digest of Statistics. Reproduced with the permission of the Controller of HMSO.

- The share of trade with 'other developed economies' has also fallen significantly, particularly on the export side. Trade with Japan, however, has grown, with the import share having risen tenfold over the period.
- The share of import trade with the oil-exporting countries (OPEC) fell substantially following the exploitation of North Sea oil reserves.
- Trade with the 'other developing countries' (particularly Commonwealth countries and Latin America) has fallen very rapidly and now accounts for only one-tenth of total trade in goods, having at one time been the UK's largest single trading partner.

Table 7.5 UK visible trade by commodity groups (%)

	1955		1969		1980		1989	
	X	M	X	M	X	M	X	M
Food, beverages and tobacco	6	36	6	23	7	12	7	10
Basic materials	4	29	4	15	3	8	3	5
Mineral fuels and lubricants	5	10	2	11	14	14	6	5
Manufactured goods	82	24	85	50	74	63	82	79
(of which: semi-manufactures)	(39)	(19)	(35)	(28)	(30)	(27)	(29)	(27)
(and finished manufactures)	(43)	(5)	(50)	(22)	(44)	(36)	(53)	(52)
Miscellaneous items	3	1	3	1	3	3	2	1

Note: Exports (*X*) are f.o.b.; imports (*M*) are c.i.f. Figures are rounded.
Source: Annual Abstract of Statistics, Monthly Digest of Statistics. Reproduced with the permission of the Controller of HMSO.

Analysis of the commodity composition of UK visible trade shows equally significant changes and trends (Table 7.5). On the export side, the UK trade in manufactured goods remains by far the largest component, with finished manufactured goods (especially vehicles, machinery and office equipment) constituting half of total visible exports. Exports of oil also became significant by the late 1970s, but the percentage share has declined recently. On the import side, a substantial decline in the share of food, beverages and tobacco, together with basic materials, has occurred, despite an increase in the volume of imports of these items. In contrast, growth in the volume of imports of manufactured goods has easily outstripped the increase in total imports, and consequently imported manufactured items now account for the majority share of visible imports. Indeed, between 1955 and 1989 imports of finished manufactured items grew by a factor of ten.

7.6.2   Trade in manufactures

An analysis of UK trade patterns indicates that over the last 30–40 years the geographical focus of the country's trade has shifted away from the Commonwealth and increasingly towards the industrialized nations of Europe, and especially the European Community countries. At the same time, there is growing evidence that the UK has been overtaken in the vitally important sector of manufacturing, to the point where it is now a net importer of manufactured goods. To consider this development and its causes, it is necessary to examine the manufacturing sector in a little more detail.

Figure 7.2 shows how the UK's share of world exports of manufactures was halved in the

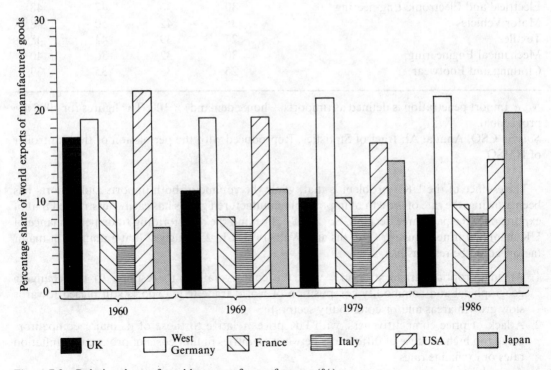

Figure 7.2   Relative share of world export of manufactures (%)
Source: based upon UN statistics, *National Institute Economic Review* (1970, 1985).

period 1960–86, a performance not matched by any of its main competitors. Over the same period, Japan's share almost tripled, while that of Germany, Italy and France tended to remain relatively constant.

At the same time, UK manufacturing industry has faced intense competition from imported goods, as seen in the Table 7.6, which examines the ratio of imports of manufactured items relative to total home demand over the period 1977–88. For manufacturing industry as a whole, import penetration rose from 25 per cent in 1977 to 35 per cent in 1988, with some of the country's key industries experiencing major problems from foreign imports. Large parts of the textile, clothing and footwear industries, for instance, have suffered a considerable decline as a result of overseas competition, with many firms going out of business in the last ten years. The picture is much the same for major export industries such as vehicles, electrical and mechanical engineering and chemicals, although in the case of vehicles the decision by a number of major Japanese multinational car manufacturers to establish facilities in the UK shows signs of reversing the trend.

Table 7.6 UK import penetration in manufactured goods (%) for selected industries

	Imports/home demand			
	1977	*1981*	*1985*	*1988*
All Manufacturing Industries	25	28	34	35
Chemicals and Man-Made Fibres	27	31	41	42
Electrical and Electronic Engineering	30	36	47	48
Motor Vehicles	35	42	50	48
Textiles	27	39	44	48
Mechanical Engineering	30	32	36	40
Clothing and Footwear	25	33	35	39

Note: Import penetration is defined as (imports ÷ home demand) × 100. The figures for 1988 are provisional.
Source: CSO, Annual Abstract of Statistics. Reproduced with the permission of the Controller of HMSO.

The essence of the UK's problem is that, while the volume of both imports and exports has been growing, the rate of growth of imports of manufactured goods has easily outstripped that of exports over the past three decades. So, what lies behind the deteriorating trade performance of UK manufacturing industry? Griffiths and Wall (1991, Ch. 23), suggest that a number of major factors could be responsible:

1. An inappropriate trade structure, with the country failing to respond to the changing geographical and commodity composition of world trade (e.g. exports still biased towards slow growth areas and/or commodity sectors)
2. A lack of price competitiveness, with UK prices relative to those of its major competitors being too high because of differences between countries in unit costs of production, inflation rates or exchange rates
3. An inability to compete in terms of non-price factors, such as marketing, design, delivery dates and product development

In discussing these factors in detail, Griffiths and Wall came to the conclusion that the main problem for the UK is its inability to compete *within* geographical areas and *within* particular commodity groupings, reflecting a decline in the country's international competitiveness. Part of the problem the authors attribute to price, and they suggest that this is particularly important on the export side, where an improvement in UK price competitiveness, *vis-à-vis* other countries, could help to increase the volume of UK exports. Similar emphasis is given to non-price factors as a determinant of UK competitiveness, and the following 'problem areas' are identified:

- Significantly higher levels of income elasticity of demand for imported manufactured goods in the UK than elsewhere, so that increases in income (and therefore demand) in the world economy will tend to cause UK imports to grow faster than exports, especially for manufactured goods
- Failure on the part of UK firms to increase capacity to meet increased demand in both the home and overseas markets, and a tendency for firms to neglect export markets where domestic demand is high
- Deficiencies in product characteristics (e.g. design, quality) and in sales characteristics (e.g. marketing, after-sales service, delivery dates)
- The tendency to export cheaper, lower-quality products, embodying 'old' technology, and to import expensive, high-quality products, embodying 'new' technology
- Insufficient resources committed to research and development and design
- Inadequate marketing and sales effort

A certain amount of evidence exists to support these propositions. Reporting on Britain's deteriorating trade position in October 1985, Michael Prowse of the *Financial Times* referred to a recent Employment Institute report by two Oxford University researchers in which they examined the country's poor manufacturing performance. The researchers argued that traditional claims of poor price competitiveness, shortages of capital and a lack of demand had not been important factors. Rather, it was poor quality that was the root cause of recurrent trade deficits and insufficient jobs. Among the reasons given for industry failing to meet the demands of consumers, the report identified three key problems: the country's failure to innovate; shortcomings in the system of education and training; and a cultural antagonism to working in the manufacturing industry. Compared with its main competitors, the UK generally spent less on R & D, had fewer managers with a business education, employed shopfloor workers with less technical expertise, and had a graduate workforce largely unwilling to take jobs in productive industries or in occupations such as engineering.

7.6.3 Trade in invisible earnings

As the balance of payments figures show, the UK has traditionally been a net exporter of invisible items, with earnings from the activities of the City of London a major contributor to the current account, along with interest, profits and dividends from overseas investments. Combined with the benefits of North Sea oil, these invisible earnings have helped to offset the growing deficit in manufactures referred to above. In 1988, for example, the UK had a physical trade deficit of over £20 billion, but after allowing for invisible earnings of £6 billion the current account deficit was reduced to £14 billion. As the *Financial Times* commented on 12 October 1989 (p. 12), the story of Britain's invisible trade in the 1980s has largely been one of success, being one area of trade where, until recently, it was possible to see steady growth.

Three separate developments appear to have caused the invisible account to weaken in recent years. First, the surplus on financial and other services has been reduced since the stock market crash of 1987, this sector having previously felt the benefits of the large-scale deregulation of the financial system at the start of the decade. Second, a large deficit on tourism has opened up as increasing numbers of Britons are holidaying abroad. Third, the cost of attracting 'hot money' into London to finance the current account deficit has affected the surplus on interest, profits and dividends that had been growing in the wake of the abolition of exchange controls in 1979. While it is too soon to say whether these developments are likely to be permanent, some commentators are worried that the UK appears to be taking an ever-declining share of a shrinking pool of invisibles. Of equal concern is the use of high interest rates to reduce domestic demand (including the demand for imports). As indicated above, such a policy may help to attract funds into Britain to finance the deficit in visibles, and this will show up in the balance of payments account as a capital item. The servicing of this investment, however, is a current item and with increasing overseas deposits in UK institutions, the interest cost is substantial.

7.6.4   The single market: 1992

As a concluding comment on UK trade patterns, we must refer to the proposed creation of a 'single market' within the European Community in 1993, since this will have direct consequences for many business organizations, as well as indirect effects on others. Under the single-market proposals, member-states of the EC have agreed to take steps to create a single internal market in which goods, services, people and resources move freely as a result of the removal of obstacles to open competition.

The idea, in effect, is to create one market within the Community which is comparable to that within the USA or Japan. To achieve this objective, the governments of member-states have agreed to a wide-ranging programme of changes, including:

- The removal or reduction of physical barriers to trade (e.g. reduced import/export documentation)
- The technical harmonization of products
- The liberalization of capital movements
- The removal of discriminatory public purchasing policies
- A closer approximation of fiscal and monetary policies
- The mutual recognition of national standards for certain products

The creation of a genuine 'common market' of over 300 million people is expected to have a number of important benefits for both producers and consumers, including:

- The reduction of travel times and, therefore, transport costs within the Community
  Reduced delays, by simplifying documentation, quicker processing at frontier posts, etc.
- Economies of scale, by agreeing Euro-standards for products, thereby making huge production runs possible
- Greater competition and wider consumer choice
- Possible price reductions (e.g. by reduced excise duties)

The Cecchini Report, for instance, predicts that, over a five-year period, EC output as a whole will rise by 7 per cent, prices will fall by up to 6 per cent, and employment will increase by 1.8 million as a result of the single-market initiatives (Cecchini *et al.*, 1988). Not all sectors, however, are likely to benefit equally. According to the *Lloyds Bank Economic Bulletin* in January 1989, the probable 'gainers' in the UK are likely to include pharmaceuticals, the food and drink industry, insurance and airlines. Many of these are industries in which the UK appears to have a comparative cost advantage and/or where technical barriers are often high. The disappearance of such barriers is thus likely to benefit these industrial sectors and will provide an incentive for firms to take advantage of their relative strength by expanding into Europe, in some cases through acquisition or merger.

An insight into the response of UK businesses to the advent of the single market is provided by the results of a survey conducted by the British Market Research Bureau for the Department of Trade and Industry (DTI) in 1990 (see *Single Market News*, 1990). Ninety-six per cent of firms interviewed confirmed that they had heard of plans for the single European market, with some 43 per cent claiming that they had already taken action to prepare for 1992 and a further 13 per cent indicating that they intended to do so. Perhaps not surprisingly, action or intended action appeared closely related to the geographical extent of trade and the size of business, with the largest firms and those with an international market significantly more proactive than smaller businesses and those that operated on a local scale. However, 23 per cent of firms felt that the single market would have little, if any, effect on their activities, and consequently they felt no need to make any special preparations. Yet even for the smallest businesses with highly localized markets, it is likely that the changes that are to be introduced will affect them both directly and indirectly; in the first case through new regulations and increased competition, and in the second through the effects of these on both their customers and their suppliers.

Table 7.7 indicates the range of measures already taken or planned by UK businesses preparing for 1992. These range from gathering information and considering the implications of the single market, to taking steps to defend the home market, expanding an existing overseas market or entering into joint ventures. Some companies, such as J. C. Bamfords (JCB), manufac-

Table 7.7 Action for 1992

	Action taken (%)	Action planned (%)
Researching, reviewing situation	66	23
Monitoring progress	64	24
Considering implications	59	21
Developing aspects of business	59	21
Meeting new standards, checking standards	59	20
Reviewing competition, taking steps to defend home market	54	21
Looking for business in Europe, exporting more	41	23
Input or communication with trade association	43	12
Diversifying	34	20
Consulting DTI/UK government	39	18
Alternatives to the European market	38	10
Training, updating staff	23	22
Joint ventures	21	22
Forming a division to develop existing business with Europe	18	12
Lobbying	14	7
Seeking acquisition of a European company	11	10
Visiting Brussels, or discussion with 'Brussels'	9	5

Source: adapted from *Single Market News* (DTI), Winter 1990.

turers of earth-moving equipment, and Laura Ashley, have set up special committees to undertake a review of how the organization will be affected by the single market, and to consider what competition they will face and what is the most appropriate form of reaction. JCB's response, for example, is to set up sales-only subsidiaries overseas, rather than manufacturing facilities, thus relying on local people who will concentrate exclusively on selling its products full time in the market. In contrast, PAL International Ltd, one of Europe's leading manufacturers and suppliers of hygiene and barrier-protection clothing, intends to establish a network of regional offices and distributors based in Europe, backed up by directly accessible linguistic sales staff at head office in England, in order to meet customer needs. In addition, the company has launched a range of products tailored for individual markets (e.g. different styles of chefs' hats for France and Germany) and is producing sales literature in a number of key European languages.

Similar responses are occurring in companies all across Europe. Volkswagen has centred the production of its SEAT models in Spain, where unit labour costs are currently lower than in most other parts of the community and has established a group purchasing process which will give it considerable economies of scale. The French multinational food group, BSN, has been involved in a number of transnational acquisitions in an effort to build up its brand names and strengthen its position as a European brand leader. Japanese companies, too, have not been slow to recognize the significance of the move towards a single European market: as mentioned above, multinationals such as Nissan have established manufacturing facilities with Europe in order to take advantage of the huge, tariff-free market that is shortly to come into existence.

As these and many other companies recognize, 1992 provides both an opportunity and a threat, with considerable implications for the marketing of goods and services. Companies failing to respond to this change in their environment will at best tend to be increasingly left behind in the battle for customers; at worst, they will cease to exist.

7.7 EXCHANGE RATES

International trade differs from domestic trade in that different currencies are involved. A British citizen holidaying in France (i.e. importing a holiday) changes pounds sterling into francs, whereas a French citizen holidaying in Britain undertakes the opposite exchange. In other words, currencies are bought and sold just like goods and services. The rate at which one currency exchanges for another in the process of making international transactions is known as the 'exchange rate'. (For a fuller discussion, see Griffiths and Wall, 1991, Ch. 22.)

The foreign exchange market is the money market on which different currencies are traded. Unlike some other markets, this market has no physical existence; instead, it consists of buyers and sellers, many of whom are in the dealing rooms of major banks, and who are in continual contact with each other on a worldwide basis. These dealers trade in currencies on behalf of clients such as governments, companies, banks and even individuals and they may undertake a transaction for completion within a few days (i.e. on the 'spot' market) or for completion at a specified date in the future, such as one, two or three months hence (i.e. on the 'forward' market). In the latter case, buying a currency for future use at a price that is fixed when the transaction takes place (e.g. today) provides a 'hedge' against the risk of a future fluctuation in the exchange rate. For this reason, many of the deals struck in the forward market tend to be on behalf of companies engaged in international trade.

Broadly speaking, the price of one currency against another (i.e. the exchange rate) may be either fixed or floating. A fixed exchange rate system is one in which the countries concerned agree to keep the exchange rates of their currencies within a very narrow band and, where necessary, to take action to maintain the agreed rate of exchange. In contrast, in a floating exchange rate system the price of one currency against another will tend to vary according to market forces and may even change from minute to minute as buying and/or selling of currencies occurs. It is, of course, possible to use both of these systems simultaneously. The UK, for example, as a member of the Exchange Rate Mechanism (ERM) of the European Monetary System (EMS), has a relatively fixed set of exchange rates against the majority of its EC partners. Against other currencies, however, including the dollar and the yen, sterling is allowed to float to different levels according to the whims of market forces—although, if necessary, government intervention in the market may occur to move the rate in either direction (known as 'managed floating').

The operation of the free market in currencies is as described in Chapter 5 and can be demonstrated with a simple example using the dollar value of the pound (Figure 7.3). UK individuals, companies or governments wishing to import US goods or invest in the US or hold US dollars, will sell sterling and purchase dollars, whilst US citizens, companies or governments wishing to do the same in the opposite direction will sell dollars and buy pounds. The net effect of these purchases and sales (i.e. demand and supply) is the formation of an equilibrium price for one currency against the other, shown in the figure as Or. Should market forces change (e.g. if the demand for the pound increases substantially), then the exchange rate will also change, in this case rising to Os. Should the demand for a currency decrease, then the opposite effect would occur.

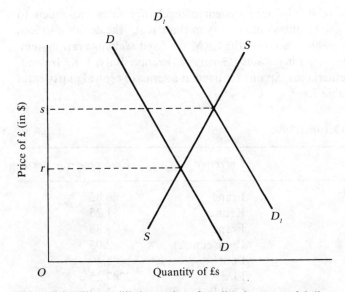

Figure 7.3   The equilibrium price of sterling in terms of dollars

Fluctuations in demand and supply, and therefore in exchange rates, can happen for a variety of reasons, including changes in the volume of trade or investment, interventions by government or movement of funds because of interest rate changes. As far as international trade and payments are concerned, such fluctuations are in theory self-correcting. For example, if the UK went into deficit with the USA because of increased imports, then the pound should depreciate (fall against the dollar), as the supply of sterling increases to buy additional dollars to purchase the imports. With a fall in the value of the pound against the dollar, UK exports to the USA would become cheaper and therefore more should be demanded; simultaneously, US exports to the UK (i.e. UK imports) would become relatively dearer and as a consequence demand for imports should fall. Taken together, these developments should, perhaps after a short time-lag, help to improve the balance of payments between the two countries concerned.

While such a system might appear attractive, from a trader's point of view fluctuations in exchange rates engender considerable uncertainty. Companies selling goods or services abroad may not be certain what revenue they will receive if they invoice in a foreign currency, since a change in the exchange rate—between agreeing the price and receiving payment—can earn them more *or* less than anticipated. Similarly, importers of goods or services (including materials, components, etc.), may be uncertain as to the final price of their purchases because of currency fluctuations, and this makes costing and pricing decisions difficult. Added to this are problems such as the impact of exchange rate changes on inflation and trade. In an open economy like the UK, which imports large amounts of materials, food and manufactured goods, a falling exchange rate tends to create inflationary pressures, since imports become relatively dearer. For a company this may result in the need to increase its prices, particularly if wages are rising in response to an increase in inflation. At the same time, a falling exchange rate not only tends to boost overseas sales by making exports cheaper on foreign markets, but also helps to reduce the competition from imports which have now become relatively more expensive because of the depreciation in the currency. Should the exchange rate move in the opposite direction, the reverse problem tends to occur: inflation tends to moderate, but exporting becomes more difficult.

From a trader's point of view, a relatively fixed system of exchange rates has much to recommend it. Hence the support by the business community in the UK for the decision to join the ERM, which occurred in October 1990. In essence, the ERM is a fixed exchange rate system, under which the currencies of the participating states (Germany, France, Italy, UK, Ireland, Denmark, Belgium, Luxembourg, Netherlands, Spain) are fixed at a series of central parity rates against each other, as indicated in Table 7.8.

Table 7.8 Central parities for the £, October 1990

Country	Currency	Exchange rate per £
Belgium/Luxembourg	Franc	60.85
Denmark	Kroner	11.25
France	Franc	9.89
Germany	Deutschmark	2.95
Ireland	Punt	1.10
Italy	Lira	2207.25
Netherlands	Guilder	3.32
Spain	Peseta	191.75

Source: Gary Cook, *Economics Update*, 1991.

Each member-currency is allowed to fluctuate by a certain percentage (in the UK's case, currently ± 6 per cent) either side of the central parity, and where necessary action is taken by member-governments to stabilize any currency within the system that looks like going out of its band. In some cases this may mean buying or selling currencies, in others altering interest rates

STRONG £ HITS EXPORTERS

Foreign travellers are familiar with the administrative costs involved in changing currencies. An article in the *Guardian* on 5 February 1991 suggested that a person starting with £100 in the UK and changing it into the local currency of every EC country visited would be left with only £28 at the end of the journey, simply as a result of the cost of currency transactions. When account is taken of the fact that exchange rates can also vary substantially, even in the short term, it is plain that anyone involved in currency changes—whether for business or pleasure—faces considerable uncertainty and potential loss of income.

Table 7.9   UK currency-related earnings (% profits)

From export		From N. America		From Europe	
Rolls-Royce	63	Wellcome	57	Unilever	45
British Aerospace	60	BAT Industries	55	GKN	42
British Steel	25	British Airways	52	RMC	42
GEC	22	Maxwell	50	Glaxo	32
ICI	22	Carlton	48	Smithkline Beecham	33

Source: James Capel & Co. Reproduced in the *Guardian*, 23 August 1990.

In an open economy such as Britain, many businesses are dependent on foreign trade, and for some, exporting is responsible for a substantial proportion of their profits, as the table demonstrates. Consequently, given the need for some businesses to engage in regular currency deals, considerable attention tends to be focused on exchange rates which can affect a company's earnings and export performance. As the pound rises against other currencies, British goods cost more abroad, making them relatively less attractive to overseas buyers. At the same time, since imports become relatively cheaper, UK businesses may also face tougher competition at home.

The exchange rate 'problem' is well illustrated by the experiences of Jaguar in 1988, which faced a strong pound in relation to the dollar. For the company—with a large market in the USA—the strength of sterling created a dilemma. Either it could maintain its prices in local currency (i.e. dollar) terms, which meant earning fewer pounds when the dollars were converted back into sterling, or it could raise its dollar prices to reflect the strengthening pound and suffer from falling sales. Either way, as Jaguar found, the strength of sterling had a substantial effect on its export earnings in the US market.

The precise effect of currency fluctuations is, of course, conditioned by a variety of factors. Temporary 'blips' in the exchange rate can be ignored, particularly by large companies who tend to work on long-term contracts whose prices may have been fixed months, if not years, in advance. Moreover, longer-term movements can be mitigated by forcing suppliers to invoice in dollars, for example. Unfortunately, such remedies tend not to be so readily available to smaller companies with less influence in the market-place. As a result, the effects of a strong pound tend to fall more heavily on small exporters than on large international businesses.

either to strengthen or weaken a currency. Alternatively, member-states may agree on a realignment of currencies by making changes in the central parity rates; but this tends to be very much a last resort, given that the main aim of the EMS is for member-states to conduct their economic policies in such a way as to avoid revaluation or devaluation of currencies.

For UK business, membership of the ERM should provide greater exchange rate stability in dealings with customers in the participating member-states, and this should make planning, cost and revenue predictions much easier. It has also been claimed that, as a consequence of membership, the country is likely to benefit at some point in the future from lower rates of interest and inflation, both of which would be of considerable advantage to businesses. Many commentators feel, however, that in the short term the picture is likely to be less rosy, with the UK needing to adjust to the discipline of fixed exchange rates through austere economic policies which squeeze living standards and create higher levels of unemployment. Should this be the case, the short-term prospects for businesses look relatively unfavourable, and some firms, inevitably, are unlikely to survive the experience.

7.8 JAPANESE TELEVISION PRODUCTION: A CASE STUDY

Prior to the mid-1970s, only a handful of Japanese manufacturing plants existed in the UK (YKK Zip fasteners at Runcorn being the first, in 1972). Today, the figure is in excess of 100. There is little doubt that this rapid growth in Japanese industrial investment was one of the most significant developments on the UK industrial scene in the 1980s and looks likely to remain so in the foreseeable future as companies like Honda and Toyota join other Japanese multinationals such as Nissan in establishing manufacturing facilities in the UK.

For the Japanese, the UK is by far their biggest European manufacturing base, accounting for about 35 per cent of the European total. Much of this investment is highly concentrated in the five clear geographical clusters: South Wales, North Wales, West Midlands, North East England and Central Scotland (Dicken, 1990). In addition to this spatial concentration, Japanese companies are highly concentrated in particular industries, with two major sectors—electronics and motor vehicles (including components)—dominating.

In total, Japanese manufacturing plants employ over 25,000 workers, and this number is set to rise substantially over the next few years. While the number directly employed is far fewer than those employed in the US manufacturing plants in the UK, there is little doubt that the Japanese manufacturing presence is of considerable significance to the UK economy, particularly at a time when the number of jobs in the UK manufacturing industry is steadily falling.

Numerous reasons have been suggested for the Japanese 'invasion' of Europe in general and the UK in particular, the single most important one being to gain direct access to the single market without having to face actual or potential trade barriers after 1992. The apparent preference for Britain over other European locations is more difficult to explain, but has been linked to a variety of economic and social factors, including the English language (compulsory in Japanese schools); competitive labour rates; a supply of highly skilled labour as a result of Britain's declining industrial base; good infrastructure; ease of access to mainland Europe; improved labour relations; fairly low corporation tax rates; a familiar legal system; government inducements; the size of the market; the warmth of the welcome. Interestingly enough, within the UK, recent Japanese investment—including the proposed Toyota plant near Derby—has tended to become more 'footloose', moving away from those parts of the country where government financial assistance has traditionally been available under regional policy. On the whole, however, most Japanese manufacturing plants tend to be found in the declining industrial areas of the country—a factor of considerable importance for the local and regional economies of the chosen locations.

Supporters of such large-scale inward investment—including the British government—point to the obvious benefits to the UK economy. Claimed advantages include the number of jobs (both direct and indirect) created; the transfer of technology; the transfer of superior working practices; improved domestic quality; the attraction of further direct investment from abroad and the benefits to UK trade. Critics, however, are less convinced and tend to stress the potential loss of jobs in certain sectors and/or locations from Japanese competition; the possibility that plants may remain 'screwdriver' operations; the lack of guarantees on 'local content' and the danger of overdependence on companies not necessarily committed to a long-term presence. Inevitably, the reality of the situation seems to lie somewhere between the two opposing views. The growing Japanese presence is likely to bring both costs and benefits at local, regional and national levels, and only time and further research will tell what the net effects are likely to be.

A good demonstration of the potential trade-off for the UK economy of Japanese inward investment can be seen by examining its effects on the current account of the UK balance of payments. Writing in the *Guardian* on 28 February 1990, Victor Keegan referred to three stages of development in UK–Japanese trading relationships. In the first stage, when UK consumers buy products directly imported from Japan, such as televisions and videos, the trade figures are adversely affected. For much of the 1980s, for example, Britain had a net deficit in the balance of trade in TV sets and videos, most of which were Japanese imports. This deficit reflected the growing overall deficit in manufactured items that the UK economy faced after 1983.

The second stage of the relationship occurs when Japanese companies establish manufacturing facilities in Britain to supply the home market directly and to use the UK as a base for exporting to the rest of Europe. The effect of this is not only to reduce Japanese imports but also to boost UK exports. In 1989, for instance, UK-based manufacturers of colour television sets achieved a trade surplus of £58 million, following a deficit of £12 million in 1988 (*Guardian*, 28 February 1990; see also *Financial Times*, 26 September 1990). Similarly, in video recorders a substantial deficit of £182 million in 1987 had been reduced to £49 million by 1989, as imports from Japan were progressively reduced.

In the third stage, when profits and other capital payments are remitted back to Japan, the balance of payments experiences an outflow of funds, predominantly from the invisibles account (i.e. interest, profits and dividends). For the UK economy, which has traditionally depended on a healthy surplus on the invisible side of the current account to finance its burgeoning deficit on visibles, such a development is potentially serious. As Keegan points out, the deficit on visible trade has recently become too large to be financed by the invisible surplus, and since the latter has been shrinking substantially of late, the overall current account of the UK balance of payments is under severe strain.

A similar analysis could be applied to the effects of Japanese investment in the UK car industry. Having once been the world's biggest exporter of cars and a net contributor to the UK balance of payments, the UK motor industry has fallen into endemic deficit. By 1988, for instance, the industry had a trade deficit of just over £6 billion, which represented more than half the UK's entire deficit in manufactured goods. Keegan predicts that this could change dramatically in future, as output and exports from UK-based overseas car manufacturers—including Nissan—increase (*Guardian*, 28 February 1990). Indeed, Nissan itself is said to have pledged that it would slice £500 million a year from the UK's annual trade deficit by 1993 (*Guardian*, 26 June 1990).

The opening of the Honda and Toyota plants also promises to reduce the number of cars imported from Japan and to boost UK car exports in the 1990s. A key consideration from a balance of payments point of view will be how much 'local content' the Japanese car manufacturers decide to use. The substitution of local suppliers for components imported from Japan, together with increased numbers of finished cars exported from British plants, would undoubtedly improve the UK's balance of trade in this sector. In this context it is worth noting that each of the companies mentioned above committed itself to achieving an 80 per cent local content, although 'local' in this case refers to the EC, not just the UK (Peck, 1990). However, given the tendency of Japanese manufacturers to operate a 'Just in Time' component supply system, it is likely that there will be limits to the geographical radius in which component suppliers are located—though this in itself does not guarantee that they will all be British, as experience with Nissan has shown.

Nor should it be forgotten that any favourable effect on the visibles side will be counteracted to some degree by the outflow of funds from the invisibles account, as profits and capital are sent back to Japan—a case illustrated by Ford UK, which generally runs a balance of payments deficit on its UK activities. What matters in global terms is the extent to which any cash drain from the UK is offset by earnings from British investments abroad. On this, the future is far from clear.

REVIEW QUESTIONS

1. To what extent does the theory of comparative cost advantage suggest that the UK should become a service-based economy?
2. Contrast the effects of the single European market on the marketing environment of the following products:
   (a) building materials
   (b) potato crisps
   (c) banking
3. What would be the advantages and disadvantages to a British manufacturer of commercial vehicles resulting from full European monetary union?
4. How would you explain the performance of the UK textile industry over the past two decades?
5. What are the attractions of investing in productive capacity within the UK to a Japanese manufacturer of computer printers?
6. What are the consequences of a volatile pound–dollar exchange rate for a UK firm exporting drilling equipment to the USA? How can the adverse consequences be mitigated?

REFERENCES

Cecchini, P. et al. (1988), *The European Challenge 1992: The Benefits of a Single Market*, Wildwood House, Aldershot.
Cook, G. C. (1991), *Economics Update*, Sterling Books, Leicester.
Dicken, P. (1990), 'Japanese Industrial Investment in the UK', *Geography*, October, pp. 351–4, vol. no. 75(**4**).
Griffiths, A. and Wall, S. (1991), *Applied Economics: An Introductory Course*, 4th edn, Longman, London.
Peck, F. (1990), 'Nissan in the North East: the Multiplier Effects', *Geography*, October, pp. 354–7, vol. no. 75(**4**).

EIGHT
THE POLITICAL ENVIRONMENT

8.1 INTRODUCTION

The political environment is one of the less predictable elements in a business organization's marketing environment. Although politicians issue manifestos and other policy statements, these have to be seen against the pragmatic need of governments to modify their policies during their period in office. Change in the political environment can result from a variety of internal and external pressures. The fact that a government has to seek re-election within five years has contributed towards a cyclical political environment. Thus, the dominant ideology since the Second World War has changed from the late 1940s situation of heavy government intervention in all aspects of the economy, including ownership of a substantial share of productive capacity, to a much more restrained hands-off approach of the 1950s; the 1960s and 1970s saw the political environment oscillating in moderation between more and less government involvement in the ways businesses are run; and, finally, the 1980s saw a significant change in the political environment with the wholesale withdrawal of government from ownership and regulation of large areas of business activity. More recently, marketers seeking to monitor the political environment have detected a shift away from the radicalism of the 1980s to the idea of a social market economy in the 1990s.

The marketer needs to monitor the changing political environment because it impinges on the marketing function in a number of ways.

At a national level, government passes legislation which directly affects the relationship between the firm and its customers and between the firm and other firms. Sometimes legislation has a direct effect on marketers, for example a law giving consumers rights against the seller of faulty goods. At other times the effect is less direct, for example where legislation requiring local authorities to put out to tender some of their duties has the effect of creating more competitive relationships between firms in a market.

In addition, the government is responsible for protecting the public interest at large, imposing further constraints on the activities of firms, for example laying down the design standards for cars to protect the public against pollution or road safety risks.

Third, as indicated in Chapter 6, the macroeconomic environment is directly affected by government-formulated policies which can influence the rate of growth in the economy and hence the total amount of spending power. Also, it is a political decision as to how this spending power should be distributed between different groups of consumers and between the public and private sectors.

Furthermore, government at both central and local levels is itself a major consumer of goods and services. In 1987 total government expenditure accounted for 41 per cent of gross domestic product, although this has been falling in recent years as a result of government policy to remove large areas of activity from the public sector.

Finally, government policies can influence the dominant social and cultural values of a country, although there can be argument about which is cause and which is effect. Government policies of the 1980s emphasized wealth creation as an end in itself and also had the effect of generating a feeling of confidence among consumers. This can be directly linked to an increase in consumer spending at a higher rate than earnings growth, and a renewed enthusiasm for purchasing items of ostentatious consumption.

Before the implications of the political environment for marketing are considered more fully, the organization and processes of government need to be analysed in some detail. This analysis can be undertaken at central government, local government and European government levels.

8.2   CENTRAL GOVERNMENT

There are four principal elements to central government in the UK: the legislature, the executive, the civil service and the judiciary. Collectively, these provide sovereign government within the UK, although, as will be seen later, this sovereignty is increasingly being subjected to the authority of the European Community.

8.2.1   Parliament

Parliament provides the supreme legislative authority in the UK and comprises the Queen, the House of Commons and the House of Lords. The House of Commons is the most important part of the legislature, as legislation has curtailed the authority in Parliament of the monarch and the House of Lords. It would be useful to consider the progress of new legislation through Parliament, from starting life as a Bill to the point where it becomes an Act of Parliament (see Figure 8.1).

Most Bills that subsequently become law are government-sponsored and often start life following discussion between government departments and interested parties. On some occasions, these discussions may lead to the setting up of a committee of inquiry, or (less frequently) a royal commission which reports to the government. The findings of such a committee can be accepted, rejected or amended by the government, which puts forward ideas for discussion in a Green Paper. Following initial discussion, government submits definite proposals for legislation in the form of a White Paper. A parliamentary Bill is then drafted, incorporating some of the comments that the government has received in response to the publication of the White Paper. The Bill is then formally introduced to Parliament by a first reading in the House of Commons, at which a date is set for the main debate at a second reading. A vote is taken at each reading, and if it is a government Bill it invariably passes at each stage. If it passes the second reading, the Bill is sent to a standing committee for a discussion of the details. This committee in due course reports back to the full House of Commons, and there is then a final debate where amendments are considered, some of which originate from the committee, some from members of the House of Commons in general. The Bill then passes to the House of Lords and goes through a similar five stages. The Lords may delay or amend a Bill, although the Commons may subsequently use the Parliament Act to force the Bill through. Finally, the Bill goes to the monarch to receive the Royal Assent, upon which it becomes an Act of Parliament.

This basic model can be changed in a number of ways. First, in response to a newly perceived

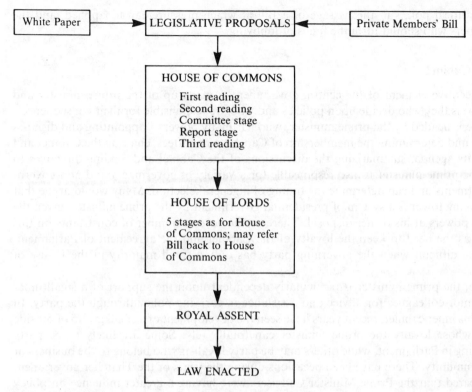

Figure 8.1   The progress of legislation through Parliament

problem, a government can introduce a Bill with very few clauses and, with agreement of party managers, can short-cut the consultation stages, speed up the passage of the Bill through its various stages and provide Royal Assent within a matter of days, instead of the months that it can typically take. This has occurred, for example, in the case of a one-clause Bill to prohibit trade in human organs, a measure that had all-party support. A second variation on the basic model is provided by Private Members' Bills. Most Bills start life with government backing; however, backbench members of Parliament can introduce their own Bills, although the opportunities for doing this are limited, and if they do not subsequently receive government backing their chances of passing all stages of the parliamentary process are significantly reduced.

In Chapter 12 on the Legal Environment, it is noted that the law affecting marketers comes from two principal sources: statute law and case law. Case law evolves gradually and is determined by judges who aim to be impartial and free from any sectional interest. The ability of the marketer to influence change in this aspect of the law is therefore very limited. However, this cannot be said of statute law passed by Parliament. The lobbying of members of Parliament has become an increasingly important activity, brought about by individuals and pressure groups to try and protect their interests where new legislation is proposed which may affect them. Recent proposals to reform the pattern of brewery ownership of pubs encountered fierce lobbying of members of Parliament by the brewing industry, with the result that the final legislation passed was what some would describe as a very much watered-down version of the government's original proposals, which were themselves based on a report of the Monopolies and Mergers Commission. Marketers, if they are to succeed in influencing their political environment, need to identify the critical points in the passage of a Bill at which pressure can be applied, and the critical members who should form the focus of lobbying.

8.2.2 The Cabinet

The main executive element of the central government is made up of the prime minister and Cabinet, for it is they who decide upon policies and who are responsible for their consequences. The executive is headed by the prime minister, who has many powers—appointing and dismissing ministers and determining the membership of Cabinet committees, chairing the Cabinet and determining its agenda, summarizing the discussions of the Cabinet and sending directives to ministers. The prime minister is also responsible for a variety of government and non-government appointments and can determine the timing of a general election. Many would argue that Britain is moving towards a system of presidential government by the prime minister, given the considerable powers at his or her disposal. There are however a number of constraints on this power, such as the need to keep the loyalty of the Cabinet and the agreement of Parliament, which may be difficult when the governing party has only a small majority in the House of Commons.

In practice, the prime minister is particularly dependent upon the support of a small inner cabinet of senior colleagues for advice and assistance in carrying policy through the party. In addition to this inner cabinet, recent years have seen the development of a small group of outside advisers on whose loyalty the prime minister can totally rely. Some are likely to be party members sitting in Parliament, while others may be party loyalists who belong to the business or academic community. There have been occasions during the years of the Thatcher government when it appeared that the Prime Minister's advisers were having a greater influence on policy than her Cabinet colleagues.

The government of the country is divided between a number of different departments of state. Each department is headed by a minister or secretary of state who is a political appointee, usually a member of Parliament. They are assisted in their tasks by other ministers whose portfolio of responsibilities frequently changes when a new government comes into being. Ministers are often given delegated authority by Parliament, as where an Act may allow charges to be made for certain health services but the minister has the delegated power to decide the actual level of the charges.

The ideological background of the prime minister and the composition of the government may give some indication of the direction of government policy. On government attitudes towards aspects of the political environment such as competition policy and personal taxation, marketers could study the composition of the government to try and predict future policy.

8.2.3 The civil service

The civil service is the secretariat that is responsible for implementing the policy of government. Civil servants are paid officials who do not change when the government changes, providing a degree of continuity to government. Although legally civil servants are servants of the Crown, technically they are employed by a separate government department and are responsible to a minister. Each department is generally headed by a permanent secretary, responsible to the Public Accounts Committee of Parliament. The permanent secretary is a professional administrator who gives advice to his or her minister, a political appointee who generally lacks expertise in the work of that department.

The fact that civil servants are relatively expert in their areas and generally remain in their

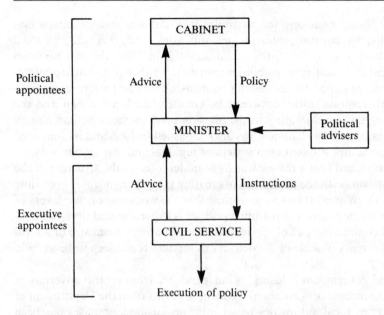

Figure 8.2 The UK government system of departmental administration: a simplified diagram

posts for much longer than their ministers has given them great power. A delicate relationship develops between the permanent secretary and the minister based on sometimes conflicting goals. The minister may view an issue in terms of broader political opportunities, while civil servants may be more concerned about their status and career prospects resulting from a change affecting their departments. The nature of the career civil servant is changing now with the emergence of agencies to take over the activities of civil service departments, for example vehicle licensing. In principle, these new executive agencies should be much freer of ministerial control, meeting longer-term performance standards with less day-to-day ministerial intervention as to how this should be achieved.

The marketer seeking to influence government policy must recognize the power that civil servants have in advising their ministers, especially on the details of proposed legislation. Civil servants are usually involved in consultation exercises, for instance on the details of proposed food regulations.

8.3 LOCAL GOVERNMENT

Local authorities are responsible for a wide range of services, from social services and education to refuse collection and street cleaning. The current structure of local government was broadly established by the 1972 Local Government Act, implemented in 1974. The largely rural areas of England were divided into counties ('shire counties'), each with their own county council. The chief responsibilities of these county councils include education, social services, emergency services, highways and refuse disposal. These areas are further subdivided into district councils (sometimes designated as borough or city councils) which have responsibilities for housing, leisure services and refuse collection. Districts in rural areas are usually further divided into parishes, with a parish council (sometimes designated as a town council) responsible for local matters such as the maintenance of playing fields.

In the larger conurbations, metropolitan counties were created. Their responsibilities were generally less than those of 'shire' counties; for example, they did not include education. Metropolitan district councils, by contrast, had greater functions—they became the local education authority and took on responsibility for social services. In 1986, the metropolitan county councils were abolished and their responsibilities transferred either to the metropolitan districts or to new joint boards governed by the district councils. A similar pattern of government existed in London, with responsibilities between the Greater London Council and the London borough councils roughly corresponding to the division between metropolitan county and district councils. The Greater London Council was also abolished in 1986 and its functions reallocated. In Scotland, the structure is based on a system of regional and district councils.

In 1990 the government announced that a review was to be undertaken of the structure of the local government system in Britain, with the possibility of creating unitary authorities providing all local government services in an area. It has been argued that the existence of two layers of local government in the shires on such issues as planning policies is expensive and time-consuming. With the development of contracting-out of services, the idea of an optimum size of a local government unit based on economies of scale in the delivery of services is not seen to be as valid as it was in the early 1970s.

It has been argued that local government is losing its independence from central government —over half of local government income now comes in the form of grants from the Department of Environment, while the ability of local authorities to set rates on business premises has been taken away from them altogether. Furthermore, their total expenditure and the freedom to set a community charge on individuals has been constrained by central government. In addition, legislation setting performance standards in education and social services, among others, has limited the independence of local government to set locally determined standards.

The process of privatization is another factor that has altered the role of local authorities, who are now being regarded more as enablers of service provision than as actual providers. The Local Government Act 1988 specified a number of activities such as refuse collection and school catering where local authorities are required to put the provision of services out to competitive tender. Local authorities have entered the market for these services as buyers of services that were previously produced internally; sometimes they are still provided internally, but by a separately accountable section within the authority.

Local authorities are also becoming increasingly marketing-orientated in the relationships with their clients. Leisure centres which were once seen as a necessary social service provided by the authority are now moving from a production orientation to a situation where consumer needs are analysed, and services are then developed to meet these needs and are priced and promoted accordingly.

NEW WAYS OF COLLECTING OLD RUBBISH

Refuse collection is one of the statutory functions of district councils in England and Wales. It was an early target in the 1980s drive by local authorities to contract out operations to the most cost-effective provider.

Stratford-on-Avon District Council has led the way in many aspects of privatization. Until 1987, refuse was collected by the Council's own direct labour force, but in that year tenders were invited for the contract to clear the area's refuse. The management and workforce of the existing council operation submitted a tender and won the contract. However, rather than operate as a separately accountable Direct Labour Organization (as happened in many other authorities), the group negotiated—and succeeded—in buying out the refuse collection operation from the

Council to form a new company—the Fosse Group Ltd. As a separate company, Fosse competed for further contracts with Stratford District Council and for other organizations, both private sector and public sector.

The Council applied a similar treatment to many more of its activities, including grounds maintenance, street cleaning, council house management and the operation of leisure centres. Faced with its changing role as an enabler rather than an actual provider of services, the Council restructured itself to draw a distinction between those employees responsible for relations with the public (the users of the service) and those responsible for procuring services to satisfy the end users' needs.

Meanwhile, the privatized refuse collection service began to run into trouble. Penalty charges imposed by the District Council for sub-standard service and the effects of high interest rates put financial pressure on the Fosse Group. By 1991 it found it difficult to continue as a separate entity and the business was taken over by Cambrian Environmental Services—a well resourced subsidiary of the newly privatized Welsh Water Company.

8.4 QUASI-GOVERNMENTAL BODIES

Some organizations are neither a private business organization nor an elected government body, yet they fulfil an executive or administrative function with the aim of creating or implementing government policy. These are known as quasi-government bodies. In Britain, quasi-government bodies exist because direct involvement by a government department in a particular area of activity is considered to be inefficient or undesirable, while leaving the activity to the private sector may be inappropriate where issues of public policy are concerned. The quasi-government body thus represents a compromise between the constitutional needs of government control and the organizational needs of independence and flexibility associated with private sector organizations.

Some quasi-governmental bodies directly implement government policy. For example, the Office of Fair Trading, the Equal Opportunities Commission and the Monopolies and Mergers Commission are not government departments, but an Act of Parliament gives them duties that allow them to act in the manner of a government department. Other quasi-governmental bodies are involved in matters that are somewhat more removed from mainstream policy and decision-making. This group of bodies is often referred to as QUANGOs (quasi-autonomous non-governmental organization). Most QUANGOs are established by an Act of Parliament or by an Order made under an Act, while others have been created by a minister's administrative act.

QUANGOs enjoy considerable autonomy from their parent department, and the sponsoring minister has no direct control over the activities of the body, other than making the appointment of the chairman. Because of this, the minister ceases to be answerable to Parliament for the day-to-day activities of a QUANGO, unlike the responsibility that a minister has in respect of a government department. The responsibilities of a QUANGO vary from being purely advisory to making important policy decisions and allocating large amounts of expenditure. Their income can come from a combination of government grant, precepts from local authorities and charges to customers. Examples of QUANGOs at a national level include the Civil Aviation Authority, the BBC, the National Economic Development Office, the Sports Council and the Arts Council. QUANGOs also have important responsibilities at a local level. Following the abolition of metropolitan county councils in 1986, residuary bodies were set up to take over some of the county-wide services such as fire and ambulance services which were not reallocated to the borough councils.

The main advantage of the QUANGO is in allowing action to be taken much more quickly than may have been the case with a government department, where it may have been necessary to receive ministerial approval before action was taken; ministers may have less time to devote to the details of policy application with which many QUANGOs are often involved, and may also be constrained to a much greater extent by broader considerations of government policy. Being relatively free of day-to-day political interference, QUANGOs are in a better position to maintain a long-term plan free of the short-term diversions that may be the result of direct control by a minister who is subject to the need for short-term political popularity. Against this are a number of potential disadvantages that QUANGOs have compared with government departments. It is sometimes argued that they are not sufficiently accountable to elected representatives for their actions, which may be a particular problem where they are delegated with the task of drawing up policy. Some would argue instead that the power of patronage enjoyed by ministers ensures that their independence may be relatively limited.

In the early 1980s there was a feeling that there were too many QUANGOs in Britain, often duplicating efforts of other government bodies or imposing unnecessary restrictions on the individual. Consequently, there was considerable change in the nature of QUANGOs during the 1980s. Some were abolished, such as the area health authorities; many more were transformed into PLC status upon privatization, such as the electricity and water authorities and the British Airports Authority. On the other hand, many new QUANGOs have been created. In response to the privatization of many state monopolies, a new generation of regulatory QUANGOs has appeared, such as Oftel and Ofgas. The abolition of metropolitan county councils has further increased the number of QUANGOs. More recently, a number of government functions previously carried out by the civil service have been transferred to executive agencies—a new form of QUANGO.

The transformation of many QUANGOs into PLCs has greatly increased the marketing activities of these organizations, often taking them into competitive markets that are beyond their core activities. For example, the British Airports Authority has changed from simply managing airports to taking an active role in hotel and retail development. Similarly, newly privatized water companies are competing in the market-place for amenity cleaning contracts and hydraulic engineering. Freshly capitalized and free from previous constraints, newly privatized organizations can significantly affect the competitive marketing environment of a sector.

8.5   THE EUROPEAN COMMUNITY

The European Community (EC) had its origins in the European Coal and Steel Community. The result of negotiations was the Treaty of Rome, signed in 1957 by the original six members of EC: France, West Germany, Italy, Belgium, the Netherlands and Luxembourg. Britain joined the EC in 1972, together with Ireland and Denmark, to be joined by Greece in 1981 and Spain and Portugal in 1986. The combined population of EC countries is now over 340 million.

8.5.1   Aims of the EC

The Treaty of Rome initially created a customs union and a common market. The creation of a customs union has involved first the abolition of tariffs between member-states and second the introduction of a common external tariff on trade with the rest of the world. When Britain joined the EC, tariffs tended to encourage UK trade with Commonwealth countries at the expense of European countries. In particular, Britain had been able to obtain a source of relatively cheap agricultural produce from Commonwealth countries, but on joining the EC was forced to phase in a common tariff for agricultural products imported from outside the EC.

The second aim of the Treaty of Rome was the creation of a common market, in which trade could take place between member-states as if it were one country. The implication of a common market is the free movement of trade, labour and capital between member-states. So far, it is only in agriculture that a genuinely common market has been created, with a system of common pricing and support payments between all countries and free movement of produce between member-states. Further development of a common market has been hampered by a range of non-tariff trade barriers, such as national legislation specifying design standards, the cost and risk of currency exchange and the underlying desire of public authorities to back their own national industries. As the previous chapter indicates, the EC aims to remove these non-tariff barriers to create a single market by January 1993.

More recently, debate has taken place over the extent to which political union should take place. The achievement of European Monetary Union would have the effect of integrating economies much more closely by taking away from national governments many of the tools of national economic management such as exchange rate, interest rate and monetary policy. An inter-governmental conference was established in December 1990 to consider modifications to the Treaty of Rome which may bring about greater political and economic unity.

The EC has also developed social goals with the Social Charter. This is a declaration of basic rights for workers, such as rights to trade union representation and minimum wages, planned for implementation in 1993. If implemented, it will have a significant effect on companies producing goods and services in the domestic market by imposing higher costs relative to much of the overseas competition. The UK government has so far dissented from these proposals.

8.5.2 Structure of the EC

The Treaty of Rome developed a structure of government whose elements reflect in part the structure of the British government. The executive or Cabinet is provided by the Council of Ministers, the secretariat or civil service is provided by the European Commission, while the legislature is provided by the European Parliament. There is also a European Court of Justice, mentioned further in Chapter 12 on the legal environment.

The Treaty of Rome places a constraint upon the policies that the institutions of the European Community can adopt. The European Court of Justice is able to rule that an action or decision is not in accordance with the Treaty. In some cases, such as competition policy, the Treaty is quite specific; for example, Articles 85 and 86 define the basic approach to be adopted in dealing with cartels and monopoly power. On the other hand, the Treaty says little more on transport policy than that there should be a common policy, giving the community institutions considerable power to develop such a policy.

The activities of the European Community are now directly funded from income received from customs duties and other levies on goods entering the Community from non-member-countries. In addition, a value added tax collected by member-states on purchases by consumers includes an element of up to 1.45 per cent which is automatically transferred to the Community budget. More recently, a new resource transfer between member-states and the Community has been introduced which is based on the gross domestic product of each member-state. The UK remains a net contributor to the Community budget.

8.5.3 The Council of Ministers

The Council of Ministers represents the governments of member-states and can be regarded as the ultimate controlling authority of the European Community, as draft regulations and draft directives become law only if the Council of Ministers agrees.

Each member-state sends one minister to the European Council of Ministers. Which minister attends will depend on the subject being discussed—for example, agriculture ministers would be sent if the Common Agricultural Policy was being discussed. The ministers of foreign affairs, and agriculture and those with budgetary responsibilities meet more frequently, making a senior body within the Council, sometimes called the General Council. The chairmanship or presidency of the Council of Ministers rotates between countries in alphabetical order, with each period of presidency lasting for six months.

The Council of Ministers draws up the major policies and decisions of the Community, acting on the basis of proposals made by the Commission. It also has the power to pass new Community legislation; but before a decision can be arrived at, it must have 70 per cent support. When the Council votes on a proposal that does not originate from within the European Commission, the support of eight of the twelve states is also necessary. The votes allocated to each minister are related to the size of the country which they represent, as Table 8.1 shows. For more important decisions, for example the entry of new members, unanimity is required. Since the Single European Act of 1987, many more decisions are taken by a simple majority vote.

Table 8.1 Voting rights within European Community institutions

Country	No. of votes in European Council of Ministers	No. of MEPs returned to European Parliament
France	10	81
Italy	10	81
UK	10	81
West Germany	10	81
Spain	8	60
Belgium	5	24
Netherlands	5	25
Greece	5	24
Portugal	5	24
Denmark	3	16
Ireland	3	15
Luxembourg	2	6
TOTAL	76	518

The Council of Ministers can generally pass laws even if the European Parliament disagrees with them, unlike the practice within the British system, where ministers must obtain approval of a majority of members of Parliament. There are two main exceptions to this authority of the

Council. First, the European Parliament has power to approve or reject the Community budget (see Section 8.5.5). Second, the Single European Act introduced a system of legislative co-operation between the Council and Parliament, obliging the Council and the Commission to take Parliament's amendments to proposals into consideration, although a unanimous vote by the Council of Ministers retains ultimate authority.

The Committee of Permanent Representatives (Coreper) complements the work of the Council of Ministers. Because ministers have responsibilities to their own national governments as well as to the European Community, they cannot give a continuing presence. To make up for this, each member-state sends one ambassador to the Committee which is based in Brussels. Proposals are discussed by Coreper and its sub-committees before they reach ministers. If Coreper reaches full agreement on the matter, it is empowered to pass it through the Council without further debate, but where disagreement occurs it is left for ministers to discuss.

8.5.4   The European Commission

Each member-state sends at least one commissioner to the Commission (the five largest members send two), who is appointed by the member-government for a renewable term of four years. They are supported in their work by a staff of about 13,000 civil servants drawn from all member-states, working mainly at the Commission's headquarters in Brussels. The Commission is headed by a president who holds office for six months. Countries take it in turn to nominate the president of the Commission. Each commissioner is given responsibility for a portfolio which could be for a policy area such as transport, or for administrative matters, such as the Commission's relations with the Parliament, while others are given a combination of responsibilities in their portfolios.

Unlike the Council of Ministers, all members of the Commission are supposed to act primarily for the benefit of the Community as a whole, rather than for the country they represent. This is spelt out in Article 157 of the Treaty of Rome, which states that Commissioners 'shall neither seek nor take instruction from any other body'.

The Commission has an initiation, mediation and implementation role. As an initiator, its task is to draft proposals for legislation which the Council of Ministers has to consider. If the Council does not accept a proposal, it can alter the draft only by a unanimous vote. If unanimity cannot be achieved, the proposal has to go back to the Commission for it to draft a revised proposal which will be acceptable to the Council of Ministers.

As a mediator, the Commission can intervene in disputes between member-states to try to find a solution through negotiation. The Commission has frequently acted as mediator in trade disputes between members, avoiding recourse to the European Court of Justice.

As an implementer, the Commission undertakes the day-to-day administration of the EC. This involves monitoring the activities of member-states to ensure that they do not conflict with community policy. In addition, the Commission implements community policies such as the Regional Development Fund and Common Agricultural Policy.

8.5.5   The European Parliament

Unlike the UK Parliament, the European Parliament is primarily consultative and has no legislative powers. Its main function is to monitor the activities of other Community institutions. It can give an opinion on Commission proposals but has powers only to amend, adopt or reject the Community budget. It also has the theoretical power to dismiss the entire Commission, for which a censure motion must be passed by a two-thirds majority of members. However, it has no control over the selection of new commissioners to replace those who had been dismissed. It does not yet have the power to initiate and enact legislation.

Members of the European Parliament are now directly elected by the constituents of each country. The Parliament has a total of 518 members, of which 81 represent UK constituencies, with other countries returning members roughly in proportion to their populations, as shown in Table 8.2. The European Parliament generally meets in Strasbourg, but parliamentary committee meetings are held in Brussels and in the capital of the country holding the presidency of the Council of Ministers.

Members of the European Parliament increasingly belong to political rather than national groupings. The political composition of the Parliament is shown in Table 8.2.

Table 8.2 Political allegiance of members of the European Parliament as at 2 May 1986

Political affiliation	No. of members
Socialists	180
European People's Party	121
European Democrats	34
European United Left	28
Liberal and Democratic Reformist Group	49
European Democratic Alliance	22
Rainbow Group	14
European Right	17
Green	29
Coalition Left	14
Non-affiliated	14

8.5.6 The European Court of Justice

The supreme legislative body of the European Community is provided by the Court of Justice. Article 164 of the Treaty of Rome gave the Court the task of 'ensuring that the law is observed in the interpretation and implementation of the Treaty'. It is the final arbiter in all matters of interpreting Community treaties and rules on disputes between member-states, between member-states and the Commission and between the Commission and business organizations, individuals or Community officials.

Although the Court can condemn violations of the Treaty by member-governments, it has no sanctions against them except that of goodwill. The Court can investigate complaints that the Commission has acted beyond its powers, and if upheld can annul decisions of the Commission.

The European Court of Justice is composed of thirteen judges, each appointed for a six-year term and each of whom must put Community interests before national interests.

The Court can be called upon to settle disputes where the persuasion and negotiations of the Commission have failed to yield results. For example, in the area of competition policy, the Commission may by decision forbid an anti-competitive practice or impose a fine. The companies concerned can appeal to the European Court of Justice for the decision to be set aside. In one case, several dye producers appealed to the European Court of Justice against the fines

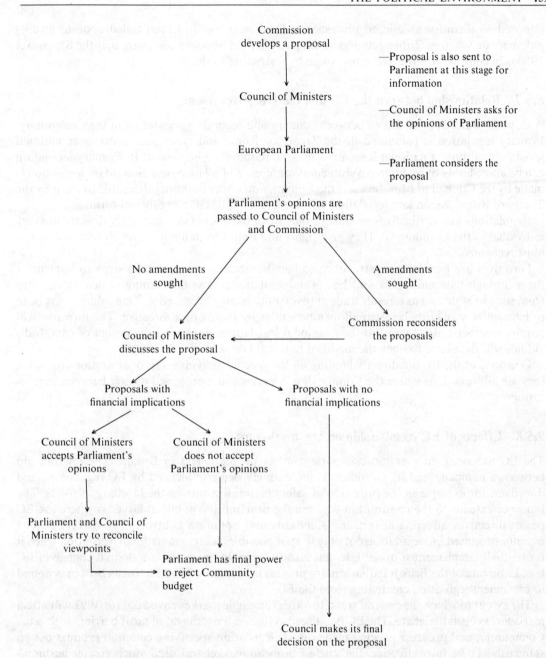

Figure 8.3 The process of European legislation

Note: This simplified diagram does not take account of Commission proposals on social and economic matters which are sent initially to the Economic and Social Committee rather than the Council of Ministers.

imposed on them for an alleged price cartel. The Court has also been called upon to give its judgment on whether British retailers seeking to open on Sundays can claim that the Shops Act 1950 is in conflict with the Treaty of Rome by restricting trade.

8.5.7   Relationship between the EC and the UK government

A distinction needs to be drawn between primary and secondary legislation of the Community. Primary legislation is contained in the Treaty of Rome and takes precedence over national legislation, although national legislation may be required to implement it. Primary legislation can be altered only by an inter-governmental conference of all members. Secondary legislation is made by the Council of Ministers and the Commission under authority delegated to them by the Treaty of Rome. Secondary legislation affects member-states in a number of forms.

Regulations automatically form part of the law of member-states and apply directly to every individual in the Community. They give rights and duties to individuals which national courts must recognize.

Directives are mandatory instructions to member-states who must take steps to implement them through national legislation. For example, national laws concerning vehicle safety vary from state to state and as a result trade across frontiers may be impeded. One solution has been to harmonize standards between all member-states by means of a directive. The directive will require member-states to amend their national legislations governing the design of cars. Individuals will then have to obey the modified national law.

Decisions of the EC are directly binding on the specific individuals or organizations to which they are addressed, as where the Commission intervenes in a proposed merger between organizations.

8.5.8   Effects of EC membership on UK marketers

The EC is having an ever more important effect on marketers in Britain. The relationship between a company and its customers is increasingly being influenced by EC regulations and directives, for example in the provision of safety features in cars or the labelling of foods. The influence extends to the relationship between the firm and the public at large, as where the EC passes directives affecting advertising standards and pollution controls. The marketer must monitor proposed EC legislation not only to spot possible changes in national legislation when it is eventually implemented in the UK, but also to lobby to bring about a desired change in EC law. Lobbying of the British parliamentary process is becoming less effective as Britain is bound to implement legislation emanating from the EC.

The extent to which the general trend towards the single market envisaged for 1992 will affect marketers is open to debate. The EC has already effected the removal of tariff barriers within the Community, and progress is being made on EC legislation specifying common product design standards. To be fully effective, the single European market will need much greater harmonization of fiscal policies and monetary union. The latter cannot be brought about without a change to the Treaty of Rome.

EUROPEAN COMMISSION GIVES PHARMACEUTICAL COMPANIES A HEADACHE OVER ADVERTISING

The pharmaceutical industry in the UK faced a very anxious period during 1990/1 when the European Commission proposed a directive covering the advertising of over-the-counter (OTC) medicines. Proposals in the draft directive would have meant the compulsory inclusion of information on side-effects, interactions with other products and other precautions in all advertising. At least 20 per cent of all advertising space would have to be reserved for such warnings. The effect of the directive would have been to make advertising of OTCs very difficult.

The pharmaceuticals industry, led by its trade body the Proprietary Association of Great Britain, fought hard to have the directive dropped. It lobbied on a number of fronts—directly to the European Commission in the hope that the proposals could be modified before being published; to the European Parliament in the hope that members would reject the proposal as being against the interests of the general public; and to the British government, especially the secretary of state for health, in the hope that Britain would use its voice in the Council of Ministers to vote against the proposals.

Had the draft directive been passed, member-states would have been obliged to pass legislation in their own countries to implement the directive. In the event, the European Parliament rejected most of the proposals, although it did accept the proposal that a warning should be included urging users to read the label carefully. This was subsequently upheld by the Council of Ministers and will be incorporated into future UK legislation. However, the European Parliament went one step further by approving its own proposal that a statement should be included on all OTC products stating that 'any medical product can be dangerous if used incorrectly—consult your doctor'. This proposal was opposed by the European Commission and is unlikely to succeed in view of the Parliament's very limited capacity in initiating legislation.

By applying pressure at a number of points in the political system, the pharmaceuticals industry had managed to reduce the impact of the proposed legislation on its members.

8.6   INFLUENCES ON POLICY FORMATION

8.6.1   Pressure groups

It was mentioned at the beginning of this chapter that policy laid out in a manifesto may be changed during a political party's period of office on account of internal or external pressure. An important role is played by pressure (or interest) groups, which represent a medium through which the government is made aware of the views of a section of the public or of a group of organizations. Marketers need to monitor the efforts of pressure groups, for if successful they will influence government policy. There are many examples of government legislation resulting directly from the efforts of pressure groups—for example, legislation requiring new cars to be capable of running on unleaded petrol was significantly influenced by the efforts of the pressure group CLEAR (the Campaign for Lead Free Air). The latter was an example of a pressure group supported by a widespread public membership. On the other hand, in addition to anticipating and responding to the political environment, marketers frequently used pressure groups to try and change the political environment in a manner that satisfies the aims of their organizations. For example, the Brewers Society is a vehicle through which individual brewers have applied pressure on the government to drop proposals to reform the system of tied houses.

Pressure groups can be divided into a number of categories. In the first place, there is a division between those that are permanent in fighting for a general cause and those that are set up to achieve a specific objective and are dissolved when this objective is met—or when there no longer seems any prospect of changing the situation. Groups set up to fight specific new road schemes fit into this category.

Pressure groups can be classified according to their functions. Sectional groups exist to promote the common economic interests of their members over a wide range of issues. Trade unions and employers' associations fall into this category—they represent their members' views to government on diverse issues such as proposed employment legislation, import controls and Sunday trading laws. This type of pressure group frequently offers other benefits to members, such as legal representation for individual members and the dissemination of information to members. Promotional groups, on the other hand, are established to fight for specific causes, such as nuclear disarmament which is represented by CND.

Pressure groups can influence government policy by three main methods. The first—propaganda—can be used to create awareness of the group and its cause. This can be aimed directly at policy-formers, or indirectly by appealing to the constituents of policy-formers to apply direct pressure themselves. This is essentially an impersonal form of mass communication.

A second option is to try and represent the views of the group directly to policy-formers on a one-to-one basis. Policy-formers frequently welcome representations which they consider could prevent bigger problems or confrontations in the future. Links between pressure groups and government could become institutionalized, as where the Department of Transport routinely seeks the views of the Automobile Association and RAC on proposals to change road traffic legislation. Where no regular contacts exist, pressure groups can be represented by giving evidence before a government-appointed inquiry, by approaching sympathetic MPs or by hiring the services of a professional lobbyist.

A third approach used by pressure groups is to carry out research and supply information. This has the effect of increasing public awareness of the organization and usually has a valuable propaganda function. An example is the British Road Federation, which frequently supplies MPs with comparative road statistics purporting to show that the government should be spending more money on road building.

Pressure groups are most effective where they apply pressure in a low-key manner, for example where they are routinely consulted for their views. The lobbying of MPs, which combines elements of all three methods described above, has become increasingly important over recent years. Yet it is not only national government to which pressure groups apply their attention—local authorities are frequently the target of pressure groups over issues of planning policy or the provision of welfare services. Increasingly, pressure is also being applied at the EC level. Again, the European Commission regularly consults some groups while other groups apply direct pressure to members of the Commission.

Marketers have achieved numerous triumphs in attempting to influence the political environment in which they operate. The pressure group representing the tobacco industry, the Tobacco Advisory Council, has had a significant effect in countering the pressure applied by the anti-tobacco lobby represented by Action on Smoking Health—as a result, proposed anti-smoking legislation has been considerably watered down.

Pressure groups are increasingly crossing national boundaries to reflect the influence of international governmental institutions such as the European Community and the growing influence of multinational business organizations. Both industrial and consumer pressure groups have been formed at a multinational level to counter these influences—a good example of the latter is Greenpeace.

8.6.2 The media

The media—press, radio and television—not only spread awareness of political issues, but also influence policy and decision-making by setting the political agenda and influencing public opinion. The broadcast media must by law show balance in their coverage of political events, but the press is often more openly partisan. Campaigns undertaken by the press frequently reflect the background of their owners—the *Daily Telegraph* is more likely to support the causes of deregulation in an industry, while the *Guardian* will be more likely to put forward the case for government spending on essential public services.

Public relations is an important tool for marketing management to try and create mutually useful relationships with the media. The media is frequently grateful for the specialized information provided by companies. It is possible that, by building up a close relationship, the media will be better informed before printing a story—partly out of ignorance—that is harmful to the company.

8.7 THE EFFECTS OF THE CHANGING POLITICAL ENVIRONMENT ON THE MARKETING ACTIVITY OF THE BUS OPERATING INDUSTRY: A CASE STUDY

The provision of bus services in Britain has been significantly influenced by the nature of the political environment, at both central and local government level. The bus industry can be used to illustrate many of the issues raised in this chapter, especially the changing attitude at central government level towards regulation of economic activity and at a local level towards the changing role of local government. In this changing political environment, the role of marketing has been transformed.

Local bus services saw rapid development during the period immediately following the First World War. The political environment of the time recognized the superiority of free markets, and bus services were therefore seen as something to be provided by market forces. The early 1920s consequently saw large numbers of small entrepreneurs operating in competition with each other, resulting in sometimes wasteful and dangerous competitive practices.

The dominant political attitude shifted during the 1920s away from a pure *laissez-faire* approach to one where state intervention in the economy was becoming more acceptable. Against this changing background, government was able to recognize that public transport was an important public service by passing the Road Traffic Act 1930. This required all bus routes to be licensed. Route licences were strictly limited in number and, in general, a licence would be granted only if the applicant could prove that there was unsatisfied demand for a service. Route licences gave the holder substantial monopoly power, and large bus operating companies emerged during the 1930s by acquiring the licences of their small competitors. The companies thus acquired territorial monopolies, which made it even more difficult for a small company to prove the need for a new service and thereby acquire a route licence. In these conditions, bus companies tended to be production- rather than marketing-led. A further recognition that public transport was an essential public service came when a large section of the bus industry was nationalized by the Labour government in 1948.

By the 1960s bus operation had ceased to be profitable outside the main corridors of movement, mainly because of the growing levels of car ownership. Faced with a deterioration in the quantity and quality of bus services, the Labour government of the late 1960s again intervened with the acquisition of the largest private sector group of companies, and the subsequent formation of the National Bus Company and Scottish Bus Group. These were given responsibility for running most of the large bus operators outside the main cities. The two companies were given strict financial rather than social objectives, although government did later intervene in a manner that appeared to make the companies an instrument of wider government policy—for instance, they were asked to keep fare increases down to help the government's anti-inflation policy.

Local authorities in a number of areas had for many years operated their own bus fleets for various reasons. Making profits to help keep down the level of rates charged to ratepayers was one objective, but in addition, local authorities provided bus services out of civic pride and to ensure that a high standard of public service was provided. Local government legislation frequently prevented them from operating outside their own boundaries. By the 1960s, local authority bus operations too had become generally unprofitable. They were often allowed to lose money if councillors decided that the service provided justified being subsidized out of rates income.

By the 1970s, a highly regulated system of route licensing and of companies having large territorial monopolies resulted in the business environment becoming increasingly production-rather than marketing-orientated. Promotion was aimed almost entirely at existing users, providing basic information rather than trying to create a favourable image among potential users. Faced with an inelastic demand among most of its users, a bus company would set its fares as high as politically possible, given the need for fare increases to be approved by the Traffic Commissioners. Innovation in new products was nearly always reactive rather than proactive. Most innovation was aimed at cutting production costs—such as reducing the need to employ conductors through one-person operation—rather than meeting the needs of consumers, such as providing faster journey times or a more reliable service.

At the same time as the market for scheduled bus services appeared to be going into decline, the market for contract hire by schools, factories and private groups remained buoyant. In this market there were no quantity restrictions on operators, only quality controls, which applied equally to operators of scheduled bus services. The market was dominated by a large number of small firms aggressively competing against each other on price and the quality of service provided. It was difficult for a production-orientated company to survive in this environment for long.

By the 1980s the question was being asked whether the unregulated environment that had encouraged a marketing orientation in the contract service sector could also be applied to the scheduled services sector to achieve the same effect. The traditional argument against deregulation was that licence-holders who had a territorial monopoly provided some element of social service—they used profits generated on one route or at one time of day to cross-subsidize loss-making routes or less profitable evening and weekend services. The National Bus Company used this argument, even though it had been given clearly defined profit rather than social goals by the government.

The political environment of the scheduled bus services sector changed significantly during the 1980s. The first change was brought about by the Conservative government's ideological belief that free and unregulated markets were inherently better than regulated ones, which were presumed to stifle innovation. The government therefore abolished the need for route licences in most parts of the country: any company could now operate a bus service subject to satisfying quality criteria. In addition, subsidies from local authorities to provide socially necessary but unprofitable bus services were to be subject to competitive tendering, rather than being allocated to the existing licence-holder.

The second major change brought about was the restructuring and gradual dismantling of public sector bus operations. The ideology of the time considered that the state was bad at providing marketable goods and services compared with the private sector. Where a social service was considered desirable, this should be explicitly identified by policy-makers in government and satisfied by market mechanisms. The first step was the breaking up of the National Bus Company and its sale to the private sector. Many of the individual companies that it comprised were sold on favourable terms to their management and employees, fulfilling another wish of the Conservative government of the late 1980s—widespread capitalism. Local authorities, which had frequently operated their bus fleets as a quasi-social service, were forced to restructure their operations by forming limited companies to which a board of directors was appointed. Cross-subsidy from the general rate fund was not allowed, and the new operating companies were required to produce an annual profit and loss account and balance sheet. The provision of a shareholding structure facilitated the introduction of private capital, or the eventual sale of the business to the private sector.

Changes in the political environment totally transformed the market for scheduled bus services during the 1980s. Marketing tools which had been used by the fast-moving consumer goods sector for many years but were ignored by this section of the bus industry became popular. Tactical pricing was used aggressively to gain market share, particularly by new entrants to a route who frequently made no charge to attract initial custom. A whole range of market-led new product developments occurred, such as high-frequency minibus services and express commuter services. Much more attention was paid to product quality, including reliability, availability of service information, training of staff and the appearance of vehicles. Corporate identity increasingly took as its starting point the values of the target customers rather than those of management.

Acquisition and merger activity during the previous decade had been quite insignificant for scheduled bus operators, but achieved a frenetic pace during the late 1980s. Many management buy-outs of National Bus Company subsidiaries left the new companies with high levels of gearing, and many sold a majority shareholding to one of the emerging holding companies that had acquired a number of former National Bus Company subsidiaries.

Local monopolies of bus services had until the 1980s been seen as beneficial by the government, recognizing the implicit public service obligations of licence-holders. Moreover, bus operators were not subject to the same vetting for anti-competitive practices as most other industries. Previously, bus companies had adjusted fares on overlapping routes at the same time; this was seen as a common-sense way of minimizing confusion to passengers. In the new political environment, this was considered a potentially anti-competitive practice which the Office of Fair Trading has investigated, warning companies who have been involved. Where take-overs have occurred, the OFT has sought to have them set aside where it felt they were against the public interest, as it argued when Stagecoach Holdings Ltd—the owner of a number of newly privatized companies—sought to acquire the local authority operations in Portsmouth, creating a potentially monopolistic situation, as it had already acquired control of Southdown Motor Services Ltd—the main competitor to the local-authority-controlled Portsmouth City Bus.

The changed political environment has resulted in profound change within bus operators. As well as having to familiarize themselves with marketing tools that had been commonplace elsewhere, bus companies have had to adapt the structure of their organizations. Faced with competition from small bus operators with low overheads and a high degree of flexibility, a major streamlining of company structures has been undertaken. Many companies could still not replicate the cultural values of smaller companies with their relative customer-centredness and low overheads, so they sought to imitate them by creating their own autonomous small business subsidiaries. The Midland Red bus company was typical of this change. As part of the state-owned National Bus Company, it had been protected from competition in most of its markets and had become production-orientated. A reorganization into five smaller operating subsidiaries in the early 1980s—Midland Red North, East, South, West and Express—had been undertaken to save overheads as much as to improve marketing performance. Faced with the prospect of deregulation, the company initially lobbied hard against the proposal. When deregulation occurred in 1986, the companies initially used their greater financial resources to see off competition by offering reduced fares on routes affected by competition. Midland Red West, for instance, frequently ran a 'free bus' to thwart the efforts of smaller companies who did not have the resources to match this tactic. Over the following years, many sought to remove competition as far as the Office of Fair Trading would allow. Midland Red South acquired two small firms—G & G of Leamington Spa and Vanguard Coaches of Bedworth—that had previously competed against it. However, instead of absorbing these businesses into its own company structure, it retained them and used their small business culture to develop their markets further.

REVIEW QUESTIONS

1. What measures can a large multinational business take to monitor the political environment in its various operating areas?
2. How can a manufacturer of potentially harmful pesticides counteract the actions of a pressure group seeking to ban the use of its product?
3. In what ways has the marketing function of district councils in England and Wales changed during the past ten years?
4. In what ways can change in government policies affect a company's marketing plan?
5. Explain the reasons for the growth in political lobbying.

REFERENCES

Alderman, G. (1984), *Pressure Groups and Government in Great Britain*, Longman, London.
Barker, A. (1982), *Quangos in Britain*, Macmillan, London.
Bryne, T. (1986), *Local Government in Britain*, Penguin, Harmondsworth.
Dunleavey, P. (1986), 'Explaining the Privatisation Boom', *Public Administration*, vol. 64, pp. 13–34.
Perry, K. (1984), *Britain and the European Community Made Simple*, Heinemann, London.

NINE

THE DEMOGRAPHIC ENVIRONMENT

9.1 INTRODUCTION

Demography is the study of populations in terms of their size and characteristics. Among the topics of interest to demographers are the age structure of a country, the geographic distribution of its population, the balance between males and females, and the likely future size of the population and its characteristics. Marketers need to study the demographic environment, because changes in the above factors will influence their decision-making in many ways.

First, on the demand side, demography helps to predict the size of the market that a product is likely to face. For example, demographers can predict an increase in elderly people living in the UK and the numbers living in the South West of the country. Marketers can use this information as a basis for predicting, say, the size of the market for retirement homes in the South West.

A second important reason why marketers should be aware of demographic trends concerns supply-side implications. The aim of strategic marketing management is to match the opportunities facing a business organization with the resource strengths that it possesses. In many businesses, labour is a key resource, and a study of demographics will indicate the resources that a company can expect to have available to it in future years. So a firm that has relied on relatively low-wage young labour—such as retailing—will need to have regard to the future availability of this type of worker when developing its product strategy. A retailer might decide to invest in more automated methods of processing transactions and handling customer enquiries rather than rely on a traditional but diminishing source of relatively low-cost labour.

The study of demographics also has implications that affect public sector services, which are themselves becoming more marketing-orientated. Changing population structures influence the community facilities that need to be provided by the government; for example, fluctuations in the number of children have affected the number of schools and teachers required, while the increasing number of elderly people will require the provision of more specialized housing and hospital facilities.

In an even wider sense, demographic change can influence the nature of family life and communities and ultimately affect the social and economic system in which businesses operate. For example, the imbalance that is developing between a growing dependent elderly population and a diminishing population of working age could affect government fiscal policy and the way in which we care for the elderly, with major implications for marketing.

Although demographics has assumed great importance in Western Europe in recent years, study of the consequences of population change dates back considerably further.

T. R. Malthus studied the effects of population changes in a paper published in 1798 entitled

'An Essay on the Principle of Population as it Effects the Future Improvement of Society'. Malthus predicted that the population would continue to grow exponentially, while world food resources would grow at a slower, linear, rate. Population growth would be held back only by 'war, pestilence and famine' until an equilibrium point was again reached at which the size of the population was just equal to the food resources available.

Malthus's model of population growth failed to predict the future accurately, and this only serves to highlight the difficulty of forecasting population levels, when the underlying assumptions on which forecasts are based are themselves changing. On the one hand, Malthus failed to anticipate the tremendous improvement in agricultural efficiency, which would allow a larger population to be sustained, while on the other hand he was unable to foretell changes in social and cultural attitudes which were to limit family size.

9.2   CHANGES IN WORLD POPULATION LEVELS

Globally, population is expanding at a rapid and increasing rate. The world population level in AD 1000 has been estimated to have been about 300 million. Over the following 750 years, it rose at a steady rate to 728 million in 1750. Thereafter, the rate of increase became progressively more rapid, doubling in the following 150 years to 1,550 million in 1900 and almost doubling again to 3,000 million in the 62 years to 1962. It is predicted that world population will double again in an even shorter period—a United Nations Report has predicted that it will have doubled to 6,000 million in 2001, in just 30 years. Despite this exponential nature of world population increase, it should be noted that there is still considerable debate about the likely world population level at the turn of the century, with many predictions being revised downwards.

The growth of world population has not been uniform, with the main growth occurring in the Far Eastern countries, especially Korea and China, and South America. By contrast, the total population levels of most Western developed countries are stable, or in some cases actually declining. An indication of the variation in population growth rates is given in Figure 9.1.

A growth in the population of a country does not necessarily mean a growth in market opportunity, for the countries with the highest population growth rates also tend to be those with the lowest gross national product per head; indeed, in many countries of Africa, total GNP is not keeping up with the growth in population levels, resulting in an ever lower GNP per head. On the other hand, the growth in population results in a large and low-cost labour force, which can help to explain the tendency for many European-based businesses to base their design capacity in Europe but locate the relatively labour-intensive assembly operations in the Far East.

9.3   CHANGES IN UK POPULATION LEVEL

The first British census was carried out in 1801, and the subsequent ten-yearly censuses provide the basis for studying changes in the size of the British population. A summary of British population growth is shown in Table 9.1.

The fluctuation in the rate of population growth can be attributed to three main factors: the birth rate, the death rate, and the difference between inward and outward migration. The fluctuation in these rates is illustrated in Figure 9.2. These three components of population change are described in more detail below.

9.4   THE BIRTH RATE

The birth rate is usually expressed in terms of the number of live births per 1,000 population. Since the Second World War, the birth rate has shown a number of distinct cyclical tendencies.

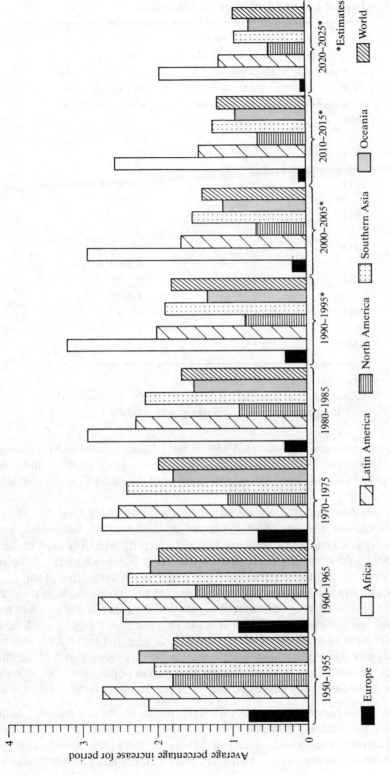

Figure 9.1 World population changes
Source: Based on UN estimates, 1985.

Table 9.1 Population growth, 1801–2003

Year	Population of England, Wales & Scotland ('000)	Ave. % increase per decade
1801	10,501	
		13.9
1871	26,072	
		9.4
1911	40,891	
		4.5
1941	46,605	
		5.8
1971	54,369	
		0.8
1984	54,910	
		1.0
1993*	55,382	
		1.3
2003*	56,138	

* Estimated.
Source: *Annual Abstract of Statistics*, 1986. Reproduced with the permission of the Controller of HMSO.

The immediate postwar years are associated with a 'baby boom', followed by a steady decrease in the number of births until 1955. Following this, the rate rose again until the mid-1960s during a second but lesser baby boom. The birth rate then fell until the mid-1970s, rising again in recent years.

In order to explain these trends, it is necessary to examine two key factors: first, the number of women in the population who are of child-bearing age, the second, the proportion of these women who actually give birth. (This is referred to as the fertility rate.) The peak in the birth rate of the early 1960s could be partly explained by the 'baby boom' children of the immediate postwar period working through to child-bearing age; and similarly, this group is itself now reaching child-bearing age, accounting for some of the recent increase in the birth rate. Greater doubt lies over reasons for changes in the fertility rate, usually expressed in terms of the number of births per 1,000 women aged between 16 and 44. This has varied from a peak of 115 at the beginning of the century to a low point of 56.8 in 1983, as seen in Table 9.2.

There are many possible explanations for changes in fertility rates, and it is our difficulty in understanding the precise nature of these changes that makes population forecasting a difficult task. Some of the more frequently suggested causes of the declining fertility rate are as follows:

1. A large family is no longer seen as an insurance policy for future parental security. The extended family has declined in importance, and state institutions have taken over many of the welfare functions concerning elderly members of the family which were previously expected of children. Furthermore, infant and child mortality has declined and consequently

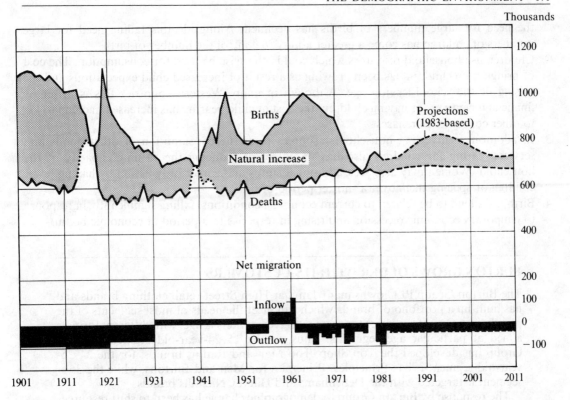

Figure 9.2   Changes in the UK birth rate, death rate and level of migration, 1901–2021
Source: Office of Population Censuses and Survey, Government Actuary's Department. ©
Crown copyright.

Table 9.2 General UK fertility rate: total births
per 1,000 women aged 15–44, 1900–1989

Year	Fertility rate
1900	115.0
1933	81.0
1951	73.0
1961	90.6
1971	84.3
1981	62.1
1983	56.8
1989	62.4

Source: *Social Trends* (1989), OPCS. © Crown
copyright. Figure 1.4.

the need for large numbers of births has declined. Alongside this falling need for large numbers of children has come a greater ability to control the number of births.

2. Children use household resources which could otherwise be used for consumption. The cost of bringing up children has been growing as a result of increased child expectations and the raising of the school-leaving age. Although in many Western countries this is offset by financial incentives for having children, the cost of child-rearing has increased in comparison to other consumer purchases.

3. In addition to diverting household resources from the consumption of other goods and services, caring for children also has the effect of reducing the earning capacity of the household. Women may also seek additional status and career progression by having fewer children or spacing them over a shorter period of time.

4. Birth rates tend to be related to current economic conditions, falling significantly in response to temporary economic recession and rising in response to a period of economic boom.

BURTON GROWS OLDER WITH ITS CUSTOMERS

The Burton Group PLC owns many familiar High Street retail clothing brands and has built up a portfolio of brands which can meet the needs of most segments of the population. One of the bases for segmenting its markets is age, with different formats aimed at particular age segments. Thus, in the 15–24-year-old segment, Burton Group has developed the Top Shop, Top Man and Radius brands; for the 24–35-year-old segment it has Principles, Principles for Men and Burtons, while the 35+ segment is targeted with the Debenhams and Harvey Nicholls brands.

The response by Burton Group to demographic change has been to shift resources to those brands serving segments facing the strongest demographic growth. During the 1970s, when the number of teenagers reached a peak (following the 1960s baby boom), heavy investment was made in expanding the Top Shop and Top Man brands. During the 1980s this bulge of births matured, carrying through with it new attitudes to fashion. In response to both the growing numbers of 24–35-year-olds and their increasing fashion consciousness, the Burton Group channelled resources into its new Principles and Principles for Men brands, both aimed at this group. During most of the 1980s, the Debenhams brand had been the 'cash cow' of the Burton Group—a relatively static business which had ceased to grow, producing steady but not spectacular profits. Its product offering was geared mainly to the older segments of the population, which had not shown the growth in spending power of younger groups. To try and bring more business back into the stores, a lot of space within Debenhams was turned into concessions for other brands within the Burton Group. This had the effect of attracting many of the younger customers into the stores.

By the end of the 1980s, however, the teenage market had gone into numerical decline, while the number of people aged over 50 was increasing not only numerically, but even more so in terms of their spending power. The Burton Group responded to this in various ways. The Debenhams chain which had been static during the 1980s received new investment with a series of new store openings. The brand emphasized older age groups' values of quality and durability—as opposed to purely fashionability—in its product offering. The space allocated within Debenhams to the younger Top Shop and Top Man has been reduced. Meanwhile, the Dorothy Perkins brand, which had previously targeted 18–40-year-old women, was refocused to meet the needs of the more discerning 30–40-year-old woman.

9.5   THE DEATH RATE

Death rates are normally expressed as the number of people in the country that die in a year per 1,000 of the population. This is sometimes called the crude death rate; the age-specific death rate takes account of the age of death and is expressed as the number of people per 1,000 of a particular age group that die in a year.

In contrast to the volatility of the birth rate during the postwar period, the death rate has been relatively stable and has played a relatively small part in changing the population level. The main feature of mortality in the UK has been a small decline in age-specific death rates, having the effect of increasing the survival chances of older people. The age-specific death rate of women has fallen more significantly than for men. The main reasons for the decline in age-specific death rates are the improved standard of living, a better environment and better health services. While age-specific death rates have been falling in most advanced industrial countries, the UK has generally experienced a slower fall than most other EC members.

9.6   MIGRATION

If immigration is compared with emigration, a figure for net migration is obtained. During most periods of this century, the UK has experienced a net outflow of population, the main exceptions being the 1930s, when emigrants to the Commonwealth returned home during the Depression; the 1940s, when a large number of refugees entered the UK from Nazi Europe; and the late 1950s/early 1960s, when the prosperity of the British economy attracted large numbers of immigrants from the new Commonwealth. Emigration has tended to peak at times of economic depression in the UK.

While migration has had only a marginal effect upon the total population level, it has had a more significant effect on the population structure. On the demand side, many immigrants have come from different cultural backgrounds and pose new opportunities and problems for segmenting markets for goods and services. Furthermore, immigrants themselves need to be segmented into various ethnic minorities, each with differing needs. Table 9.3 indicates the extent of the main ethnic minorities in the UK.

In some cases, completely new markets have emerged specifically for ethnic minorities, such as the market for black sticking plasters. It has sometimes proved difficult for established businesses to gain access to immigrant segments. Many companies have not adequately researched the attitudes and buying processes of these groups, with the result that, in markets as diverse as vegetables, clothing and travel, ethnic minorities have supported businesses run by fellow members of their own minority groups. On the supply side, immigrants have tended to be of working age and have filled a vital role in providing labour for the economy. Moreover, some Asian minorities have brought vital entrepreneurial skills to the economy. Balanced against this is the fact that the emigrants that Britain has lost have tended to be highly trained and dynamic.

9.7   THE AGE STRUCTURE OF THE POPULATION

It was noted earlier that the total population of the UK—and indeed, of most countries in the EC—is fairly stable. Within this stable total, there has been a more noted change in the composition of particular age groups. The age distribution of the population can be shown by means of a histogram.

Figure 9.3 shows the distribution of age groups at yearly intervals and for males and females. Some bulges in the distribution are evident, and these have a number of marketing implications.

Table 9.3 Great Britain population by ethnic group, 1981–9

	Number ('000)	% of UK population
Indian	787	1.44
West Indian or Guyanese	495	0.91
Pakistani	428	0.78
Chinese	125	0.23
African	112	0.20
Bangladeshi	108	0.19
Arab	73	0.13
Mixed	287	5.26
Other	163	2.99
Total ethnic minorities	2,577	4.72
Not stated	472	0.86
White	51,470	94.40
Total population	54,519	100.00

Source: 'Estimates of the ethnic minority populations of Great Britain, 1987–89' in 'In Brief', *Population Trends*, Spring 1991, no. 63. Figures derive from the Labour Force Surveys for 1981, 1987, 1988 and 1989. Office of Population Censuses and Surveys. © Crown copyright.

The shortage of 8–15-year-olds will in due course pose problems for businesses serving the young adult market as well as depriving firms of a traditional source of relatively low-cost labour. The declining presence of this group may alter many of the values of our youth-orientated culture; for example, the emphasis on fashion and short-life products may give way to an emphasis on quality and durability as the growing numbers in the older age groups increasingly dominate cultural values. Another major issue that may affect the cultural environment of marketing is the growing imbalance between the size of the working population and an increasingly large dependent population.

9.8 EC COMPARISONS

Although the population of most EC countries is stable, a number of structural differences can be noted between member-states. From Table 9.4, it can be seen that an exporter to the Irish Republic will face a much younger age structure than that in the domestic UK market, and an even younger age structure than that in West Germany. Also, the total population of the Irish Republic is likely to grow the most rapidly, in contrast to Belgium and West Germany, which are expected to fall.

9.9 HOUSEHOLD STRUCTURE

Marketers focus a lot of attention on the household as the unit of consumption. It is therefore vital to understand the components of the household and hence the resulting decision-making unit. In household structure, several important trends can be noted.

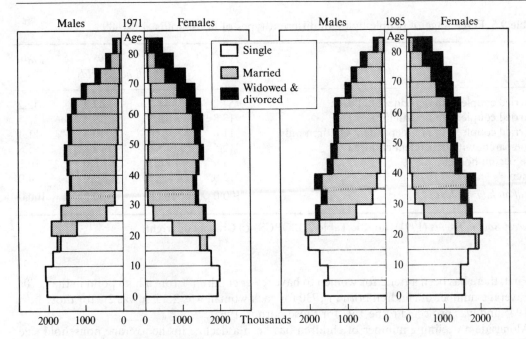

Figure 9.3 Age distribution of the population of England and Wales by sex, age and marital status in 1986
Source: Population Census, 1971 and 1985, Office of Population Censuses and Surveys.
© Crown copyright.

[1] Figures for 1985 are on the new census base and definition of population, which includes residents absent from Britain and excludes overseas visitors. The reverse was the case in 1971.
[2] 'Married' includes separated people.

Table 9.4 Population structure of the EC, 1985

	Population	Birth rate	Death rate	Percentage aged under 15	Percentage aged 60+	% increase 1985–90	% increase 1985–2000
UK	56.6	13.3	11.8	19	21	1.23	4.06
Belgium	9.9	11.6	11.2	19	20	− 1.02	− 2.06
Denmark	5.1	10.5	11.4	18	20	0.00	1.96
France	55.2	13.9	10.0	21	19	1.63	4.89
W. Germany	61.0	9.6	11.5	15	20	0.00	− 0.82
Greece	9.9	11.7	9.3	21	18	1.01	4.04
Irish Republic	3.5	17.6	9.4	30	15	5.70	14.28
Italy	57.1	10.1	9.5	19	19	3.50	1.75
Luxembourg	0.4	11.2	11.3	17	18	0.00	0.00
Netherlands	14.5	12.3	8.5	19	17	2.75	7.58
Portugal	10.3	12.8	9.6	23	17	1.01	7.77
Spain	38.6	12.1	7.7	23	17	1.55	5.44

Source: Statistical Office of the European Communities.

Table 9.5 Percentage of people living in different types of households, 1961–89

	1961	1971	1981	1989
		(% of all households)		
Married couple with dependent children	52.2	51.7	47.4	42.2
Married couple with no children	17.8	19.3	19.5	22.4
Married couple with non-dependent children only	11.6	10.0	10.3	11.4
Lone parent with dependent children	2.5	3.5	5.8	5.8
One-person household	3.9	6.3	8.0	10.2
Other	12.0	9.2	9.0	8.0
Total all households	100.0	100.0	100.0	100.0

Source: Social Trends (1991), no. 21, Table 2.3. OPCS. © Crown copyright.

First, there has been a trend for women to have fewer children. From a high point in the 1870s, the average number of children born in 1930 for each woman was 2.35; it was 2.2 for those born in 1945 and was projected to be 1.97 for those born in 1965.

Alongside a declining number of children has been a decline in the average household size. This has fallen continuously, from an average of 2.91 people in 1971 to 2.56 in 1985. There has been a particular fall in the number of large households with five or more people (down from 18 per cent of all households in 1951 to 9 per cent in 1986) and a significant increase in the number of one-person households (up from 11 per cent to 25 per cent over the same period). A number of factors have contributed to the increase in one-person households, including the increase in solitary survivors, later marriage and an increased divorce rate. The marketing implications of the growth of this group are numerous, ranging from an increased demand for smaller units of housing to the types and sizes of groceries purchased. A single-person household is likely to use different types of retail outlets compared with the household buying as a unit; the single person may be more likely to use a niche retailer than the (typically) housewife buying for the whole family whose needs may be better met by a department store or supermarket.

The typical family is often portrayed as comprising a husband, a wife and two children. In fact, marketers cannot afford to ignore the many significant deviations from this apparent norm. Table 9.5 shows that only 42 per cent of all households comprise a married couple with dependent children. The proportion of single-person households now accounts for one-tenth of all households.

The role of the woman in the household structure has also been changing, with 59 per cent of all wives having some form of employment in 1985 (compared with 54 per cent in 1973). Along with this has been the emergence of a large segment of career-minded women who are cash-rich but time-poor. This has created new opportunities for labour-saving consumer durables in the home and for convenience foods. It has also resulted in women becoming important target markets for products that were previously considered to be male preserves, such as new cars.

9.10   GEOGRAPHICAL DISTRIBUTION OF THE POPULATION

The population density of the UK of 231 people per square kilometre is one of the highest in the world. However, this figure hides the fact that the population is dispersed very unevenly and the distribution is not static.

9.10.1 Regional distribution

The major feature of the regional distribution of the UK population is the dominance of the South East of England, with 30 per cent of the population, and the industrial regions of the West Midlands, Lancashire and Yorkshire. By contrast, the populations of Scotland, Wales and Northern Ireland account in total for only 17 per cent of the total population.

Movement between the regions tends to be a very gradual process. In an average year, about 10 per cent of the population will change address, but only about one-eighth of these will move to another region. Nevertheless, there have been a number of noticeable trends. First, throughout the twentieth century there has been a general drift of population from the North to the Midlands and South. More recently, there has been a trend for population to move away from the relatively congested South East to East Anglia, the South West and the home counties. This drift of population is illustrated in Figure 9.4. It can be partly explained by the increased cost of industrial and residential location in the South East, the greater locational flexibility of modern industry, and the desire of people for a pleasanter environment in which to live.

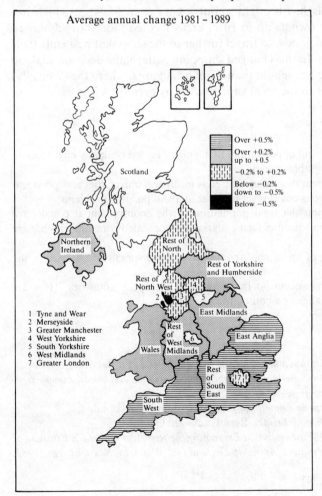

Average annual change 1981 – 1989

Over +0.5%

Over +0.2%
up to +0.5

−0.2% to +0.2%

Below −0.2%
down to −0.5%

Below −0.5%

Scotland

Northern
Ireland

Rest of
North

Rest of Yorkshire
and Humberside

Rest of
North West

East Midlands

1 Tyne and Wear
2 Merseyside
3 Greater Manchester
4 West Yorkshire
5 South Yorkshire
6 West Midlands
7 Greater London

Rest
of
West
Midlands

East Anglia

Wales

Rest
of
South
East

South
West

Figure 9.4 Average annual population change in UK by region, 1981–1989
Source: Office of Population Censuses and Surveys; General Register Office (Scotland); General Register Office (Northern Ireland)

9.10.2   Urban concentration

Another trend has been a shift in the proportion of the population living in urban areas. Throughout most of Western Europe, the nineteenth and twentieth centuries have been associated with a drift from rural areas to towns. In the UK, this has resulted in the urban areas of Greater London, Greater Manchester, Merseyside, Greater Glasgow, West Midlands, West Yorkshire and Tyneside having just one-thirtieth of the UK's surface area, but nearly one-third of the total population. More recently, the trend towards urbanization has been partly reversed, with many of the larger conurbations experiencing a decline in population since the 1960s, combined with a deterioration in many inner-city areas. Those moving out have tended to be the most economically active, leaving behind a relatively elderly and poor population. Much of the movement from the conurbations has been towards the rural areas just beyond the urban fringe; for example, London has lost population to the home counties of Berkshire, Buckinghamshire, Hertfordshire and Essex. The increasingly large dormitory population of these areas remains dependent on the neighbouring conurbation.

Movement from urban to rural areas has brought about a change in life-style which has implications for marketing. Higher car ownership in rural areas has led more households to make fewer shopping trips for household goods, to travel further to the shop that best suits their life-style, and to spend more on each trip. In this changed shopping pattern, the decision-making unit may comprise more members of the household than in an urban area, where the (typically) wife may have made more frequent trips to the local supermarket by herself.

REVIEW QUESTIONS

1. Examine some of the marketing problems and opportunities that a major record company might face in changing its strategy in response to demographic trends.
2. Consider some of the implications of current demographic trends on British universities and polytechnics. Suggest ways in which these institutions could react in order to avoid possible problems.
3. Migration may have had little effect upon the total population of the country, but it could have significant effects on the problems and opportunities facing marketing-orientated companies. What are these problems and opportunities?
4. What are the implications for marketing of an increasing number of career-orientated women in the population?
5. Migration from urban to rural areas has occurred in many West European countries. How are consumers' spending patterns likely to change as a consequence?

FURTHER READING

Barker, T. and Drake, M. (eds) (1982), *Population and Society in Britain, 1850–1980*, Batsford, London.

Champion, A. *et al.* (1987), *Changing Places: Britain's demographic, economic and social complexion*, Edward Arnold, London.

Findlay, A. and White, P. (1986), *West European Population Change*, Croom Helm, London.

Joshi, H. (ed.) (1989), *The Changing Population of Britain*, Basil Blackwell, Oxford.

Office of Population Census and Surveys (1983), *Population Estimates: the Registrar General's Estimate of the Population of Regions and Local Government Areas of England and Wales by Sex and Age, 1981*, HMSO, London.

UN, *Statistical Pocket Book* (1985), 9th edn, NY.

THE SOCIAL AND CULTURAL ENVIRONMENT

10.1 INTRODUCTION

People are vital to business organizations, and, as Chapter 9 on demography illustrates, it is important for marketers to consider the supply-side as well as demand-side aspects of this factor. On the supply side, individuals represent a key organizational resource and one on which the success (or otherwise) of an enterprise largely depends. On the demand side, it is individuals or groups of individuals who are a company's customers or potential customers, and marketers are seeking not only to retain the loyalty of existing buyers, but also to convert the latter into the former. A critical requirement for any business enterprise is to appreciate that demand-side and supply-side aspects are mutually interdependent, given that inputs generate output and output generates inputs. As Kotler and others have argued, it is the key role of strategic management to develop and maintain an effective match between an organization's resources (including people) and its market opportunities, and in doing so to permit the organization to achieve its objectives (see Kotler and Armstrong, 1989, Ch. 2).

In particular, marketers need to consider what factors influence a person's behaviour, especially with regard to consumption. Why, for example, does one person choose one brand of a product while another chooses a different brand—or, for that matter, does not consume the product at all? In seeking an answer to such a question, one may initially be led to consider differences in income or sex or age, and these indeed may explain some differences in consumer behaviour. For most consumer purchases, however, it is likely that a number of other factors will be significant, including the influence of a person's social and cultural environment. As the discussion below illustrates, while for the most part these variables cannot be controlled by the marketer, an understanding of their influence on buying behaviour can help marketers to select the most effective product design, method of promotion, price, channels of distribution and other aspects of the marketing programme.

10.2 SOCIAL INFLUENCES

10.2.1 Social class

Individuals in society can be categorized in a number of ways. One such category is social class. The basic idea of class is that a society can be divided into broad strata which comprise individuals whose members share certain common features, such as type of occupation, income level, educational background and/or other generally acceptable variables. Allocating people to a particular class category usually involves one of three approaches (see Chisnall, 1985, Ch. 7):

1. The subjective approach—where participants are asked to decide their own social class
2. The reputational approach—where individuals are asked to determine the social class of others in the community
3. The objective approach—where non-participants allocate individuals on the basis of various predetermined factors (e.g. occupation, education, income and wealth, life-style)

In general, the objective approach tends to be the one most readily used, given that it is relatively easy to apply and is thought to be the most accurate.

Through this means of social differentiation, social scientists are able to build up a picture of a society's class structure and to distribute individuals among particular class categories. While in some societies an individual may not be able to change his or her social position, in others the boundaries between social classes are relatively flexible and individuals may change classes over their lifetimes. Either way, marketers are interested in the idea of social class because class is seen to be a key determinant of a person's behaviour—including buying behaviour.

A number of examples of social class categories are given below. Table 10.1 shows the system of classification used by the Institute of Practitioners in Advertising (IPA), which bases its class categories on the occupation of the head of the household, and which is used as a main method of classification in British media audience studies.

Table 10.1 Social class: IPA definition

Class category	Occupation
A	Higher managerial, administrative, or professional
B	Intermediate managerial, administrative or professional
C1	Supervisory or clerical, and junior managerial, administrative or professional
C2	Skilled manual workers
D	Semi- and unskilled manual workers
E	State pensioners or widows (no other earners), casual or lower-grade workers, or long-term unemployed.

Source: *Social Trends* (1991). Reproduced with the permission of the Controller of HMSO.

A similar system is used for the General Household Survey in Britain, which defines socio-economic groupings in occupational terms, based on the Registrar General's classification of occupations for 1980 (see Table 10.2). Non-manual occupations comprise SEGs 1–6 and 13; manual occupations comprise SEGs 7–12, 14 and 15.

In the USA, one system of classification (Kotler and Armstrong, 1989) identifies seven social class categories ranging from 'Upper Uppers' through 'Middle Class' to 'Lower Lowers'. 'Upper Uppers' are individuals who live on inherited wealth, normally have well-known family backgrounds, give large donations to charity and send their children to the finest schools. The 'Middle Class' refers to those white- and blue-collar workers on average pay, who live on the better side of town in a nice neighbourhood with good schools. In contrast, 'Lower Lowers' are individuals on welfare, who are visibly poverty-stricken and out of work or working in the dirtiest, lowest paid jobs. Allocation of individuals to the different class categories takes place on the basis of a range of indicators, including income, wealth, occupation, life-style and, even attitudes.

Table 10.2 Socioeconomic groups in Britain

Descriptive definition	Socioeconomic group numbers (SEGs)
Professional	3, 4
Employers and managers	1, 2, 13
Intermediate non-manual	5
Junior non-manual	6
Skilled manual and own account non-professional	8, 9, 12, 14
Semi-skilled manual and personal service	7, 10, 15
Unskilled manual	11

Source: *General Household Survey* (1988). Reproduced with the permission of the Controller of HMSO.

Empirical evidence indicates that individuals' buying behaviour is often more strongly influenced by the class to which they belong, or to which they aspire, than by their incomes alone, and consequently marketers use social class as one means of market segmentation. Kotler and Armstrong (1989, Ch. 5) suggest that social classes have distinct product and brand preferences in such areas as clothing, home furnishings, leisure activities and cars, and that these preferences tend to change as a person moves from one social class to another. 'Upper uppers', for example, are an important market for jewellery, antiques, expensive homes and holidays, and are said to serve as a reference group, to the extent that their consumption habits are often imitated or aspired to by other social classes. In contrast, those in the 'middle class' often buy products that are popular, own imported cars and are seen to be particularly concerned with fashion, seeking the better brand names and keeping up with trends in consumption.

Evidence on social trends in Britain substantiates this link between consumer behaviour and social class. In a survey of leisure activities in 1987, the General Household Survey found that people in professional occupations were at least three times more likely than those in unskilled occupations to visit art galleries or museums, stately homes, castles, cathedrals or other historic buildings (see Table 10.3). Similarly, holiday habits in 1989 were shown to be linked to class differences, with individuals in classes A and B not only more likely to take a holiday than those in social classes D and E, but also five times more likely to have three or more holidays than those in these class categories.

These examples illustrate that social class is one factor influencing buyer behaviour, and that marketers can benefit from acquiring knowledge of the characteristics and typical behaviour patterns of each social class. This applies not only to the types of product bought or to differences in the level of consumption, but also to such things as product design, the kinds of outlets used, methods of selling and selection of advertising media. Studies of social class in Chicago in the 1950s found that customers in the 'lower class' tended to prefer overstuffed or ornate house furnishings and looked on the salesperson as a friend and adviser, whereas the 'middle' and 'upper classes' were more receptive to plain and functional styles and treated the seller as an impersonal guide (McCarthy, 1971, Ch. 7). More recently (1990) a survey by Mintel of beer consumption in Britain found important differences in habits and attitude between the different social classes (*Marketing Intelligence*, February 1991). For example, when questioned

Table 10.3 Attendance at arts and entertainment performances and visits to art galleries, museums and historic buildings; by socioeconomic group, 1987

	Professional	Employers and managers	Inter-mediate and junior non-manual	Skilled manual and own account non-professional	Semi-skilled manual and personal service	Unskilled manual	All groups
	(% in each group participating in each activity in the 4 weeks before interview)						
Arts and entertainments							
Film	15	11	12	8	8	5	11
Plays, pantomimes or musicals	13	10	10	4	4	3	7
Ballet or modern dances	1	1	1	1	—	1	1
Operas or operettas	2	2	1	—	—	—	1
Classical music	6	3	3	1	1	1	2
Jazz, blues, soul, reggae	2	2	2	1	1	—	2
Other music shows	9	7	8	7	6	5	7
Galleries, museums, historic buildings							
Art galleries or museums	15	11	11	6	5	4	8
Stately homes, castles, cathedrals or other historic buildings	14	11	10	6	5	4	8

Source: *Social Trends* (1991). Reproduced with the permission of the Controller of HMSO.

about the benefit of low-alcohol beers, Mintel found that it was the higher socioeconomic groups that responded positively to this idea rather than people in class categories C2, D and E. According to the survey, this reflected differences in perceptions of health, as well as the fact that the higher socioeconomic groups are more likely to possess a car and hence be more concerned with the question of drink-driving.

10.2.2   Reference groups

Reference groups are groups that have either a direct (i.e. face-to-face) or indirect influence on a person's attitudes, values, opinions and/or behaviour. In some cases, the individual may be a member of the group, and this will have a direct influence on his or her behaviour patterns, with the group(s) serving as a 'frame of reference' for the individual member. In other cases individuals may aspire to membership of a group to which they do not currently belong, and this too can influence the way they behave and react. Membership groups include the family, friends and work colleagues with whom regular and informal interaction takes place (known as 'primary groups'), as well as those groups such as trade unions, religious groups and clubs with whom interaction tends to be more restricted and more formal (termed 'secondary groups'). 'Aspirational groups' are those to which the individual wishes to belong and which can range from a gang or terrorist group to a sporting team or even a particular social class.

   While a person may not be influenced by all the attitudes or behaviour patterns of a particular reference group, the fact that such influence occurs at all makes it important for marketers to try to identify the reference groups of the target markets they are selling to. Naturally, the importance of group influence will tend to vary across products and brands, but it appears to be at its greatest where only a few people own a particular product (e.g. a 'luxury') or where other individuals are able to 'see' a product or brand that is being consumed (Kotler and Armstrong, 1989, Ch. 5). In the case of a product that is consumed by a limited number of individuals and in which the consumer's choice is visible, group influence is likely to affect not only the choice of product but also the choice of brand (e.g. membership of a particular golf club).

Marketers have recognized that, in cases where group influence is strong, informal face-to-face advice can often be more influential in deciding consumer behaviour than advertising. In this context the identification of group opinion leaders becomes critical. Opinion leaders are those members of a reference group who, because of some particular characteristic (e.g. knowledge, skill, experience, personality), are able to exert influence over others. If marketers are able to identify such individuals, and to direct their promotional activities at influencing the influencers, then a significant opportunity exists for increasing consumer purchases—a point not lost on companies who use media or sporting personalities to 'endorse' their products and brands.

10.2.3 Family

For the vast majority of people, the family is a vital reference group and one that influences a person's perceptions and behaviour. Apart from the central role as a transmitter of cultural values and norms, the family can exercise a strong influence on an individual's buying behaviour, and this influence may persist even if the individual no longer has much contact with his or her parents. As individuals move from being children in a family to being parents, it is likely that family influences *by* them and *on* them will change, and this fact has been recognized in the notion of the 'family life-cycle'. Accordingly, marketers often use life-cycle stages as a means of defining their target markets in order to develop appropriate offerings and marketing strategies.

Studies of family buying behaviour have indicated that an individual's role and influence in the purchase decision can vary quite considerably between products and over time and that it is important to distinguish, *inter alia*, who makes the buying decision, who influences the buying decision, who make the physical purchase and who uses the product. For example, with expensive products and services (e.g. holidays), husbands and wives are more likely to engage in joint decision-making than in the case of more routine purchases, where either person may be the sole or dominant decision-maker. Marketing planners, however, need to be constantly vigilant as changes in economic, social or cultural circumstances may result in changes in the roles and relative influence of family members in the buying process. Food and household items, for instance, have normally been seen as products predominantly purchased by wives, while car purchases are generally associated with husbands. And yet, as recent surveys have shown, these buying roles have undergone considerable change as a result of such factors as increased female participation rates, later marriages, growing numbers of single-parent families and changing cultural attitudes.

It is not difficult to see that, if marketers can understand the dynamics of the family decision-making process and identify the roles and relative influences of different individuals, then they can be more effective in targeting their products and messages at the right family members. It is no coincidence that in the period before Christmas leading manufacturers of toys and games advertise their brands during peak children's TV viewing times, since it is widely accepted that parents' purchase decisions for these products are influenced by their children's expressed preferences.

10.2.4 Life-styles

Life-styles are the ways in which people live and spend their money. Chisnall (1985, Ch. 6) describes them as distinctive or characteristic ways of living adopted by certain communities or sections of community, particularly with regard to their general attitudes and behaviour towards the use of time, money and effort. In effect, they represent an attempt to classify individuals on the basis of their interests, activities and opinions, as well as their demographic characteristics. The proposition is that, by examining an individual's behavioural traits, one can build up a clearer picture of how a person acts and interacts in the world, and in doing so can infer certain things about that person's habits and behaviour. Perhaps not surprisingly, marketers have seen life-style analysis as a useful tool in the examination and segmentation of markets. Consequently, marketing programmes and communications have often been designed to appeal to specific life-style groups.

A well-known example of a life-style classification system is the SRI values and life-styles (VALS) typology, which classifies Americans into nine life-style groups, according to how they behave, their values, interests and opinions. These are: survivors, sustainers, belongers, emulators, achievers, egotists or 'I-am-Me's', experientials, societally conscious, and integrated. 'Belongers' are traditional, conformist and family-orientated, with a strong need for acceptance and a preference for following rather than leading. In contrast, 'achievers' are people whose drive has taken them to the top and who are hard-working, successful, self-confident and pleased with themselves and their accomplishments. The supposition is that individuals in these different life-style groups may consume different products or buy in different ways or may be receptive to different types of marketing message, and that a knowledge of these differences can help a company to improve its marketing strategy. However, it should not be forgotten that an individual may pass through several life-style groups during the course of a lifetime and may even exhibit traits associated with several different life-styles at one time. Nor should it be assumed that every member of a group will respond in exactly the same way to the stimuli they receive, since a wide range of social, psychological and other factors also influence a person's behaviour.

10.3 CULTURAL INFLUENCES

10.3.1 Macroculture

Culture refers to a complex set of values, beliefs, attitudes, customs, symbols and artefacts which are handed down from generation to generation and which help individuals to communicate, interpret and evaluate as members of a given society. Defined in this way, culture can be seen to have three important features:

1. It comprises both abstract (e.g. symbols, rituals, values) and material elements (e.g. human artefacts including literature, art, music, buildings).
2. It is socially transmitted and learned.
3. It influences human behaviour.

Since part of this behaviour involves consumption, culture represents an important influence on consumer behaviour in both a general and a specific way. As Oliver (1990, Ch. 3) argues, at a general level it may provide standards that direct a person's life-style; specifically, it may encourage or discourage consumption of particular products or services.

It is easy to underestimate the extent to which a person's behaviour is culturally determined. A child growing up in a society learns about its values, norms and acceptable forms of behaviour from the family and a range of other socio-cultural institutions, and these agencies of socialization provide behavioural guidelines for the individual. Some of these guidelines tend to be relatively enduring and represent 'core' values and beliefs, which are central to understanding a person's attitudes and behaviour. Others may be of 'secondary' importance and are therefore more susceptible to change over time. In Britain, for example, the acceptance of monogamy represents a core belief and one that few if any would disagree with. At the same time, the growing incidence of divorce and the increasing number of single-parent families suggest that attitudes towards the sanctity of marriage have undergone considerable change in recent years.

An understanding of culture and, in particular, an appreciation of cultural differences is clearly important for marketers. Individuals from different cultures not only buy different products, but may also respond in different ways to the same product because of cultural influences. (For instance, eating horsemeat is acceptable in France but not in Britain.) Culture may also affect marketing practices in other ways, including:

- Deciding who does the buying or how it is bought or where it is bought (e.g. women are the predominant purchasers of household products in some, but not all, cultures)
- Determining which colours are acceptable, because of symbolic associations (e.g. the colour associated with mourning/bereavement varies across cultures)
- Influencing how a sale takes place (e.g. bribes are acceptable in some cultures)
- Shaping the nature of the marketing message or deciding on the most appropriate medium of communication (e.g. in Britain a single shared language makes it possible to communicate through national media)
- Determining cross-cultural marketing strategies (e.g. designing products and promotions that avoid clashes with foreign cultures)

In short, culture not only conditions an individual's response to products and influences the nature of the purchase process, but it also exercises considerable influence on the structure of consumption within a given society. As such, it provides both opportunities and challenges for marketing organizations that should not be overlooked.

Nor should it be forgotten that culture itself is marketable. A report produced for the British Invisibles Cultural Sector Working Party in March 1991 estimated that Britain was making a small fortune from its cultural exports, with overseas earnings from culture and arts-related tourism having soared from £4 billion in 1984–5 to £6 billion in 1988–9. This increase put the cultural sector on a par with export earnings from the oil industry and placed it among the leading invisible contributors to the British balance of payments (see e.g. the *Guardian*, 16 March 1991).

10.3.2 Microculture (sub-culture)

No society is totally homogeneous. Every culture contains smaller sub-cultures, or groups of people with shared value systems which are based on common experiences and situations. These identifiable sub-groups may be distinguished by race, nationality, religion, age, geographical location or some other factor, and attitudes and behaviour in such groups will often reflect sub-cultural influences. In Britain, nationality groups such as the Welsh, the Irish and the Scots, together with more recent migrants, are readily apparent, and the spatial concentration of these groups helps to reinforce sub-cultural differences, including language, traditions and life-styles. Similarly, large groupings of ethnic minorities in particular parts of the country have given rise to a truly multicultural society that is reflected in differences in attitudes, values, eating habits, styles, customs, taboos, etc. In Leicester, for example, where a quarter of the population is Asian, a large number of retailers cater for the particular taste of this ethnic minority, and this provision extends to services as well as goods (e.g. bureaux for arranged marriages). As Kotler and others have indicated, these and many other sub-cultures often represent important market segments, and marketers can find it advantageous to provide products and marketing programmes tailored to the needs of the various sub-cultural groups.

10.4   REGIONAL VARIATIONS

Different classes and cultural groups are not usually spread evenly across a country. It is more normal for local and regional variations to occur, and it is important for marketers (and, for that matter, political parties) to recognize these differences when planning their marketing activities. In this context, their task tends to be made much easier by data on regional variations produced by a range of public and private agencies in most countries.

Table 10.4 Population in private households, by ethnic groups, 1986–8

| | Ethnic minority groups | | | | White | All ethnic groups[a] | Ethnic minority population as % of all ethnic groups |
| | West Indian or African | Indian, Pakistani or Bangladeshi | Other | Total | | | |
			(thousands)				
UK	607	1,323	648	2,577	51,470	54,519	4.7
North	2	26	13	42	2,982	3,042	1.4
Yorkshire & Humberside	28	137	40	205	4,610	4,847	4.2
East Midlands	18	107	32	157	3,708	3,899	4.0
East Anglia	4	17	19	41	1,925	1,982	2.1
South East	410	603	382	1,395	15,438	16,997	8.2
South West	16	13	25	54	4,406	4,494	1.2
West Midlands	87	248	42	377	4,729	5,140	7.3
North West	34	137	57	228	5,989	6,289	3.6
England	599	1,288	611	2,499	43,788	46,690	5.4
Wales	4	12	19	35	2,739	2,804	1.2
Scotland	3	23	17	43	4,943	5,025	0.9

[a] Includes white and ethnic groups not stated.
Source: *Regional Trends* (1990) compiled by CSO. Reproduced with the permission of the Controller of HMSO.

A good example of what information is available can be seen in Table 10.4, which shows the regional distribution of the population in Britain by ethnic group for the period 1986–8. As the table shows, ethnic minority groups such as West Indians and Asians tend to be concentrated in particular regions of the country, especially the North West, Yorkshire, the Midlands and parts of the South East. Further analysis of these regions indicates that within each area the greatest concentration of these ethnic sub-cultures is in major cities and towns, such as Bradford, Leeds, Leicester, Birmingham and London.

THE ETHNIC FOOD BUSINESS

Research by Saker and Brooke into Asian and Afro-Caribbean food businesses that were located in the West Midlands has provided some interesting insights into the ethnic business community (Saker and Brooke, 1989). The project had been commissioned by a consortium of small business support agencies based in Birmingham in light of the high failure rate found in the ethnic minority food sector. The researchers sought to test the hypothesis that business failures were the result of poor equipment and production techniques, which resulted in poor-quality products and a failure to attract customers. Their research covered food manufacturers, wholesalers, restaurants/take-aways and sweet centres.

The research's main finding was that business survival appeared linked to the market orientation adopted by the respective businesses, rather than to equipment or production techniques. Those businesses that relied essentially on the 'ethnic market' (e.g. Afro-Caribbean bakeries and some restaurants) had a much higher failure rate than those that took a broader market stance (e.g. wholesalers, non-ethnic-orientated restaurants). An interesting exception was sweet centres, which were predominately ethnic-orientated but which had the longest average survival rate of any of the categories.

Saker and Brooke come to the conclusion that it was the characteristic of a particular market that was a key factor in business success, and that reliance on the ethnic market alone was insufficient to sustain many small ethnic businesses. While sweet centres benefited from their ethnic orientation by operating predominately as contract caterers for Asian weddings, religious festivals and family parties, other types of businesses could not be supported by the minority community on its own. An apparently large and concentrated market could not provide enough customers, given the high propensity for members of the ethnic minority, say, to eat in a family home rather than in restaurants. In effect, those businesses that were deliberately ignoring the ethnicity of their particular market appeared to be the ones most likely to survive.

These findings give rise to the question of why different ethnic businesses have different market orientations. What socio-cultural factors help to determine why a large percentage of entrepreneurs in the ethnic food business choose an operation that appears to lead eventually to business failure?

Saker (1989) suggests that, when comparing businesses with an ethnic and non-ethnic orientation, two main differences become evident. First, ethnic-market-orientated businesses tend to exploit more readily the social network found in the ethnic community during the start-up process (e.g. using funds from family and friends, employing family or near-family); in contrast, non-ethnic market businesses often seek finance, equipment and staff from more conventional business sources (e.g. banks, estate agents). While the former makes it easier for ethnic businesses to become established, it may lead the entrepreneur to take for granted the existence of an adequate market, rather than to seek to justify and explore the market's potential—something that is likely to be required where a business has to justify a loan from a financial institution.

Second, the non-ethnic-orientated businesses tended to be owned by individuals with better academic qualifications, though not invariably in marketing or management. The significance of this difference appears related to the willingness and/or ability of individuals to seek access to the conventional small business support network. Individuals with superior qualifications probably felt less marginalized and had a greater opportunity to exploit agencies outside their own social network, thus helping to condition their approach to start-up and hence their subsequent market orientation. In short, the research indicates the importance of social influences in small business decision-making within this sector of the ethnic business community.

Table 10.5 Distribution of household income, 1987–8

	% of households in each weekly income group								Ave. income per household (£/wk)
	Under 60	60 but under 80	80 but under 100	100 but under 150	150 but under 200	200 but under 300	300 but under 400	400 and over	
UK	10.8	7.5	6.0	11.4	9.8	19.6	14.8	20.0	270.0
North	14.9	10.4	7.1	11.2	9.7	20.2	12.8	13.7	220.1
Yorkshire & Humberside	11.6	9.7	7.2	12.0	8.7	22.2	14.8	13.8	232.8
East Midlands	10.9	6.8	6.4	13.2	10.8	20.3	17.6	14.0	241.3
East Anglia	8.8	7.6	7.4	10.0	12.3	23.3	14.4	16.2	256.8
South East	8.2	5.7	4.2	9.0	8.7	17.6	15.6	30.9	338.6
South West	8.0	6.0	5.0	12.9	11.0	21.8	17.0	18.3	273.7
West Midlands	12.2	8.0	7.1	12.0	10.0	19.7	15.1	15.9	241.7
North West	12.3	8.5	7.2	13.5	9.6	18.0	13.1	17.7	245.8
England	10.3	7.3	5.9	11.2	9.6	19.5	15.2	21.1	277.4
Wales	11.0	7.3	7.4	13.6	12.7	22.1	13.0	13.1	227.5
Scotland	14.5	9.1	6.1	13.0	9.4	19.3	13.3	15.3	234.2
Northern Ireland	13.9	10.2	7.8	9.8	12.2	22.4	10.2	13.5	224.8

Source: *Regional Trends* (1990) compiled by CSO. Reproduced with the permission of the Controller of HMSO.

Data on occupational background and other socioeconomic indicators confirm the importance of regional variations in class and culture, and these data are often produced at a relatively high level of specificity. For example, in Table 10.5, the regional distribution of household income is shown across a range of income levels from under £60 per week to £400 and over. Presented in this way, it becomes evident that there is a much larger concentration of high-income households in the South East than elsewhere, and this is reflected in the average weekly income per household, which is around 40–50 per cent higher than many other parts of Britain.

Differences such as these clearly have implications for consumption patterns, and this is well illustrated by Table 10.6, based on a survey carried out by the British Market Research Bureau (BMRB) for Mintel in 1989. Examining patterns of ownership of selected kitchen appliances,

Table 10.6 Ownership of cooled storage equipment by TV region, 1987

Television region	Freezer	Fridge-freezer	Refrigerator only
London/TVS	44	57	8
Anglia/Central	44	47	17
Harlech/TSW	36	53	15
Yorkshire/Tyne Tees	33	59	11
Granada	32	53	16
Scotland	25	54	14

Source: Mintel Special Report, *Chilled Cabinet*, 1990.

BMRB/Mintel's survey suggested that overall ownership of some of these appliances reflected a North/South divide with regard to income levels, with differences being particularly marked in the case of free-standing freezer units.

While it is not being suggested that social and cultural factors alone can account for such regional variations in the consumption of durable goods, it is readily accepted that these factors have a part to play. This may provide a justification for differential marketing policies and strategies in order to achieve the most effective use of organizational efforts and resources.

10.5   SOCIAL AND CULTURAL CHANGE

Social and cultural influences tend to change over time in response to changes in educational opportunities, income, the availability of information, intergenerational factors and a range of other variables. Marketers need to be alert to such changes—and may even be responsible, in part, for causing them—if they are to adjust their programmes to meet new market conditions. Fortunately, regular surveys of social and cultural trends by agencies in both the public and private sectors provide a wealth of data and information for any marketing-orientated organization.

Table 10.7 identifies some of the discernible changes in Western society in recent years and suggests possible marketing implications. While the list is by no means exhaustive, it does stress the importance of attempting to measure and monitor social and cultural developments and the need to consider how these might affect a business organization's target markets, offering, distribution methods, pricing and promotional activities.

Table 10.7 Key cultural changes affecting marketers in Western countries

Changes	Marketing implications
1. Increased time devoted to leisure activities	Growth in demand for time-saving products (e.g. fast foods, microwave ovens); catalogue
2. Increased concern for healthy living	Increased demand for sporting facilities and products; low-fat products; natural foods; private medical services
3. Emphasis on 'quality of life'	Changes in life-styles; 'environmentally friendly' products; new magazines stressing elegance, country life-styles; increased demand for classical music, gourmet food
4. Changing role of women	Increased demand for convenience products; changing shopping habits; child-care facilities
5. Changing home and family life, especially more informal relationships	Single portions, houses for single people
6. Desire for convenience	More ready-to-use products; more convenient sizes; easier methods of payments
7. Greater concern for the environment	Environmentally friendly products; new production methods; changes in packaging and advertising; recycled products
8. Greater informality	Increased demand for casual clothing; less formal restaurants; less formal furnishings
9. Increased life expectancy	Demand for products and services catering for the elderly, e.g. entertainment, food, health products, holidays, etc.

As a final word, it should be noted that many of the changes identified in Table 10.7 have not occurred overnight, but have developed slowly—often over many years—and marketers may have adequate opportunity to respond to such social and cultural shifts. It is perhaps surprising, therefore, that some businesses tend to take a uniquely short-term perspective when drawing up their plans, when a longer-term view might be equally, if not more, appropriate.

REVIEW QUESTIONS

1. Examine advertisements in a range of popular magazines. Can you identify any core values or attitudes to which these may be appealing?
2. How might the area or region a person lives in influence his or her buying behaviour? Give examples.
3. The sale of male deodorants in Britain has increased significantly over the last twenty years, but there are still parts of the country where such products are treated with suspicion. How would you account for:
   (a) the general increase in sales?
   (b) the existence of pockets of resistance to such products?
4. The 1990s is likely to see a growing concern with the environment. How is this likely to be reflected in the marketing of goods and services?

REFERENCES

Chisnall, P. M. (1985), *Marketing: A Behavioural Analysis*, 2nd edn, McGraw-Hill, Maidenhead, Berks.

Engel, J. F. *et al*. (1986), *Consumer Behaviour*, 5th edn, Dryden Press, Hinsdale, Ill.

Foxall, G. R. (1980), *Consumer Behaviour: A Practical Guide*, Croom Helm, London.

Kotler, P. and Armstrong, G. A. (1989), *Principles of Marketing*, 4th edn, Prentice-Hall, Englewood Cliffs, NJ.

McCarthy, E. J. (1971), *Basic Marketing*, 4th edn.

Oliver, G. (1990), *Marketing Today*, 3rd edn, Prentice-Hall, Hemel Hempstead.

Saker, J. (1989), 'Ethnic Food Business Revisited', *British Food Journal*, **91**(6), pp. 26–7.

Saker, J. and Brooke, B. (1989), 'Ethnic Food Businesses: Success and Failure', *British Food Journal*, **91**(2), pp. 22–4.

Wilkie, W. L. (1986), *Consumer Behaviour*, John Wiley, NY.

ELEVEN
THE TECHNOLOGICAL ENVIRONMENT

11.1 INTRODUCTION

The aim of this chapter is to explain how changes in the technological environment influence marketing decisions. The word 'technology' can be easily misunderstood as simply being about computers and hi-tech industries such as aerospace. In fact, technology has a much broader meaning and influences our everyday lives. It impacts on the frying pan (Teflon-coated for non-stick), the programmable central heating timer, cavity wall insulation, the TV, video, washing machine, car—in fact, just about everything in the home. The impact at work can be even greater, as technology changes the nature of people's jobs, creating new jobs and making others redundant. It influences the way we shop, our entertainment and leisure, and the treatment we receive in hospital. Marketing managers and other executives who fail to evaluate technological progress and assess the potential impact on their industry, company and products may find that the competition has gained a competitive advantage.

11.2 WHAT IS TECHNOLOGY?

Technology is defined in the Longman *Modern English Dictionary* as 'the science of technical processes in a wide, though related, field of knowledge'. Pride and Ferrell (1987) define technology 'as the knowledge of how to accomplish tasks and goals'. Technology, then, embraces mechanics, electrics, electronics, physics, chemistry and biology and all the derivatives and combinations of them. The technological fusion and interaction of these sciences is what drives the frontiers of achievement forward. It is the continuing development, combination and application of these disciplines that give rise to new processes, manufacturing systems, products and ways of storing, processing and communicating data. The fusion and interaction of knowledge and experience from different sciences is what sustains the 'Technological Revolution' (see Figure 11.1).

Kotler (1988) uses the 'demand–technology life cycle' to help explain the relevance to marketing of technological advances. Products are produced and marketed to meet some basic underlying need of individuals. An individual product or group of products may be only one way of meeting this need, however, and indeed is likely to be only a temporary means of meeting this need. The way in which the need is met at any period is dependent on the level of technology prevailing at that time. Kotler cites the need of the human race for calculating power. The need has grown over the centuries with the growth of trade and the increasing complexity of life. This is depicted by the 'demand life cycle' in Figure 11.2, which runs through the stages of emergence (E), accelerating growth (G_1), decelerating growth (G_2), maturity (M) and decline (D).

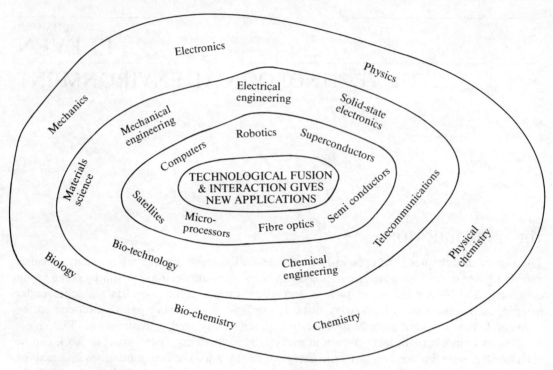

Figure 11.1 Technological fusion and interaction

Over the centuries, the need for calculating power has been met by finger-counting, abacuses, ready-reckoners, slide rules, mechanical adding machines (as big as an office desk), electrical adding machines (half the size of an office desk), electric calculators (half the size of a typewriter), battery-powered hand calculators, and now pocket-sized computers. Kotler suggests that 'each new technology normally satisfies the need in a superior way'. Each technology has its own 'demand–technology life cycle', shown in Figure 11.2 as T_1 and T_2, which serves the demand cycle for a period of time. Each demand–technology life cycle will have a history of emergence, rapid growth, slower growth, maturity, and decline, but over a shorter period than the more sustainable demand cycle.

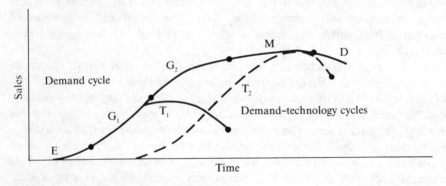

Figure 11.2 Demand–technology life-cycle

Marketing managers and other executives need to watch closely not only their immediate competitors, but also emerging technologies. Should the demand technology on which their products is based be undermined by a new demand technology, the consequences may be dire. If the emerging demand technology is not recognized until the new and superior products are on the market, there may be insufficient time and money available for the firm to develop its own products using the competing technology. Companies making mechanical typewriters, slide rules, gas lights and radio valves all had to adjust rapidly or go out of business. One way executives can scan the technological environment in order to spot changes and future trends is to study technology transfer.

The term 'technology transfer' can be used in a number of contexts. It is used to refer to the transfer of technology from research establishments and universities to commercial applications. It may be also used in the context of transfers from one country to another, usually from advanced to less well advanced economies. Transfers also occur from one industry to another; technology then permeates through the international economy from research into commercial applications in industries that can sustain the initially high development and production costs. As the costs of the new technology fall, new applications become possible. Thus, the technology permeates through different industries and countries. Applications of technology first developed for the US space programme, for example, may now be found in many domestic and industrial situations. NASA (the National Aeronautics and Space Administration) established nine application centres in the USA to help in transferring the technology that was developed for space exploration to other applications (Kotler and Armstrong, 1989).

The rate at which technology is being enhanced and the rate at which it permeates through the world economy is of importance to the marketing manager. Product life-cycles are typically becoming shorter. Expertise in a particular technology may no longer be a barrier preventing competitors from entering an industry. New entrants into an industry may benefit from the falling costs of technology or may be able to bypass the traditional technology by using some new and alternative technology.

The marketing manager, then, should be interested in the degree to which technology influences his or her business. As we have all learned, the environment is always changing and throwing up new challenges. Bic produces a disposable plastic razor to challenge Wilkinson and Gillette; Imperial Typewriters are no longer in business but Olivetti, once a typewriter manufacturer, now produces computers; and so on. The fountain pen is challenged by the ball-point, and in turn the ball-point is challenged by the fibre-tip. Failure to identify changes in technology soon enough may cause severe and sometimes terminal problems for companies. Although there can be sudden changes in technology which impact on an industry, it is the gradual changes that creep through the industry that may be harder to detect. Companies that anticipate, identify and successfully invest in emerging technologies should be able to develop a strategic advantage over the competition. As the demand–technology cycle goes through the stage of rapid growth, they will grow with it. As growth slows and the cycle matures, competitors will find it increasingly hard to gain a foothold in the new and by now dominant technology.

11.3   EXPENDITURE ON RESEARCH AND DEVELOPMENT

Between 1985 and 1989, expenditure on research and development in the UK rose by only 10.6 per cent, according to a government survey (Table 11.1). Expenditure as a percentage of gross domestic product (GDP) declined from a peak of 1.6 per cent in 1986 to 1.4 per cent in 1989.

In real terms, expenditure declined in mechanical engineering, electronics, electrical engineering, motor vehicles and aerospace (Table 11.2). Increases in expenditure were recorded only

Table 11.1 UK expenditure on R &D, based on 1985 prices and as a percentage of gross domestic product

	1985	1986	1987	1988	1989
£ million	5,122	5,745	5,837	5,940	5,664
% of GDP	1.4	1.6	1.5	1.5	1.4

Source: *Business Bulletin*, 28 February 1991 (CSO). Reproduced with the permission of the Controller of HMSO.

Table 11.2 UK expenditure on R &D by industry group, based on 1985 prices

	1985	1989	% change
	£ million		
All product groups	5,122	5,664	10.6
All manufactured products	4,673	4,774	2.2
Chemicals	942	1,326	40.2
Mechanical engineering	263	157	− 40.3
Electronics	1,759	1,662	− 5.5
Electrical engineering	126	77	− 38.9
Motor vehicles	372	365	− 1.9
Aerospace	818	655	− 20.0
Other manufactured products	395	502	27.0
Non-manufactured products	448	920	105.4

Source: *Business Bulletin*, 28 February 1991 (CSO). Reproduced with the permission of the Controller of HMSO.

in chemicals, other manufactured products and non-manufactured products, thus reflecting the serious decline of manufacturing industry referred to previously.

The source of funds for industrial R & D has also changed over the period. The UK government's funding has fallen from 23 per cent of the total in 1985 to 13 per cent in 1989. This is much reduced from the figures seen in the 1970s of over 45 per cent of government funding of R & D.

The UK government uses internationally agreed guidelines and definitions, produced by the Organisation for Economic Cooperation and Development (OECD), for measuring the expenditure on R & D. There are three components to the definition of R & D:

1. *Basic or fundamental research* is work undertaken primarily for the advancement of scientific knowledge without a specific application in view.
2. *Applied research* is work undertaken with either a general or specific application in mind.
3. *Experimental development* is the development of fundamental or applied research with a view to the introduction of new, or the improvement of existing, materials, processes, products, devices and systems.

These internationally agreed definitions aid comparison between nations, although caution still needs to be exercised when using international statistics. The variations in the exchange rate, the purchasing power of the currency in the domestic market and the reliability and comparability of the statistics all give grounds for caution. Various organizations publish international statistics, and UNESCO publishes data on R & D activities in most countries of the world in its *Statistical Year Book*. Table 11.3 summarizes some of these data for the USA, Japan, West Germany, France and the UK.

Table 11.3 Selected indicators for scientific and technical manpower and personnel engaged in R & D development

Country	Year	Per capita expenditure ($)	% of GNP	Scientists and engineers per million of population
USA	1982	354	2.7	3,025
Japan	1982	220	2.5	4,189
W. Germany	1981	276	2.5	2,078
France	1979	194	1.8	1,363
UK	1978	120	2.1	1,550

Source: adapted from UNESCO *Statistical Year Book*, 1984, Table 5.14. Reproduced by permission of The UNESCO Press, Paris.

These figures do not make happy reading for UK industrialists and politicians. The figures for the UK's R & D expenditure in manufacturing are particularly bad, with a decline in expenditure in almost every sector. The UK is well down the international league table on expenditure and on the numbers employed in R & D. All its main international competitors are well ahead in this area. Add to this the controversy surrounding cuts in academic research budgets affecting UK universities, and the picture looks even worse. Research and development is the seed-corn for the new technologies, processes and products of the future. Failure in this area is likely to mean that UK companies will be less competitive in the future. Larry Elliott (1991) writing in the *Guardian*, sums up the picture nicely: 'Five Japanese companies—Toyota, NEC, Matsushita, Hitachi, and Toshiba—spent more money on civil research and development last year [1990] than the whole of British industry.'

Having taken the broad macro view of technology thus far, the rest of this chapter looks more specifically at how technology impacts on a business, and where it may be applied to improve marketing and business operations. These are: product design, manufacturing and processing systems, storage and distribution, order and payment processing, materials handling, document handling, computerized information and control and communications, and the individual's office (see Figure 11.3).

11.4 PRODUCT DESIGN

The design of the product is influenced by its components and materials, their price and availability. Components and materials incorporating new technology may be more expensive

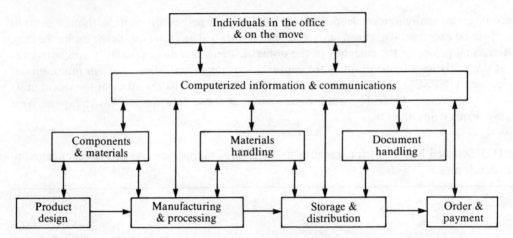

Figure 11.3 Impact of technological change on company operations

than older components or traditional materials. They may also be in short supply. Using new components or materials may involve increased risks or delay the product launch because of more extensive testing. Products should be designed with a view to keeping material, manufacturing, handling and storage costs to a minimum. These issues should be considered at the outset of the design brief and not as an after-thought. Reducing product costs by 5 or 10 per cent can mean huge savings over the life of a product. In many industries computer-aided design (CAD) gives more flexibility and a speedier response to customer needs. As production methods may now give greater flexibility, it is possible to produce a wider variety of styles, colours and features based on a basic product. These planned variations should be designed in at the initial design stages, even though they may not be incorporated until much later.

It is argued that the life expectancy of products has generally tended to shorten as technology has advanced. The product life-cycle (PLC) is a means of plotting sales and profits over time (see Figure 11.4) in such a way that different stages in the life-cycle can be identified and appropriate marketing strategies thus applied.

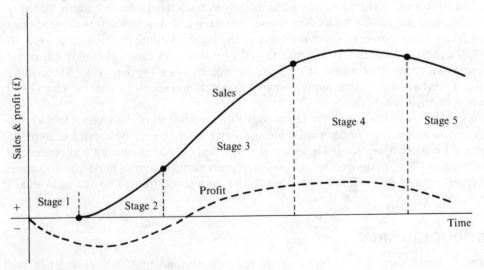

Figure 11.4 The product life-cycle

Five stages in the product life cycle can be identified:

1. Product *development* prior to launch: at this point, sales are zero and development and investment costs are rising.
2. *Introduction* of the product into the market: this means expensive launch costs and promotion. Profitable sales may take some time to develop.
3. *Growth* stage: this is when the product is fully accepted into the market and healthy profits begin to materialize on the strength of increasing sales.
4. *Maturity*: this refers to the period over which sales growth begins to slow and eventually stop. Profits may begin to decline as increasing competition puts pressure on prices and forces up promotional expenses to defend the market share.
5. *Decline*: at this point sales begin to fall off and profits decline due to lower volume of production.

Kotler (1988) makes a useful distinction between product category (say, typewriters), product forms (e.g. manual, electric and electronic) and brands (individual product brands offered by particular manufacturers). According to him, product categories tend to have the longest PLCs and to stay in the mature stage for very long periods. They may begin to decline only with significant and fundamental changes in technology (as when typewriters come to be replaced by personal computers) or shifts in consumer preferences (away from smoking, for example). Product forms tend to show a more classical PLC, with each subsequent form showing a similar history to the previous one. For example, manual typewriters move through the stages of introduction, growth and maturity, and enter decline as electric typewriters are introduced. These then follow a similar history until they begin to decline as electronic typewriters are introduced. The whole product category is now entering a decline stage as the new product category of personal computers has come well into the growth stage. Individual brands follow the shortest PLC, as companies are constantly attempting to update their products to keep abreast of changes in technology, fashion, customer preferences and competitors' offerings.

Rapid advances in technology may mean shortening product life-cycles in some industries. In consumer electronics, for example, advances in technology have allowed manufacturers to add more and more product features and reduce prices as costs have fallen. Brands in this product category may have a life expectancy of only 18 months before they are withdrawn and replaced.

11.5 MANUFACTURING AND PROCESSING

Technology impacts on manufacturing or processing systems particularly in computerized numerical control (CNC) machine tools, computer-aided manufacturing (CAM), integrated manufacturing systems (IMS) and just-in-time (JIT) systems. With CNC, the machine tool is directly linked to a microprocessor so that the instructions can be created and stored. This gives greater reliability and quicker change-over times. Previously the machine would have been controlled by punch cards or cassette tapes. CAM involves linking computers to a number of machine tools and assembly robots which are interfaced with computer-controlled material handling systems. Sections of the manufacturing process are thus integrated into the same production control system. CAD/CAM (computer-aided design/computer-aided manufacturing) is where parts designed on the computer can be programmed directly into the machine tool via the same computer system. These systems can save hundreds of hours over previous methods involving the separate activities of design, building models and prototypes and then programming separate machines for production.

Integrated manufacturing systems (IMS) enable a number of CAM sub-systems to be integrated together within a larger computer-controlled system. A number of manufacturers are attempting to integrate the total manufacturing process. This, however, is very difficult to do in practice, as plant and equipment are often of different ages, were designed by different companies and use different control systems. While it is possible to design a total IMS from scratch, the investment costs are likely to be prohibitive for most companies. JIT systems are designed to limit stockholding and handling costs. A supplier is expected to deliver components to the right delivery bay, at a specific day and time. There may be heavy penalties for failing to deliver on time. Components can then be moved directly on to the production floor ready for use on the line. This requires close co-operation between the manufacturer and supplier and usually is made possible only by the use of computerized information systems and data links.

These developments in technology impact on small companies and large, and on traditional industries such as textiles and shoes as well as on new ones. Generally speaking, modern manufacturing systems allow production lines to be run with greater flexibility and higher quality, making it easier to produce product variations and allowing a speedier change-over between products, thus minimizing down-time.

At first sight, it may not be obvious why marketing managers should be interested in these developments in production technology. However, such developments present companies with a number of opportunities for gaining a competitive advantage. First, developments in these areas are likely to contribute to a reduction in costs. Aiming to be a low-cost manufacturer should help in achieving a higher return on investment by allowing a higher margin and/or a higher volume of sales at lower prices. Second, modern manufacturing techniques allow for greater flexibility in production; thus, a wider variety of product variations may be produced without incurring onerous cost penalties. Third, lead times between orders and delivery can be improved. Finally, it is possible to ensure that the quality of the product is more consistent and of a higher standard if desired. Recent advances in integrated manufacturing systems using computer-controlled industrial robots has meant that some Japanese car makers, for example, can produce totally different models on the same production line. Thus, low-volume/high-value cars can be produced more cheaply by utilizing an automated line set up for the high-volume output of another model. The company can take a higher profit margin or pass on lower prices to its customers, or a combination of both.

11.6 STORAGE AND DISTRIBUTION

The storage and distribution of goods has benefited also from advances in technology. In particular, the increased capacity and reliability of computerized data processing and storage, combined with improved data transmission and computer-controlled physical handling systems, have led to reductions in costs and improvements in service. It is now possible to hold less stock at all stages in the distribution chain for a given product variety. From the retailers' perspective, they can reduce the amount of stock on the sales floor and in the back room.

These developments would not have been possible, however, without a great deal of co-operation and the integration of other technologies. The systems developed depend on each individual product having a unique code number and the equipment at the point of sale being able to read that number. Manufacturers, retailers and other interested parties co-operated under the auspices of the Article Number Association (ANA)[1] to devise a numbering system, allocate numbers and set standards for the use of what have become known as 'barcodes'. Each product item is allocated a unique number so that each product variation by size and colour can be identified. In the words of the Article Number Association, 'A 430 g can of peas, for example, has a different number from a 300 g can. A tin of blue paint has a different number from the same size can of red paint.' Membership of the ANA now totals over 7,000 firms, and it is estimated that there are over 4,000 scanning stores in the UK. According to the ANA, nearly 100 per cent of grocery products now carry a barcode on the packaging, and over 50 per cent of general merchandise.

At first, these barcodes were read by light pens and were only suitable for outlets with a medium volume of daily sales such as clothing retailers. Very high-volume outlets such as supermarkets had to wait for the development of the laser scanner, which can now be seen in most modern grocery stores. The product is simply passed over the scanner at the check-out so that the computerized till can read the barcode. It is these systems that provide itemized till receipts.

For a national clothing retailer, the improved service and reduction in costs is achieved by linking computerized tills to a central computer and stock control system which connects all stores and warehouses (Figure 11.5). In some cases large suppliers may be linked directly into the system. Items purchased are read with a light pen at the till, which in addition to logging the price identifies the item. At the end of the day's trading, or periodically during the day, the central computer checks on the sales through each till. Replacement orders can then be placed with the nearest warehouse by the computer, and if necessary the warehouse stock will be replenished by calling off further orders from the supplier.

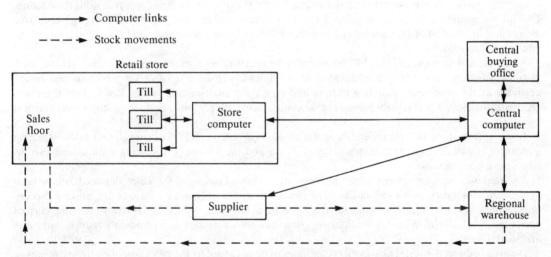

Figure 11.5 Systems linking the retail store, the warehouse and head office

In the warehouse, orders can be processed overnight or the next day and delivered the following evening or early the next morning. On delivery to the store, most of the items will be placed directly on to the rack on the sales floor, thus considerably reducing the need for back-room storage. This allows for a greater range of items to be stocked in a given floor space as the stock on the rack for each item is reduced; the space previously given over to back-room storage (up to a third of the total space in a High Street store) can now be opened up as part of the sales floor. Thus, the total selling space is increased, sales turnover per square metre is increased, and the range of items carried is increased. There is less overstocking, fewer out-of-stock situations and less shrinkage. Immediate price changes can be introduced, and there is generally tighter price control. The tighter financial control, higher sales turnover and increased profits help pay for the investment in computers, new out-of-town warehousing and transport/

physical handling systems. The systems that are dependent on these computerized tills are known as EPOS (electronic point of sale), and are discussed further in Section 11.7.1.

Other benefits to these systems are obtained from the sales information collected and stored by the computer. Sales of individual product items can be analysed. For fast-moving fashion items, this is vital information. In the past, a whole season's estimated sales had to be ordered in advance from the supplier—a risky business in the fashion world. Now initial orders from the supplier may be kept relatively low. Fast-selling lines can be identified using the computerized information and projections of sales made; further orders can then be placed with the supplier. This may be based on the first few days of a line being placed on sale. The whole process of business is thus speeded up. The links between store, warehouse, buying office and supplier become much more dynamic. Stockholding by the individual store may be as low as two days' sales, compared with a week in the late 1970s.

Another example is provided by Tesco PLC, which operates nearly 400 superstores and supermarkets in the UK. Tesco has been investing heavily in recent years in new systems to improve its operations, reduce costs and increase profits. This is what the company had to say about technology in its 1988 *Annual Report*:

TECHNOLOGY
Branch computing, which provides electronic stock ordering, has now been installed into 103 stores. Measurements continue to confirm that the original benefits expected are being enjoyed by all these stores. Benefits are mainly in the areas of reduced stock levels and wastage and higher sales through improved availability. By the end of 1988 a total of 160 stores will have branch computing and the programme will be continued into 1989/90.

A new electronic point-of-sale (EPOS) scanning project has been developed and a pilot scheme with Nixdorf was very successfully implemented at the Flitwick store. Extensive services provided to the customer at the check-out, including cheque and credit slip printing and weigh scales, have been well received. Installation is currently planned in 30 stores during 1988/9 and a further 70 stores over the next two years.

Tesco is developing electronic funds transfer at point-of-sale (EFTPOS) systems. Our latest scanning equipment is well designed to accommodate EFTPOS and the tests in petrol filling stations and various stores have been valuable.

A warehouse computer system, which provides stock control functions for Tesco depots, has now been installed in all grocery, non-food and bonded wines and spirits depots. For various fast-moving grocery lines, stores are now receiving daily deliveries with a lead-time of 24/48 hours, whilst the current computerised Home 'n' Wear replenishment system has been amended to significantly reduce lead-times and stock levels.

The area of direct deliveries by suppliers continues to be advanced by the provision of electronic means of order transmission. The number of main suppliers involved in this scheme continues to grow. Our participation in the nationwide Tradanet scheme, for which we were a pilot member, has proven successful.

A trial of computerised vehicle scheduling facilities has confirmed the operational benefits of such an approach.

These facilities determine optimum routes and delivery schedules to meet store requirements while maximising driver and vehicle utilisation. A system is being developed for installation in 1988.

(Tesco PLC Annual Report and Accounts 1988, p. 10)

This investment in new technology now means that the morning stock check for a whole superstore can be completed by 10 am. (Figure 11.6). A hand-held data capture unit with a light pen is used to scan the barcode on the shelf prior to entering the amount of stock sold of the item. The stock room is checked in a similar way. Between two and four people can complete the stock check for a large superstore, carrying 30,000 items, in less than three hours. This is then down-loaded into the branch computer in a few minutes. The stock figures are then checked and adjusted/confirmed ready for 10 am. The head office mainframe computer can capture the data from all the branch computers by 10.30 am. The orders are then processed and the order picking lists are sent by the mainframe computer to the warehouse computers located around the country or direct to some large manufacturers. Pickers in the warehouse load directly on to wheeled pallets. These are then easily wheeled on to the vehicles for overnight delivery. On arrival at the store, the pallets can be wheeled straight on to the sales floor, ready for the evening and night shift workers to stack the shelves. The time between stock check and delivery to the store can be as little as 24 hours. As fast-moving items can be delivered every night, the stock on the shelves is kept to a minimum and the superstores' back-room storage is used only for bulky items or small-volume lines.

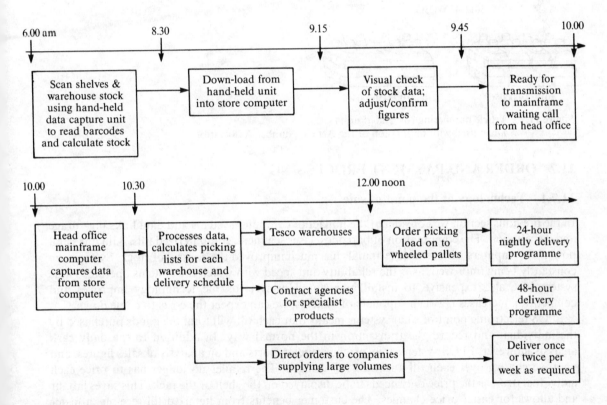

Figure 11.6 Tesco's system of electronic stock ordering

Barcode scanning systems are also used throughout the distribution chain. Outer cases are referred to as 'traded units' and can include pallets. The ANA co-ordinates the allocation of numbers that are used for traded units as well as consumer units. These barcodes for the 'traded units' are also machine-readable, so the outer cases can be controlled more effectively at every stage in the distribution channel, from the manufacturer to the retailer or customer. According to the Article Number Association, 'Every traded unit which differs by the nature or quantity of its contents must have a different number' (Figure 11.7).

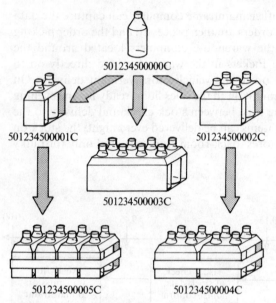

501234500000C

501234500001C   501234500002C

501234500003C

501234500005C   501234500004C

Figure 11.7   Article numbering for traded units
Source: used with permission of the Article Number Association.

11.7   ORDER AND PAYMENT PROCESSING

11.7.1   Technology at the point of sale

In the previous section we considered the impact of computer systems and data links on storage and distribution. The combination of barcodes, laser scanners, computerized tills, data links and powerful computers with remote terminals has much improved the control of stock. Systems are constantly being improved, as is the reliability and speed with which the systems operate. These systems are also expensive to install and run. However, as the technology improves and competition increases between suppliers of systems, we can expect the costs to come down.

EPOS (electronic point of sale) systems means that each till will total the goods purchased by the individual and record the transaction in the normal way. In addition to the daily cash analysis, however, EPOS systems may provide stock reports and an analysis of sales figures, and improve control over each till and the staff using it. The retailer no longer has to price each individual item, as the price only needs to be displayed on the shelf or the rack. This saves labour and allows for easier price changes. The customer benefits from itemized till receipts, a faster check-out, greater choice and fewer items out of stock.

EFTPOS (electronic funds transfer at point of sale) has all the benefits of EPOS plus electronic funds transfer. This means that the computerized till is now fitted with a card reader, and data links into the banking system can transfer funds electronically. The customer's credit card such as Mastercard (e.g. Access) and Visa (e.g. Barclaycard) or debit card (e.g. Switch) is presented in the normal way, the cashier swipes this through the card reader, the till prints out the slip for signature, and the customer retains the top copy. The customer's credit card company or current account (depending on the card used) is debited with the sale and the retailer's account is credited. The convenience for customers and retailers is enhanced, the accuracy of transactions is increased, cash handling is reduced, and the costs of processing the sale are also significantly reduced. These systems have now been applied to many types of retailing operations, including for example supermarkets, DIY superstores, clothing retailers, petrol stations, book shops and hotels. Such systems are set to expand rapidly in the retailing industry during the next decade. Changes are also impacting on business-to-business transactions in a similar way with electronic data interchange (EDI).

11.7.2 Business-to-business sales

In business-to-business transactions the speed at which orders can be captured and processed by the companies' systems denotes the speed at which orders and invoices can be dispatched and payment collected. Closely associated and inseparable from the system is the document handling, which includes orders, manufacturing dockets, picking notes, dispatch/delivery notes, invoices and statements. Advances in technology will continue to influence all these aspects of the business. Two examples illustrate what is possible with 1990s technology.

The first is provided by Golden Wonder Crisps, a UK manufacturer of crisps and snacks. The van sales representative takes the order from the local shop and drops off the goods. The order is entered into the van sales representative's portable computer, which will then print out a delivery note to leave with the buyer. In the evening the sales representative phones through to the head office mainframe computer and couples his portable computer to the phone using an acoustic coupler. The mainframe draws out the sales data and passes back any messages. Next day the invoice is raised and posted so as to arrive the third day after delivery.

When these systems were first developed in the early 1980s, it would take up to 20 minutes to down-load these data. Today it takes only a few minutes with new portable computers, and the transmission is much more of a two-way process. It is possible for the mainframe to input into the representative's portable the sales journey cycles for the coming weeks, relevant customer information, update on products and prices, notes on special promotional deals and messages from the manager.

This system is now being used for the direct sales force serving the larger retailer and cash-and-carry. Orders received one day are down-loaded to the mainframe the same evening. Overnight or the next day (day 2), the mainframe raises the picking and dispatch notes. On day 3 the order is dispatched, and the invoice is printed and posted. In the late 1970s this whole process would have taken between seven and ten days.

The second example comes from RS Components, a UK-based company with international operations. In the UK market the company is the largest distributor of electronic and electrical components and associated products. Its products are sold via a catalogue to industrial, educational, research and public sector organizations. Its particular unique selling proposition is the range of products stocked and the speed of delivery.

This is how it works. Regular customers have their own customer number. The customer phones RS and the call should be answered instantaneously. With 20 phone lines and a computer-controlled exchange which places the call to one of the telesales staff, the call should not ring more than three times. The customer gives a customer number, order number, part numbers of products ordered and quantity ordered—that is all. This information is typed directly into the computer by the telesalesperson. The total call should not take more than a few seconds. The computerized telephone system handles 7,500 calls per day. The computer prints out the invoice/order picking document. The order picking document starts its run through a part-computerized warehouse to its bin. A barcode is attached to the front of the bin which directs it along a conveyor system only to those bays holding stock for that order. The order is packed and shipped the same day, and the invoice, folded and placed in an envelope by document-handling equipment, is also posted the same day. Express delivery companies are used to ensure next-day delivery. The speed and efficiency of a system such as this which can handle 10,000 separate orders per day with same-day dispatch of goods and invoice is staggering. It was simply not possible ten years ago.

11.7.3 Electronic data interchange (EDI) transactions

A huge volume of transactions taking place daily between businesses in the UK has prompted a number of companies to encourage the development and use of electronic transactions. A number of systems are now in place. Previously the limitations of telecommunications, the problems of incompatible computers and their software, and the lack of legal status for electronic documents prevented business-to-business communication via computers and electronic mail. These technical and legal problems are now behind us, and the Article Number Association (ANA), along with the support of a number of leading organizations, has set standards for and promoted the use of electronic communication. TRADACOMS (Trading Data Communications) is the term used to cover the standards developed by the ANA.

Standards are set at two levels. First, common standards are applied to all the paper documents in terms of layout, which ensures clarity and improved efficiency. Second, the way in which these paper documents are configured electronically into computerized documents is standardized. This allows electronic data interchange (EDI), which means that data can be transmitted directly between one company's computer system and another's for automatic processing. This computer-to-computer communication improves speed, accuracy and efficiency of document transmission between manufacturers and their customers and the carriers (Figure 11.8). Documents and data that can be transmitted directly from computer to computer

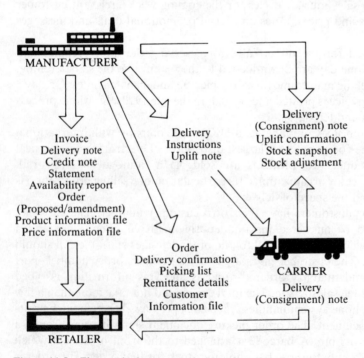

Figure 11.8 Electronic data transmission of trading documents
Source: used with permission of the Article Number Association.

include orders, picking instructions, invoices, credit notes, delivery notes, statements, general text, availability reports, remittance advice, stock adjustments, product information, prices and customer details.

Major computer and telecommunication companies are involved in providing the system interchange services. These allow direct computer-to-computer communications (even between different hardware and software) via the telecommunications system. TRADANET is one such system (Figure 11.9). Companies can transmit or collect data from this electronic mailbox at any time. Transmissions to any number of receivers need only be input into the system once, 'leaving the TRADANET service to route and distribute the data quickly and in absolute security to each recipient's electronic mail box' (the Article Number Association).

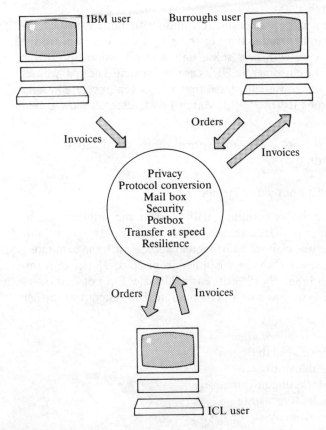

Figure 11.9   How TRADANET works
Source: used with permission of the Article Number Association.

There are a number of such systems now operating in the UK and throughout Europe. In addition to the well established TRADACOMS standard and the TRADANET network, which provide a general service, there is ODETTE (Organization for Data Exchange by Teletransmissions in Europe), which provides a European service (see Fletcher, 1990). Various systems have been designed to serve specific industries such as motor manufacturing, pharmaceuticals, electronics and chemicals. These services are set to expand rapidly in the 1990s and will help simplify domestic and international trade.

11.8 COMPUTERIZED INFORMATION AND COMMUNICATION SYSTEMS

Developments in these areas will influence manufacturing, processing, distribution, sales and order/payment systems. The examples already discussed illustrate some of the links between computer systems used for processing and storing data and those used for communicating within and between different sites via telecommunications. The power of computers continues to increase and their size and price continues to reduce. Developments in satellites, optic fibre cable, exchanges and the miniaturizing of electronic components have given us satellite TV, fax machines, the car phone and now the mobile phone. Telecommunication networks have had to be increased in capacity to deal with huge volumes of electronic data generated by computers. Hewlett-Packard provides an example of what is now possible with improved information and communication systems (*HP World*, March 1988).

Hewlett-Packard (HP) has been working on the project since the mid-1980s, initially in the USA and more recently in the UK, to increase the productivity of the sales force and improve the service to the customer. As is often the case with field sales, only a small proportion of the representative's total time was spent with the customer, in HP's case 26 per cent. The goal was set to increase this by 25 per cent, and from this it was calculated that a 5 per cent increase in sales volume would pay for the system. According to *HP World* (March 1988), research showed that the field sales representatives required:

- Personal productivity solutions such as word processing, spread sheets and databases
- Price and product availability information
- Order status reports
- Access to HP company-wide communications via electronic mail

Sales representatives were issued with a portable computer with modem and printer so as to access the company database from home or the customer's office. This first stage, a pilot involving 104 representatives in the USA, was claimed to be a great success with the computerized representatives, increasing the time spent with the customer from 26 to 35 per cent (an increase of 30 per cent) (*HP World*, March 1988). By 1987 the entire US sales force of 2,100 sales representatives had been converted to the system at a cost of $6 million. The system was further enhanced to provide:

Personal tools	*Access to information*
- Word processing	- Price availability
- Memo maker	- Order status
- Spread sheet	- Marketing information
- Electronic mail	- Sales forecasting
- Budgetary quotes	- Sales analysis
- Proposal generation	- Customer information
- Printer	- Lead distribution and tracking

These developments in the field would not have been possible without enhancement of the company's customer databases and the reorganization of the marketing support operation. Two new support centres were established. The installed base centre (IBC) holds the records of all existing customers and their systems. The field sales personnel can access this through their portable PCs. In addition to providing information, it is used as a resource for telemarketing and for screening customer enquiries to see if a personal call by the sales representative is really necessary. The main benefits claimed by HP for this centre are; field sales call per order down 25 per cent, costs per order down 10 per cent, and sales volume up 15 per cent.

The second support centre is the customer information centre (CIC), which is used to manage new enquiries resulting from marketing activities such as mailings, seminars and exhibitions. HP in the USA receives a total of 500,000 enquiries annually by phone and mail. These need to be screened before a sales representative is dispatched, to establish that a personal visit is necessary and that the call will be viable. According to HP, the volume of sales leads being passed to field sales has been reduced to 5 per cent of enquiries with this new system. The quality of the leads is much higher, and the speed at which they are passed on is much faster, down from weeks to days. The CIC uses a closed-loop system to handle this huge volume of enquiries. Figure 11.10 shows how the qualified leads resulting from the marketing activity and screening by the customer information centre are passed electronically to the field sales representative's portable computer via the 'funnel management account book'. The lead cannot be removed from the file by the representative without the result first being passed back to the CIC database. The result win/loss and new contacts is used to update the database files—promotion analysis, win/lose analysis, forecasting, market analysis and list management.

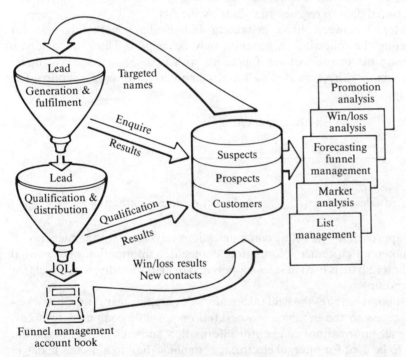

Figure 11.10   Field sales and marketing closed-loop information system
Source: *HP World* (March 1988), used with permission of Hewlett-Packard.

The advances in technology, then, are allowing companies to manage huge volumes of information in databases which can be accessed easily and speedily by non-technical personnel from locations outside the office. The sales representative is better informed about the customer, his company's products, prices, quotations, orders, delivery lead times, competitors and market conditions. Personal efficiency is increased and sales productivity is up, as is sales volume and profit.

The power of computers to store and manipulate huge volumes of information in databases, and the ability to transmit this to people remote from the office, presents marketing managers with a new marketing tool. As can be seen from the examples provided above, the potential uses for the database far exceed those of direct mail. Database marketing will be a major growth area in the next ten years.

11.9 DATABASE MARKETING

During the 1980s and early 1990s a whole new industry has emerged. As yet it is so new and is still changing so rapidly that it is difficult to define precisely. 'Direct marketing' is a term that is now used to encompass marketing activities which are designed to induce a direct response from mail order, direct mail, direct response advertising and telemarketing. These activities developed rapidly in the 1980s and have been reliant on the production of mailing lists. As the use of computers has expanded, so has the production, sale and purchase of lists multiplied. The capture of personal data and its subsequent use, including the sale of the lists for mailing purposes, has provoked a number of governments to introduce legislation to protect the individual's rights. In the UK the Data Protection Act 1984 was introduced, which requires organizations holding personal data to register and abide by the Act.

A difference has developed between direct marketing and database marketing, and for students studying marketing the following explanation may be helpful. Think of 'database marketing' (DBM) as being the broader of the functions, with two sub-activities of 'direct response marketing' (or simply 'direct marketing') and computer-aided sales support. The following then becomes apparent:

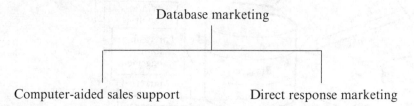

DBM is an interactive approach to marketing communications relying on the maintenance of accurate customer and potential customer information, competitor information and internal company information. The database is used in sales support and to identify individual targets for use in direct response marketing.

Computer-aided sales support requires the field sales team, sales support team and telemarketing team to have direct access to the database via desktop or portable computer, to access customer/potential customer information, competitor information and company information. The system is also likely to be used for internal electronic communication to aid sales management. Personal tools such as memo writing, spread sheets, records, proposal/quotation generation, etc., would also be available.

Direct response marketing involves the use of the database in addressable communications (such as direct mail, mail order and telemarketing), targeted at existing and potential customers, and direct-response advertising—the purpose being to stimulate a response such as an order, a request for information or a visit, or the provision of information for market research purposes.

11.9.1 Computer-aided sales support

A number of marketers and writers still tend to take a narrow view of DBM as being wholly about direct-response marketing. However, as can be seen by the examples of Hewlett-Packard and Golden Wonder given earlier in this chapter, when the database is made accessible to the sales teams, it has the potential to enhance their performances substantially. Thus, DBM is relevant both to business-to-business marketing and to the marketing of consumer products and services.

For companies producing products and services for other businesses, the database may hold company information such as product listings, specifications, part numbers, availability and lead times as well as pricing details. Customer and potential customer details may also be made available, such as buyer details, contract details, quotations outstanding, order status, previous purchases, installed equipment and competitor purchases. It is also possible to store competitor information on the database, thus making it directly accessible to the field sales force where it is most needed, rather than being hidden away in inaccessible files. As in the case with Hewlett Packard, if this database is made readily accessible to the field sales force by telecommunications, modems and portable personal computers, then productivity and effectiveness can be seen to rise. Such databases may also be used for direct-response marketing in order to generate sales leads from direct mail and telemarketing, thus supplementing leads generated from more traditional means such as exhibitions and advertising in trade journals.

11.9.2 Direct-response marketing

Direct-response marketing including such activities as direct mail, mail order, telemarketing and direct-response advertising. Direct mail is targeted at a specific address and delivered by the public postal system. It is likely to include a letter, usually addressed to a named individual, a leaflet or brochure, and some response mechanism such as a coupon or order form and envelope. Mail order relies on the use of the database to identify specific target customers who would find the particular catalogue of interest. The 1980s saw a huge growth in the distribution of slim, specialist catalogues aimed at very specific target groups, while the traditional full shopping catalogues aimed at the C2 and D social groups were experiencing sluggish sales. The mail order business was reshaped in the 1980s as the very powerful databases were developed. Telemarketing involves the use of the database and modern specialist telephone exchanges linked to computers which can automatically dial numbers and record the results. The term 'telemarketing' is used as it encompasses sales activity and market research. Direct response advertising uses the print or TV media in the usual way, but the customer is asked to order direct from the supplier via the telephone or coupon. Information gained from customers and enquirers in this way can then be added to the database.

The company's database is likely to be constructed from a number of sources including its own trading records, bought-in lists and bought-in database services from very specialized companies. The company then purges and merges the lists to form its own database. This last activity is most important, as it removes duplicate names and those who do not want to be or should not be contacted. Fletcher (1990) cites the Neilson Clearing House as an example of a specialist service company which has constructed a database from respondents to sales promotion offers found on grocery products; this would be of interest, then, to manufacturers of fast-moving consumer products (FMCGs). Other specialist companies operating in the UK include International Communications & Data PLC, who operate the National Consumer Database (NCD). This database is compiled from:

- The Electoral Roll, listing 42 million adults
- Investor data from 630 company share registers, comprising 8.5 million individuals
- Life-style data from the company's Facts of Living Survey Programme, which establishes life-style and product purchasing data and holds one million records

- Home data, including details on 350,000 properties such as value, location, size, etc.
- Telephone data, matching telephone numbers and addresses for 14 million individuals

A wide number of services are offered to clients from this database. For instance, a client may have a need for a profile analysis. The client provides a profile of current customers or enquirers which is then matched against the National Consumer Database. According to the company, a number of reports can then be produced, showing the quality of the client's file (from the accuracy of postcoding to the level of 'gone aways'), the penetration of the client file into its target markets, and a new target mailing list.

A growing number of companies now offer such services in the UK. As is often the case with retail audits, data can be purchased in such a way that it can be input directly into the client's own computerized marketing information system.

11.10 CONCLUSIONS

This chapter has considered technological change from the macro perspective and examined the impact of technology on different aspects of the business at the micro level. In both cases the relevance of technological change to marketing has been stressed. Marketing managers, however, are not the only executives who need to anticipate, identify and evaluate the impact of technological change.

At the macro level of technological change, the key points to remember concern the demand–technology life-cycle. This will be influenced by the level of research and development expenditure, not only in a particular industry, but in related and sometimes unrelated industries. The fusion and interaction of different technologies results in new applications and processes which eventually may give rise to whole new industries. Technology permeates through from academic and research institutions into industry, from one industry to another, and from one economy to another. However, if the UK manufacturing sector has become a follower rather than a leader, then it will have lost a much needed competitive advantage in world markets. Marketing managers should be just as concerned with the long-term prospects of their company as with yesterday's sales. Research and development is too important to be left to the technical boffins. Production, finance and marketing people need to be involved in the R & D process along with the scientists and development engineers. The board of directors needs to show serious interest and should be seen to be giving it the priority it requires.

At the micro level, the chapter has considered the impact of technology on the company's products and operations; product design, manufacturing and processing; storage and distribution; order and payment processing; information and communication systems; and database marketing. With regard to the specific areas of marketing and company operations referred to throughout the chapter, marketing managers and other executives may look to the medium-term horizon for planning purposes. The aim is not only to improve efficiency of the business operations, but also to ensure that the benefits are passed on to the customer.

These customer benefits may include better pre-order services such as product availability and specification information, faster quotations, and quicker design/customizing. Improved post-order services may include shorter delivery times, delivery to just-in-time (JIT) requirements, installation, training, electronic data interchange (EDI) and itemized till receipts.

Overall, the reduction of costs and the move to low-cost production relative to the competition will benefit shareholders and customers alike. The opportunity to increase the efficiency of operations such as materials handling and distribution is there. Marketing activities such as direct response marketing and computer-aided sales support have much room for future development. A more knowledgeable sales force with easy access to the right information and the modern tools to do the job will be a more productive and cost-efficient sales force.

The technological environment is a constantly changing environment. In many industries during the 1990s and beyond, change will be the norm rather than the exception. Companies that adhere to the marketing concept and that focus on customer needs, competitor activity and technological developments, rather than simply aiming to sell what the factory makes, are more likely to succeed.

11.11 ELECTRON BEAM METALLIZING: A CASE STUDY

This case study illustrates the opportunities presented by new technology and the way a UK company evaluated the market potential.

What is metallizing?

Metallizing is the popular term for vacuum coating under very high temperatures, a process used to apply ultra-thin coatings (thinner than a human hair) to a variety of materials. The coating material—in this case metallic aluminium—is vaporized in a vacuum and condensed on to a film made from another material, in this case plastic film. Aluminium imparts a bright finish but also gives plastic film a good barrier to light, oxygen, moisture and odours. Not only does packaging look good on the shelves, but it extends the shelf life of the product. In addition to the packaging industry, uses include bottle tops, gift wrapping, car trims and insulation.

Packaging is the largest single market in tonnage. The required combinations of attractiveness and effectiveness means that the metallized film is especially of interest to firms in the fast-moving consumer goods (FMCG) industries, which are often looking for new ideas. Metallized packaging film has become more popular in recent years, particularly in the food industry, where it is now used for example on biscuits, tea bags and crisps. These customers, though, are price-sensitive, as a small rise in packaging costs can have a significant impact on selling price.

Metallizing at Bonar Teich

Bonar Teich Flexibles, of Derby, part of the Low and Bonar Group, has been producing metallized plastic films for packaging since 1983. In 1987 it was producing to capacity, its products were well established, and the company was considering further investment in metallizing. Market research was undertaken, and the size and growth rates of the European market were established. Research from a number of sources showed:

Market size

- The overall market size for metallized plastic film in Western Europe in 1986 was 21,000–23,000 tonnes.
- Packaging accounted for approximately 50 per cent.
- Growth was estimated to be 13 per cent per annum.
- Some products were expected to grow by up to 40 per cent per annum.

Market shares

Company	UK (%)	W. Europe (%)
Camvac (UK)	50	30
Convertec (UK)	20	10
Bonar Teich (UK)	10	3
MF & P (UK)	10	3
Others (European)	10	54

Source: Bonar Teich

The company was aware that, if it were to extend its applications into more price-sensitive sectors, such as packaging for grocery products, then prices and therefore costs would have to be lower. Alternative technologies for metallizing were investigated. A new machine was available, but the technology was new and not in commercial production and thus presented some development risks. Close co-operation with the suppliers of the machine dependent on the new technology would be required. Teething problems could be expected. Development and commissioning trials using the new technology could be expected to take longer than with the proven technology. Once the new machine was in commercial production, there was the risk that its performance might never quite match the initial expectations or claims of the manufacturer.

The estimated performance of the new technology, then, had to be matched against the proven reliability and performance of the conventional machines. Financial projections had to be made on the basis of this technical judgement. A summary of the competing technologies follows.

The metallizing process: conventional technology versus new technology

All commercial metallizing is done on a batch process as rolls of material are loaded on to the machine for processing. However, there are some important differences between the conventional process and the new technology (see Figure 11.11). With the conventional method of 'resistance-heated evaporation', the roll of material is loaded into the processing chamber and the vacuum pumped down. The vacuum reduces the evaporation temperature of the coating material and prevents oxidation. The material is processed by unwinding the material in such a way that it passes over the aluminium which is vaporized at a very high temperature. This process coats the plastic film with the aluminium, and the now metallized material is received on to the rewind drum. The vacuum is then broken so that the finished product can be removed from within the machine. The efficiency of the process, i.e. the actual running time of the machine to total time from start to finish of the operation, is 50 per cent. This is because of the time taken to load the machine and then pump down the vacuum at the start, and to allow cooling at the end before the roll of metallized material can be removed. The actual speed at which the machine can process the material is 450 metres per minute. The machine can use only aluminium as a coating material as the maximum temperature at the source of evaporation is 1500 °C. The consumable costs are 0.235 pence per square metre. The machine is mechanically complex but of proven technology with a known reliability.

The new technology uses an 'electron beam evaporation' process. The principles by which the machine works are the same as with the conventional machine. The roll of material is unwound and passed over a heat source where the coating material is vaporized. The now metallized material is then received on to the rewind drum. There are a number of important differences,

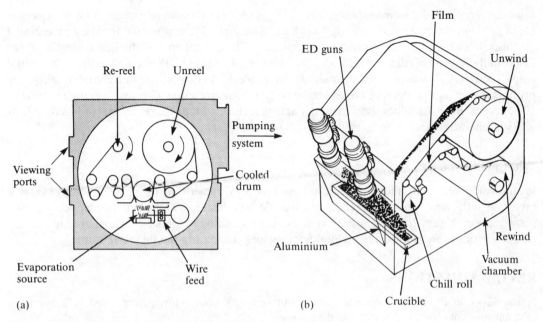

Figure 11.11 Conventional versus new technology in metallizing
(a) Resistance heated evaporation (conventional)
(b) Electron beam evaporation (new technology)
Source: Bonar Teich.

though. First, the roll of material and the rewind drum are located outside the vacuum chamber, so that there is no need for waiting time to break the vacuum and allow for cooling. The evaporation energy is provided by two electron beams which can give a higher operating temperature, up to 2200 °C. This means that other materials, in addition to aluminium, can be used in the metallizing process if desired. The machine can operate up to speeds of 600 metres per minute. Very thick coatings can be applied at full speed if desired.

Financial estimates

The parent company of Bonar Teich was prepared to invest in its packaging business if projects gave a worthwhile return. The financial estimates for the investment are shown in Table 11.4. No

Table 11.4 Financial projections for investment in new metallizing plant

	Year 3	Year 4	Year 5	Year 6
Sales (£ '000)	820	1,315	1,750	1,750
Profit (%)				
Electron beam	120	234	328	328
Conventional	100	200	283	283
ROCE (%)				
Electron beam	13.0	26.5	34.5	38.5
Conventional	12.0	25.5	32.5	36.5

sales for years 1 and 2 were assumed, and sales of £1.75 million were judged to be the electron beam's maximum capacity on five-day working. The same figure was used for the conventional machine, but an element of overtime was assumed. The capital cost of the new technology was £1.60 million, and of the conventional machine £1.45 million. Profit and return on capital employed (ROCE) was projected as shown in Table 11.4. For reasons of confidentiality, the profit is shown as a percentage based on the conventional machine with year 3 being the base of 100 per cent. Both machines showed a satisfactory return, with payback periods of less than four years of operation and an increase in manning of ten.

What would you do?

Would you invest in another conventional machine staying with the proven technology? Or risk investing in the new, but commercially untried, electron beam machine with its claimed superior performance? You will find it useful to assess the technology balance by summarizing the key characteristics of the competing technologies, before comparing the financial figures.

REVIEW QUESTIONS

1. Should we in the UK be concerned about our relatively poor showing (compared with our main competitor countries) in research and development?
2. Should marketing managers be involved in the R & D process, and if so what should their role be?
3. Can you identify any product class that has been recently affected by changes in the demand–technology life-cycle, and if so, what has been the impact of the change?
4. Identify some recent technological developments and discuss the benefits these have brought to the consumer.
5. How have recent advances in technology helped companies improve their marketing operations?
6. What are the ingredients that led to the successful development and implementation of 'article numbering' in the UK?

NOTE

1. The Article Numbers Association (UK) Ltd., 6 Catherine Street, London WC2B 5JJ

REFERENCES

Elliott, L. (1991), 'Lesson for Britain as Sun Rises on Ideas in Japan', *Guardian*, 20 April 1991, p. 14.

Fairlie, R. (1990), *A Marketing Person's Guide to Database Marketing and Direct Mail*, Exely Publications, Watford, Herts.

Fletcher, K. (1990), *Marketing Management & Information Technology*. Prentice-Hall International, London.

Kotler, P. (1988), *Marketing Management: Analysis, Planning, Implementation, and Control*, 6th edn, Prentice-Hall, Englewood Cliffs, NJ.

Kotler, P. and Armstrong, G. (1989), *Principles of Marketing*, 4th edn, Prentice-Hall, Englewood Cliffs, NJ.

Pride, W. M. and Ferrell, O. C. (1987), *Marketing: Basic Concepts and Decisions*, 5th edn, Houghton Mifflin, Boston.

TWELVE
THE LEGAL ENVIRONMENT

12.1 INTRODUCTION

The legal environment impinges on the marketing activities of a business organization at various levels:

1. The nature of the relationship between the organization and its customers is influenced by the prevailing law. At one time, the two parties were considered to be equal partners, both being able to look after their affairs by their own means. Over time, however, there has been a tendency for the law to give additional rights to the buyer of goods and additional duties to the seller, especially in the case of transactions between businesses and private individuals. Whereas the nineteenth-century entrepreneur in Britain would have had almost complete freedom to dictate the terms of the relationship with his customers, developments in statute law and common law now require—for example—the supplier to ensure that the goods are of merchantable quality and that no misleading description of them is made.

    Furthermore, the expectations of an organization's customers have changed over time. Whereas previous generations may have resigned themselves to suffering injustice in their dealings with a business, today the expectation is increasingly for perfection every time. Greater awareness of the law on the part of consumers has produced an increasingly litigious society.

2. In addition to the direct relationship that a company has with its customers, the law also influences the relationship that it has with other members of the general public. The law may, for example, prevent a firm having access to certain sectors of the market, as where children are prohibited by law from buying cigarettes or drinking in public houses. Also, the messages that a company sends out in its advertising are likely to be picked up by members of the general public, and the law has intervened to protect the public interest where these messages could cause offence—adverts that are racially prejudicial, for example. The law is imposing increasing duties on businesses in their dealings with the general public.

3. The legal environment influences the relationship between business enterprises themselves, not only in terms of contracts for transactions between them, but also in the way they relate to each other in a competitive environment. The law has increasingly prevented companies from joining together in anti-competitive practices, such as legislation that regulates the activities of monopoly providers of public utilities.

4. Companies need to develop new products, yet the rewards of undertaking new product development are influenced by the law. The laws of copyright and patent protect a firm's investment in fruitful research.

5. From a wider perspective, the legal environment influences the production possibilities of an enterprise and hence the products that can be offered to consumers. These can have a direct effect—as in the case of regulations stipulating car safety design requirements—or an indirect effect, as where legislation to reduce pollution increases the manufacturing costs of a product, or prevents its manufacture completely.

The legal environment of marketing is very closely related to the political environment. Law derives from two sources. The common law develops on the basis of judgments in the courts: a case may set a precedent for all subsequent cases to follow; the judiciary is independent of government; and the general direction of precedents tends gradually to reflect changing attitudes in society. Statute law, on the other hand, is passed by Parliament and to a much greater extent reflects the prevailing political ideology of the government.

The law is a very complex area of the marketing environment. Most marketers would call upon expert members of the legal profession to interpret and act upon some of the more complex elements of the law. The purpose of this chapter is not to give definitive answers on aspects of the law as it affects marketers—this would be impossible and dangerous in such a short space. Instead, the aim is to raise the marketer's awareness of legal issues so that he or she can recognize in general terms the opportunities and restrictions which the law poses for them, and the areas in which they may need to seek the specialized advice of a legal professional.

12.2 THE LAW OF CONTRACT

The first area to consider in examining the legal environment is the nature of the contract governing the relationship between the business organization and its customers.

There can be no direct legal relationship between a company and customers unless it can be proved that a contract exists. An advertisement on its own only very rarely creates a legal relationship. The elements of a contract comprise: offer, acceptance, intention to create legal relations, consideration, and capacity.

12.2.1 Offer

An offer is a declaration by which the offeror intends to be legally bound on the terms stated in the offer if it is accepted by the offeree. The offer may be oral, in writing or by conduct between the parties, and must be clear and unambiguous. It may be made to a particular person or to the whole world. It is extremely important that it be distinguished from an 'invitation to treat', which can be defined as an invitation to make offers. Normally, all advertisements are regarded as invitations to treat, as is illustrated in a case in which a man was charged with offering for sale live birds, bramble finches (*Partridge* v. *Crittendon* [1968] 1 WLR 286). A person reading the advert wrote, enclosing the money for the bird which was duly sent. The advertiser was charged with the offence of offering wild birds for sale, but it was held that the advertisement was not an offer but an invitation to treat and therefore he escaped the charge.

Of importance to the consumer is the rule that priced goods on display in supermarkets and shops are not offers but invitations to treat. Therefore if a leather jacket is priced at £20 (through error) in the shop window, it is not possible to demand the garment at that price: as the display is an invitation to treat, it is the consumer who is making the offer which the shopkeeper may accept or reject as he wishes.

12.2.2 Acceptance

Acceptance may be made only by the person(s) to whom the offer was made, and it must be absolute and unqualified; i.e. it must not add any new terms or conditions, for to do so would have the effect of revoking the original offer. Acceptance must be communicated to the offeror unless it can be implied by conduct. In the case of *Carlill* v. *Carbolic Smoke Ball Co.* ([1893] 1 QB 256 CA), the defendants were the makers of a smoke ball which was purported to prevent influenza. The advertisement stated that £100 would be given to any person catching influenza after having sniffed their smoke ball in accordance with the instructions given. The manufacturers deposited £1,000 at a bank to show that their claim was sincere. Mrs Carlill bought a smoke ball in response to the advertisement, complied with the instructions but still caught influenza.

In Mrs Carlill's case, her purchase implied her acceptance, for this was an offer to the world at large and it was not therefore necessary to communicate her acceptance in person to the offeror. She sued for the £100 and was successful. It was argued by the defence that the advertisement was an invitation to treat, but in this rare instance it was held to be an offer.

12.2.3 Intention to create legal relations

The above case turned on the third element of a contract—the intention to create legal relations. It was held that, because the company had deposited the £1,000 in the bank, this was evidence of its intention to be legally bound and therefore here the advertisement constituted an offer. Generally, in all commercial agreements it is accepted that both parties intend to make a legally binding contract and therefore it is unnecessary to include terms to this effect.

12.2.4 Consideration

This factor is essential in all contracts unless they are made 'under seal'. Consideration has been defined as some right, interest, profit or benefit accruing to one part or some forbearance, detriment, loss or responsibility given, suffered or undertaken by the other—i.e. some benefit accruing to one part or a detriment suffered by the other. In commercial contracts generally, the consideration takes the form of a cash payment. However, in contracts of barter, which are common with Eastern bloc countries, goods are often exchanged for goods.

12.2.5 Capacity

The final element is that of capacity. Generally, any persons may enter into an agreement which may be enforced against them. Exceptions include minors, drunks and mental patients; for this reason, companies usually exclude people under 18 from offers of goods to be supplied on credit.

An offer may be revoked any time prior to acceptance. However, if postal acceptance is an acceptable means of communication between the parties, then acceptance is effective as soon as it is posted provided it is correctly addressed and stamped.

12.3 STATUTORY INTERVENTION

Prior to 1968, there was very little statutory intervention in the relationship between the business organization and its customers, with a few exceptions such as those that came within the scope of the Food and Drugs Act 1955.

Every advertisement is now governed by the Trade Descriptions Acts 1968 and 1972, which make it an offence for a person to make a false or misleading trade description.

12.3.1 Trade Descriptions Act 1968

The Trade Descriptions Act 1968 imposes an obligation on local authorities for enforcement and creates three principal offences.

A false trade description to goods Under s. 1, this states that 'a person who, in the course of business, applies false trade descriptions to goods or suppliers or offers to supply goods to which a false description has been applied is guilty of an offence'. Section 2 defines a false trade description as including 'any indication of any physical characteristics such as quantity, size, method of manufacture, composition and fitness for purpose'.

A description is regarded as false when it is false or, by s. 3(2), misleading to a material degree. In one case it was held that to describe as 'new' a car that had sustained damage while in the manufacturer's compound was not an offence because of the excellent repair work carried out on the car which rendered the vehicle 'good as new' (*R.* v. *Ford Motor Co. Ltd* [1947] 3 All ER 489).

In some cases consumers are misled by advertisements that are economical with the truth. A car was advertised as having one previous 'owner'. Strictly this was true, but it had been owned by a leasing company who had leased it to five different buyers. The divisional court held this was misleading and caught by s. 3(2) of the Trade Descriptions Act. (*R.* v. *South Western Justices* ex parte *London Borough of Wandsworth, Times* [20 January, 1983].)

A false statement of price Section 11 makes a false statement as to the price of an offence. If a trader claims that his prices are reduced, he is guilty of an offence unless he can show that the goods have been on sale at the higher price during the preceding six months for a consecutive period of 28 days.

A false trade description of services Section 14 states that it is an offence to make false or misleading statements as to services. An example of this is illustrated in the case of a store that advertised 'folding doors and folding door gear—carriage free'. This statement was intended to convey to the consumer that only the folding door *gear* would be sent carriage-free on purchase of the folding doors. It was held that the advert was misleading and that it was irrelevant that it was not intended to be misleading (*MFI Warehouses Ltd* v. *Nattrass* [1973] 1 All ER 762).

Defences under the Trade Descriptions Act are set out in s. 24(i):

(a) that the commission of the offence was due to a mistake or to reliance on information supplied to him or to the act or default of another person, an accident or some other cause beyond his control; *and*
(b) that he took all reasonable precautions and exercised all due diligence to avoid the commission of such an offence by himself or any person under his control.

For the defence to succeed, it is necessary to show that both subsections apply.

In a case concerning a leading supermarket, a brand of washing powder was advertised as being 5p less than the price marked in the store. The defendants said that it was the fault of the store manager who had failed to go through the system laid down for checking shelves. The court held that the defence applied; the store manager was another person (s. 24(i)(*a*)), and the store had taken reasonable precautions to prevent commission of the offence (*Tesco Supermarkets Ltd* v. *Nattrass* [1971] 2 All ER 127).

12.3.2 Sale of Goods Act 1979

What rights has the consumer if on purchase he discovers that the goods are faulty or are different from those ordered? The Sale of Goods Act (SOGA) contains implied terms specifically to protect the consumer. A party deals as a consumer according to s. 12 Unfair Contract Terms Act 1977 if:

(a) he neither makes the contract in the course of a business nor holds himself out as doing so; and
(b) the other party does make the contract in the course of a business; and
(c) in the case of a contract governed by the law of sale of goods or hire purchase, . . . The goods passing under . . . the contracts are of a type ordinarily supplied for private use or consumption.

Section 13 of the Sale of Goods Act 1979 states that 'Where there is a contract for the sale of goods by description there is an implied condition that the goods will correspond with the description.' The sale is not prevented from being a sale by description even if the goods are on display and selected by the buyer. It is important to note that s. 13 applies to sales by private individuals and businesses.

In a case concerning a 1961 Triumph Herald, advertised for sale in the paper, it was discovered that the car was made up of two halves of different Triumph Heralds, only one of which was a 1961 model, and in the Court of Appeal the plaintiff's claim for damages was upheld (*Beale* v. *Taylor* [1967] 1 WLR 1193).

The goods, then, must for example be as described on the package. If a customer purchases a blue long-sleeved shirt and on opening the box discovers that it is a red short-sleeved shirt, then he is entitled to a return of the price for breach of an implied condition of the contract.

A recent example that illustrates the operation of s. 13 is a case concerning the sale by one art dealer to another of a painting that both assumed genuine. It later transpired that the painting was a forgery. The buyer brought an action relying on a breach of s. 13(i) and s. 14(2) of SOGA. It was however held that the contract was not one for the sale of goods by description within s. 13(1) because the description of the painting as regards its author did not become a term of the contract. It was clearly fit for the purpose for which art is commonly bought and therefore of merchantable quality. In this case, 'by description [it] was held to imply that the description must have been so important a factor in the sale to become a condition of the contract' (*Harlingdon & Leinster Enterprises Ltd* v. *Christopher Hull*/Fine Art Ltd [1990] 1 All ER 737.)

Section 14(2) states:

Where the seller sells goods in the course of a business, there is an implied condition that goods supplied under the contract are of merchantable quality except that there is no such condition

(a) as regards defects that are specifically drawn to the buyer's attention before the contract is made; or
(b) if the buyer examines the goods before the contract is made as regards defects which that examination ought to reveal.

(The moral for the consumer is therefore: examine thoroughly or not at all.)

Section 14(6) defines 'merchantable quality' as follows:

'Goods of any kind are of merchantable quality within the meaning of subsection (2) above if they are as fit for the purpose or purposes for which goods of that kind are commonly bought as it is reasonable to expect having regard to any description applied to them, the price . . . , and all other relevant circumstances.'

The implied term of merchantability applies to sale goods and second-hand goods, but clearly, the consumer would not have such high expectations of second-hand goods. For example, a clutch fault in a new car would make it unmerchantable, but not so if the car were second-hand.

In a second-hand car—again, depending on all the circumstances—a fault would have to be major to render the car unmerchantable. Thus, the question to be asked is, Are the goods merchantable in the light of the contract description and all the circumstances of the case?

It is often asked for how long the goods should remain merchantable. It is perhaps implicit that the goods remain merchantable for a length of time reasonable in the circumstances of the case and the nature of the goods. If a good becomes defective within a very short time, this is evidence that there was possibly a latent defect at the time of the sale.

In one case, a new car which on delivery had a minor defect that was likely to, and subsequently did, cause the engine to seize up while the car was being driven was neither of merchantable quality nor reasonably fit for its purpose under s. 14. The purchaser could not however rescind the contract and recover the price because it was held that he had retained the car 'after the lapse of a reasonable time' without intimating to the seller that he had rejected it even though the defect had not at that time become obvious (*Berstein* v. *Pampson Motors (Golders Green) Ltd* [1987] 2 All ER 220 N3). It was held that s. 35(i) SOGA did not refer to a reasonable time to discover a particular defect: rather, it meant a reasonable time to inspect the goods and try them out generally. Thus, the owner, having been deemed to have accepted the car, was entitled to damages to compensate him for the cost of getting home, the loss of a tank of petrol and the inconvenience of being without the car while it was being repaired. Had there been any evidence that the car's value had been reduced as a result of the defect, he would obviously have been entitled to damages for that too. The moral here is to examine thoroughly immediately on purchase.

Under s. 14(3), there is an implied condition that goods are fit for a particular purpose:

Where the seller sells goods in the course of a business and the buyer, expressly or by implication, makes known to the seller . . . any particular purpose for which the goods are being bought, there is an implied condition that the goods . . . are reasonably fit for that purpose, whether or not it is a purpose for which goods are commonly supplied, except where the circumstances show that the buyer does not rely, or that it is unreasonable for him to rely, on the skill or judgment of the seller.

Thus, if a seller, on request, confirms suitability for a particular purpose and the product proves unsuitable, there would be a breach of s. 14(3); if the product is also unsuitable for its normal purposes, then s. 14(2) would also be breached. If the seller disclaims any knowledge of the product's suitability for the particular purpose and the consumer takes a chance and purchases it, then if it proves unsuitable for its particular purpose there is no breach of s. 14(3). The only circumstance in which a breach may occur is, again, if it were unsuitable for its normal purposes under s. 14(2).

In business contracts, implied terms in ss. 13–15 Sale of Goods Act 1979 can be excluded. Such exclusion clauses, purporting for example to exclude a term for reasonable fitness for goods (s. 14), are valid subject to the test of reasonableness provided that the term is incorporated into the contract (i.e. that the buyer is or ought reasonably to be aware of the term).

Where consumer contracts are concerned, then such clauses that purport to limit or exclude liability are void under s. 6(2) Unfair Contract Terms Act 1977. Obviously, the goods purchased must come within the scope of consumer goods, and thus items such as lorries or machinery would take the transaction outside the scope of a consumer sale.

The case of *R & B Customs Brokers Co Ltd* v. *United Dominions Trust Ltd* ([1988] 1 All ER 847) is of some importance to the business world. Here, a company operating as shipping brokers and freight forwarding agents purchased a car for use by a director in the business. The sale was held to be a consumer sale within the meaning of s. 12 of the Unfair Contract Terms Act 1977 (UCTA); therefore a term for reasonable fitness for purposes under s. 14 SOGA 1979 could not be excluded from the contract of sale (s. 6(2) UCTA). The Court of Appeal followed the decision in a Trade Descriptions Act case in which a self-employed courier traded in his old car in part-exchange for a new car. The mileometer registered 18,100 miles, but it was evident that the true mileage was 118,000 miles. The owner was therefore prosecuted for having applied a false trade description to the car and was convicted by the magistrate's court. The divisional court allowed the appeal on the grounds that the vehicle was not disposed of in the course of a business—the point on which the prosecution turned. Lord Keith held that the expression 'in the course of a trade or business' in the context of an Act having consumer protection as its primary purpose conveys the concept of some degree of regularity. He said that the requisite degree of regularity had not been established here because a normal practice of buying and disposing of cars had not been established at the time of the alleged offence in the case. From this it follows that, had R & B Customs Brokers been dealing in cars, then the purchase of a director's car would not have been a consumer purchase. It is clear then that the self-employed—the sole traders—who no doubt assume that they are dealing in the course of a business are extremely well protected under the Sale of Goods Act and the Trade Descriptions Act. How anomalous it is when one considers that R & B Customs Brokers would no doubt be horrified if the Inland Revenue held that they were not operating in the course of a business and refused capital allowances on the director's car.

Where the buyer is dealing otherwise than as consumer, any exclusion or limitation clause will be valid subject to the tests of reasonableness contained in s. 11 and schedule II Unfair Contract Terms Act 1977.

The Supply of Goods and Services Act 1982 (SGSA) offers almost identical protection where goods are passed under a Supply of Goods and Services contract in s. 3 (which corresponds to s. 13 SOGA) and s. 4 (which corresponds to s. 14 SOGA). Where exclusion clauses are incorporated that relate to the supply of goods, then s. 7 Unfair Contract Terms Act replaces s. 6, previously discussed.

Section 13 SGSA provides that, where the supplier of a service under a contract is acting in the course of a business, there is an implied term that the supplier will carry out the service with reasonable care and skill. Reasonable care and skill may be defined as 'the ordinary skill of an ordinary competent man exercising that particular act'. Much will depend on the circumstances of the case and the nature of the trade or profession.

12.4 MISREPRESENTATION

If a consumer cannot find a remedy under statute, there is a possibility that in certain circumstances he may be able to rescind the contract or claim damages arising from misrepresentation. Even though the essential elements of a contract are present, the contract may still fail to be given full effect.

Generally it is assumed that statements which are made at the formation of the contracts are terms of that contract, but many statements made during the course of negotiations are mere representations. If the statement is a term, the injured party may sue for breach of contract and will normally obtain damages that are deemed to put him in the position he would have been in if the statement had been true. If the statement is a mere representation, he may be able to avoid the contract by obtaining an order—known as rescission—which puts the parties back in the position they were in prior to the formation of the contract.

Statements of opinion and mere 'puffs' (e.g. advertising jargon) are not statements of fact and consequently are not actionable. For a long time estate agents have been free to describe houses for sale in unjustifiably glowing terms without fear of redress as the terms were mere puffs.

However, as a result of growing pressure from the public, in March 1991 the House of Commons debated a Private Members' Bill to make misleading property particulars illegal. The Bill, which has the support of both the Consumers Association and the government, could signal the end of such gems as 'easily managed garden' (meaning a 2 ft × 2 ft yard at the back) and 'in need of some restoration' (meaning derelict). The most common complaints from estate agents' descriptions include incorrect room sizes, misleading photographs and deceptive descriptions of local amenities in the area—in one case the agents blocked out in the photograph an ugly gasworks which overshadowed a house they were trying to sell.

Once it has been established that the statement in question is a representation and not a term of the contract, it is necessary to consider whether it is actionable. An actionable misrepresentation may be defined as 'a false statement of existing or past fact made by one party to the other before or at the time of making the contract, which is intended to, and does induce the other party to enter into the contract'.

A representation has no effect on a contract unless it was intended to cause and has caused the representee to make the contract.

12.4.1 Remedies for misrepresentation

The main remedy for all types of misrepresentation is the equitable remedy of rescission. Obviously it is not always possible to make rescission. It cannot occur where the plaintiff has by his actions affirmed that he is continuing with the contract, where restitution is impossible, where there are supervening third-party rights, or where there is a lapse of time without any step towards repudiation being taken. In these cases, damages form the principal remedy.

When considering the availability of damages for misrepresentation, it is necessary to distinguish between the position before and after the Misrepresentation Act 1967. Prior to the Act there were two types of misrepresentation: fraudulent and innocent.

Fraudulent misrepresentation could be defined as a statement made knowingly, or without belief in its truth, or recklessly, i.e. careless as to whether it was true or false. If the representee could prove fraud, then in addition to rescission he could also claim damages.

Innocent misrepresentation was any misrepresentation prior to the 1967 Act for which fraud could not be proved, and there was no remedy in damages for innocent misrepresentation. Since the 1967 Act, however, it has been necessary to maintain a clear distinction between negligent misrepresentation and wholly innocent misrepresentation.

Section 2(1) states:

Where a person has entered into a contract after a misrepresentation has been made to him by another party and as a result has suffered loss, then, if the person making the representation would be liable to damages in respect thereof had the misrepresentation been made fraudulently, that person shall be so liable not withstanding that the misrepresentation was not made fraudulently, unless he pleads that he had reasonable grounds to believe and did believe up to the time the contract was made that the facts represented were true.

Section 2(2) states:

Where a person has entered into a contract after a misrepresentation has been made to him otherwise than fraudulently, and he would be entitled, by reason of the misrepresentation, to rescind the contract, then if it is claimed, in any proceedings arising out of the contract, that the contract ought to be or has been rescinded, the court or arbitrator may declare the contract subsisting and award damages in lieu of rescission, if of the opinion that it would be equitable to do so having regard to the nature of the misrepresentation and the loss that would be caused by it if the contract were upheld, as well as to the loss that rescission would cause to the other party.

The 1967 Act introduced a different type of misrepresentation (negligence under s. 2(i)), but this is misleading because negligence does not have to be proved, as Bridge LJ held in *Howard Marine and Dredging Co Ltd* v. *Ogden and Sons (Excavations) Ltd*:

the liability of the representor does not depend on his being under a duty of care the extent of which may vary according to the circumstances in which the representation is made. In the course of negotiations leading to a contract the 1967 Act imposes an absolute obligation not to state facts which he cannot prove he had reasonable grounds to believe.

Section 2(2) empowers the court to refuse rescission or to reconstitute a rescinded contract and award damages in lieu.

To sum up, rescission is a remedy for all three types of misrepresentation. In addition to rescission for fraudulent misrepresentation, damages may be awarded under the tort of fraud, and in respect of negligent misrepresentation damages may be awarded under s. 2(1) of the 1967 Act. Under s. 2(2) damages may also be awarded at the discretion of the court, but if so, these are in lieu of rescission.

12.5 NON-CONTRACTUAL LIABILITY

Consider now the situation where the consumer discovers that his goods are defective in some way but is unable to sue the retailer because the consumer is not a party to the contract. The only possible course of action was to sue the manufacturer. This situation was illustrated in 1932 in the case of *Donaghue* v. *Stevenson*, where a man bought a bottle of ginger beer manufactured by the defendant. The man gave the bottle to his female companion, who became ill from drinking the contents as the bottle (which was opaque) contained the decomposing remains of a snail. The consumer sued the manufacturer and won. The House of Lords held that on the facts outlined there was remedy in the tort of negligence.

To prove negligence, there are three elements that must be shown:

1. That the defendant was under a duty of care to the plaintiff
2. That there had been a breach of that duty
3. That there is damage to the plaintiff as a result of the breach which is not too remote a consequence

In the case, Lord Atkin defined a duty of care thus:

A manufacturer of products, which he sells in such a form as to show that he intends them to reach the ultimate consumer in the form in which they left him with no reasonable possibility of intermediate examination, and with the knowledge that the absence of reasonable care in the preparation or putting up of the products will result in an injury to the consumer's life or property, owes a duty to the consumer to take reasonable care. . . .

You must take reasonable care to avoid acts or omissions which you can reasonably foresee would be likely to injure your neighbour. Who then is my neighbour? The answer seems to be persons who are so closely and directly affected by my act that I ought reasonably to have them in contemplation as being so affected when I am directing my mind to the acts or omissions which are called in question.

The law of negligence is founded almost entirely on decided cases, and the approach adopted by the courts is one that affords flexibility in response to the changing patterns of practical problems. Unfortunately, it is unavoidable that with flexibility comes an element of uncertainty. Whether or not liability will arise in a particular set of circumstances appears to be heavily governed by public policy, and it is not clear exactly when a duty of care will arise. At present, the principles or alternatively the questions to be asked in attempting to determine whether a duty exists are:

- Is there foreseeability of harm, and if so,
- Is there proximity—a close and direct relationship—and if so,
- Is it fair and reasonable for there to be a duty in these circumstances?

Having established in certain circumstances that a duty of care exists, defendants will be in breach of that duty if they have not acted reasonably. The question is, What standard of care does the law require? The standard of care required is that of an ordinary prudent man in the circumstances pertaining to the case. For example, in one case it was held that an employee owed a higher standard of care to a one-eyed motor mechanic and was therefore obliged to provide protective goggles—not because the likelihood of damage was greater, but because the consequences of an eye injury were more serious (*Paris* v. *Stepney BC* (1951)). Similarly, a higher standard of care would be expected from a drug manufacturer than from a greetings cards manufacturer because the consequences of defective products would be far more serious in the former case.

Where a person is regarded as a professional—i.e. where he sets himself up as possessing a particular skill, such as a plumber, solicitor, surgeon—then he must display the type of skill required in carrying out that particular profession or trade.

With a liability based on fault, the defendant can only be liable for damages caused by him. The test adopted is whether the damage is of a type or kind that ought reasonably to have been foreseen even though the extent need not have been envisaged.

The main duty is that of the manufacturer, but cases have shown that almost any party who is responsible for the marketing of goods may be held liable.

The onus of proving negligence is on the plaintiff. Of importance in this area is s. 2(1) of the Unfair Contract Terms Act 1977, which states: 'a person cannot by reference to any contract term or notice exclude or restrict his liability for death or personal injury resulting from negligence', and s. 2(2): 'in the case of other loss or damage, a person cannot so exclude or restrict his liability for negligence except in so far as the contract term or notice satisfies the test of reasonableness'. Thus, all clauses that purport to exclude liability in respect of negligence resulting in death or personal injuries are void, and other clauses, e.g. 'goods accepted at owner's risk', must satisfy the test of reasonableness.

12.6   THE CONSUMER PROTECTION ACT 1987

The Consumer Protection Act 1987 came into force in March 1988 as a result of the government's obligation to implement an EC directive and provides a remedy in damages for anyone who suffers personal injury or damage to property as a result of a defective product. The effect is to impose a *strict* (i.e. whereby it is unnecessary to prove negligence) tortious liability on producers of defective goods. The Act supplements the existing law; thus, a consumer may well have a remedy in contract, in the tort of negligence or under the Act if he has suffered loss caused by a defective product.

A product is defined in s. 12 as 'any goods or electricity'; s. 45(i) defines goods as including substances (natural or artificial, in solid, liquid or gaseous form), growing crops, things compressed in land by virtue of being attached to it, ships, aircraft and vehicles.

The producer will be liable if the consumer can establish that the product is defective and that it caused his loss. There is a defect if the safety of the goods does not conform to general expectations with reference to the risk of damage to property or risk of death or personal injury. The general expectations will differ depending on the particular circumstances, but points to be taken into account include the product's instructions, warnings and the time elapsed since supply, the latter point to determine the possibility of the defect being due to wear and tear.

The onus is on the plaintiff to prove that his loss was caused by the defect. A claim may be made by anyone, whether death, personal injury or damage to property has occurred. However, where damage to property is concerned, the damage is confined to property ordinarily intended for private use or consumption and acquired by the person mainly for his own use or consumption, thus excluding commercial goods and property. Damage caused to private property must exceed £275 for claims to be considered. It is not possible to exclude liability under the Consumer Protection Act.

The Act is intended to place liability on the producer of defective goods. In some cases the company may not manufacture but may still be liable, as follows:

1. Anyone carrying out an 'industrial or other process' to goods that have been manufactured by someone else will be treated as the producer where 'essential characteristics' are attributable to that process. Essential characteristics are nowhere defined in the Act, but processes that modify the goods may well be within the scope. It is important to note here that defects in the goods are not limited to those caused by the modifications, but encompasses any defects in the product.
2. If a company puts its own brand on goods that have been manufactured on its behalf, thus holding itself out to be the producer, that company will be liable for any defects in the branded goods.
3. Any importer who imports goods from outside EC countries will likewise be liable for defects in the imported goods. This is an extremely beneficial move for the consumer.

The Act is also instrumental in providing a remedy against suppliers who are unable to identify the importee or the previous supplier to him. If the supplier fails or cannot identify the manufacturer's importee or previous supplier, then the supplier is liable.

It should be noted that if the product itself is defective the remedy lies in contract (usually SOGA 1979).

12.7 CONSUMER CREDIT

Obviously, in paying for goods there are several methods of payment apart from a direct settlement. Nowadays a common method of payment is hire purchase, now regulated by the Consumer Credit Act 1974 which is a consumer protection measure to protect the public from, among other things, extortionate credit agreements and high-pressure selling off trade premises. The Act became fully operational in May 1985, and much of the protection afforded to those affecting hire purchase transactions is extended to those obtaining goods and services through consumer credit transactions. It is important to note that contract law governs the formation of agreements coming within the scope of the Consumer Credit Act. Also, the Act is applicable only to credit agreements not exceeding £15,000 or where the debtor is not a corporate body.

12.7.1 Consumer credit agreements

Section 8(i) states: 'A personal credit agreement is an agreement between an individual ('the debtor') and any other person ('the creditor') by which the creditor provides the debtor with credit of any amount.'

Section 8(2) defines a consumer credit agreement as a personal credit providing the debtor with credit not exceeding £15,000.

Section 9 defines credit as a cash loan and any other form of financial accommodation. There are two types of credit. The first is a running account credit (s. 10(a)), whereby the debtor is enabled to receive from time to time, from the creditor or a third party, cash, goods and services to an amount or value such that, taking into account payments made by or to the credit of the debtor, the credit limit (if any) is not at any time exceeded. Thus, running account credit is revolving credit, where the debtor can keep taking credit when he wants it subject to a credit limit. Any example of this would be a Visa or Mastercard.

The second type is fixed-sum credit, defined in s. 10(b) as any other facility under a personal credit agreement whereby the debtor is enabled to receive credit. An example here would be a bank loan.

The Act then covers hire purchase agreements (s. 189), which are agreements under which goods are bailed or hired in return for periodical payments by the person to whom they are bailed or hired and where the property in the goods will pass to that person if the terms of the agreement are complied with and one or more of the following occurs:

* The exercise of an option to purchase by that person
* The doing of any other specified act by any party to the agreement
* The happening of any other specified event

In simple terms, a hire purchase agreement is a contract of hire which gives the hirer the option to purchase the goods. The hirer does not own the goods until the option is exercised.

In addition to hire purchase agreements, also within the scope of the Act are conditional sale agreements for the sale of goods or land, in respect of which the price is payable by instalments and the property (i.e. ownership) remains with the seller until any conditions set out in the contract are fulfilled, and credit sale agreements, where the property (ownership) passes to the buyer when the sale is effected.

12.7.2   Restricted use and unrestricted use credit

Unrestricted use credit is where the money is paid to the debtor direct and the debtor is left free to use the money as he wishes. Restricted use credit is where the money is paid direct to a third party (usually the seller), e.g. via Barclaycard or Access.

12.7.3   Debtor–creditor and debtor–creditor–supplier agreements

Every agreement regulated by the Act must be either a debtor–creditor or debtor–creditor–supplier agreement. The latter relates to the situation where there is a business connection between creditor and supplier—i.e. a pre-existing arrangement—or where the creditor and the supplier are the same person.

Formalities   Section 55 and ss. 60–65 deal with formalities of the contract, their aim being that the debtor be made fully aware of the nature and the cost of the transaction and his rights and liabilities under it. The Act requires that certain information must be disclosed to the debtor before the contract is made. This includes total charge for credit, and the annual rate of the total charge for credit which the debtor will have to pay expressed as a percentage. All regulated agreements must comply with the formality procedures and must contain:

* Names and addresses of the parties to the agreement
* Amount of payments due and to whom payable
* Total charge for credit
* Annual rate of charge expressed as a percentage

- Debtor's right to pay off early
- All the terms of the agreement
- The debtor's right to cancel (if applicable)

All further copies of the agreement must contain the same, and the debtor and creditor must then sign. Sections 62 and 63 provide for the debtor and the hirer to receive a copy or copies of the agreement. The consumer should always receive one copy when he signs the agreement. A second copy must be sent if the agreement was not actually made on the occasion he signed it.

If the consumer credit agreement is drawn up off business premises, then it is a cancellable agreement designed to counteract high-pressure doorstep salesmen. If an agreement is cancellable, the debtor is entitled to a cooling-off period, i.e. to the close of the fifth day following the date the second copy of the agreement is received. If the debtor then cancels in writing, the agreement and any linked transaction is cancelled. Any sums paid are recoverable, and he has a lien on any goods in his possession until repayment is made.

12.8   CODES OF PRACTICE

Codes of practice do not in themselves have the force of law. They can however be of great importance to marketers. In the first place, they can help to raise the standards of an industry by imposing a discipline on their members not to indulge in dubious marketing practices, which—although legal—act against the long-term interests of the industry and its customers. Second, voluntary codes of practice can offer a cheaper and quicker means of resolving grievances between the two parties compared with more formal legal channels—for example, the holiday industry has its own arbitration facilities which avoid the cost of taking many cases through to the courts. Third, business organizations are often happy to accept restrictions imposed by codes of practice as these are seen as preferable to restrictions being imposed by laws. The tobacco industry has more influence over restrictions on tobacco advertising if they are based on a voluntary code rather than imposed by law.

The post of Director General of Fair Trading was established by the Fair Trading Act 1973 and is instrumental in encouraging trade associations to adopt codes of practice. An early example of a voluntary code is provided by the Motor Trade Association. On advertising, the code prohibits misleading comparisons of models and fuel consumption. Any statement must be substantiated by reference to the methods of testing and statements as to price must show clearly what is or is not incorporated in the figure. The code insists that unexpired warranties must be transferable and repair work must be capable of being carried out by any franchised dealer—not solely the dealer from whom the car was purchased. Similar criteria apply to used cars. Here the code states that mileage must be verified or the customer made aware. In the event of a dispute between a customer and a member of the Association, a conciliation service is available which reduces the need to resort to legal remedies.

A HOUSE FULL OF VOLUNTARY CODES

Many purchases of household durables are covered by a voluntary code of one form or another. The following examples serve to illustrate.

Home improvements

The Glass and Glazing Federation's Code of Ethical Practice was established in 1981. It provides that products and installations must comply with BSI Codes of Practice.

It lays down rules regarding delivery and completion dates, and where the customer has stated time to be of the essence (i.e. where the customer has specified a date by which the work must be completed) then any work that remains uncompleted after six weeks may be cancelled without the consumer incurring any penalty.

Furniture

This code of practice was established in August 1978 and covers the manufacture and selling of furniture. The code ensures that full information regarding price, measurements and cleaning is available with each product. It also provides realistic dates for delivery to customers and gives details of a conciliation scheme with a testing service. The fee for this independent service will be returned where any complaint is upheld.

Association of Manufacturers of Domestic Electrical Appliances

The code here requires that calls regarding servicing should be responded to within three days and that 80 per cent of servicing should be completed on the first visit, the balance to be finally completed within 15 days. Manufacturers are expected to carry a comprehensive supply of spare parts and to ensure that the spare parts are available up to a minimum specified period after the particular models are no longer produced.

Useful leaflets published by the Office of Fair Trading giving information regarding codes of practice can be obtained free of charge from local Consumer Advice Bureaux.

12.9   CONTROLS ON ADVERTISING

There are a number of laws that influence the content of advertisements in Britain—for example, the Trade Descriptions Act makes false statements in an advertisement an offence, while the Consumer Credit Act lays down quite precise rules about the way in which credit can be advertised. However, it could be argued that the content of advertisements is influenced just as much by voluntary codes as by legislation. Contrary to popular belief, there is no law stating that cigarettes should not be advertised on television or that health warnings should be printed on all newspaper advertisements for cigarettes. Both of these are examples of restrictions imposed on advertisers by voluntary code.

For printed media, the Advertising Standards Authority (ASA) oversees the British Code of Advertising Practice which states that all advertisements appearing in members' publications should be legal, honest, decent and truthful. Thus, an advertisement by a building society offering 'free' weekend breaks was deemed to have broken the code by not stating in the advertisement that a compulsory charge was made for meals during the weekend. An advert by the fashion retailer H & M Hennes depicting a reclining female model dressed in underwear with the caption 'Last time we ran an ad for Swedish lingerie 78 women complained—no men' was held to be offensive, inaccurate and sexist. The penalty for breaching the ASA code is the adverse publicity that follows, and ultimately the Authority could ban a business from advertising in all members' publications.

A stronger voluntary code is provided by the Independent Television Commission, which govern all terrestrial television broadcasting. Although the ITC is a statutory body, the Broadcasting Acts have devolved to the Commission the task of developing a code for advertisers. Like the ASA code, it too is continually evolving to meet the changing attitudes and expectations of the public. Thus, on some products restrictions have been tightened up—cigarette advertising is now completely banned on television, and loopholes have been closed which allowed tobacco brand names to be used to promote non-tobacco products offered by the manufacturers, such as sportswear and overseas holidays. Restrictions on alcohol advertising have also been tightened up, for example by insisting that young actors are not portrayed in advertisements and by not showing them when children are likely to be watching. On the other hand, advertising restrictions for some products have been relaxed in response to changing public attitudes. Adverts for condoms have moved from being completely banned, to being allowed but only in very abstract form, to the present situation where the product itself can be mentioned using actors in life-like situations. Similarly, restrictions on adverts for women's sanitary products have been relaxed, although, as for condoms, the ITC code stipulates that adverts should not be shown when children are likely to be viewing.

Numerous other forms of voluntary controls exist. As mentioned previously, many trade associations have codes of conduct which impose restrictions on how they can advertise. Solicitors, for example, were previously not allowed to advertise at all, but can now do so within limits defined by the Law Society. The health warnings that appear on packets of cigarettes are the result of a voluntary agreement between the government and the tobacco industry. The latter illustrates an important reason for the existence of many voluntary codes—namely, that an industry would prefer a code over which it has some influence rather than a law over which it has none. Government is saved the task of passing legislation and policing the law, while knowing that if the voluntary code fails to work it could still step in to pass legislation. In the field of advertising, the EC is currently proposing directives that will ultimately have the effect of giving legal effect to many of the voluntary codes that currently exist.

12.10 PROTECTION FOR A COMPANY'S INTANGIBLE ASSETS

The value of a business enterprise can be measured not only by the value of its physical assets such as land and buildings: increasingly, the value of a business reflects its investment in new product development and strong brand images. To protect the company from imitators reaping the benefits of this investment but bearing none of its cost, a number of legal protections are available.

12.10.1 Patents

A patent is a right given to an inventor which allows him exclusively to reap the benefits from his invention over a specified period.

To obtain a patent, application must be made to the Patent Office in accordance with the procedure set out in the Patents Act 1977. To qualify for a patent, the invention must have certain characteristics laid down—it must be covered by the Act, it must be novel, and it must include an inventive step.

Nowhere does the Act define what is patentable, but it does specify what is not under s. 1:

- s. 1(2)(a)—discoveries, scientific theories or mathematical methods
- s. 1(2)(b)—literacy, dramatic, musical or artistic works or any other aesthetic creations (obviously, works such as these are protected by copyright)
- s. 1(2)(c)—schemes, rules or methods for performing a mental act, playing a game, doing business; or a program for a computer
- s. 1(2)(a)—the presentation of information

Obviously, to qualify for a patent the invention must be novel in that it does not form part of the state of the art at the priority date (i.e. the date of filing for a patent, not the date of invention).

State of the art (s. 2(2)) comprises all matter that has at any time before that date been made available to the public anywhere in the world by written or oral description, by use or in any other way.

An inventive step (s. 3) is apparent if it is not obvious to a person skilled in the art having regard to the prior art other than co-pending patent applications which are deemed to be prior art for the purpose of testing for novelty only.

The effect of the Patents Act 1977 has been to bring UK patent law more into line with that of the EC in accordance with the provisions of the European Patent Convention.

As a result of the implementation of the convention, there are almost uniform criteria in the establishment of a patent in Austria, Belgium, Switzerland, Germany, France, the UK, Italy, Liechtenstein, Luxembourg, the Netherlands and Sweden. A European Patent Office has been set up in Munich which provides a cheaper method to obtain a patent in three or more countries, but it should be noted that, if the patent fails as a result of an application to the European Patent Office, the rejection applies to all member-states unless there is contrary domestic legislation which covers this part.

12.10.2 Trademarks

The Trade Marks Act 1938 provides protection for trademarks. (They are also protected under the common law of passing off.) The Act gives the owner of the mark exclusive rights to its use. A trademark can be defined as words or symbols used to signify a connection in the course of trade between the owner of the mark and the goods imprinted with the mark. It is possible to register only marks used in connection with goods (s. 68).

The Trade Marks Register consists of two parts. Registration under Part A applies to marks 'adapted to distinguish goods or services with which the proprietor is connected from those with which he is not'. It is easier to obtain registration under Part B but the protection afforded is less. To obtain registration under Part A, the trademark must conform to at least one of the criteria set out in s. 9 as follows. It must contain:

- s. 9(i)(a)—the name of a company's individual or firm, represented in a special or particular manner
- s. 9(i)(b)—the signature of the applicant for registration or of some predecessor of his in business
- s. 9(i)(c)—an invented word or words
- s. 9(i)(d)—a word or words having no direct reference to the character or quality of the goods, and not being according to its ordinary meaning, a geographical name or surname
- s. 9(i)(e)—any other distinctive mark; however, a name signature or word other than those covered by ss. 9(a)–(d) above is not registerable except on evidence of distinctiveness

If the trademark is infringed in any way, a successful plaintiff will be entitled to an injunction and to damages.

12.11   SUNDAY TRADING

Most of us are very familiar with the way traders 'bend' the law with 'bargain offers' for which price comparisons are meaningless and 'closing down sales', which suggest very good bargains to the public with the closing-down sale taking place on occasions over a period of years. With

Sunday trading there is a deliberate flaunting of s. 47 of the Shops Act 1950, which provides that every shop, unless otherwise provided, is to close for the serving of customers on Sunday. The Act has been constantly ridiculed by the media since its inception forty years ago. It has been described as 'unworkable', 'incomprehensible' and 'downright stupid'—not surprisingly so, as it is legal to buy some products on Sundays but not others. For example, one may purchase *Playboy* magazine but not the Bible; fish and chips may be obtained from an Indian takeaway but not from a fish and chip shop. The anomalies are many and various, bearing little relation to either common sense or customer convenience.

Recently, however, the thrust of the argument has changed and is based less on what may be lawfully purchased and more on the fact that many people want shops to be open on Sundays.

Leicester Polytechnic Business Law students had the task of running an assignment on this very subject during the autumn term of the 1990/1 session, and the results confirmed what so many opinion polls over the years have shown: i.e. that the great majority of those polled wish for complete relaxation (therefore repeal) of the Shops Act 1950. The students' research revealed two interesting things: first, around 98 per cent of those polled wanted to be able to shop on Sundays without restrictions of any kind (only 2 people objected on grounds of religion), and second, of those who did not already work on Sundays, less than half would be willing to work, notwithstanding increased pay and other 'perks'.

That this statute is honoured more in its breach than in its observance, both by members of the shopping public and by shopkeepers, has become perfectly clear; and it is also clear that many large chains do not wish to open every Sunday but probably would like the legal right to open on some Sundays, particularly those immediately prior to major public holidays such as Christmas and Easter.

Before the issue of Sunday trading can be resolved, there are some problems that need to be faced by the community. Allowing shops to open on Sundays will mean an increase in noise. It will also pose extra demands on public transport, leading to further policing requirements. Not least of these social considerations is the major issue of eligibility of those employed for state benefits such as unemployment benefits, maternity pay and state pensions.

It should not be thought that everyone in the country is demanding full shopping rights on every day of the week throughout the year: indeed, some groups (e.g. the Sunday Observance Society) have campaigned against it vociferously.

It is interesting to note the experience in Sweden, where 30 per cent of households shop regularly on Sundays, and in New Zealand, where a rather simplified version of our Shops Act 1950 is operating: there, all shops may open six days a week from 7 am to 9 pm with limited goods (on an approved list) available in some shops on Sundays. Although this may bear close investigation because of Britain's cultural affinity with New Zealand, the fact is that our trading ties and onward social progress are closely allied with Europe and that the continental experience is vastly different; for example, in North Rhine Westphalia, Germany, shops are closed on most Saturday afternoons and are open for the whole of Saturdays only on the first Saturday in the month. (This however may have to be revised, in the light of European commitments and 1992.) (Hewlett NJL, 1986.)

In the B & Q case (*Stoke-on-Trent* v. *B & Q Retail PLC* (1990)), the judge said:

The Treaty of Rome is the supreme law of this country, taking precedence over acts of Parliament . . . Parliament surrendered its sovereign right to legislate contrary to the Treaty.

. . . the purpose of the Treaty was to bring about a European common market but not to interfere with national laws and customs which did not constitute obstacles to the establishment of such a market.

It would appear therefore that, notwithstanding the 1992 commitments to the Common Market, the burden of reform or amendment will lie with our own Parliament. Therefore, as more pressure is brought to bear to support Sunday trading, it may well be that a change in the legislation will arise.

12.12 COMPETITION—RESTRAINT OF TRADE

Politicians have determined the nature of competition that should take place between business organizations, varying from a preference for centrally planned natural monopolies in the late 1940s to a belief in the 1980s that competition is inherently favourable. This political preference has been expressed in legislation that on the one hand (for example) created the nationalized industries of the early postwar period, and on the other hand allowed companies to compete for providing telephone services.

Aspects of competition policy are considered more fully in Chapter 3. This section considers the law in relation to restraint of trade which can affect all businesses, regardless of the market structure in which they operate.

Restraint of trade is a contractual term which restricts or completely stops a person from trading or carrying on his business or profession. Generally in English law parties may make an agreement on any terms they see fit subject to one major exception: any term in restraint of trade. Since it is in the public interest that people should not fetter their future rights to be free, such covenants in restraints of trade are prima facie void, unless:

(a) it can be shown by the covenantee (i.e. the person in whose interests the covenant is made) that it is reasonable between the parties
   and
(b) it can be shown by the covenantor (i.e. the person agreeing to the restriction) that it is unreasonable in the interests of the public.

There are four such categories:

1. Any situation in which a person agrees to limit his own future employment—e.g. where an employee will agree not to work for a rival employer after he has left his employment (this is the means by which those in business protect themselves from future competition)
2. Terms whereby the vendor of a business limits his freedom to compete with a purchaser
3. Agreements whereby an employee agrees not to undertake employment with any other employee
4. A situation in which a trader agrees to restrict his source of supply

Whether such restraints are valid or void depends on two factors. In considering the interests of the parties, the court will identify, first, whether or not the employer pleading the clause has a genuine proprietary interest to protect and, second, whether it is in the public interest that the restrictive term be upheld. Confusion abounds regarding a definition of 'public interest' and in effect this has been barely recognized by the courts. It is a complex area and definitions vary according to the social and political climates that exist at the time. However, as far as the first two categories are concerned, the courts have a settled view over what constitutes reasonableness.

It is clear from cases that an employer is able to protect his proprietary (property) rights. Proprietary rights exist in trade connections and trade secrets.

Trade connections can be defined as the employer's goodwill with particular customers. For example, if a hairdresser leaves a business in which she has been working for two years, it is extremely likely that she will take her own clients with her to the detriment of her employer.

There are certain businesses where it cannot be argued that customers do not constitute trade connections, in that the commodity the business is selling is not such that the customer would go to that establishment as opposed to any other—e.g. petrol stations.

Even where it can be said that customers are particular to that business—e.g. solicitors, estate agents, accountants—employers will not be able to impose a term in restraint of trade unless the employee is in a position to influence customers so as to draw them away from the employer on leaving. This is evidenced by cases concerning, first, an estate agent's clerk who covenanted not to work for any other estate agents within a five-mile radius for a specified time and, second, a similar case but where the material difference was the position of the employee in the firm in question. In the first case the employee met most of the firm's customers and was therefore in a position to develop a fairly close relationship with them, whereas in the second case no such relationship was possible.

If during the course of his employment an employee learns a secret process which the employer uses in the course of his business, then this is a proprietary right (a trade secret) which the employer is entitled to protect. However, mere knowledge of office organization was held not to amount to a trade secret for the purpose of this rule.

It has to be demonstrated that a term in restraint of trade is reasonable in time and area and that it will obviously be dependent on the nature of the proprietary interest to be protected. If the customers, i.e. trade connections, are in Leicester, obviously a term restraining an ex-employee from setting up in competition in Newcastle would be void, but if the proprietary interest was based on trade secrets, then a restraint in wider geographical terms may be justified.

If the court rules that one aspect in a term in restraint of trade is void, it does not necessarily mean that the term ceases to be binding for any other purposes. The court may excise any offending term but cannot amend what remains of the term as to do so would be to interfere with freedom of contract. In one case the clause stipulated that the employer was not to work for any other employer within an area of 25 miles of Islington. The court identified the offending element to be 'within 25 miles of Islington'. However, to excise this term would render the whole situation worse and therefore the whole term must be declared void.

As businessmen can never be certain whether or not such a clause will be valid or void until the ex-employee starts up in competition, it is imperative that they ensure that the term is written in such a way that any offending term can be excised without making the whole term invalid.

What will the legal consequences be where, for example, a garage owner agrees to restrict his source of supply—a contract known as 'a solus agreement'? Such an agreement normally contains a tying covenant by which the garage owner agrees, in return for a rebate on the price, to sell only that supplier's brand of petrol; a compulsory trading covenant which obliges the garage owner to keep the garage open at reasonable hours; and a continuity covenant which requires him, if he sells the business, to procure the acceptance of the agreement by the purchaser. In one instance a garage owner had two garages and a solus agreement in respect of each. The first was for four years and the second for 21 years. In 1963 the petrol company allowed garages to cut prices, and the garage owner found that his profits were threatened and changed to a different petrol company in defiance of the agreements. The case came before the House of Lords, who held that the essence of the solus agreements was to restrict the garage proprietor's freedom of trading. In deciding whether the agreements were reasonable and therefore valid, they stressed the importance of taking into account the public interest and held the four-year agreement reasonable but the 21-year agreement too long and therefore unreasonable and invalid.

REVIEW QUESTIONS

1. Mrs Andrews was persuaded to part with her vacuum cleaner in exchange for a super new model priced by a salesman calling at her house. She signed a hire purchase agreement, paying a deposit of £200, made up of £100 and a £100 allowance for her old vacuum cleaner.

   Mrs Carstairs visited the salesman's shop two days later and bought Mrs Andrews' old vacuum cleaner for £150 on terms that she pay £50 in cash and the balance by six monthly payments. She signed the hire purchase agreement in the shop.

   Both ladies are now regretting their decision and wish to avoid the transactions and recover their deposits. Mrs Andrews also wants her old vacuum cleaner returned.

   Advise both parties.

2. Philip, shopping at a large department store, sees a colourful spinning top which he buys for his grandson Harry. While purchasing the toy, he sees a prominent notice in the store which states: 'This store will not be held responsible for any defects in the toys sold.'

   The box containing the spinning top carries the description 'Ideal for children over 12 months, safe and non-toxic.' (Harry is 15 months old.) Within four weeks the spinning top has split into two parts, each with a jagged edge, and Harry has suffered an illness as a result of sucking the paint.

   Philip has complained vociferously to the store, which merely pointed to the prominent notice disclaiming liability.

   Philip has now informed the store that he intends to take legal action against it.

   Draft a report to the Managing Director setting out the legal liability of the store.

3. Glazit Ltd is a company that supplies and fits replacement windows. Charles is employed as a salesman and is provided with a company car. Charles has strict instructions not to carry passengers in the car. However, his wife Diana often travels with him as he goes from customer to customer, assisting with paperwork as each order is finalized. She does not wear a seat-belt as it hampers her work completing order forms.

   While Charles is returning to the office at the end of the day his attention is distracted by questions from Diana. His car hits a man who is wheeling his bicycle across a zebra crossing. The man's leg is broken and Diana's skull is fractured.

   Draft a report to Glazit Ltd setting out their legal liability.

   Would the position be different if Charles and Diana had made a detour to drop off Diana at her hairdresser's?

4. Sharon visits Betterbuy supermarket with her children Wayne and Kylie. Consider the following scenarios.

   (a) Wayne, aged 3 years, takes some sweets from the low-level display by the checkout and puts them in his mother's basket. Sharon replaces the sweets on the display. The manager tells her she must pay for them as she put them in her basket.

   (b) Sharon chooses a large packet of washing powder marked 'Bargain offer—only 45p'. When she goes to the checkout the cashier tells her that it costs £1.45. Can Sharon demand that it be sold to her for 45p?

5. Simon, a haulage contractor, buys a second-hand car—a 1983 Jaguar which has done 60,000 miles—for £3,000. He signs a contract under which he acknowledges that the dealer is not liable for any defects in the car.

   Three weeks after purchase the battery has to be replaced at a cost of £50, and two weeks later the engine seizes up completely and has to be replaced at a cost of £600.

   (a) Advise Simon as to any claims he may have against the dealer.

   (b) What difference would it make if
      (i) the vehicle were a van?
      (ii) the car was brand new?

6. James works as an elocution teacher for the Centre of Speech and Drama. A clause in his contract of employment stipulated that on leaving the Centre of Speech and Drama he could not teach on his own account, or own or work in any organization that provided elocution lessons, for a period of one year.

He now wishes to leave and teach freelance at his home, which is only four miles from the centre.
   Advise James.

REFERENCES

Bradgate, J. R. and N. Savage (1991), *Commercial Law*, Butterworths, London.
Charlesworth, J. (1991), *Mercantile Law*, 16th edn, eds C. M. Schmitthoff and D. A. G. Sarre, Stevens & Son, London.
Davies, F. R. (1991), *Contract: Concise College Texts*, 6th edn, Sweet & Maxwell, London.
Harvey, B. W. and D. L. Parry (1987), *Law of Consumer Protection and Fair Trading*, Butterworths, London.
Phillips, J. (1986), *Introduction to Intellectual Property*, Butterworths, London.
Treitel, G. H., (1991) *The Law of Contract*. Sweet & Maxwell, London 8th Edn.

THIRTEEN
ANALYSING THE MARKETING ENVIRONMENT

13.1 INTRODUCTION

The purpose of this chapter is to examine how business organizations can interpret the marketing environment and develop frameworks within which decisions on future courses of action can be made. The aim is to progress from perceiving how a company can have a general understanding of the environment to how it can use specific methods of assessment. The emphasis will be on methods of predicting environmental change and of their impact on an enterprise, rather than on assessing the internal rate of return of a project to a business.

13.2 THE MARKETING AUDIT

It has been customary for business organizations to undertake financial audits to check on their financial health. Increasingly, the principles of the independent, objective financial audit are being applied to the marketing function of companies. The following definition of a marketing audit is given by Kotler (1988):

A marketing audit is a comprehensive, systematic, independent and periodic examination of a company's—or business unit's—marketing environment, objectives, strategies and activities with a view to determining problem areas and opportunities and recommending a plan of action to improve the company's marketing performance.

The marketing audit is not itself a framework for decisions: it is essentially a set of procedures by which an organization explicitly asks questions about the internal and external environments in which marketing operates, as well as the performance of the marketing functions themselves (such as the firm's distribution and pricing effectiveness). The process begins by the appointment of an independent person to undertake the audit. This could be a consultant from outside the organization, or somebody from another position within the firm, either sideways or above the function being audited. A self-audit could be undertaken, but at the risk of a loss of objectivity.

A large part of the audit is devoted to an objective analysis of the external environment, both indirect and immediate. In the case of the indirect environmental factors, the audit would independently verify or challenge any assumptions that the company had been making—for instance about the likely rate of economic growth or the speed of change in the technological environment. In the case of the immediate external environment, the person undertaking an audit of the distribution environment could proceed by asking retailers themselves about how they perceive the company's products and future trends in retailing for that type of product.

The marketing audit would also look inwardly to examine the relationships within the marketing function and between it and other functional areas of the firm. Organizational structures and decision-making procedures would be objectively assessed for effectiveness.

13.3   MARKETING INFORMATION SYSTEMS

Some of the elements of marketing research were examined in Chapter 1. Information is of such importance to marketing management that its collection and dissemination needs to be undertaken in a systematic way. It has been suggested by Christopher et al. (1980) that 'Good information is a facilitator of successful marketing and indeed, seen in this light, marketing management becomes first and foremost an information processing activity'.

Piercy (1985) has argued that processing information should be regarded as the fifth P of the marketing mix. Information represents a bridge between the business organization and its environment and is the means by which a picture of the changing environment is built up within the company. Marketing management is responsible for turning information into specific marketing plans.

A marketing information system is a subsystem of a company's management information system; other systems are concerned with production, finance, personnel, etc. An important requirement for an effective marketing information system is that all the elements of it are driven by meeting decision-makers' needs, rather than the needs of people producing information. Clear aims must be set; these might include the need for information on the size and characteristics of markets, customer attitudes and awareness of brand names and the effectiveness of the firm's pricing and distribution policies, to name but a few. Aims should specify the frequency with which information is to be collected, the speed with which it is to be transmitted, the level of accuracy required, whom it is to be given to and who is responsible for acting on the information.

The marketing information system could have a number of possible functions covering the planning, implementation and control of marketing programmes. A practical problem for environmental analysis is that information is typically much more difficult to obtain to meet strategic planning needs than it is to meet operational and control needs. There can be a danger of the marketing information system being focused too heavily on information that is easily available at the expense of that which is needed. At an operational level, the system might, for example, monitor the performance of individual sales personnel or brand awareness levels among a company's target market. These are not the direct concern of this chapter as far as marketing information systems are concerned—rather, the emphasis is on turning observations about the marketing environment into information that management can act upon.

The complexity of the task of gathering information about the marketing environment will vary between individual firms. Ansoff (1984) attributes this variation to two principal factors. First, firms will perceive varying levels of uncertainty in the environment as measured by the rate of environmental change. Second, the extent of complexity will also be affected by the range of activities the company is either involved in, or likely to be involved in in the future.

The information collection exercise can be seen as comprising four main elements which make up a company's marketing information system: a marketing research system, an internal reporting system, an intelligence gathering system and an analytic market modelling system (Figure 13.1).

The internal reporting system is concerned primarily with the reporting of operational and control matters rather than the changing state of the marketing environment. The tools of the marketing research system were described in some detail in Chapter 1, where it was noted that they could be used to provide both routine information about marketing effectiveness—such as

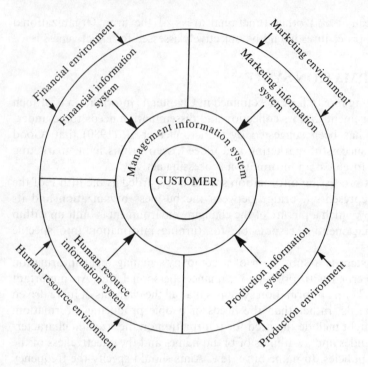

Figure 13.1   The marketing information system

brand awareness levels or delivery performance—and external environmental information, such as changing attitudes towards diet or the pattern of income distribution. The latter could be collected either routinely or as a series of discrete exercises, through both primary and secondary data collection.

The intelligence gathering system comprises the procedures and sources used by marketing managers to obtain pertinent information about developments in their marketing environment. It complements the marketing research system, for, whereas the latter tends to focus on structured and largely quantifiable data collection procedures, the intelligence gathering system concentrates on picking up relatively intangible ideas and trends. Marketing management can gather this intelligence from the following sources:

1. Where no specific information is sought, intelligence can be acquired through exposure to general sources of information (such as daily newspapers and television news programmes).
2. Selected sources may be recognized as being particularly valuable for throwing up information highly pertinent to the firm's environment. Marketing management may arrange for these to be scanned routinely and for cuttings of new developments to be fed into the marketing information system. Trade journals fit into this category of intelligence; exhibitions and conferences are also recognized as a valuable method of collecting intelligence.
3. People employed in the company beyond the marketing management function may be valuable sources of intelligence. Sales personnel are in daily contact with the firm's marketplace and are in a good position to pick up valuable news such as competitors' activities and the changing attitudes of customers—information that could not be accommodated within a standard sales report. Some businesses have used unstructured discussion groups among sales personnel to pick up intelligence.

4. In a similar manner, a company may formalize procedures for collecting information from firms within its immediate external environment, especially distributors and suppliers. Many manufacturers arrange seminars for their distributors which have the function not only of selling the product range, but also of picking up comments about the market-place in general.
5. The business organization may require intelligence on a specific subject about which its routine intelligence-gathering system described above has provided insufficient information. It may then enter into a more formal search, either by referring to specialized publications or by employing a consultant to provide the required information.

For those enterprises that have set up marketing intelligence systems, their effectiveness will be determined by three factors:

1. *The accurate description of the information needs of the enterprise* Needs can themselves be difficult to identify, and it can be very difficult to identify the boundaries of the firm's environments and to separate relevance from irrelevance. This is a particular problem for large multi-product firms. The mission statement of the business may give some indication of the boundaries for environmental search—the TSB Bank, for example, has a mission statement which includes an aim for it to be the dominant provider of financial services in the UK. The information needs therefore include anything related to the broader environment of financial services rather than the narrower field of banking.
2. *The extensiveness of the search for intelligence* A balance has to be struck between the need for information and the cost of collecting it. The most critical elements of the marketing environment must be identified and the cost of collecting intelligence on that element weighed against the cost of an inaccurate forecast. (See the following section on probability assessment.)
3. *Speed of communication* The marketing intelligence system will be effective only if information is communicated quickly and to the appropriate people. Deciding which information to withhold from an individual and concisely reporting relevant information can be as important as deciding what information to include if information overload is to be avoided.

The fourth element making up a company's market information system—the analytic marketing modelling system—is discussed below.

13.4 FRAMEWORKS FOR ANALYSING THE MARKETING ENVIRONMENT

There are two aspects to be considered when describing an analytic framework:

1. A definition of the elements that are to be included in the analysis
2. The choice of methods by which these input elements are to be used in predicting outcomes

The nature of the framework used bears a relation to the nature of the dominant business environment at the time. In the relatively stable environment that existed during the early years of this century, management could control its destiny by controlling current performance; in the turbulent environment of the 1980s, control became dependent upon mangement's ability to predict the future and respond to change.

Diffenbach (1983) has argued that detailed environmental analysis became important only in the mid-1960s. Prior to that, the marketing environment was analysed primarily for the purpose of making short-term economic forecasts. The development to include a longer-term appreciation of the wider economic, technological, demographic and cultural elements of the environment came about in three stages:

1. An increased appreciation of environmental analysis was encouraged by the emergence of professional and academic interest in the subject.
2. Awareness of the concepts of environmental analysis led to academic analysis of the subject.
3. Eventually, the concepts that had been vindicated by subsequent academic analysis were taken on board by business organizations and used as a tool for strategic decision-making.

As frameworks for analysis have developed in sophistication, so has the paradox that, by the time sufficient information has been gathered and analysed, it may be too late for the firm to do anything about the opportunities or threats with which it is faced. Ansoff (1984) has put forward a framework which helps to overcome this decision-making dilemma. His model allows the firm to respond rapidly to problems whose precise details are a surprise, but whose general nature could have been predicted. Ansoff's model of strategic issue analysis is shown in Figure 13.2. The central feature of the model is the continuing monitoring of the firm's external and internal environments for indicators of the emergence of potentially strategic issues which may significantly influence the firm's operations in future. The focal point for Ansoff's analysis is the *issue*—such as the emergence of environmentalism—rather than the conventional headings of the economic, technological environments, etc. The model allows for a graduated response: as soon as weak signals are picked up, steps are taken to allow for the possibility of these issues developing further. Responses become more precise as the signals become more amplified over time. In other words, Ansoff's model avoids the need for a firm to wait until it has sufficient information before taking a decision—it responds gradually as information emerges.

13.4.1 Choice of framework

A wide range of analytic frameworks are available for companies to use in analysing their marketing environment and making strategic marketing decisions. The choice of framework will depend upon four factors.

First, the *level of turbulence* in the marketing environment will vary between firms operating in different markets. For example, the marketing environment of an undertaker has not been—and in future is even less likely to be—as turbulent as that of a brewery. An extrapolation of recent trends might be adequate for the former type of business, but the latter must seek to understand a diverse range of changing forces if it is to be able to accurately predict future demand for its products.

Second, the *cost* associated with an inaccurate forecast will reflect the capital commitment to a project. A clothing manufacturer can afford to trust his judgement in running off a small batch of jackets—the cost of making a mistake will probably be bearable, unlike the cost of building a chemical refinery on the basis of an inaccurate forecast. The latter situation calls for relatively sophisticated analytic techniques.

Third, more sophisticated *analytic techniques* are needed for long time scale projects where there is a long time lag between the planning of the project and the time it comes into production. The problem of inaccurate forecasting will be even more acute where an asset has a long lifespan with few alternate uses.

Finally, *qualitative and quantitative techniques* may be used as appropriate. In looking at the future, facts are hard to come by. What matters is that senior management must be in the position to make better informed judgements about the future in order to aid decision-making and planning.

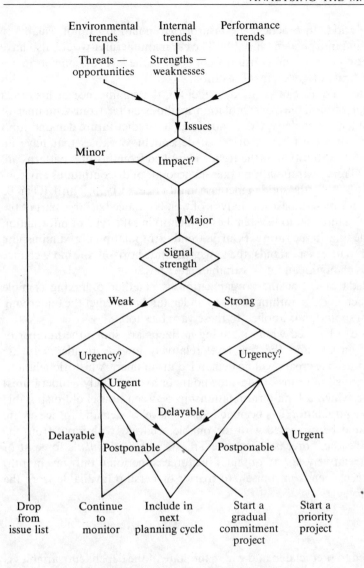

Figure 13.2 Ansoff's model of strategic issue analysis
Source: based on H. I. Ansoff (1985) *Marketing Strategy and Management*. Reproduced by permission of Macmillan Ltd. © H. I. Ansoff 1979.

13.4.2 Trend extrapolation

At its simplest level, a firm identifies an historic and consistent long-term change in demand for a product over time. Demand forecasting then takes the form of multiplying current sales by an historic growth factor. In most markets, this can at best work effectively only in predicting long-term sales growth at the expense of short-term variations.

Trend extrapolation methods can be refined to recognize a relationship between sales and one key environmental variable. An example might be an observed direct relationship between the sale of new cars to the private buyer sector and the level of disposable incomes. Forecasting the demand for new cars then becomes a problem of forecasting what will happen to disposable incomes during the planning period. In practice, the task of extrapolation cannot usually be reduced to a single dependent and independent variable. The car manufacturer would also have to consider the relationship between sales and consumer confidence, the level of competition in its environment and the varying rate of government taxation.

While multiple correlation techniques can be used to identify the significance of historical relationships between a number of variables, extrapolation methods suffer from a number of shortcomings. First, one dependent variable is seldom adequate to predict future demand for a product, yet it can be difficult to identify the full set of dependent variables that have an influence. Second, there can be no certainty that the trends identified from historic patterns are likely to continue in the future. Trend extrapolation takes no account of discontinuous environmental change, as was brought about by the sudden increase in oil prices in 1973. Third, it can be difficult to gather information on which to base an analysis of trends—indeed, a large part of the problem in designing a marketing information system lies in identifying the type of information that may be of relevance at some time in the future. Fourth, trend extrapolation is of diminishing value as the length of time used to forecast extends: the longer the time horizon, the more chance there is of historic relationships changing and new variables emerging.

Trend extrapolation as applied by most business organizations is a method of linking a simple cause with a simple effect. As such, it does nothing to try to understand or predict the underlying dependent variables, unless extrapolation is applied to these variables too.

At best, trend extrapolation can be used where planning horizons are short, the number of dependent variables relatively limited and the risk level relatively low. A retailer may use extrapolation to forecast how much ice cream will be demanded in summer. A historic relationship between the weather (quantified in terms of sunshine hours or average daily temperatures) may have been identified, on to which a long-term relationship between household disposable income and the domestic freezer population has been added. The level of demand for ice cream during the following month could be predicted with reasonable accuracy with input from the Meteorological Office on the weather forecast, from the Treasury or *Economist*'s forecast of household disposable incomes (relatively easy to obtain if the forecast period is only one month) and from statistics showing recent trends in household freezer ownership (available from the Annual General Household Survey).

13.4.3   Expert opinion

Trend analysis is commonly used to predict demand where the state of the dependent variables is given. In practice, it can be very difficult to predict what will happen to the dependent variables themselves. One solution is to consult expert opinion to obtain the best possible forecast of what will happen to these variables.

In Diffenbach's (1983) study of US corporations, 86 per cent of all firms said they used expert opinion as an input to their planning process. Expert opinion can vary in the level of specialty, from an economist being consulted for a general forecast about the state of the national economy to industry-specific experts. An example of the latter are the fashion consultants who study trends at the major international fashion shows and provide a valuable source of expert opinion to clothing manufacturers seeking to know which types of fabric to order, ahead of a fashion trend.

Expert opinion may be unstructured and come either from a few individuals inside the organization, or from external advisers or consultants. The most senior managers in companies of reasonable size tend to keep in touch with developments by various means. Paid and unpaid advisers may be used to keep abreast of a whole range of issues such as technological developments, animal rights campaigners, environmental issues, government thinking and intended legislation. Large companies may employ MPs or MEPs (Members of the European Parliament) as advisers as well as retired civil servants. Consultancy firms may be employed to brief the company on specific issues or monitor the environment on a more general basis.

In today's modern economy, it is essential that businesses monitor not only the domestic environment, but the European Community and the international environment. Today as much legislation affecting companies comes from the EC as from the UK government. Legislation passed in the USA can have a direct affect on UK companies even though their products may not be intended for sale in America. What is happening in America today may be happening in Europe next year.

Relying on individuals may give an incomplete or distorted picture of the future. There are, however, more structured methods of gaining expert opinion. One of the best known is probably the Delphi method. This involves a number of experts, usually from outside the organization, who (preferably) do not know each other and who do not meet or confer while the process is in play. A scenario or number of scenarios about the future are drawn up by the company. These are then posted out to the experts. Comments are returned and the scenario(s) modified according to the comments received. The process is run through a number of times with the scenario being amended on each occasion. Eventually a consensus of the most likely scenario is arrived at. It is believed that this is more accurate than relying on any one individual, because it involves the collected wisdom of a number of experts who have not been influenced by dominant personalities.

13.4.4 Scenario building

Scenario building is an attempt to paint a picture of the future. It may be possible to build a small number of alternative scenarios based on differing assumptions. This qualitative approach is a means of handling environmental issues which are hard to quantify because they are less structured, more uncertain and may involve very complex relationships.

Often the most senior managers in a company may hold no common view about the future. The individuals themselves are likely to be scanning the environment in an informal way, through conversations with colleagues and subordinates within the organization and through business acquaintances and friends outside. The general media and business and technical publications will also shape a person's 'view' of the future. Individuals will vary in their sensitivity to the environment. Such views may never be harnessed in any formal way, but they may be influencing decisions taken by these individuals. Yet the views each person holds may never have been exposed to debate or challenge in a way that would allow the individual to moderate or change his or her view.

Scenario building among senior management will help individuals to confirm or moderate their views. A new perspective may be taken on issues or forthcoming events. A wider perspective may be taken by individuals who may become more sensitive to the environment and the impact it can have on business. A more cohesive view may be adopted by senior management which may help strategy formulation and planning. The scenarios may be built up over a number of meetings which may be either totally unstructured or semi-structured with each meeting focusing on different aspects of the environment. The approach may be used at different levels of management in a large organization; a multinational company may build scenarios at the global, regional and country level, for example. Johnson and Scholes (1984) cite the example of Shell UK Ltd which has used this approach on a number of occasions. In the early 1980s it was used as part of the company's methodology for attempting to assess the demand for oil depending on a number of alternative scenarios (see Section 13.6).

13.4.5 Influence diagrams and impact grids

A more applied approach is to assess the likely impact of specific aspects of environmental change on the business. One method is to construct *influence diagrams* (Narchal *et al.*, 1987), so that a better understanding of the relationships between environmental forces can be obtained. If the price your company has to pay for raw materials is a critical factor, then the forces that influence the price of raw materials will be of interest to you; by monitoring these you will have an earlier warning about price rises than if you were to wait until your supplier told you of the price increase. In the influence diagram (Figure 13.3) a positive relationship means that if the value of one force rises then the pressure on the dependent factor will be in the same direction. A negative relationship means that if the value of the environmental force rises then the pressure on the dependent factor is the opposite direction—downwards.

A number of specific influence digrams may be used to improve the understanding of how forces in the environment may influence particular aspects of the business. To gain a broader view, *impact grids* can be constructed. Specific environmental forces or events are identified and their impact on particular aspects of the business are assessed (see Jenster, 1987). Weighting the assessment on a simple scale—say, 1 equals no effect and 10 equals substantial or critical impact—will help decision-making. A simple grid can then be constructed as in Figure 13.4.

For those companies that wish to structure the environmental analysis in a more detailed way, there are two different but complementary methods of impact analysis. The simplest is trend impact analysis (TIA), where the movements in a particular variable are plotted over time and the projected value is assessed (Figure 13.5).

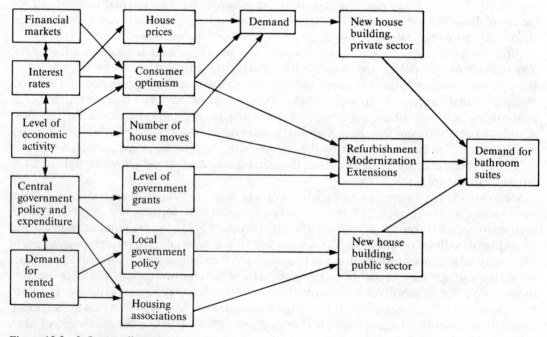

Figure 13.3 Influence diagram

Environment change Impact on UK car market	Government raises VAT	EC directive to limit exhaust emissions	EC announces plans for single currency	Japanese car makers abandon voluntary limits on imports to Europe	Technological breakthrough for battery cars
UK demand					
EC demand					
UK production levels					
Prices					
Production costs					
Marketing costs					

Figure 13.4   Environment impact grid
0 = no effect; 10 = substantial or critical impact

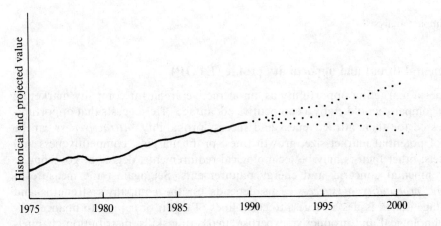

Figure 13.5   Trend impact analysis

Cross-impact analysis (CIA) is used in an attempt to assess the impact of changes in one variable on other variables. This is much more difficult to do but at the minimum it will help managers to understand the possible relationships between forces in the environment. At best, it will provide key information in order to aid strategic decision-making (see Figure 13.6). According to Glueck (1980), the General Electric Company (USA) uses these impact grids as an aid to writing scenarios.

Possible events / Wild cards	OPEC force price of oil to $30/barrel	OPEC fall out: oil drops to $12/barrel with over-supply	Economic downturn becomes recession and lasts 5 years	Government increases car and petrol taxes	
Clean-burn petrol engine developed					
Japanese launch first mass-produced battery-powered car					
Environment deteriorates suddenly; car drivers in Western world limited to 30 miles per day					

Figure 13.6   Cross-impact analysis

13.4.6   Environmental threat and opportunity profile (ETOP)

Kotler (1988) defines a marketing opportunity as 'an attractive arena for company marketing action in which the company would enjoy a competitive advantage'. He suggests that opportunities should be assessed for their attractiveness and success probability. *Attractiveness* can be assessed in terms of potential market size, growth rates, profit margins, competitiveness and distribution channels; other factors may be technological requirements, degree of government interference, environmental concerns and energy requirements. Set against the measure of attractiveness is the *probability of success*. This depends on the company's strengths and competitive advantage—such issues as access to cash, lines of credit or capital to finance new developments. Technological and productive expertise, marketing skills, distribution channels and managerial competence will all need to be taken into account. A simple matrix (Figure 13.7) can be constructed to show the relationship between attractiveness and success probability.

In 1991 a new opportunity arose in the UK for companies to bid for commercial television breakfast franchises issued periodically by the government. Since the last issue in 1981 the government has changed the regulations (Broadcasting Act) for commercial television and the criteria by which bidders for the franchise will be judged. In short, the government's intention is to create more competition in the bidding to raise revenue and to curtail broadcasting monopolies. The franchise will now go to the highest bidder subject to a minimum 'quality threshold'. According to the *Observer* (Twisk and Brooks, 1991), a number of new bidders were attempting to take the franchise away from TV-am—in particular, a consortium called Daybreak, whose partners included ITN, the Daily Telegraph, MAI (an advertising group), Carlton Communications, NBC (American TV network) and Taylor Woodrow (a construction company). With the experience held by consortium members, it is likely that its probability of success will be high. Other bidders are likely to be a consortium that includes London Weekend Television, STV (Southern Television) and Broadcast Communications (owned by the Guardian newspaper and Disney).

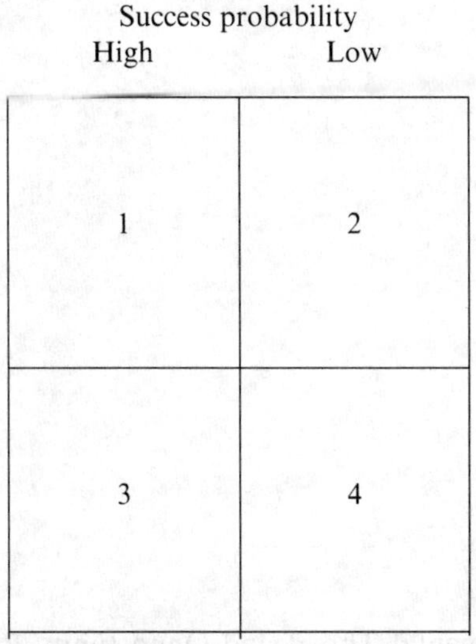

Success probability
High   Low

1	2
3	4

Figure 13.7 Opportunity matrix
1. Attractive opportunity which fits well with company's capabilities.
2. Attractive opportunity but low probability of success; poor fit with company's capabilities.
3. High probability of success if company takes this opportunity, but not an attractive market.
4. Let's forget this one.

Kotler describes an environmental threat as 'a challenge posed by an unfavourable trend or development in the environment that would lead, in the absence of purposeful marketing action, to the erosion of the company's or industry's position'. In this case the threats should be assessed according to their seriousness and the probability of occurrence. A threat matrix can then be constructed (Figure 13.8).

Again, using the example of an existing TV franchise holder, a number of threats have developed in the late 1980s. The Broadcasting Act means that the next time the franchise comes up for renewal the bidding will be much more competitive. Advertising revenues have been under pressure because of stagnant advertising spending resulting from the recession. The government is still talking about creating another new channel, Channel 5. There is pressure from some quarters for the BBC to be allowed to carry advertising so as to reduce its dependence on the public purse. Satellite TV is up and running and gaining in popularity. Production costs continue to rise. Sponsorship of programmes has been slow to take off.

In order for the environmental analysis to have a useful input into the marketing planning process, a wide range of information and opinions needs to be summarized in a meaningful way. This is particularly so if a number of the techniques described in this chapter have been used in a wide-ranging analysis. The information collated from the detailed analysis needs to be simplified

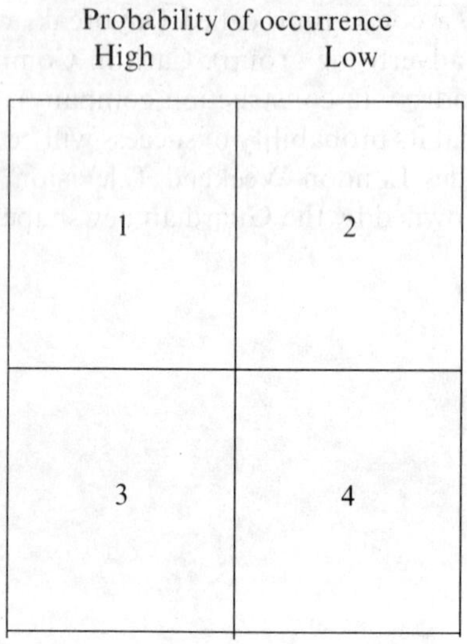

Probability of occurrence
High   Low

1	2
3	4

Figure 13.8 Threat matrix
1. Competitor launches superior product.
2. Pound sterling rises to $3.
3. Higher costs.
4. Legislation to cover 'environment-friendly' claims on labels.

and summarized for planning purposes. The Environmental Threat and Opportunity Profile (ETOP) provides a summary of the environmental factors that are most critical to the company (Figure 13.9). These provide a useful report to stimulate debate among senior management about the future of the business. Some authors suggest trying to weight these factors according to their importance and then rating them for their impact on the organization.

Marketing and business texts often refer to the SWOT analysis, which refers to Strengths, Weaknesses, Opportunities and Threats. As with ETOP, it is used to summarize the main environmental issues in the form of opportunities and threats facing the organization. With this technique, though, these are specifically listed alongside the strengths and weaknesses of the organization. The strengths and weaknesses are internal to the organization and the technique is used to put realism into the opportunities and threats. For example, the environment may be assessed as giving rise to a number of possible opportunities, but if the company is not capable of exploiting these because of internal weaknesses, then perhaps they should be left alone. Kotler (1988) suggests that these strengths and weaknesses be grouped under marketing, financial, manufacturing and organizational factors. The marketing audit discussed earlier in this chapter is one systematic method of assessing the strengths and weaknesses of the company.

13.5   FORMING A VIEW OF ENVIRONMENTAL INFLUENCE

The pace at which senior managers believe the environment is changing and the nature of that change is likely to influence their decision-making and planning. Four broad patterns of environmental change may be considered, as shown in Figure 13.10. In part (a) of the figure senior management believes that there is a stable environment with little change; in part (b) senior management believes that there is incremental change at a known and predictable pace; in

Factor	Major opportunity	Minor opportunity	Neutral	Minor threat	Major threat	Probability
Economic						
Interest rates rise 15%					✓	0.8
£ falls to $1.40	✓					0.4
Disposable incomes do not rise for 5 years				✓		0.3
Political						
Change of political party — more spending on education & public transport			✓			0.9
Legal						
EC bans flavouring additives in snacks				✓		0.1
Market						
Competitor launches major TV campaign				✓		0.5

Figure 13.9 Environmental Threat and Opportunity Profile (ETOP)
Probability scale from 0.1 (very unlikely to happen) to 0.9 (very likely to happen)

part (c) the pace of change is quickening and becoming harder to anticipate; in part (d) the environment may be subject to sudden change as a major factor has a dramatic impact on other environmental forces—for example sudden steep increases in oil prices.

Other considerations for senior management are whether the environment is simple or complex and stable or dynamic (Figure 13.11). Here it is the relationship between the company and its environment that is in question, and whether this is changing. Is the environment moving from being simple to becoming more complex, for example? Or is it moving from a period of stability into one of dynamism?

In the UK a number of industries have undergone significant changes in their environment. How would you assess the changes in the telephone industry, for example, or television broadcasting, or defence, or electricity?

13.6 SHELL OIL COMPANY: A CASE STUDY

The Shell Oil Company is a multinational organization with business interests in all geographic areas of the world, ranging from the exploration of energy resources through to the downstream marketing of energy and chemical-related products to groups that include private consumers, industry, agriculture and governments. Shell has a history of being one of the world's most profitable companies. The company illustrates how traditional demand forecasting methods are being replaced by methods that take into consideration a much closer examination of environmental change.

The traditional approach used by Shell planners to forecast the amount of refinery capacity it would need to meet consumer demand for refined oil-based products was to extrapolate from recent patterns of demand, on the assumption that recent trends would by and large continue.

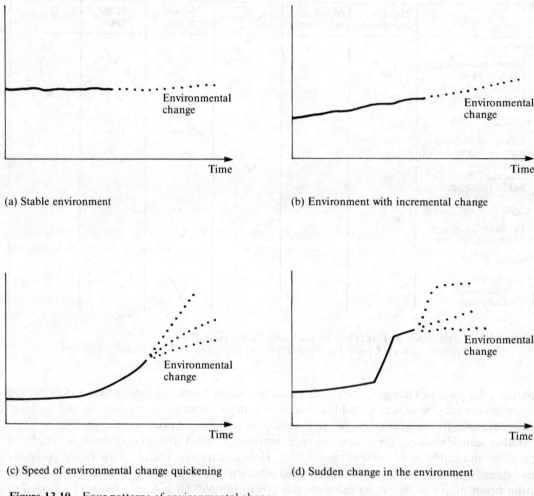

Figure 13.10 Four patterns of environmental change
(a) Stable environment
(b) Environment with incremental change
(c) Speed of environmental change quickening
(d) Sudden change in the environment

Like most oil companies, Shell had been caught largely unaware in 1973 by the actions of OPEC, a cartel which had used its monopoly power to increase crude oil prices threefold. This represented a very severe discontinuity in recent trends, and left most oil companies facing much lower levels of demand than they had previously planned for. Most oil companies were not much better prepared for the second sudden OPEC price rise which occurred in 1979.

Today, Shell tries to manage its future by developing a range of possible scenarios of future business environments. From these scenarios, managers can develop plans of action to meet each eventuality that can be envisaged. Identifying the nature of scenarios can be a challenge to managements' creativity.

One example quoted by Shell to justify it scenario-based approach to planning is the oil price collapse that occurred in 1986. In 1984 crude oil prices stood at $28 a barrel. Other oil companies using trend extrapolation predicted that oil prices would rise over the next two years to the

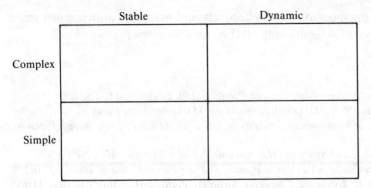

Figure 13.11   Simple/complex and stable/dynamic environments

$25–$30 a barrel level. The prospect of it falling to $15 may have seemed far-fetched to many planners, yet in February 1986 the world market price of oil fell first to $17 a barrel, and then drifted down to a low point of $10 two months later.

Shell claimed it was much better prepared for this price collapse, as it had envisaged a scenario in which this occurred and had developed a contingency plan of action in the event of its taking place. This covered, for example, alternative plans for investment in new energy sources and renewal plans for its shipping fleet. For most of its activities, Shell was trading in commodity markets in which product differentiation was either very difficult or impossible. The ability to learn and react rapidly to environmental change gave Shell its only major advantage over its competitors.

More recently, Shell's approach to scenario building demonstrated its value during the Gulf War. Although Shell had not foreseen the details of the conflict that followed the invasion of Kuwait by Iraq, it had envisaged a scenario in which there was a serious disruption to oil supplies in the Gulf region, whether this arose from war, accident or something else. Contingency plans allowed the company to rapidly replace oil supplies from alternative sources and to redeploy its tanker fleet. The speed with which the company could adjust the forecourt price of petrol to the consumer in response to volatile spot market prices had been increased with improved internal communications.

For the future, Shell feels that attitudes towards the environment represent an opportunity for alternative scenario building. The company has developed two scenarios. In the first, the world moves towards sustainable growth, with a change in attitudes towards consumption among consumers throughout the world and increasing controls on pollution-creating processes. The second scenario envisages a drop in environmentalism as an issue, with increasing emphasis on the need to generate economic wealth; at a national level, governments may seek to stimulate employment even if this results in greater environmental damage, while concern for world-wide approaches to the control of pollution may give way to increasing trade barriers as countries struggle for short-term economic survival. The marketing contingency plan for the former eventuality might include shifting resources to increase the production of wind-generated electricity or biodegradable packaging.

The development of scenario building methods has seen the increasing importance attributed within Shell to the forecasting of business environments. It has attributed its high and stable level of profits to this approach. The first business environment planners at Shell were regarded as eccentric mavericks whose conclusions were seen as relatively marginal to achieving the short-term aims of most managers. Today, the findings of the business environment planners at Shell are communicated within the organization more effectively and managers attach much more significance to the scenarios presented by drawing up their own response plans.

REFERENCES

Ansoff, H. I. (1984), *Implementing Strategic Management*, Prentice-Hall, Englewood Cliffs, NJ.

Christopher, M., McDonald, M. and Wills, G. (1980), *Introducing Marketing*, Pan, London.

Diffenbach, J. (1983), 'Corporate Environmental Analysis in US Corporations', *Long Range Planning*, **16**(3), pp. 107–16.

Glueck, W. F. (1980), *Business Policy and Strategic Management*, 3rd edn, McGraw-Hill, New York.

Jenster, P. V. (1987), 'Using Critical Success Factors in Planning', *Long Range Planning*, **20**(4), pp. 102–9.

Johnson, G. and Scholes, K. (1984), *Exploring Corporate Strategy*, Prentice-Hall International, Hemel Hempstead.

Kotler, P. (1988), *Marketing Management: Analysis, Planning, Implementation and Control*, 6th edn, Prentice-Hall International, Hemel Hempstead.

Narchal, R. M. *et al.* (1987), 'An Environmental Scanning System for Business Planning', *Long Range Planning*, **20**(6), pp. 96–105.

Piercy, N. (1985), *Marketing Organisation: An Analysis of Information Processing, Power and Politics*, Allen and Unwin, London.

Twisk, R. and Brooks, R. (1991), 'Ex-BBC chief spearheads breakfast bid with blast at "Terrible TV-am"', *Observer*, 28 April 1991, p. 1.

INDEX